Magic Land *of* Toys

Magic Land *of* Toys

BY ALBERTO MANGUEL

The Vendome Press
New York

To Gottwalt Pankow and Lucie Pabel

EDITORIAL CONCEPTION:
Xavier Barral
Dorothée Charles
and Eric Reinhardt

SCENIC DESIGN: Jean Haas
SCENIC ASSISTANT: Simon Saulnier

PHOTOGRAPHY: Michel Pintado

GRAPHIC DESIGN: Atalante-Paris

First published in the United States of America in 2006 by
The Vendome Press
1334 York Avenue
New York, NY 10021

ISBN–10: 0–86565–176–0
ISBN–13: 978–0–86565–176–0

LIBRARY OF CONGRESS CATALOGING-IN-PUBLICATION DATA

Manguel, Alberto.
  Magic land of toys / by Alberto Manguel ; photography by Michel Pintado.
    p. cm.
  ISBN–13: 978–0–86565–176–0 (hardcover : alk. paper)
  ISBN–10: 0–86565–176–0 (hardcover : alk. paper)
  1. Toys—History—19th century—Catalogs. 2. Toys—History—20th
century—Catalogs. 3. Toys—France—Paris—Catalogs. 4. Musée des arts
decoratifs (France)—Catalogs. I. Pintado, Michel. II. Title.
  NK9509.5.F8P376 2006
  745.592074'44361—dc22
                    2006018550

PRINTED AND BOUND IN ITALY

ONE HUNDRED YEARS OF ADVENTURES

This book invites kids and grown-ups on a fantastic voyage through a century of childhood, courtesy of the toy collection of the Musée des Arts Décoratifs, Paris.

Begun when the museum opened in 1905, this collection contains twelve thousand toys and games dating from the mid-19th century to the present day. But how best to illustrate this exceptional collection in book form? In a meeting between the publishers Xavier Barral and Éric Reinhardt, and the curator of the Department of Toys, Dorothée Charles, the idea was born: to bring the toys together within the setting of children's bedrooms from the late 19th century to the present, and so to breathe the life back into these sleeping treasures. By recreating more than one hundred years of the intimate world of playtime, with its furniture, decor and accessories, the toys are put back into context, and the dreams of the children who once played with them come alive once again.

Inside the studio of photographer Michel Pintado, over a period of six months, the set designer Jean Haas and his assistant Simon Saulnier worked with seven hundred toys and, with the painstaking precision of children, built up around a hundred scenes, using some ten purpose-built sets.

To plunge yourself back into childhood is to remember the hours spent arranging your own parade of cars, animals, soldiers or cyclists, then scattering them all on the ground, playing mother with dolls, building up blocks and knocking them down, starting up a train set or electric racetrack, making a hill from a cushion and getting dolls to walk up it, making a plane fly with your bare hands, re-enacting the moment when the clown walks out into the circus big top, sending armies to war, capturing the bad guys, killing the good guys, making the prince and princess meet and fall in love, and then cruelly separating them, playing the same video game over and over again.... Brought to life by the invisible hand of a child, a universal child who has spent a whole century at play, toys become the heroes in a series of tales that may be original, funny, scary, comical or poetic, cruel or angelic, simple or complex, and as changeable and varied as a Sunday afternoon.

These photographs do not only chronicle the playtime habits of children but also provide an amazing encapsulation of the 20th century: they echo changes in society and lifestyles, the technical advances and the scientific discoveries, as well as the great events of history.

In parallel to this visual world, the book is led by the gaze and imagination of Alberto Manguel. Through his childhood memories and scholarly commentary, he shows us the extent to which toys allow us to 'grasp the world.'

Many thanks for the talent and enthusiasm of everyone who has been a part of this adventure.

Béatrice Salmon
Director, Musée des Arts Décoratifs

*O God, I could be bounded in a nutshell,
and count myself a king of infinite space....*
HAMLET, ACT II, SCENE II

Everything is here. The family of Father Bear, Mother Bear and Baby Bear. The dolls who play, cook, work, dress beautifully, live in perfect houses. The wild beasts that roam places too far away to seem real. The farm animals with their uneventful lives. The soldiers engaged in wars that have no beginning and no end and no reason. The train that constantly creates its own geography. The robots, no longer inhabitants of the future. The stuffed creatures who share our beds and carry our scent. The television characters for whom new stories must be imagined. The elemental objects: the ball, the hoop, the top, the cube. The blocks from which the world is made.

Everything is here. The little god, the overseer, the general of conflicting armies, the headmaster, the lord of the manor, the Great Mother, the destroyer, the matron, the monarch, the hand of fate, the beginning and the end.

Everything is here. Comfort, conflict, nightmares, experience, hierarchies, anarchy, freedom, discipline, beginnings, adventures, prejudices, creation, scientific research, social rituals, prohibition, transgression, sex, metaphysics, knowledge, death.

This nutshell is the world. What isn't here does not yet exist.

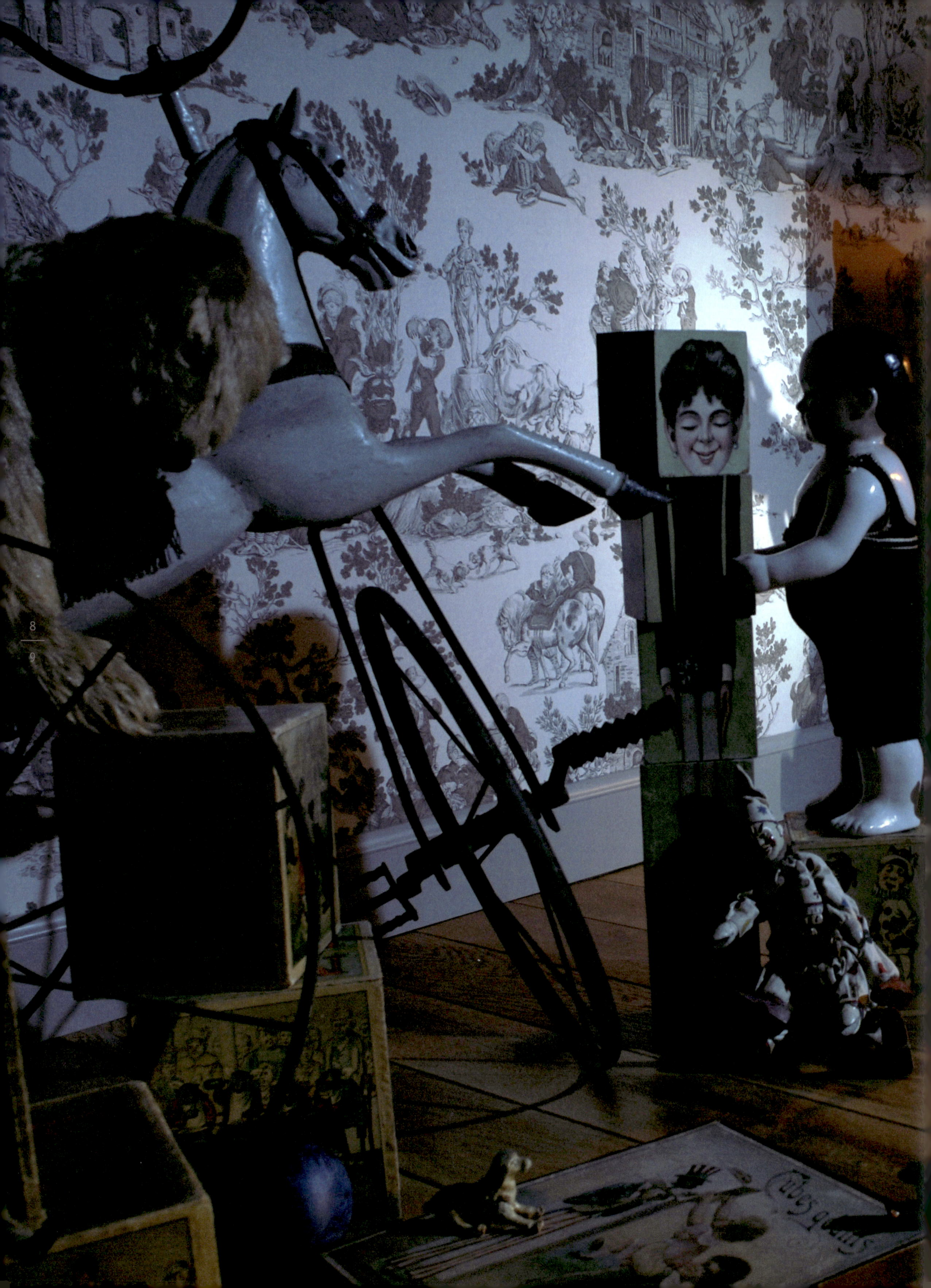

8
9

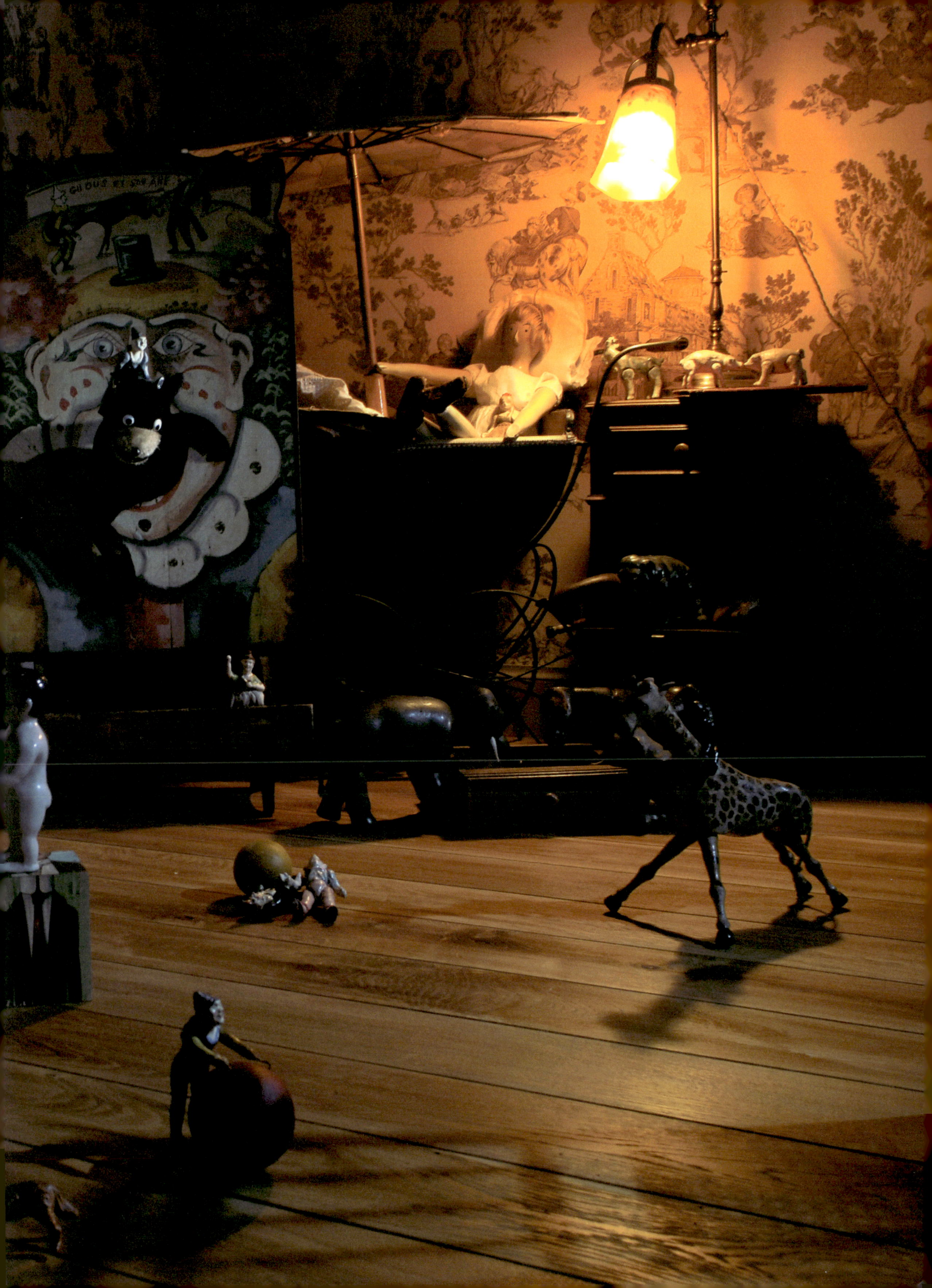

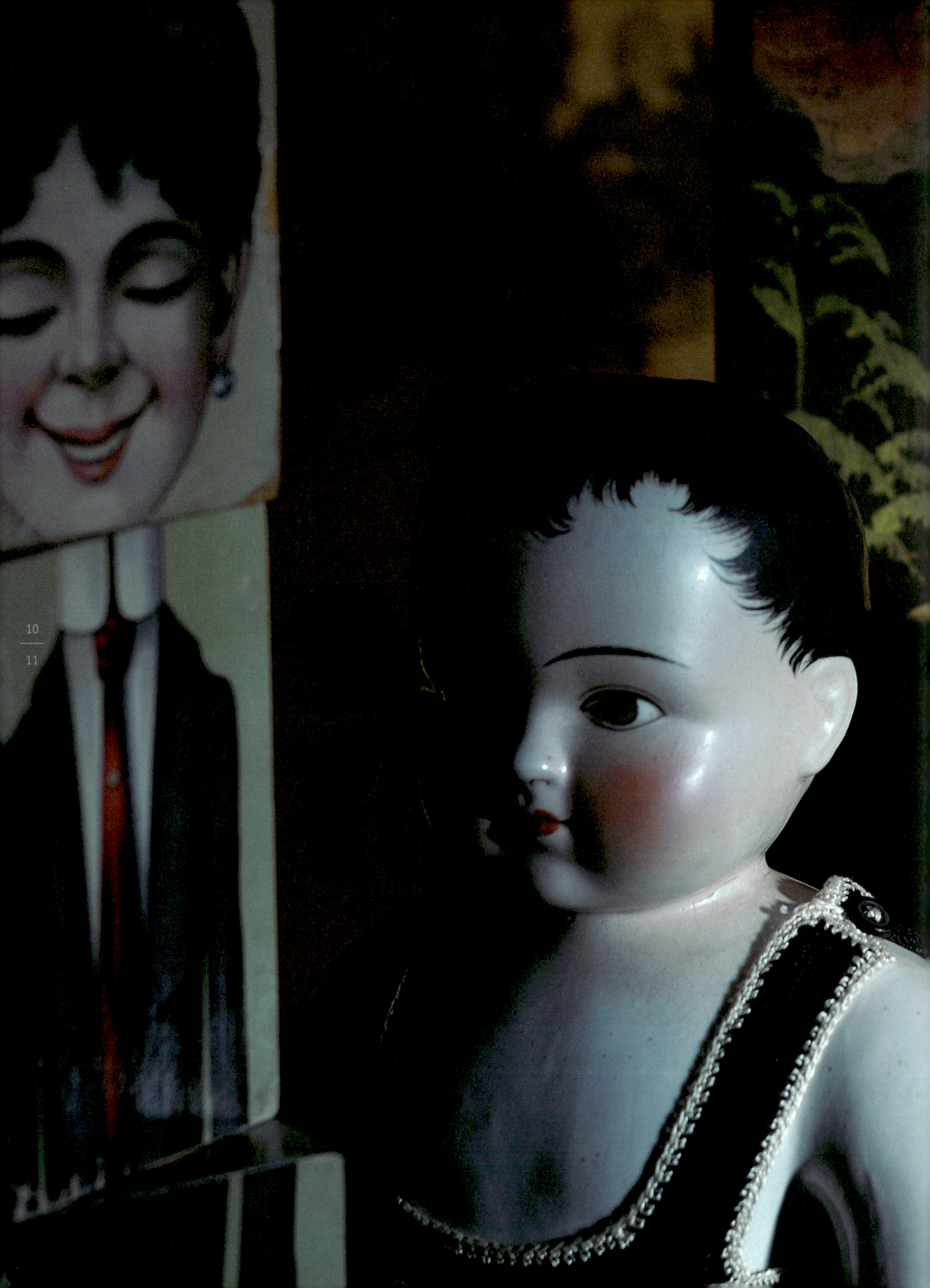

10
—
11

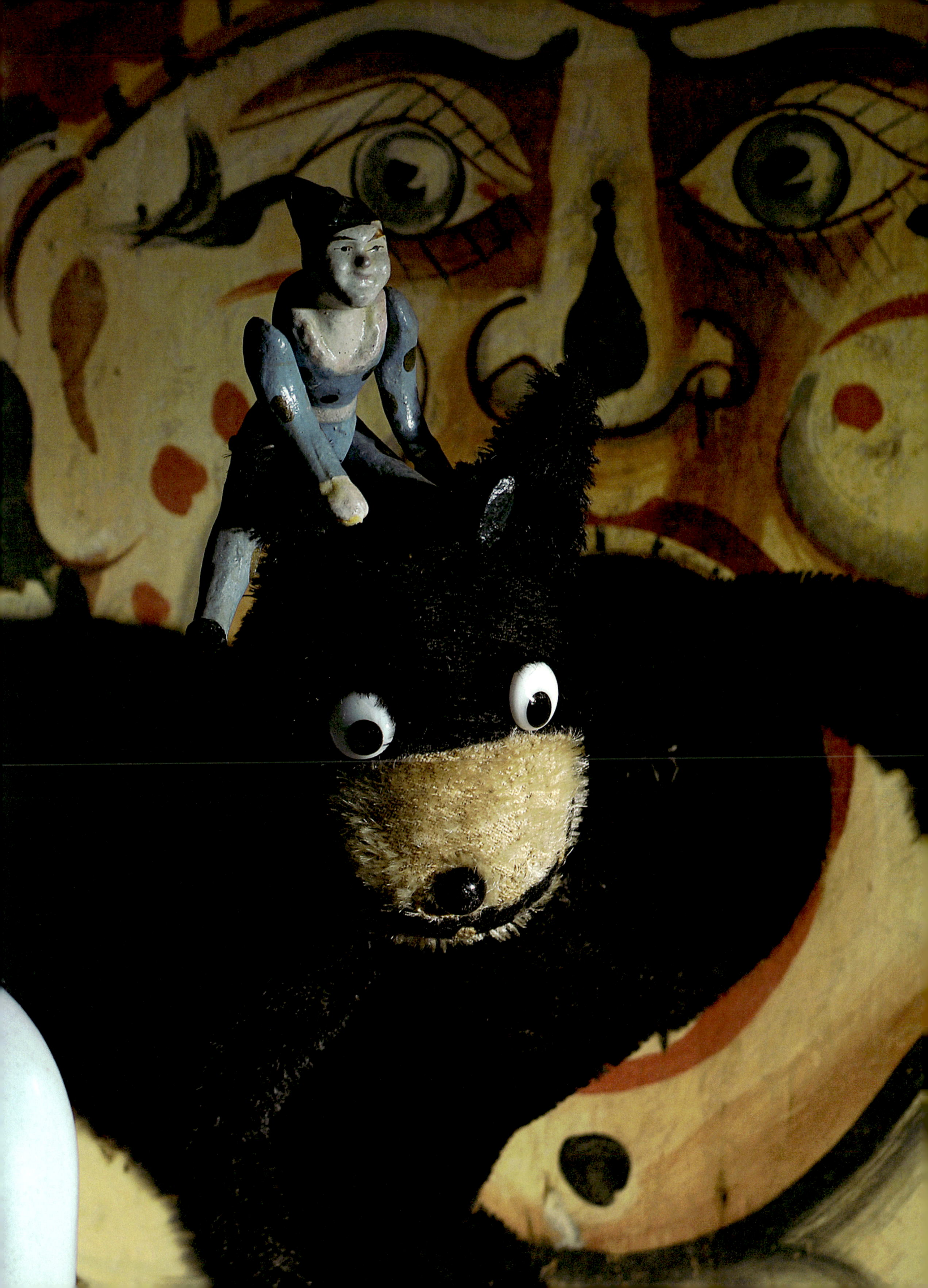

uilding blocks are a species by themselves. Meccano, Lego, wooden blocks and plastic slotted chips, these toys that allow the child to construct houses and towers, monuments and castles, bridges and walls, are one of the primordial things, like the wheel or the knife.

The story of Babel records the punishment for the ambition to go higher; the box of building blocks, the punishment's failure. Every time a child begins to pile his wall of blocks skywards, he acknowledges that the lesson has not been learned. Building echoes the act of standing up, of lifting oneself from the ground and defying the law of gravity. Everything must fall, our human nature tells us, but everything wants to rise, like trees or waves or swells of rock.

The limit of the building game is determined only by the number of blocks in a set. Since out there, on the shelves of the world, are innumerable sets, the limit (in the greedy realm of a child's desires) is very close to infinity. Within the four walls of the child's room, that knowledge, that the *possibility* of an evergrowing tower is his, appears to be sufficient. The shadow of Babel, of a triumphant Babel, falls on every playroom floor.

oys are symbols of identity: they tell us who we are. To take a toy in one's hand and play with it, to command it, possess it, make it do what one wills, conjures up the mirror image: that we too were held in someone's hand, that we too were commanded, possessed, made to obey. In the realm of make-believe, toys become scapegoats in a ritual of atonement or revenge. Suddenly the child's game of power reflects the power games of adults: the child treated as puppet, soldier, doll, dog, clown.

Like Gulliver or Pantagruel, the child is a giant among pygmies, pulling his toys out of a box, holding them on his lap, turning his body into a stage for their performances, cuddling them to his breast or throwing them about, deaf to any protest. The child is a mountain in the playroom; in the bath, he's an island; in bed, he's the waves of the sea or a monstrous avalanche.

But Gulliver in Lilliput is the flipside of Gulliver in Brobdingnag. In the world of adults, the child too is like a toy, prey to giant whims, subject to their care or carelessness, confronted with the huge and brutal nakedness of his captors. Their bare flesh (Gulliver tells us) was 'very far from being a tempting Sight, or from giving me any other Motions than those of Horror and Disgust. Their Skins appeared so coarse and uneven, so variously coloured when I saw them near, with a Mole here and there as broad as a Trencher, and Hairs hanging from it thicker than Pack-threads; to say nothing further concerning the rest of their Persons.'

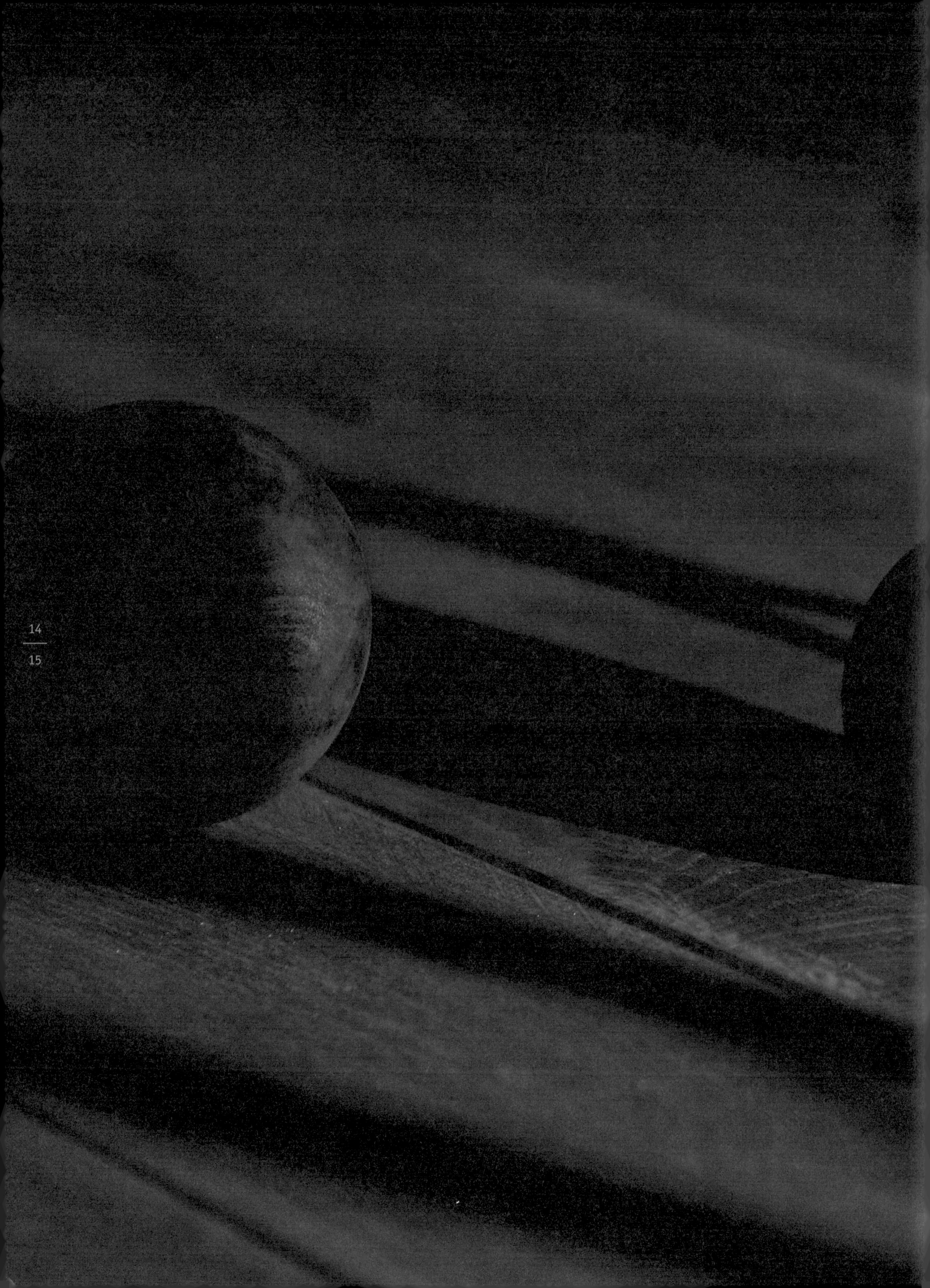
14
15

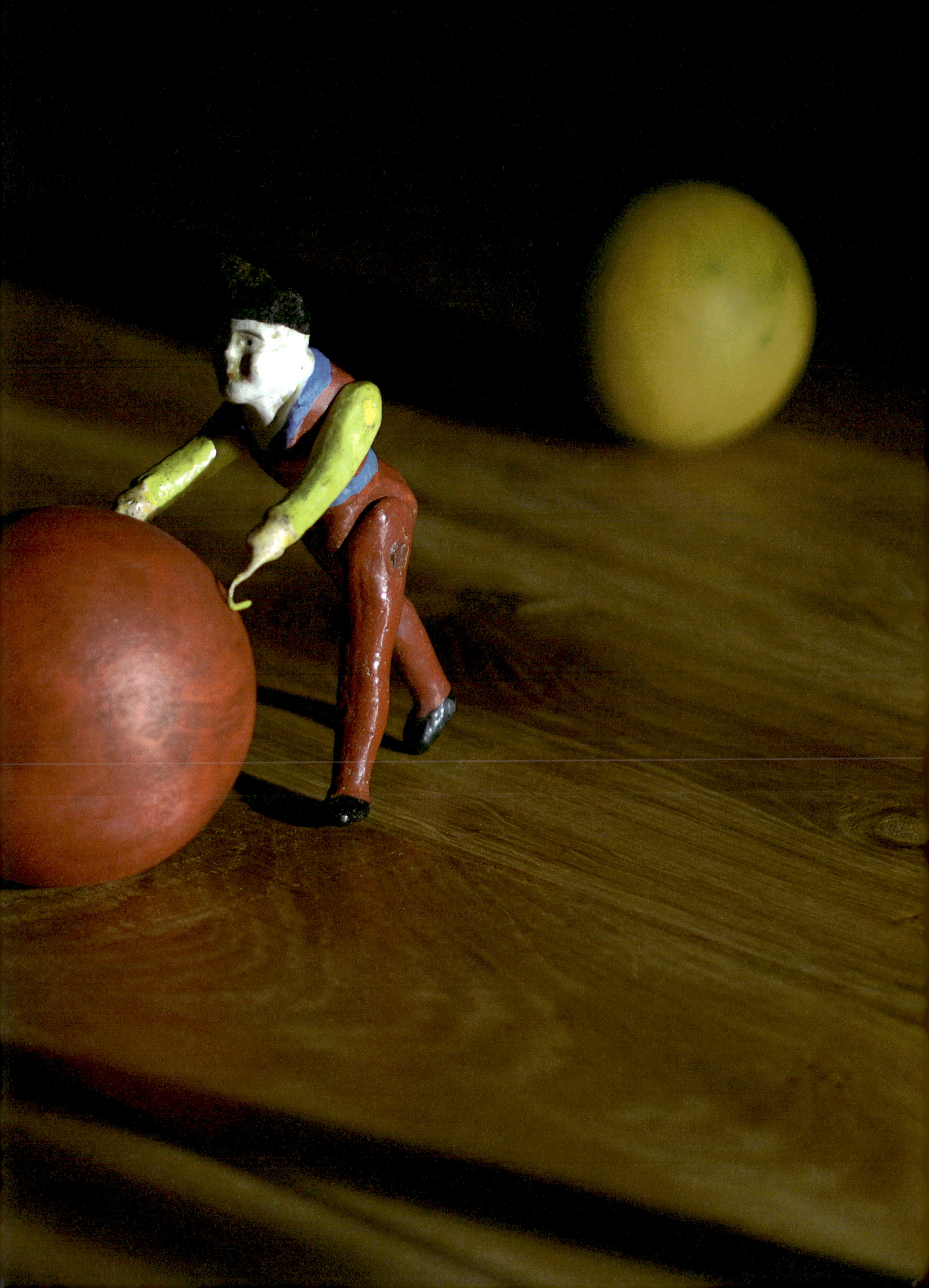

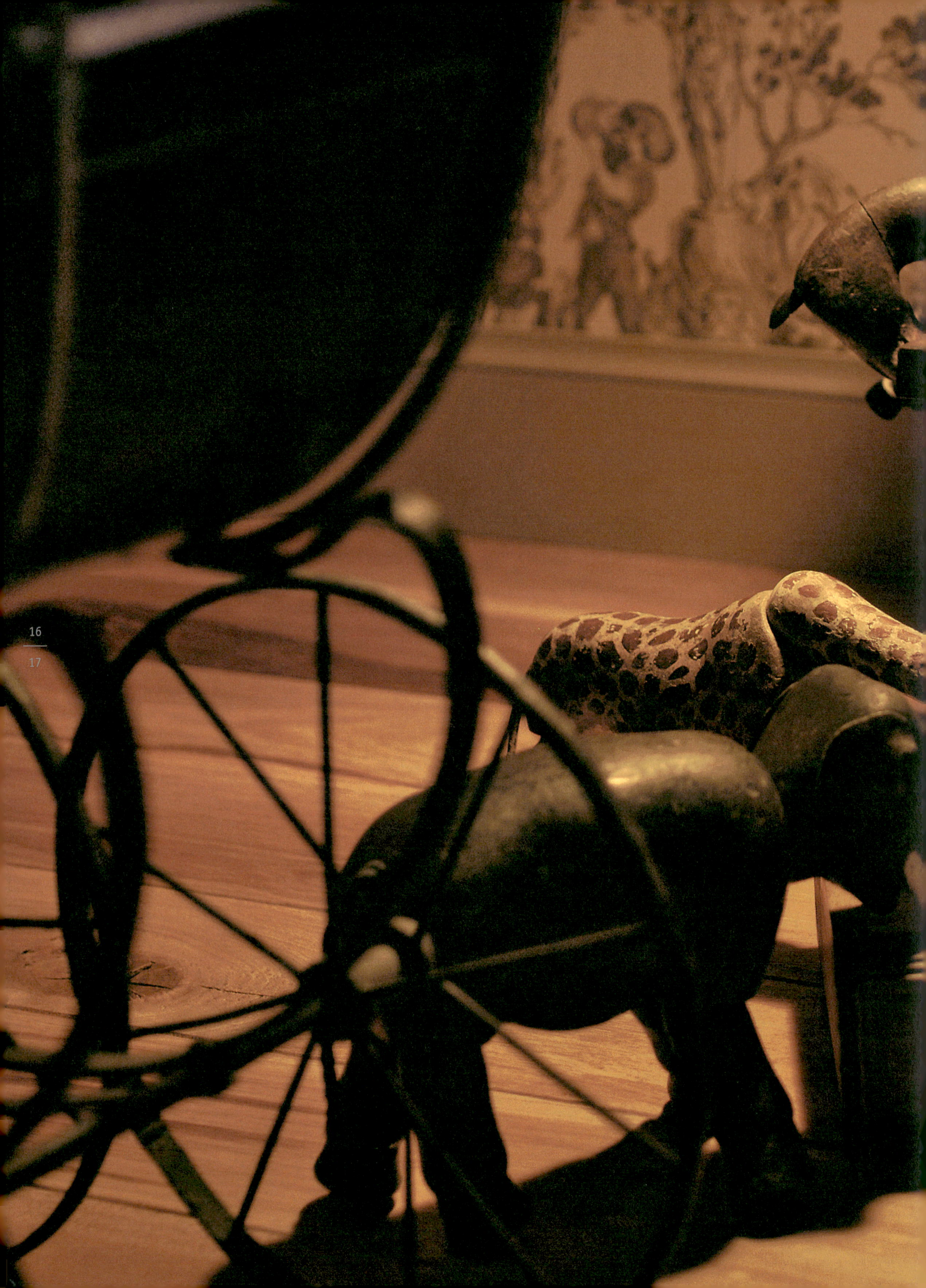

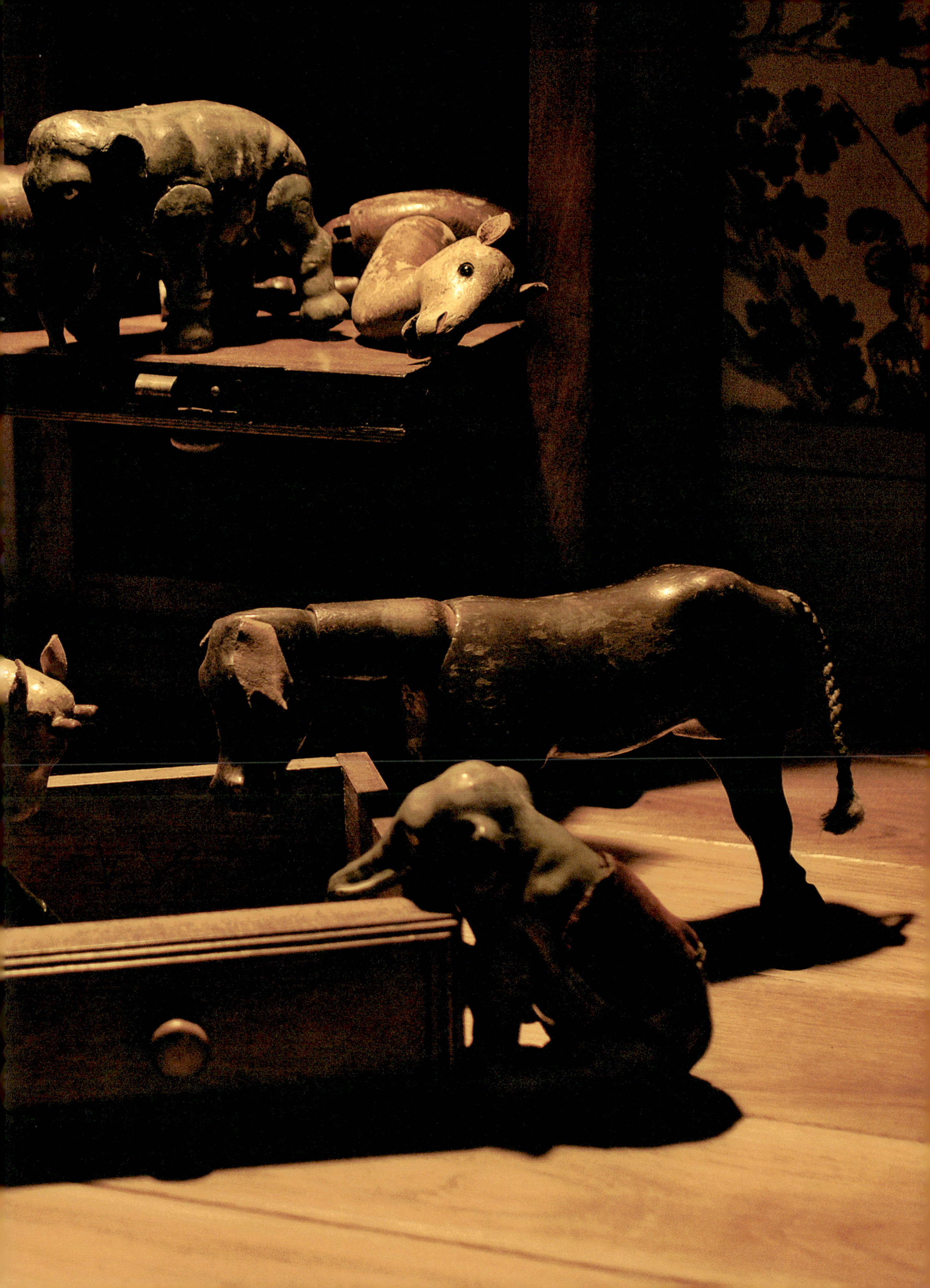

n 1902, Margarete Steiff invented the Teddy Bear, the first of a vast family
of bears. No stuffed animal has ever been as successful: lions and tigers, dogs
and rabbits, kangaroos and elephants, cannot compete with the popularity of
the bear. Something in its double nature, almost human and almost monstrous, hairy and
soft, wild and companionable, is irresistibly seductive. Its identity is both neutral and
specific: it can dress up in a national costume, in a motorcyclist's leathers, in a policeman's
uniform, in a tutu. It can serve as a badge or symbol, change size or colour. Three years
after Steiff's death, in 1912, when the *Titanic* sank, the Steiff company produced all-black
'mourning' bears exclusively for the British public.

The bear is the outsider, the almost-human, the beast who carries that which society must
exclude in order to be lawful. In the oldest story of all, Gilgamesh, the civilized man, must
meet the wild man Enkidu and, after fighting him, become his loving friend. Only then
is Gilgamesh complete. Every child who takes his toy bear to bed secretly repeats the
story of Gilgamesh.

he doll's house is the house within the house, the rooms within the room. In this ideal space of perfectly organized compartments – the upstairs bedrooms, the bathroom, the dining room, living room, library and kitchen – everything is visible, above board. Harmoniously divided and rigorously furnished, the doll's house is a miniature Arcadia: here no one is afraid, no one shouts or becomes violent, no one is jealous, spiteful, cowardly, no one is a torturer or a bully. Everyone fulfils a storybook role; everyone has his or her place. In the doll's house children are loved, parents are admired, dogs are well treated.

Sometimes, however, a darker atmosphere fills the place. The mood changes, the rules of the game are altered. Furniture is shifted, shutters are closed, wild animals are allowed to roam about. One of the dolls is found in the wrong room doing something unexpected, another upsets the table so beautifully set for tea, a third one trips on the stairs and tumbles down with a crash, a fourth climbs up on the roof and gets stuck in the chimney. The baby puts Mummy to bed, Daddy sticks his head into the oven, the dog is in the cupboard and won't come out. A fire-engine crashes into the side wall. A dinosaur stands at the entrance waiting to pounce on anyone trying to leave. Then, without warning, the game comes to an end.

In Queen Mary's doll's house in Windsor Castle is a toy nursery with a toy doll's house. This doll's house suggests a spiralling *mise-en-abîme*. Nestled within a castle where a real family lives is this perfect simulacrum of a house fit for a princess, in which no doll ever suffers, everyone is happy and toy children play with a toy doll's house. The question is this: inside the toy doll's house, is there another doll's house? Within that happy house, is there another house in which dreadful things take place, a toy house that holds tragedies too terrible to utter, and from which the only refuge is somewhere more secret still, a smaller house in a smaller nursery, a tiny haven in which all is well, Mummy and Daddy have their bedroom, the dog is in the kitchen sleeping, the children are happily inventing a game where, in an even tinier doll's house, among even more minuscule furniture, someone too small to be seen lets out a piercing, anguished, agonizing scream?

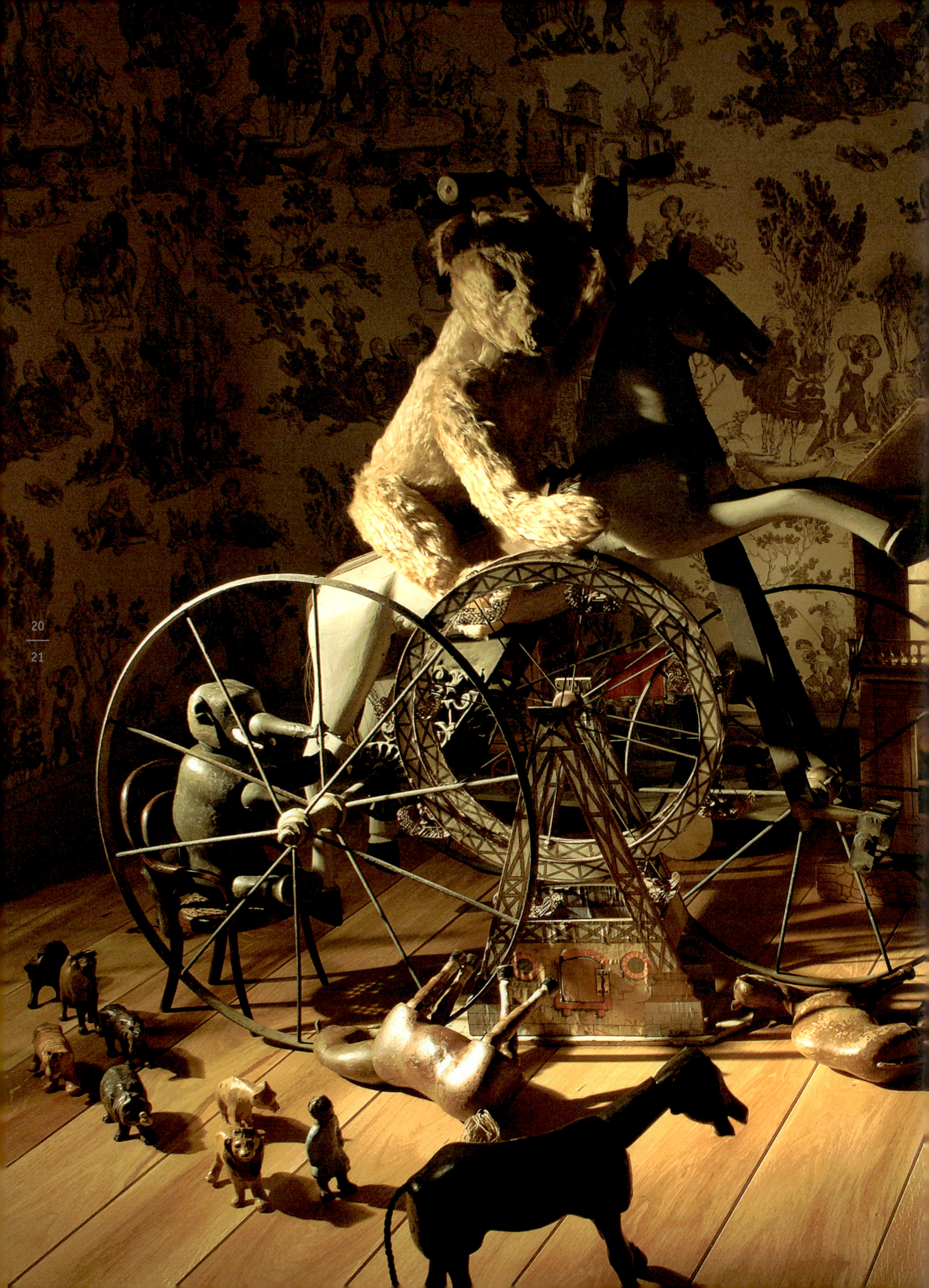

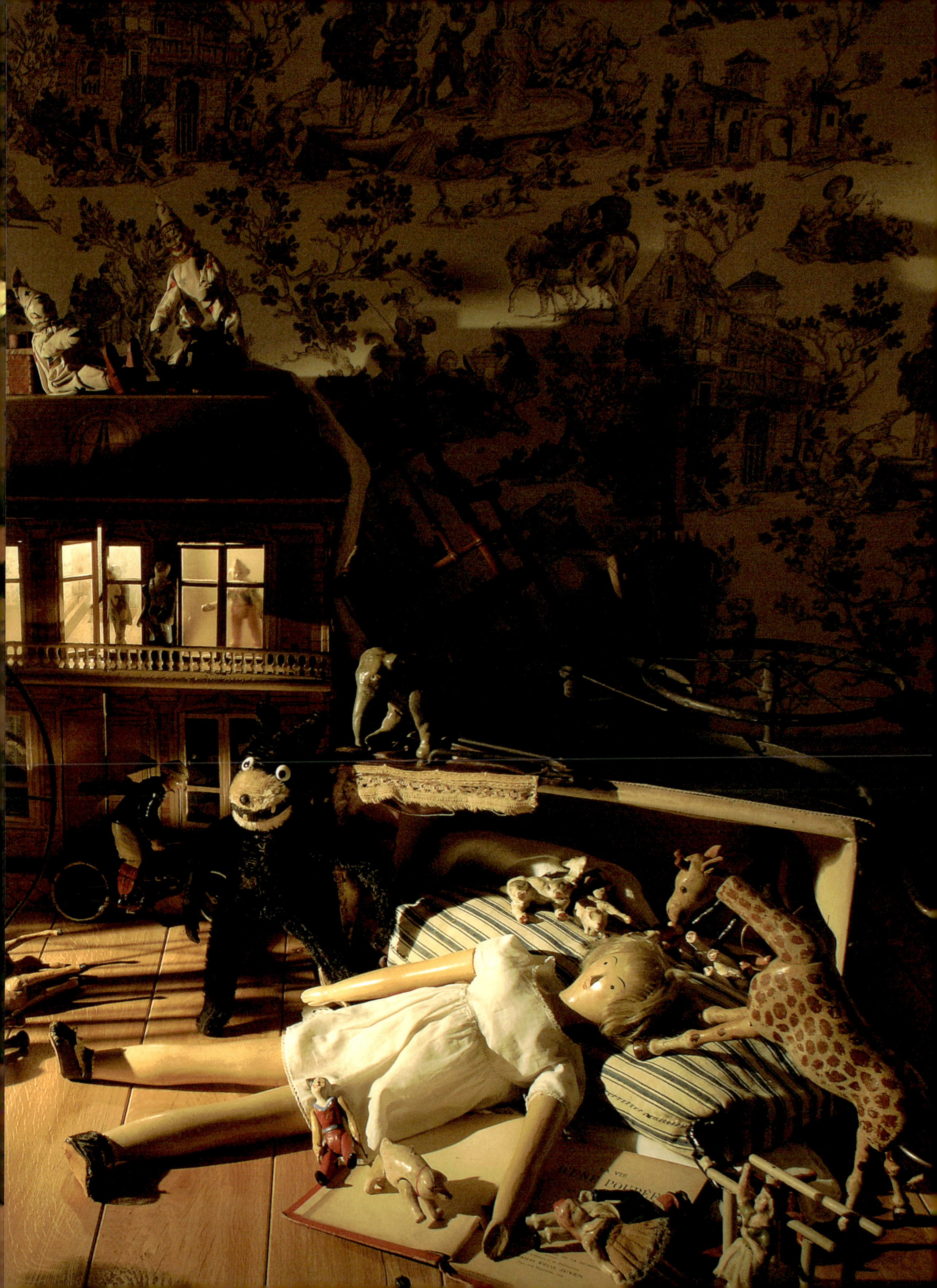

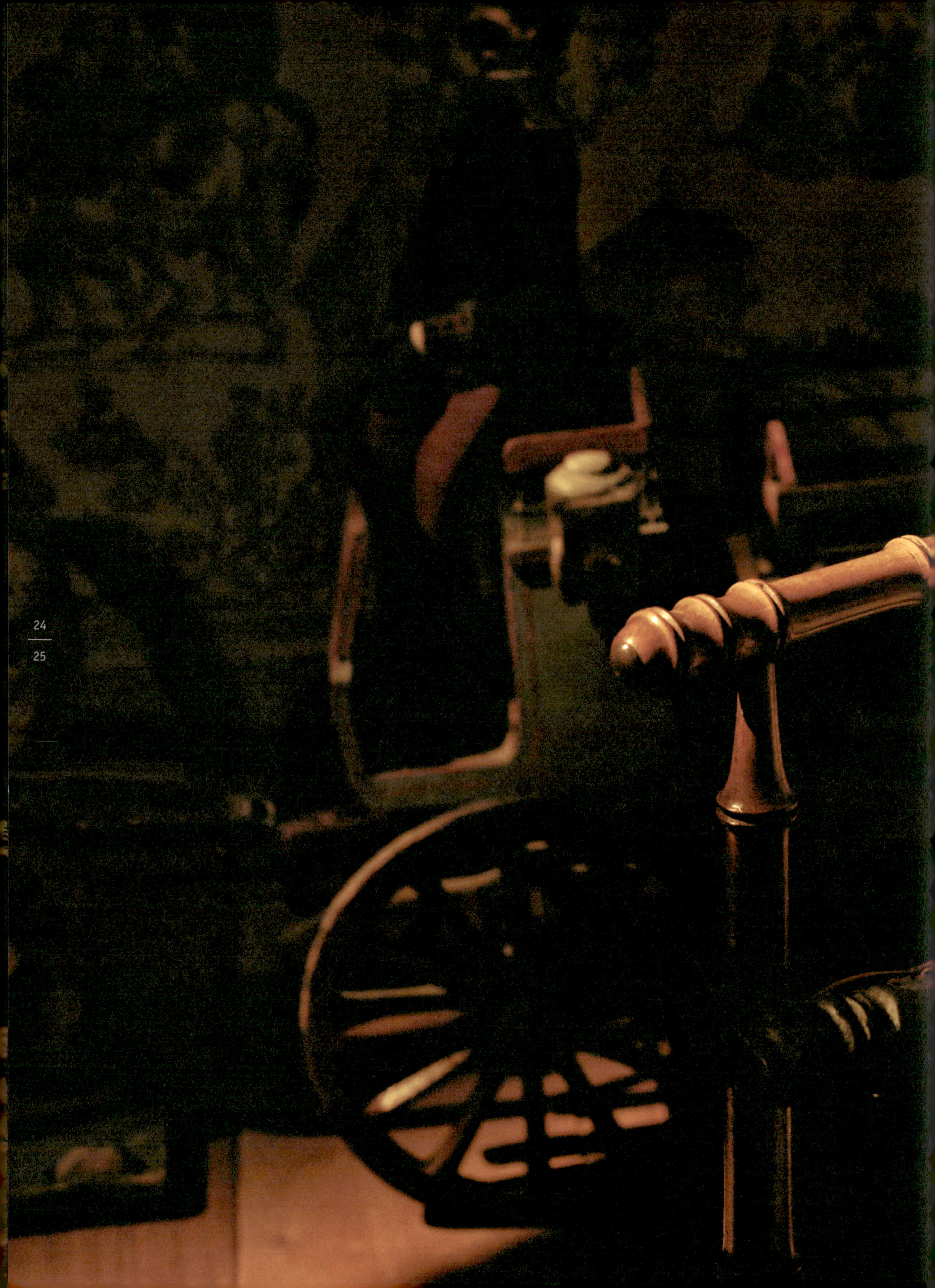

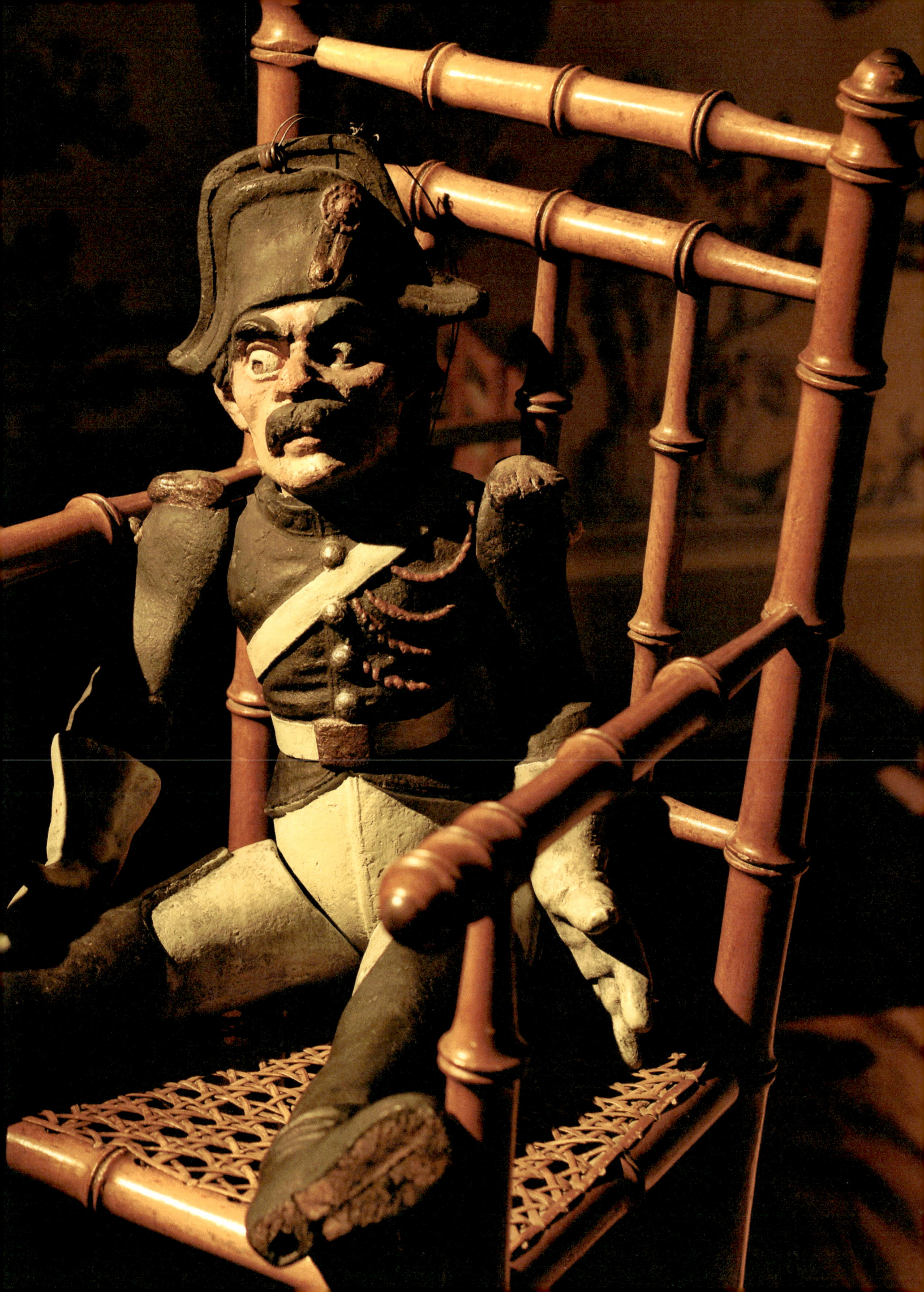

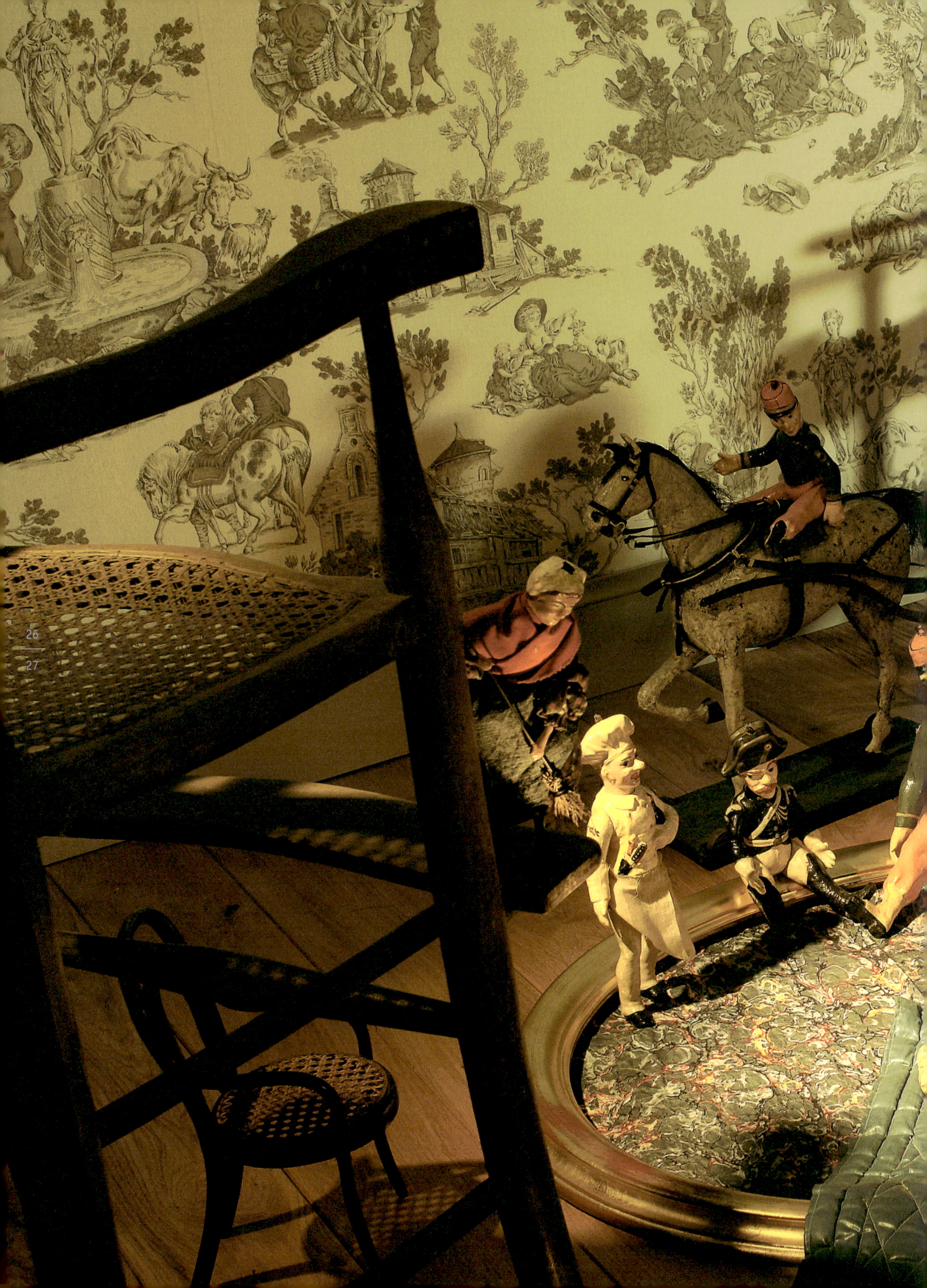

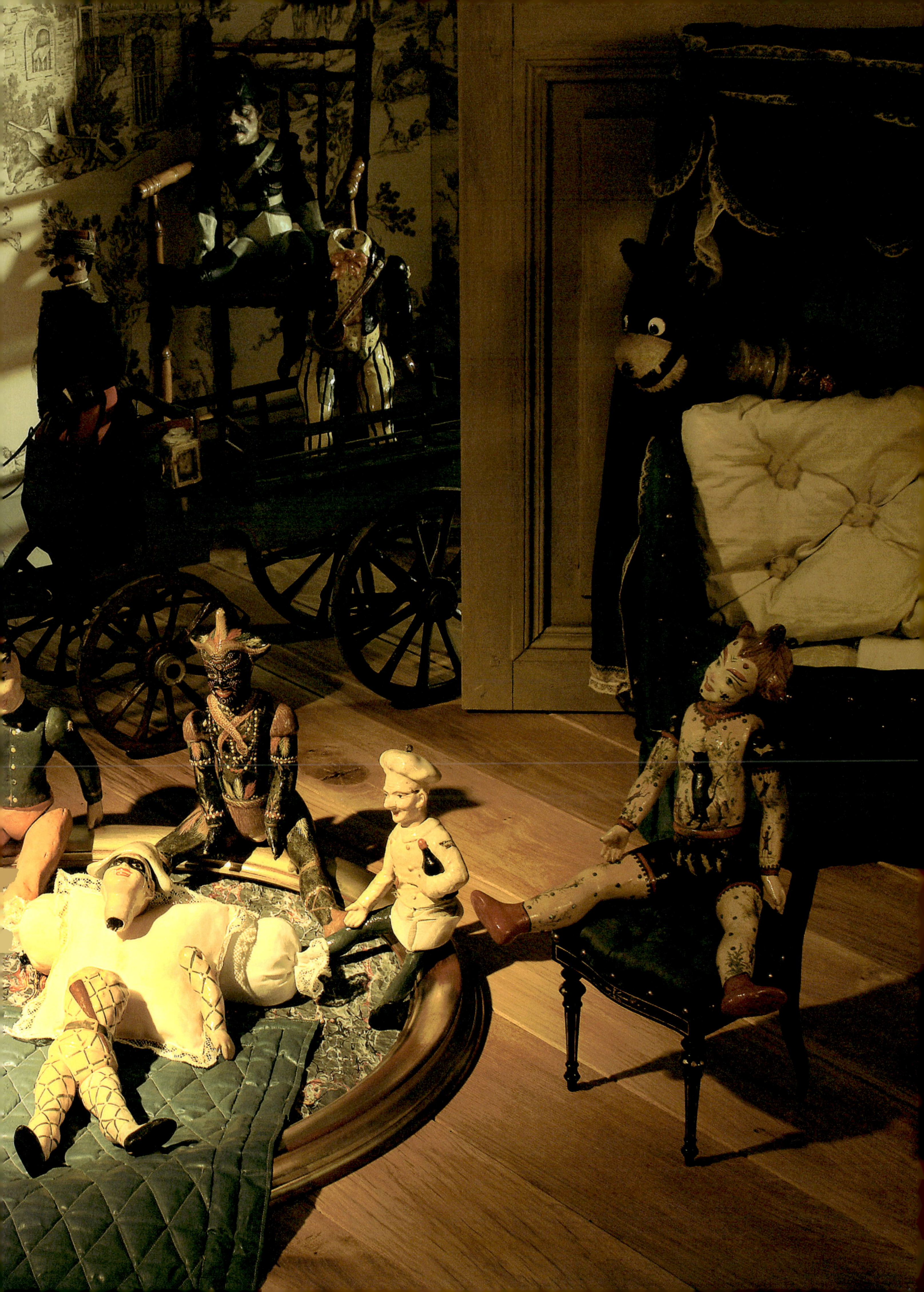

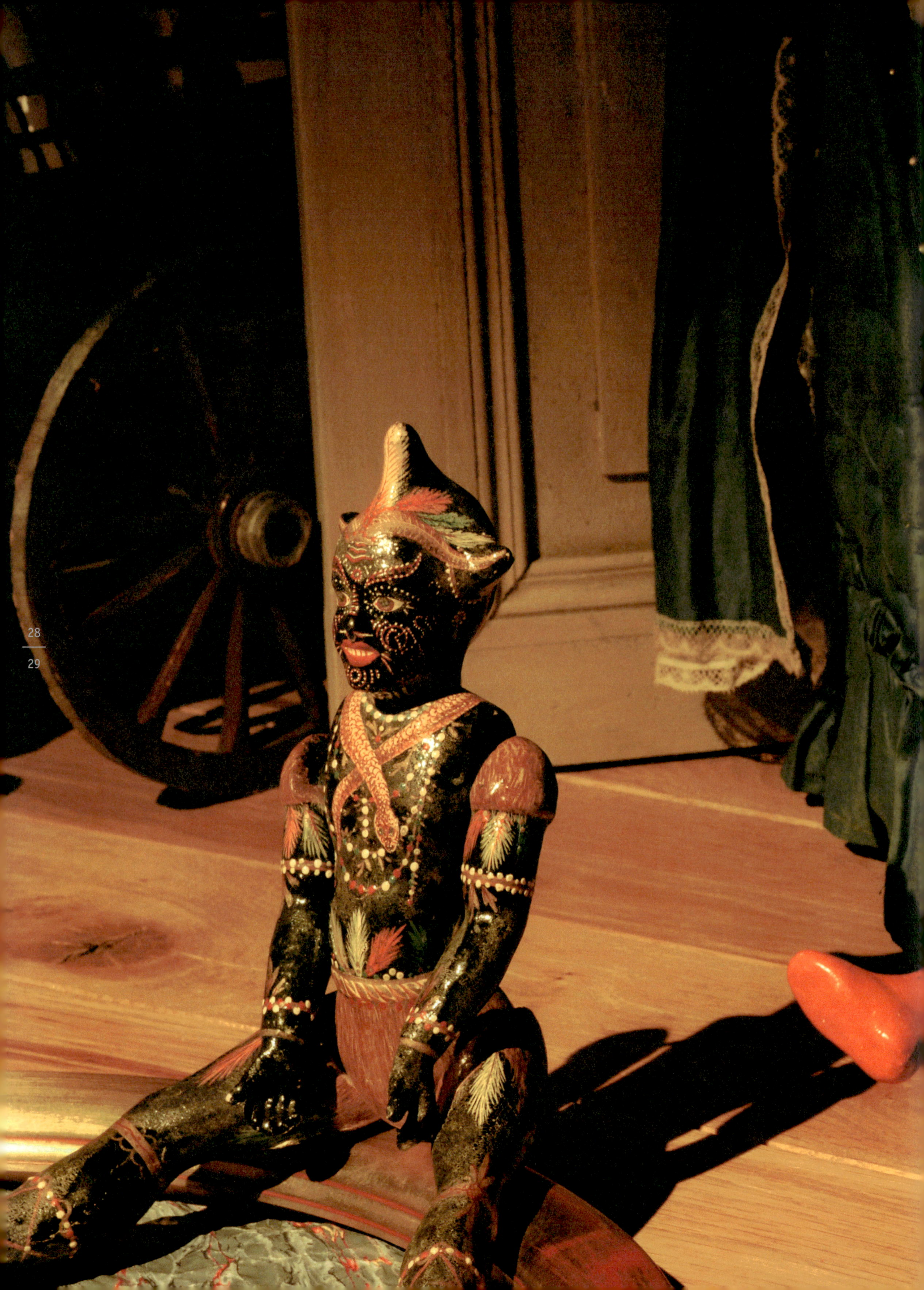

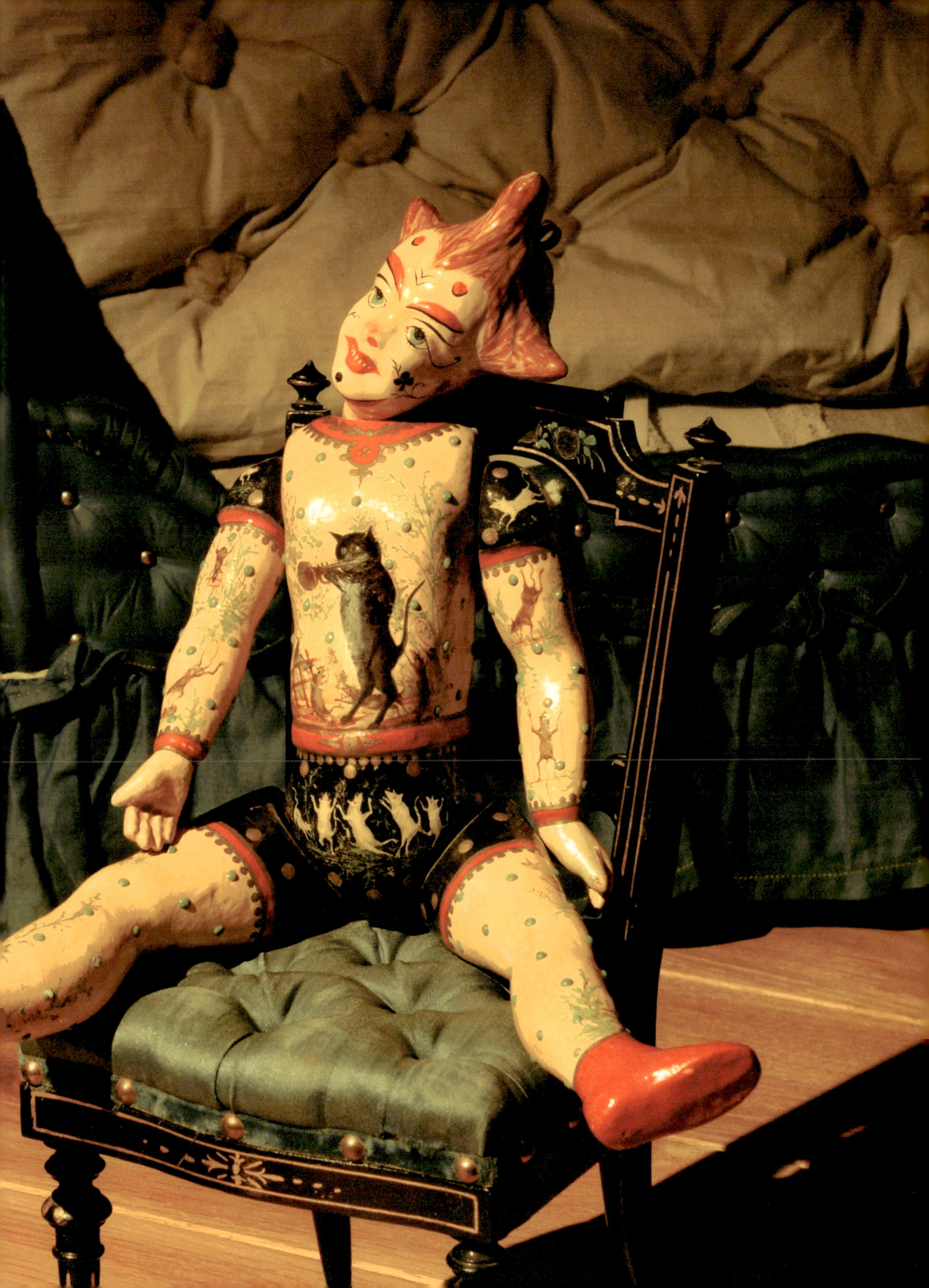

Children invent toys and also play with toys that others have invented for them. Why relinquish the absolute pleasure of creating and possessing your creation? Because the temptation of perfection is great, and who will not give up a kicked-about tin in exchange for a smooth rubber ball, even if it means accepting adult rules implicit in the toy received? Play is not always the exercise of freedom and sometimes, in order to break free from impositions, the rules of the game must be subverted, the toy repossessed.

The toys of Goethe's son August exemplify these two different species. On the one hand, we are told that August played with simple chestnuts which he threaded and hung from his neck, pretending that they were garlands of precious jewels and he a powerful oriental monarch. On the other, August enjoyed setting up an elaborate toy theatre with conventional cardboard figures representing Harlequin, Columbine, Doctor Faustus and other characters. To these (and here is the act of subversion) August would add a live cat during his performances, 'for the sake of realism'.

On one occasion, Goethe decided to buy for August a toy guillotine and asked his mother to order one from an enterprising Frankfurt manufacturer. Goethe's mother refused. 'Dear son,' she wrote. 'Everything that you wish for is fine and pleases me, but buying this abominable killing-machine is something I won't do under any circumstances. If I were the authorities, its makers would be put in chains and I'd have the executioner burn the machine in public. What an idea, to have young people play with something so frightful! To put in their hands murder and bloodshed as an entertainment – no, certainly not!'

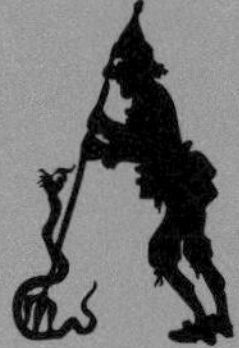 baby doll or a teddy bear, a toy sailor or a robot possess their own singular nature, but also acquire other personalities during the time of play. Every collection of toys is a repertory theatre.

In various languages the word 'play' is associated with the concepts of fun and mockery. In Arabic, *la'iba* means 'to play' and 'to make fun of'. In Hebrew, *sahaq* means 'to play' and 'to laugh out loud'. In Latin, *ludere* is both 'to play' (as a child) and 'to perform' (in the theatre). The English word 'play' retains these two last meanings. Every game is a representation, an act of magic that imitates or acts out another. Since it cannot be the original, there is in the imitation an undercurrent of fun or even, making fun of that which is seriously real.

A hand can make a toy plane fly, a tin soldier walk, a stuffed tiger pounce: that is magic. What happens in the adult world (like that which takes place on the TV or video screen) is in a sense too real. Magic requires a few imperfections, certain gaps through which the fantastic can enter. The doll that sleeps as the child sleeps, the clown that sits as the child sits, the horse that is wheeled along at the child's pace, the stories acted out by creatures of plastic and wood in the infinite space of the room tell him, over and over again, that nothing is impossible, only unbelievable, and that a game of mirrors will reveal to him 'how it's done'.

Play is imitation only in the sense that a magician imitates the creative processes of the world. The child does not merely want to observe: he wants to act out what he observes, bringing it to life again, starting afresh. Experience lies not in experience itself but in the imitation of experience.

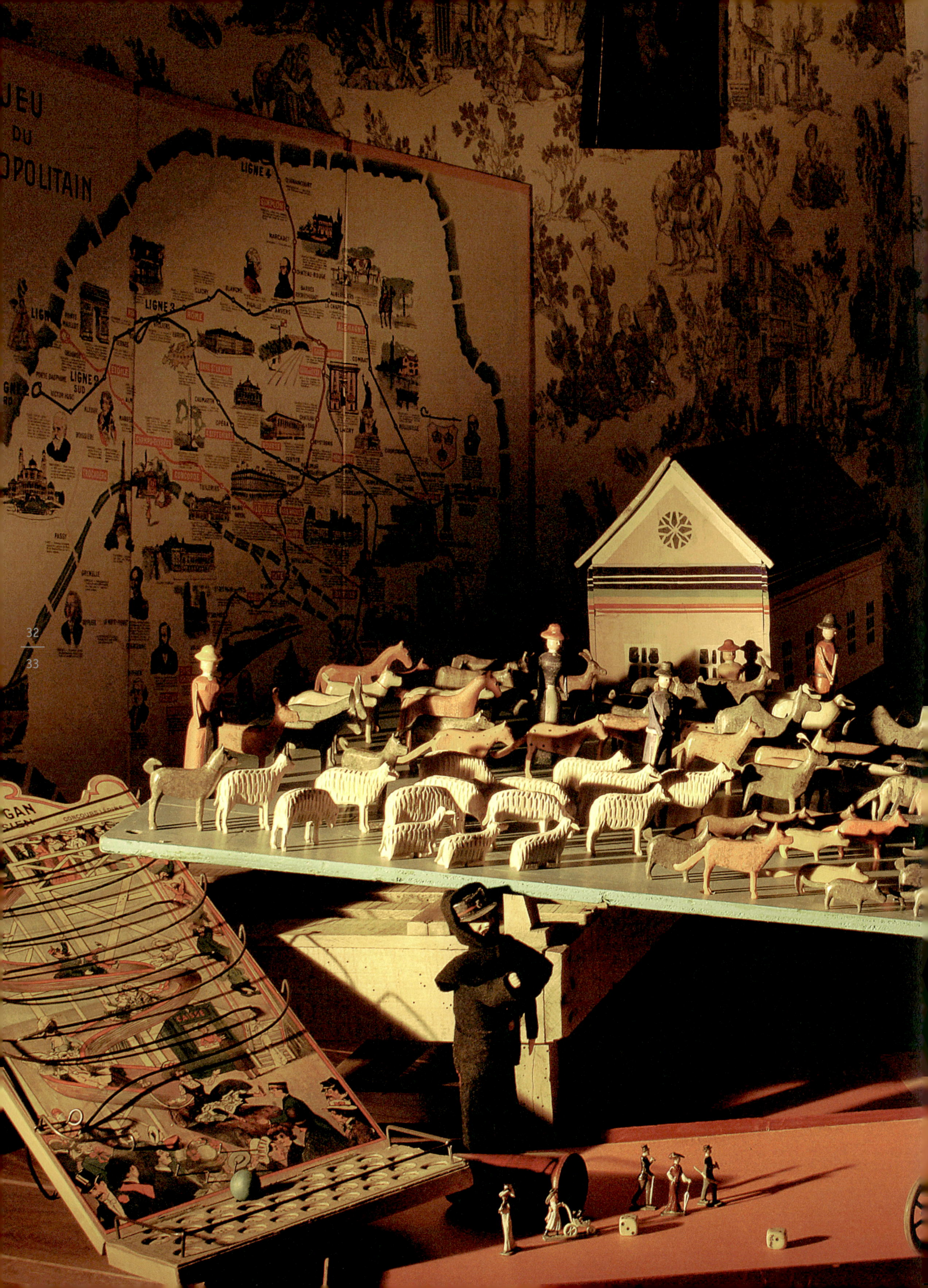
JEU
DU
OPOLITAIN

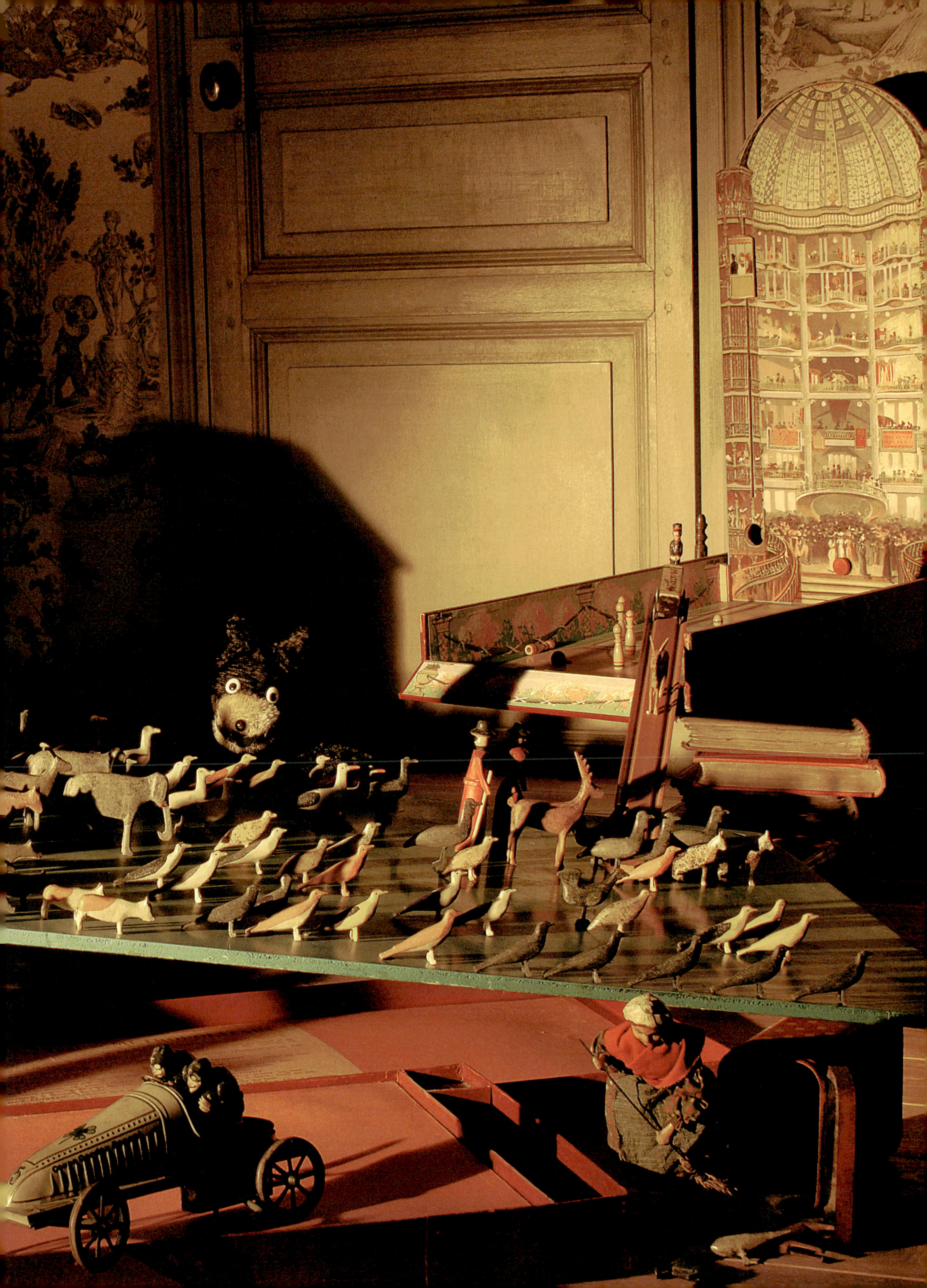

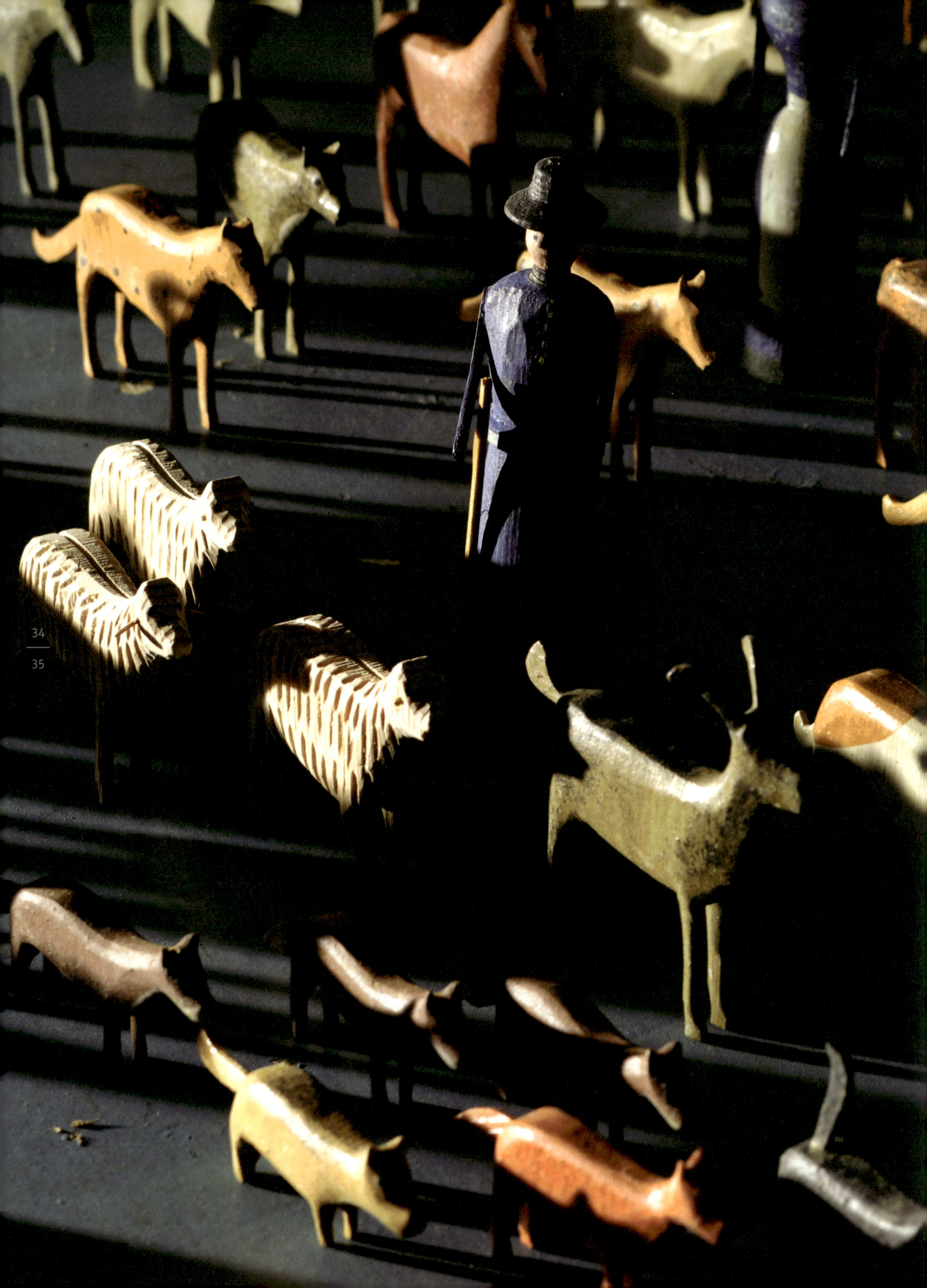

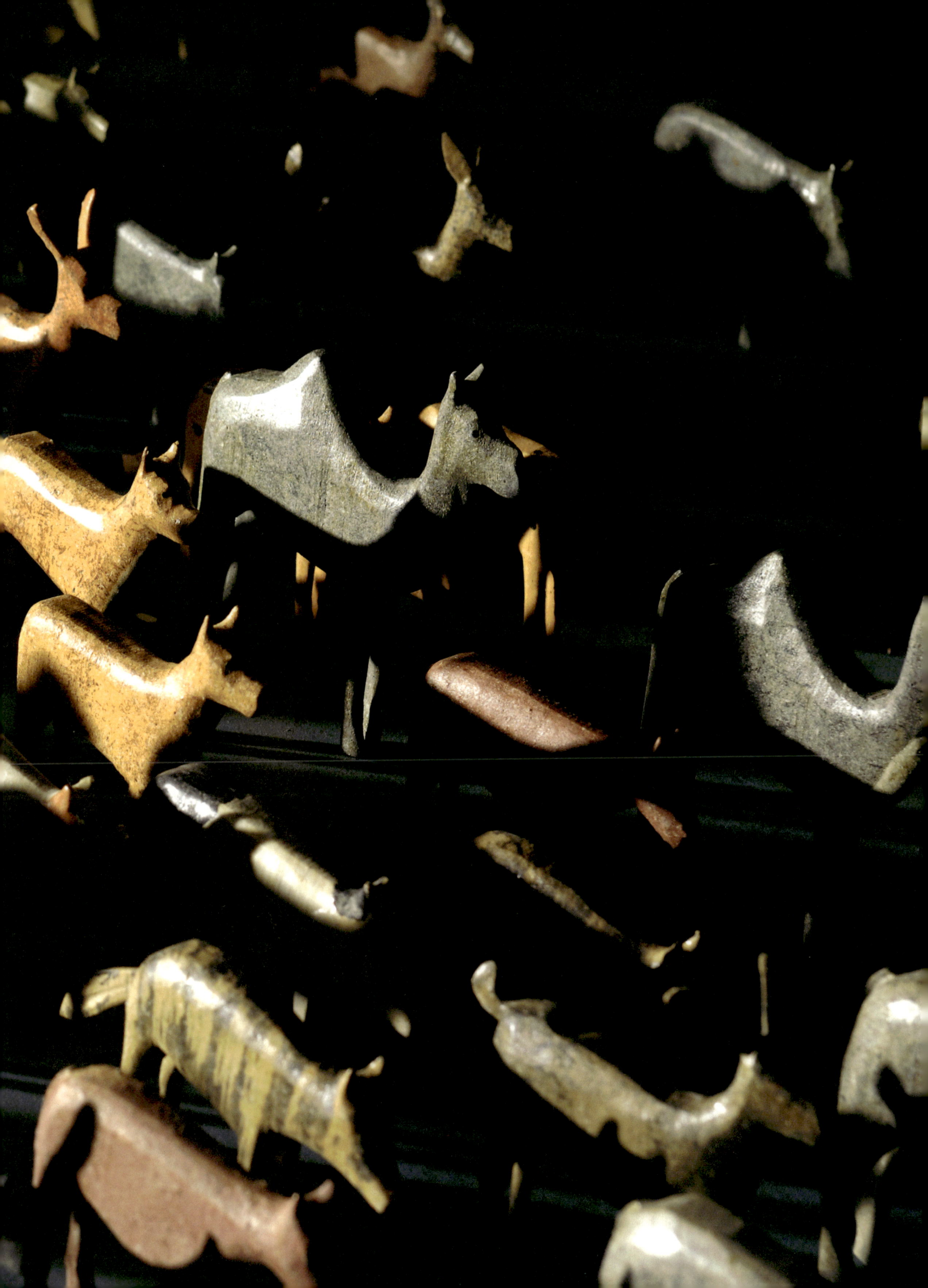

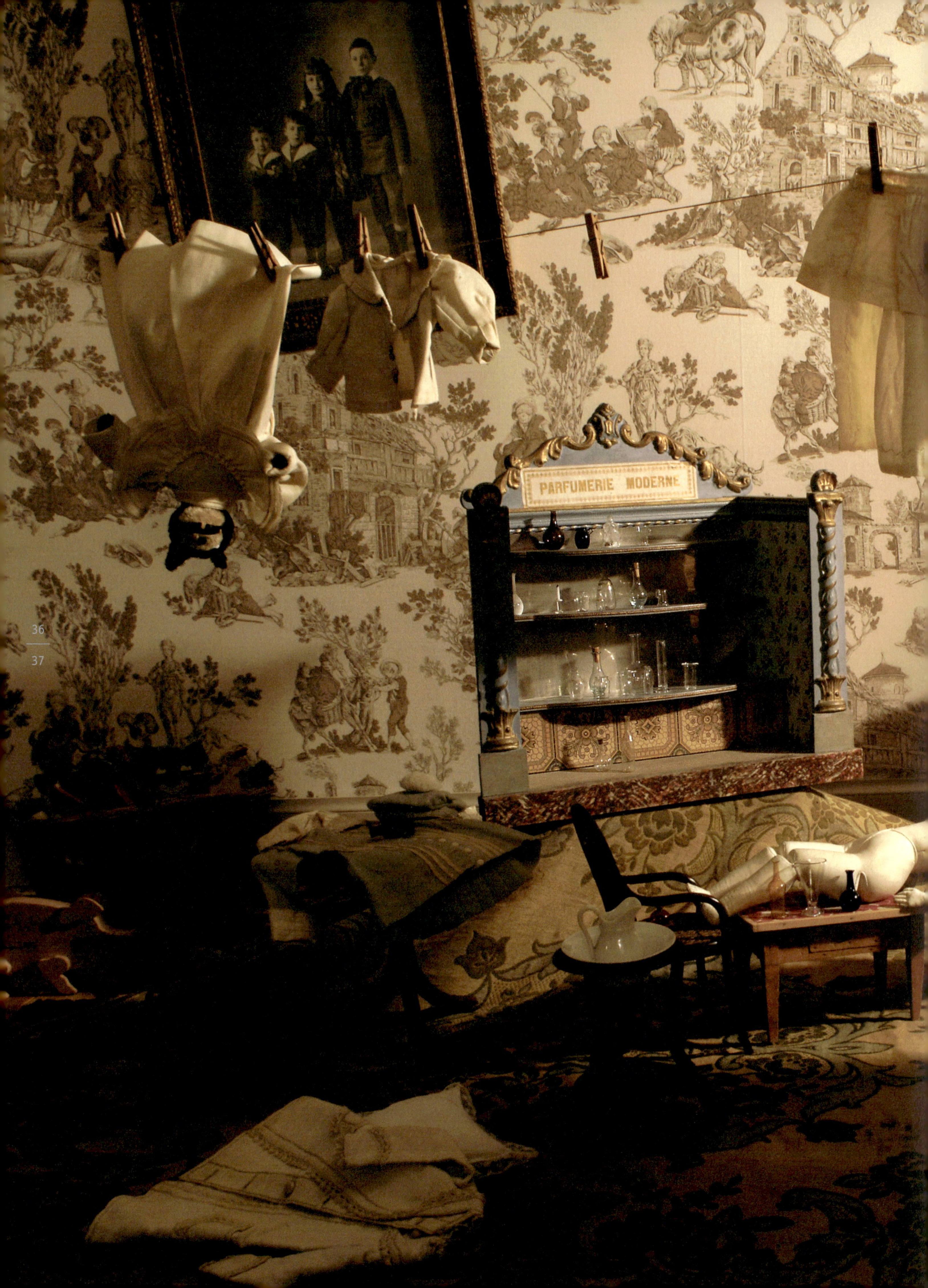

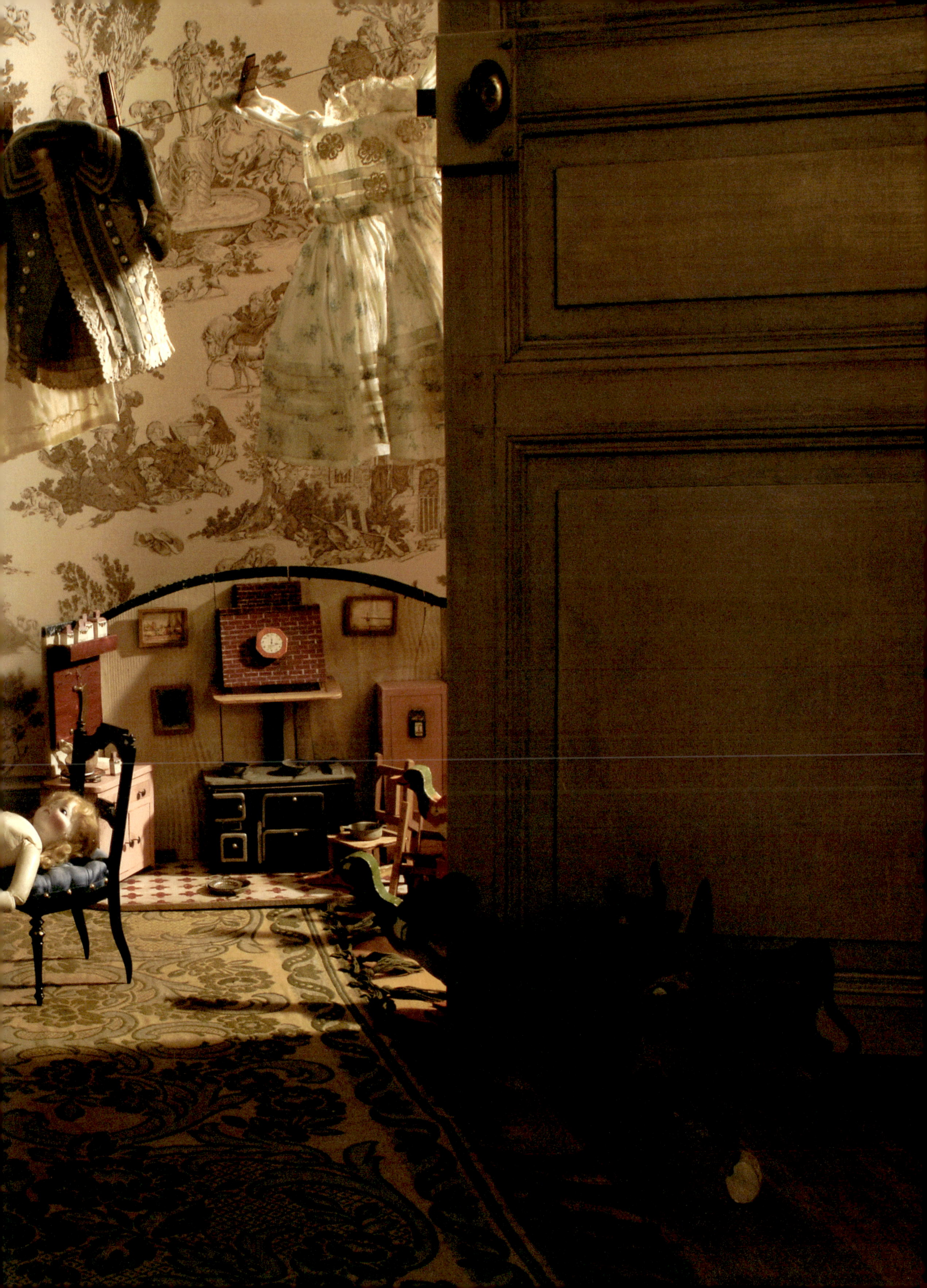

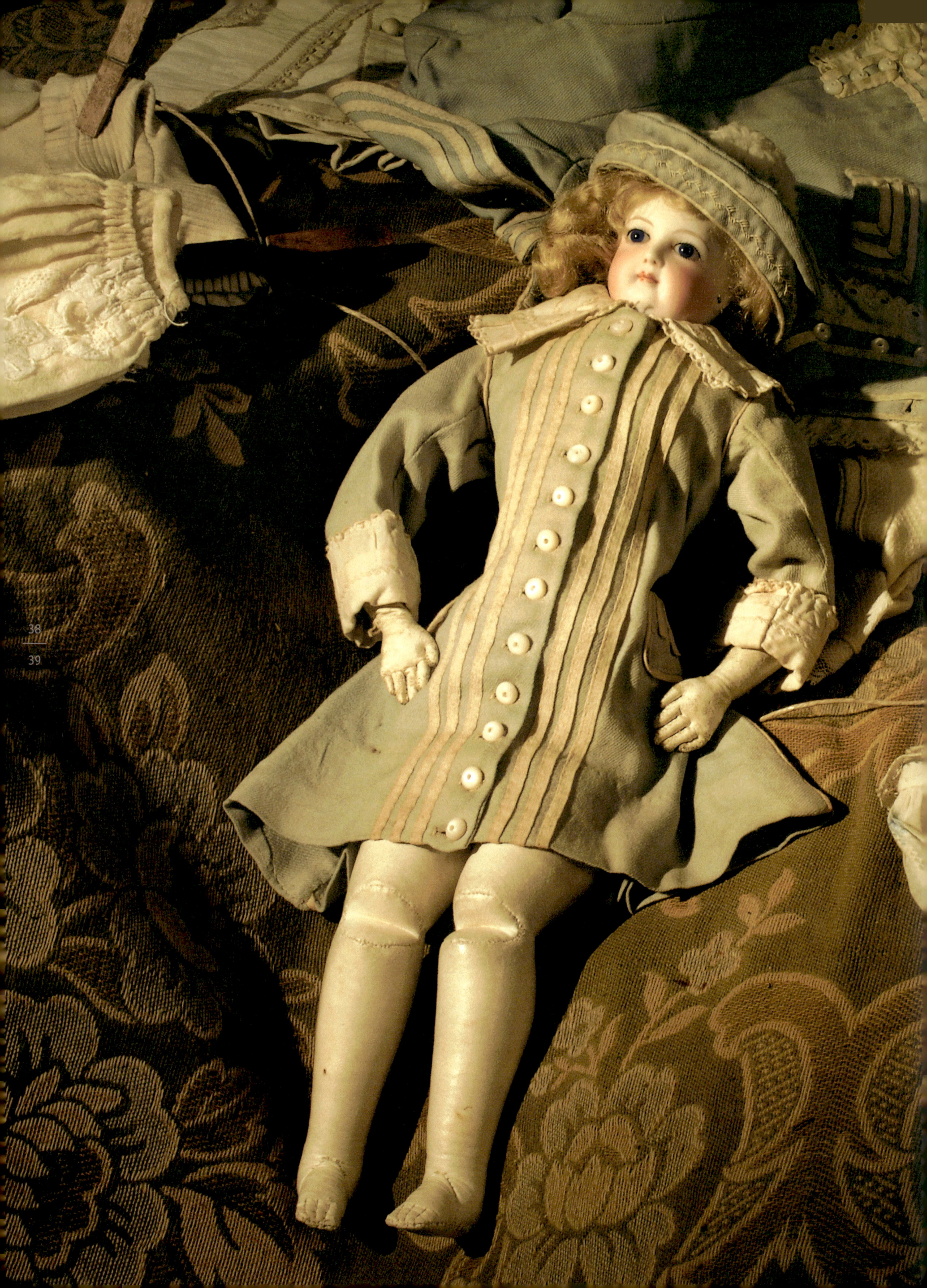

38
39

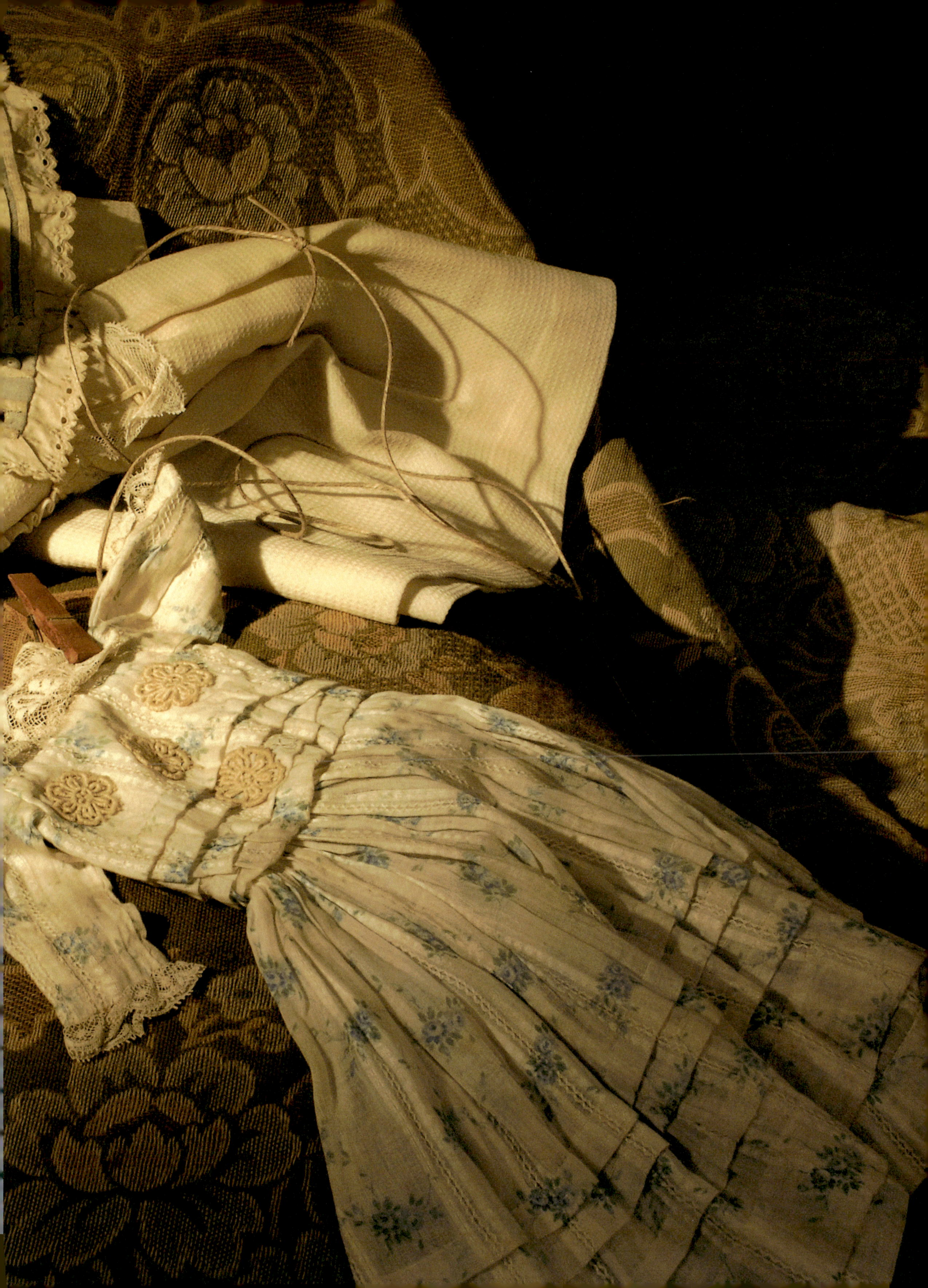

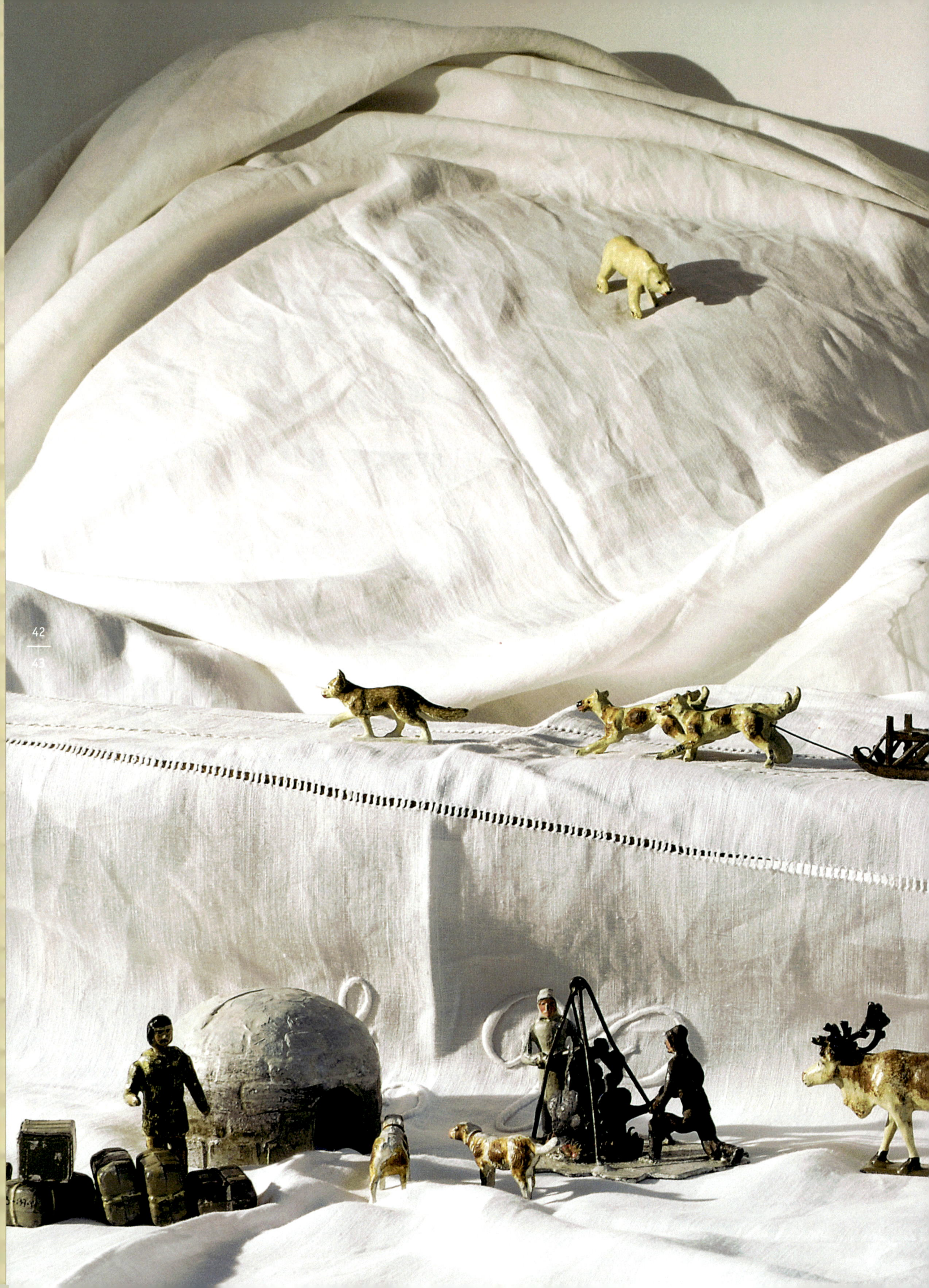

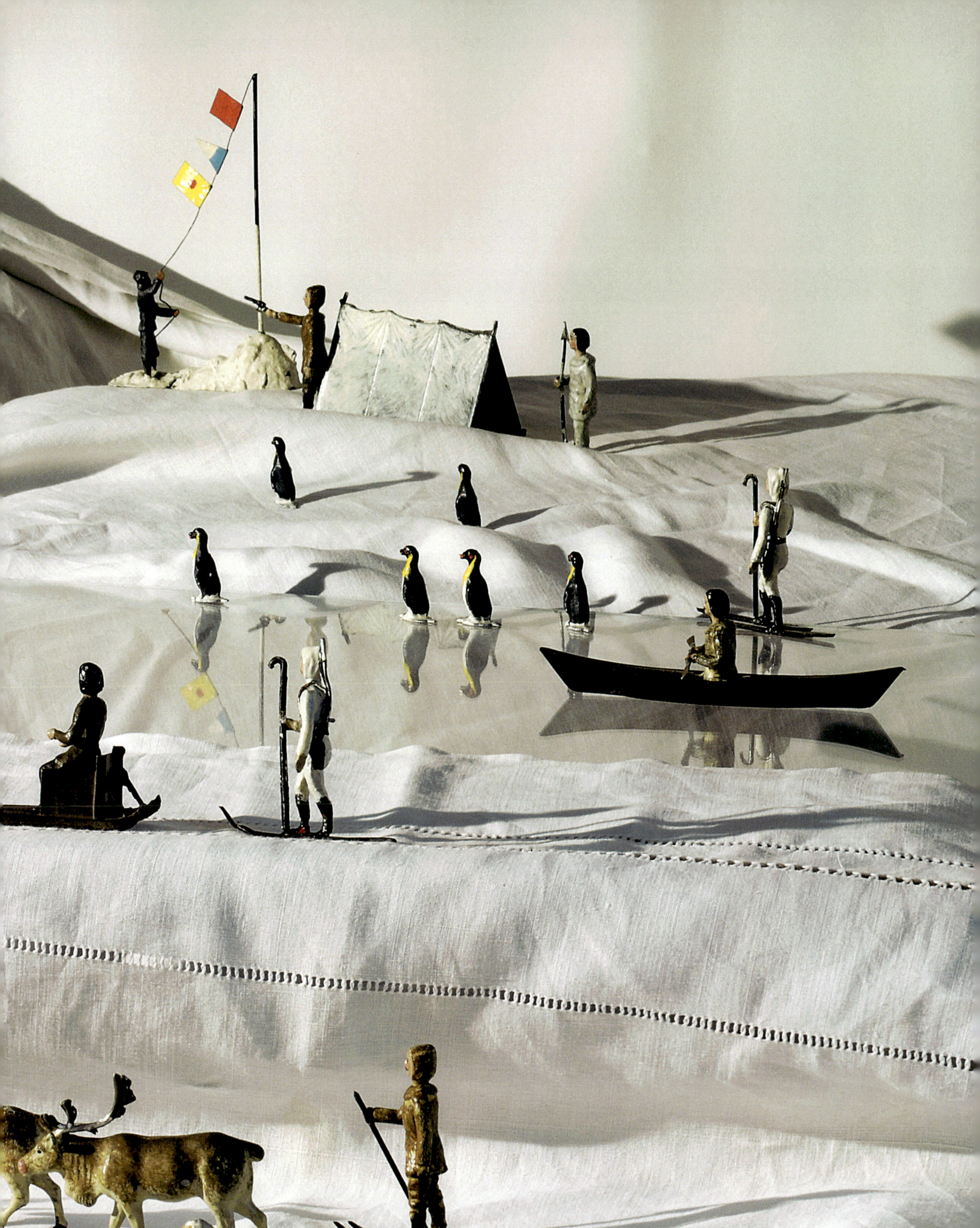

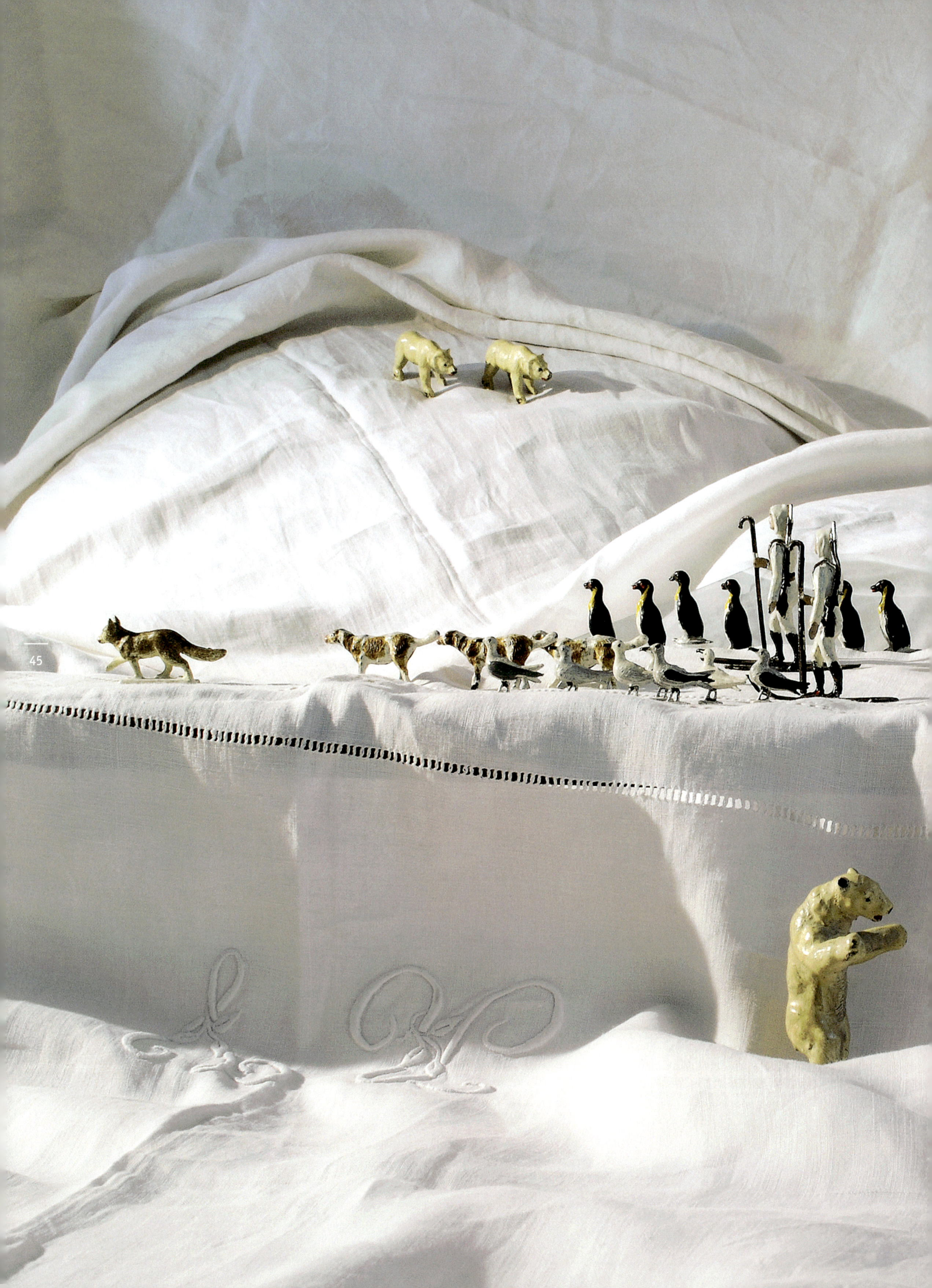

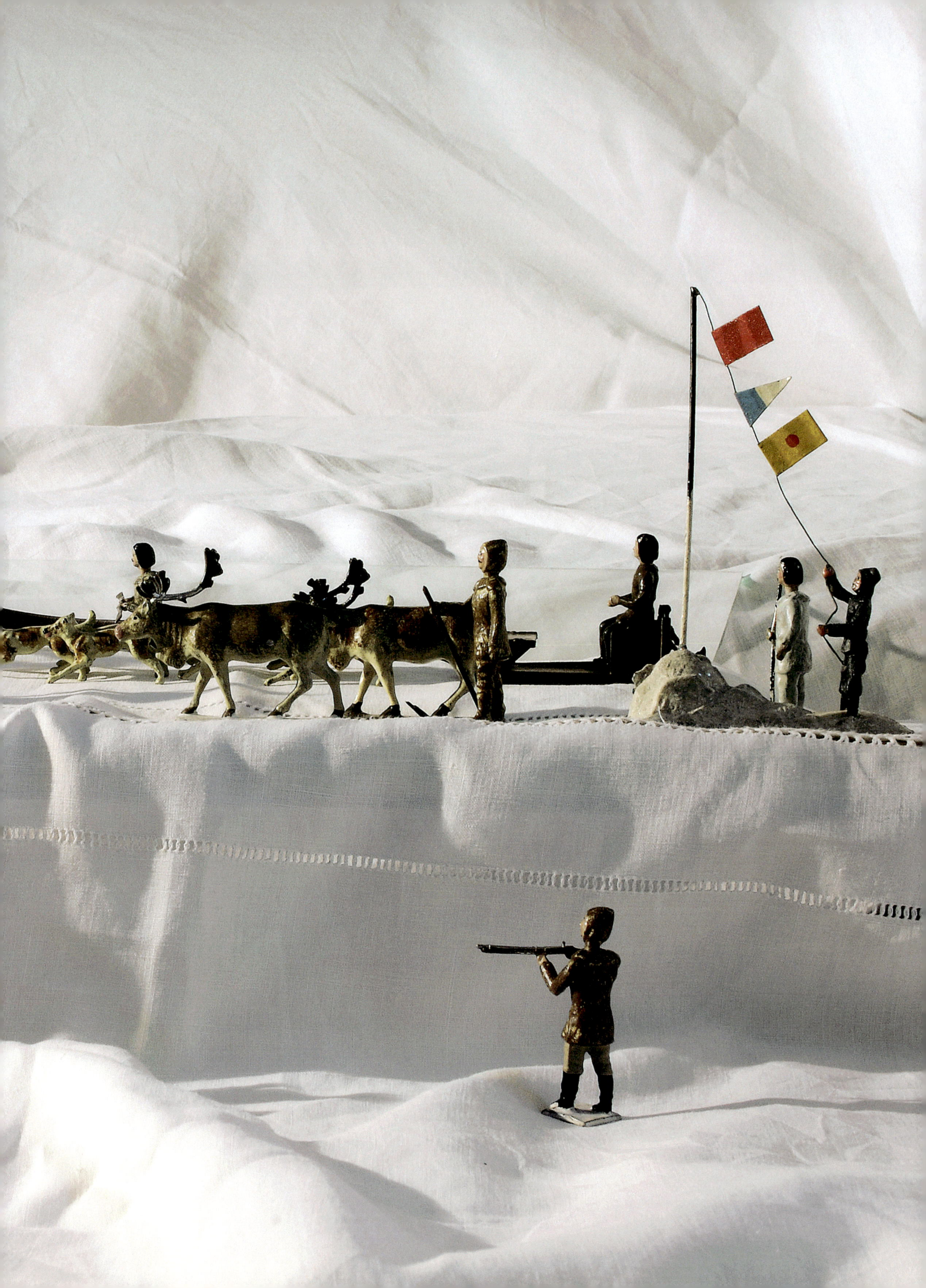

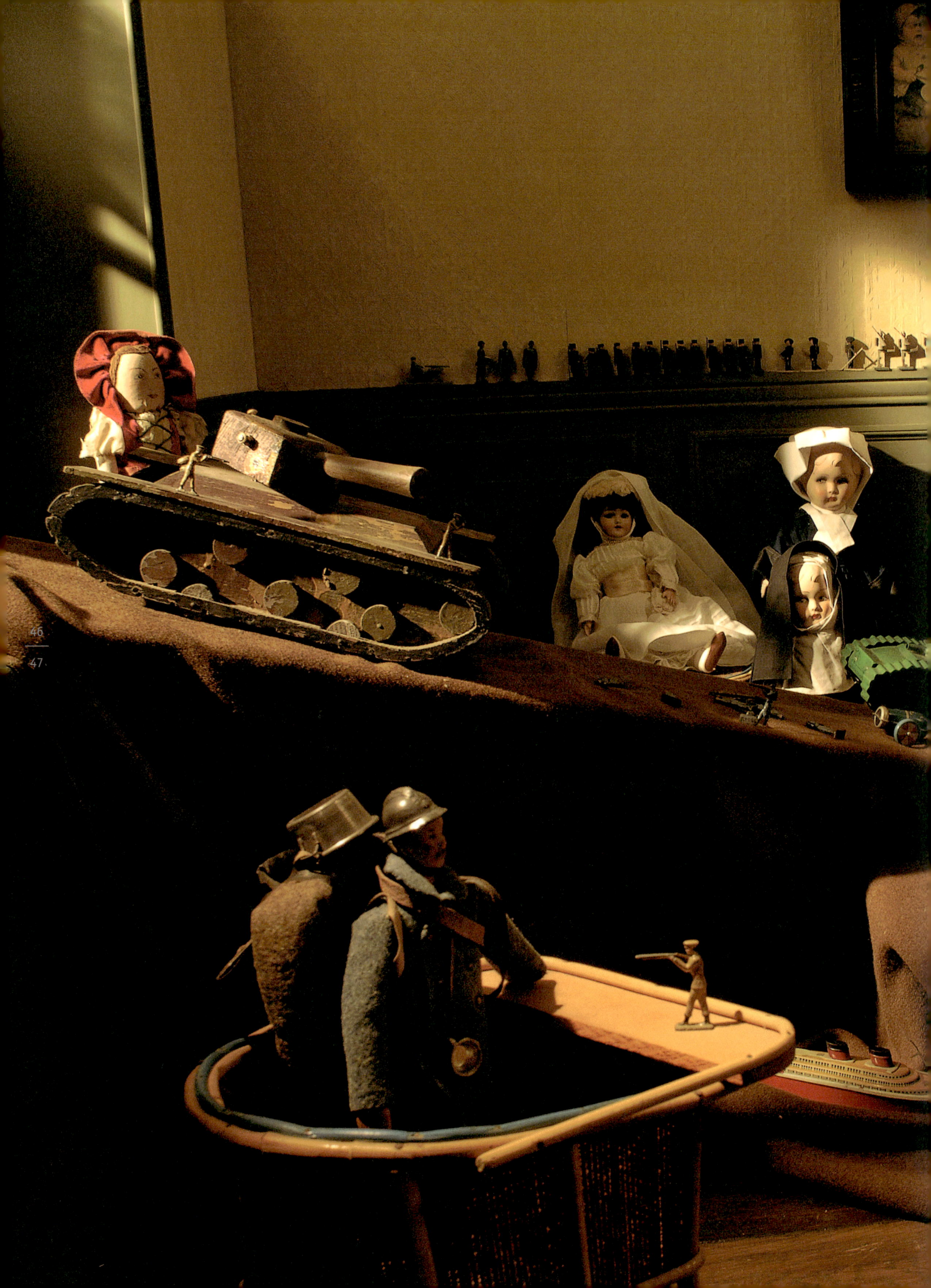

46
47

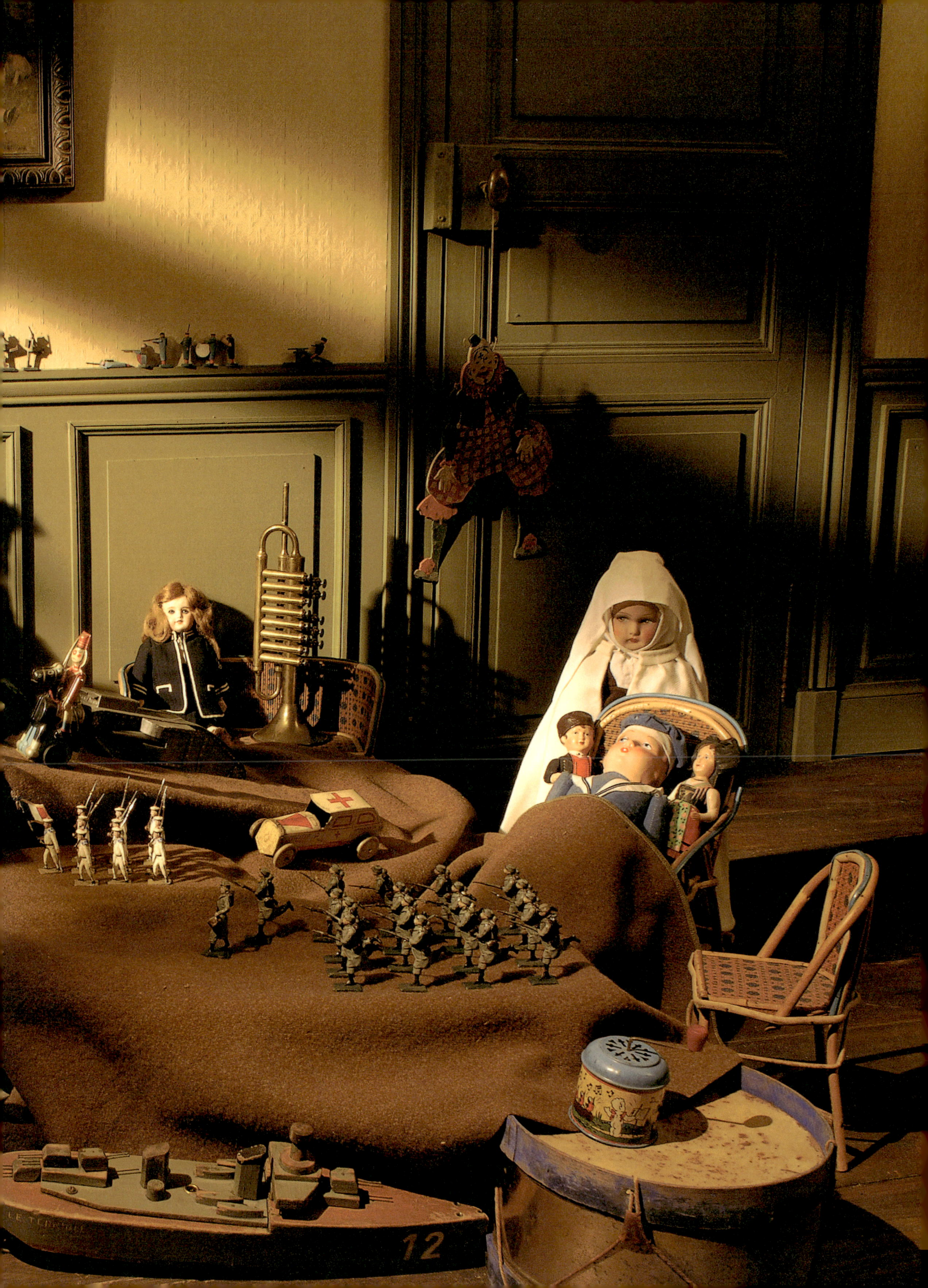

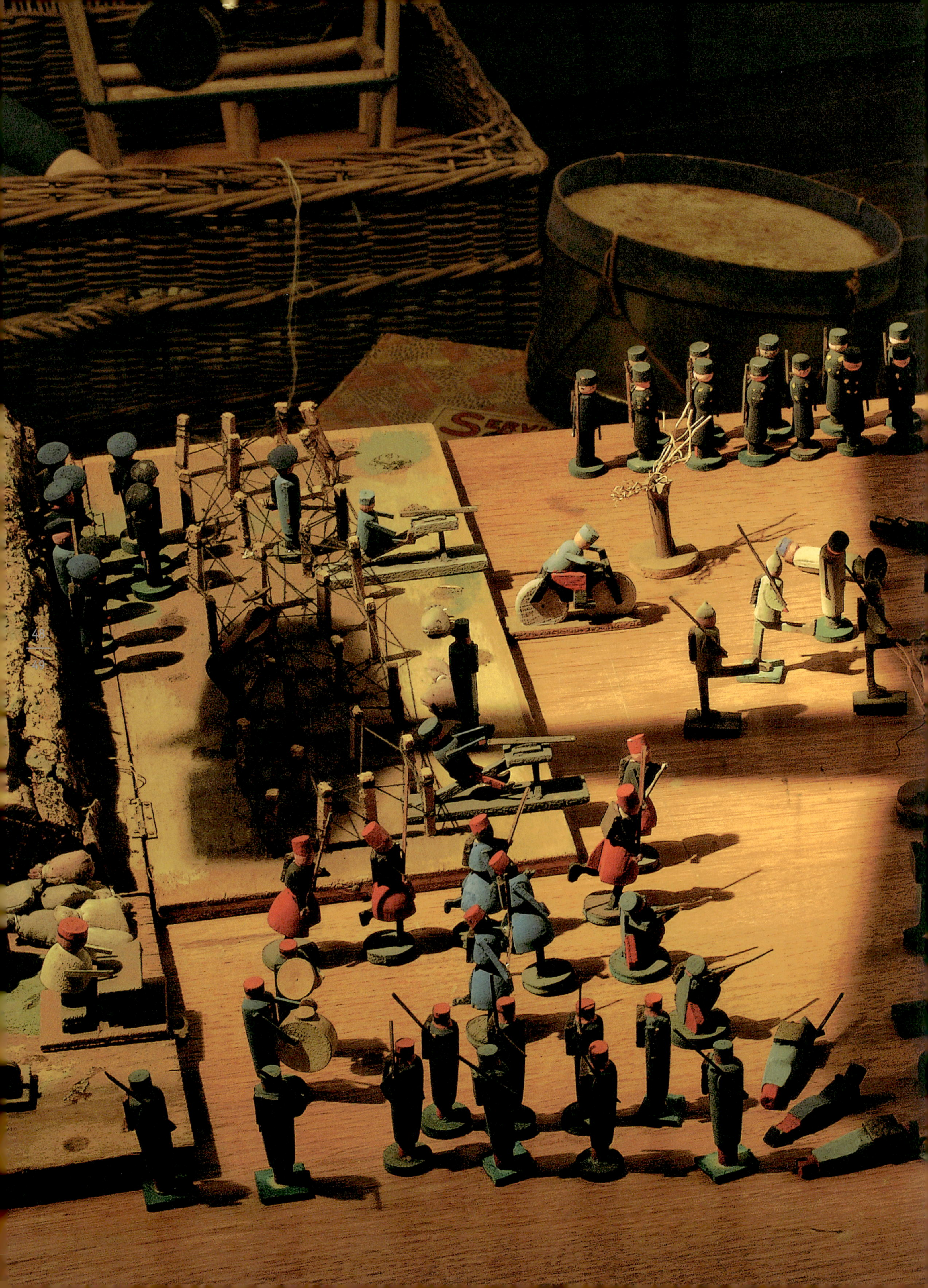

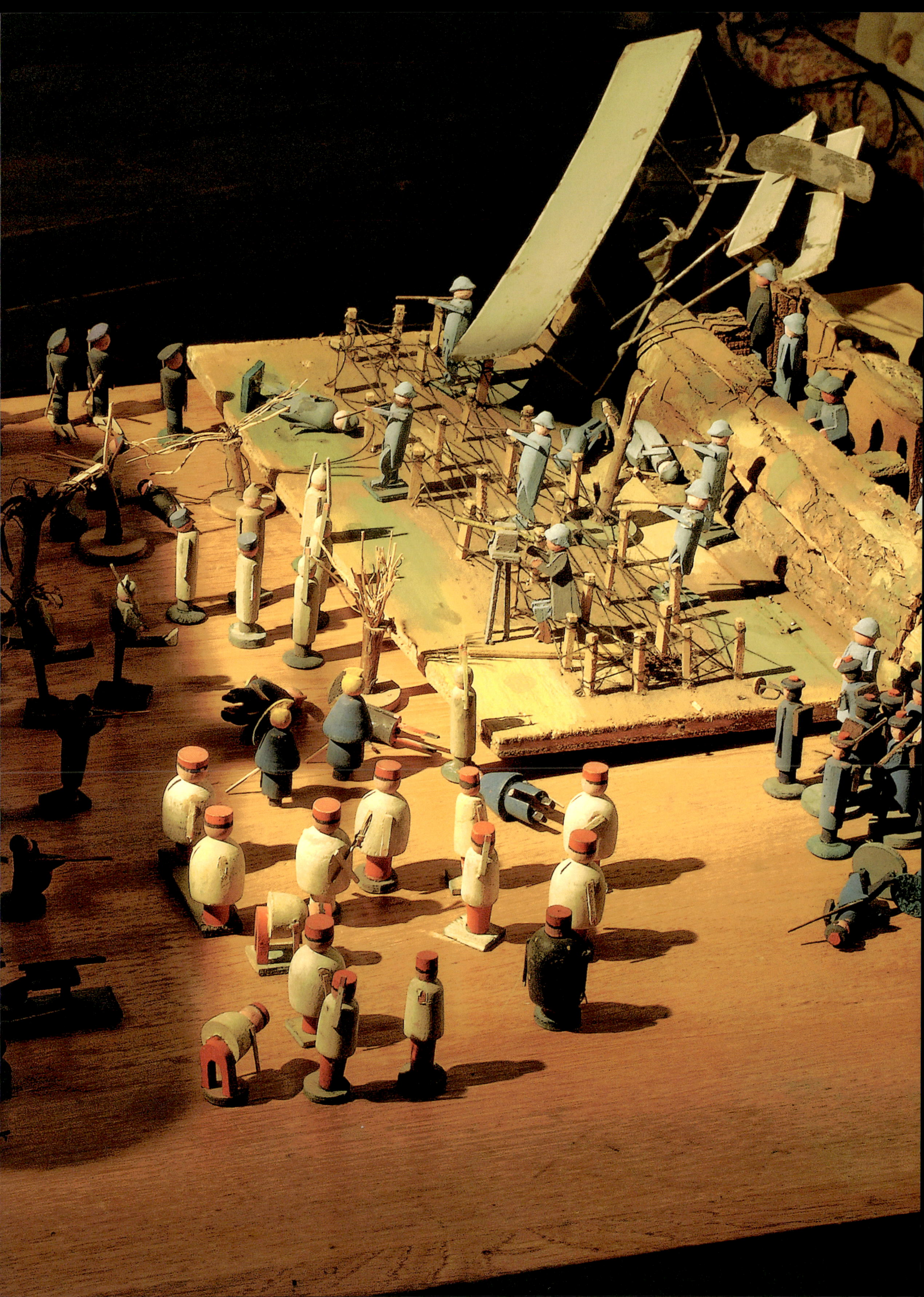

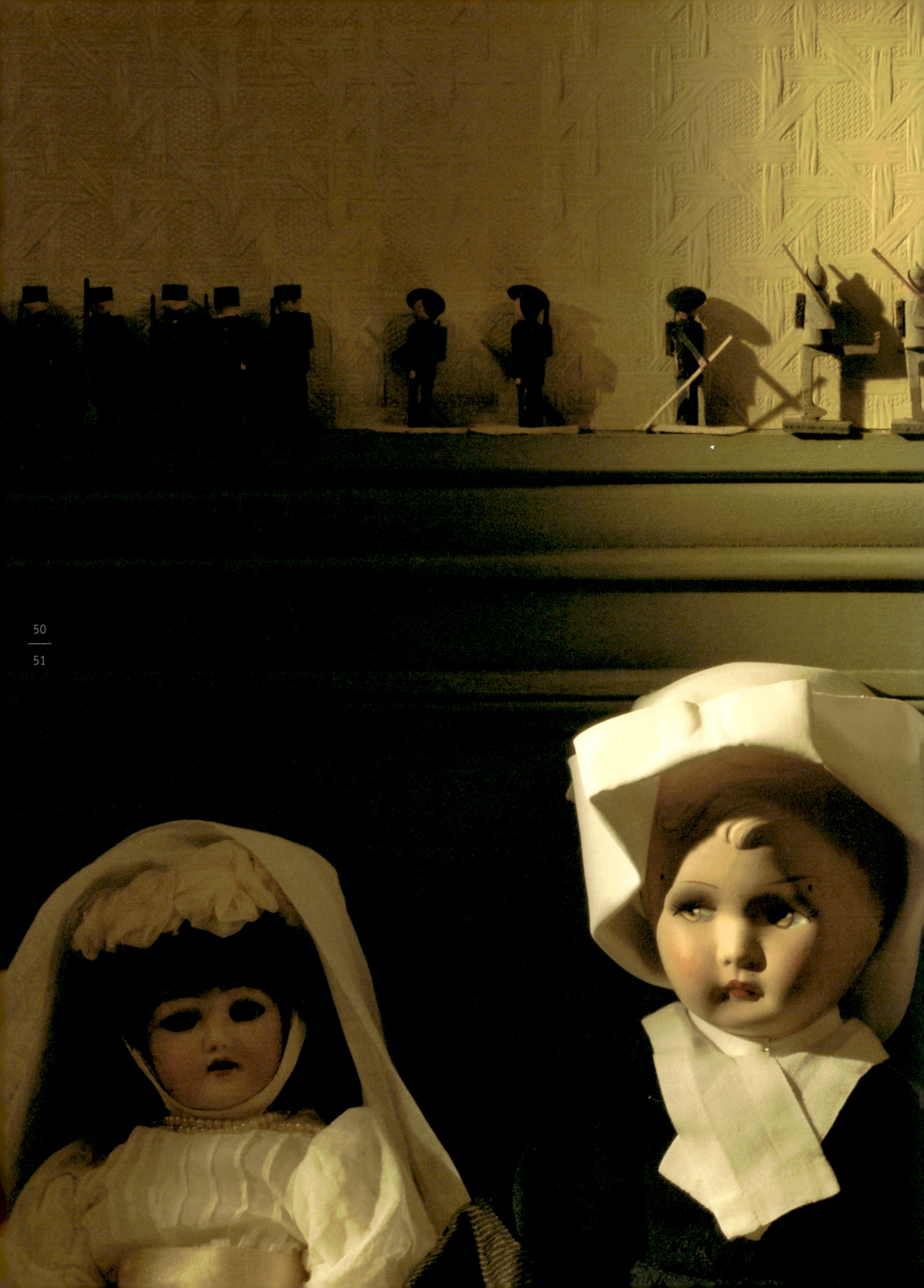

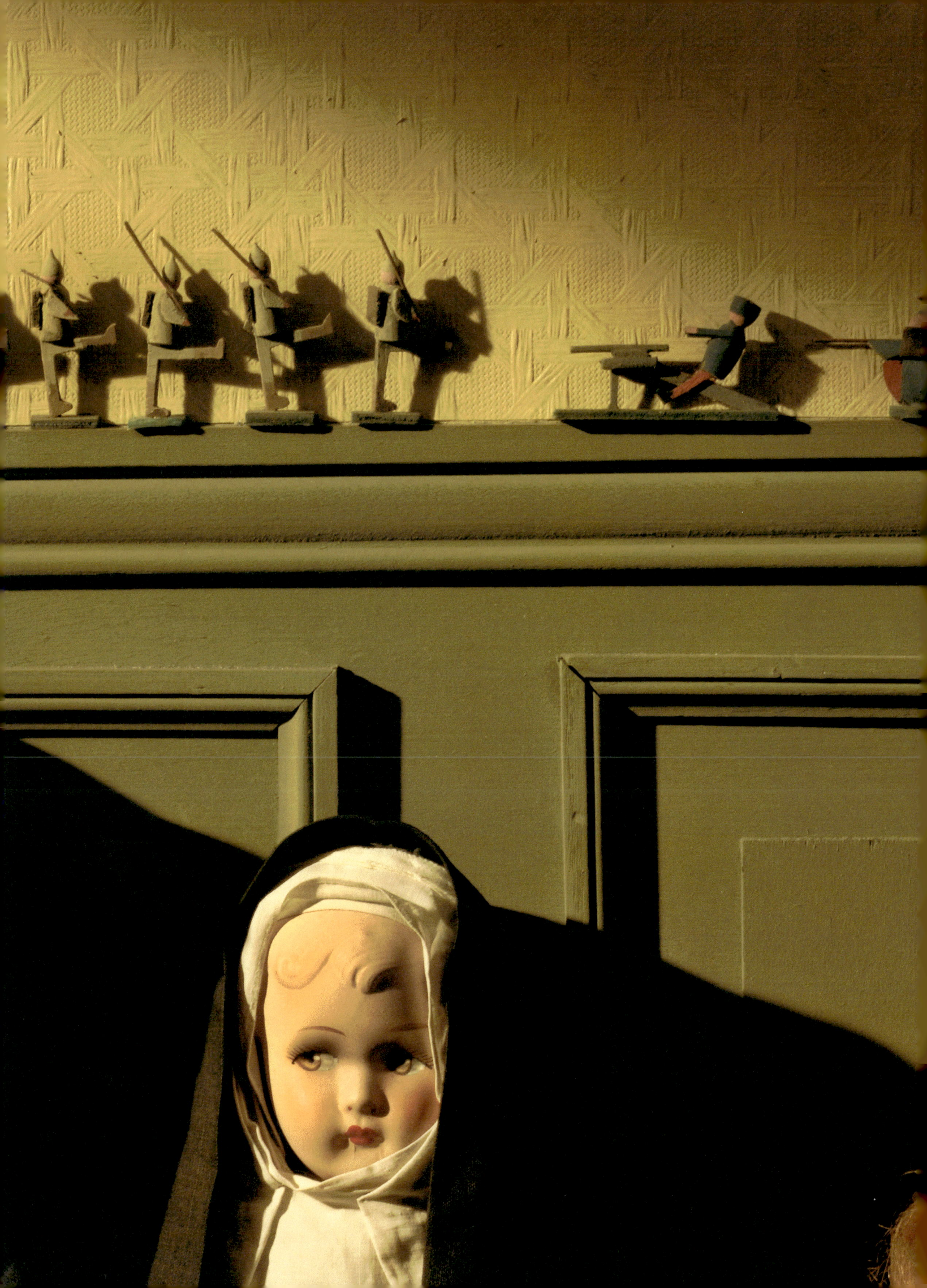

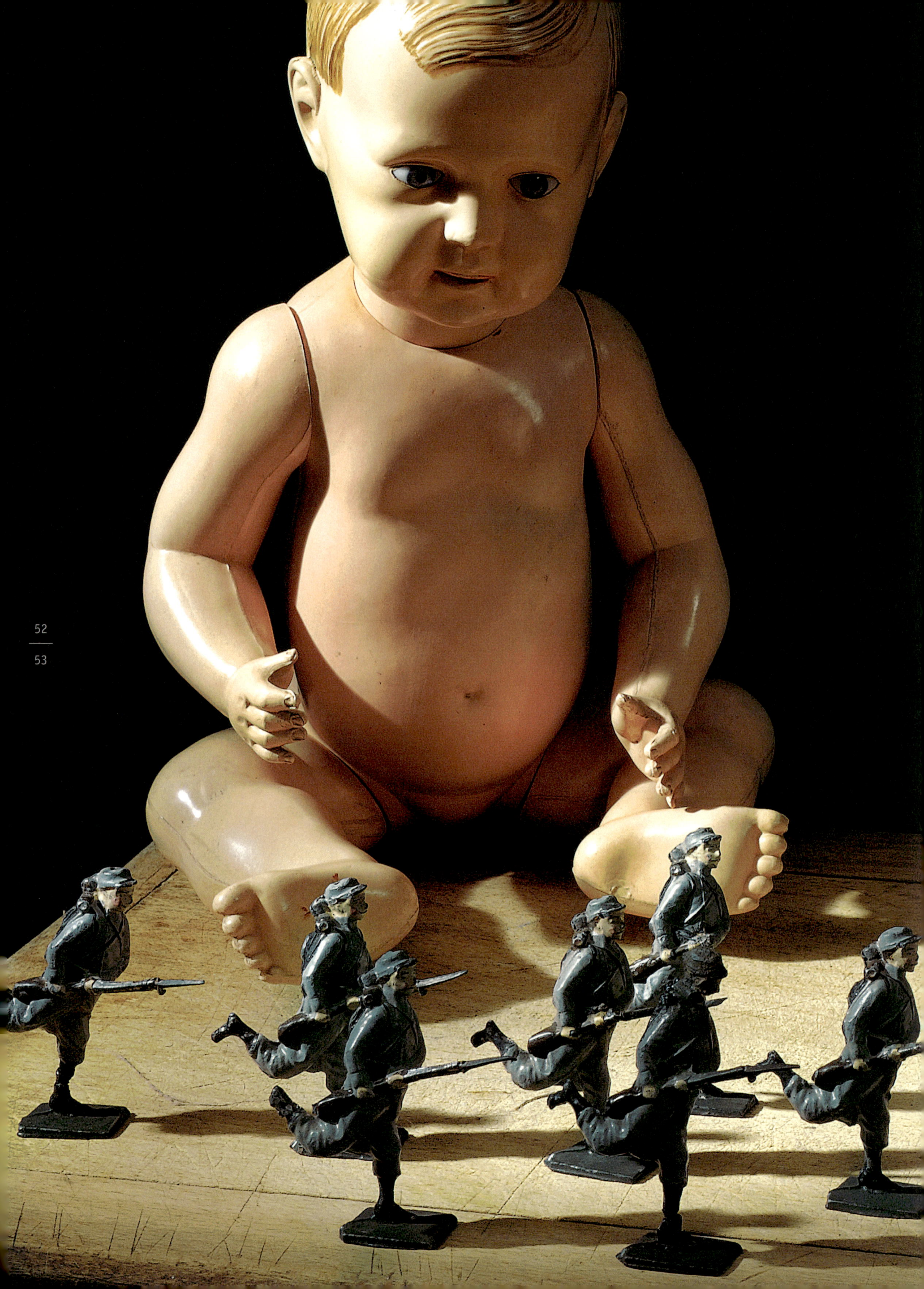
52
53

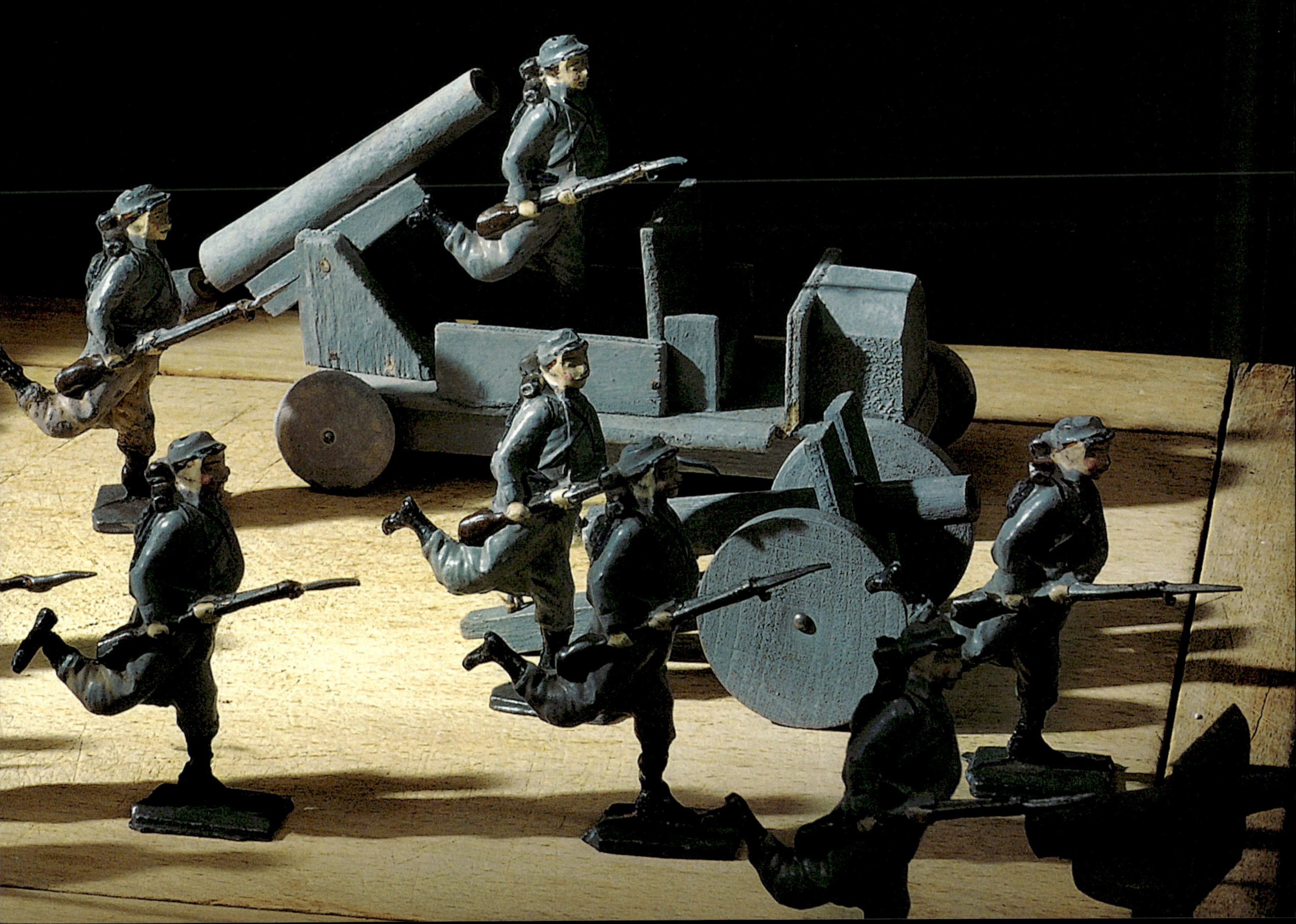

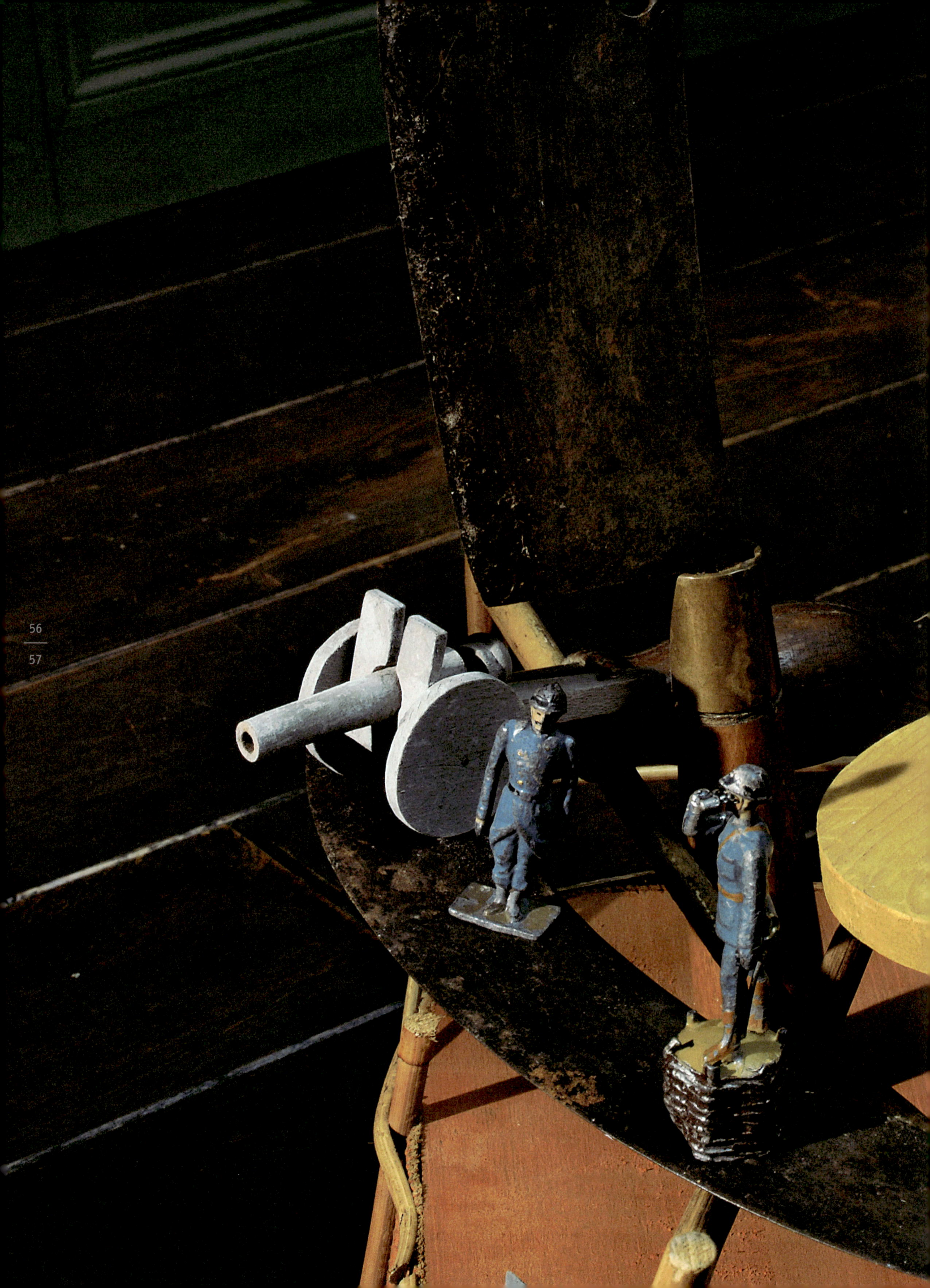

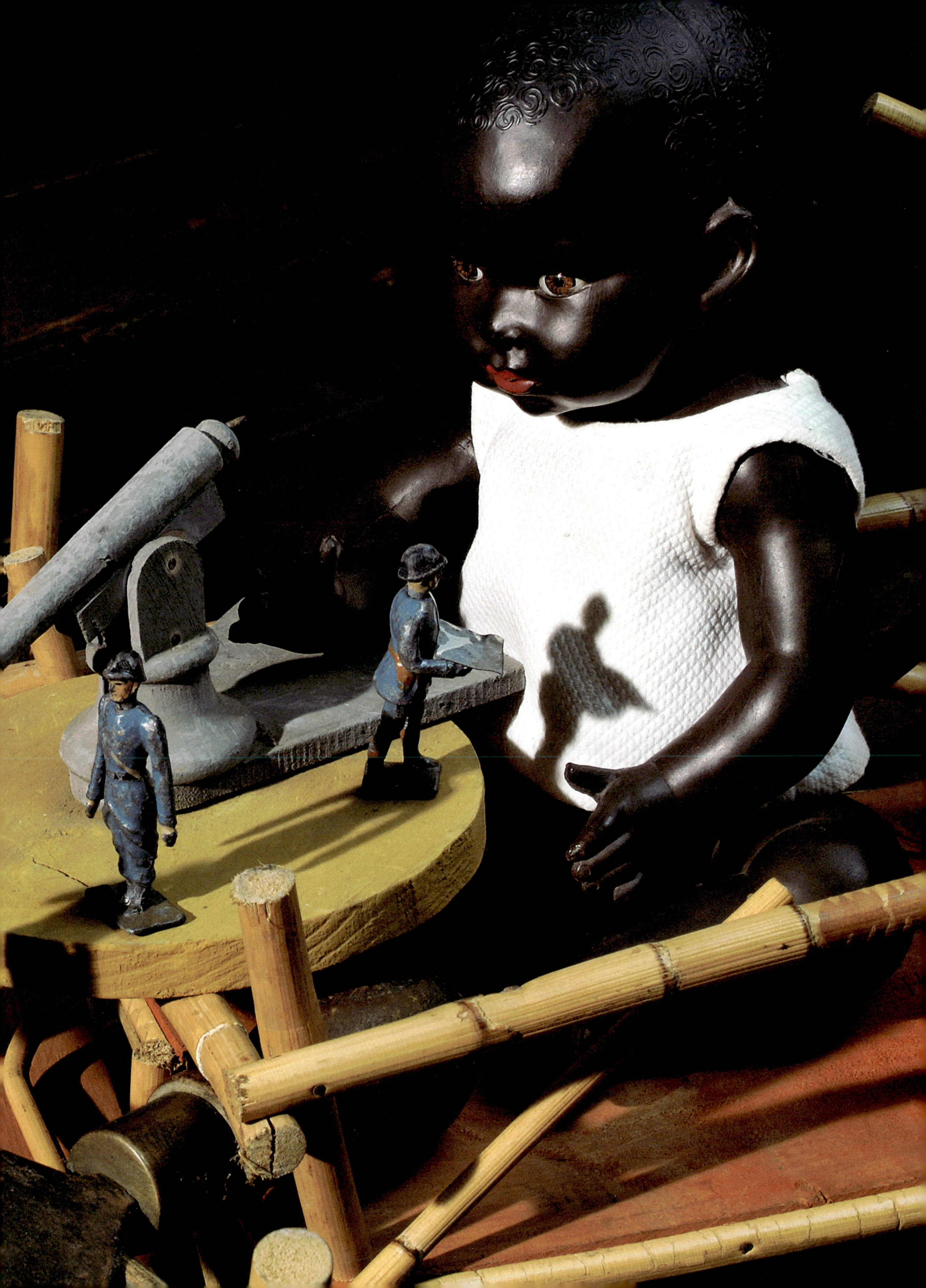

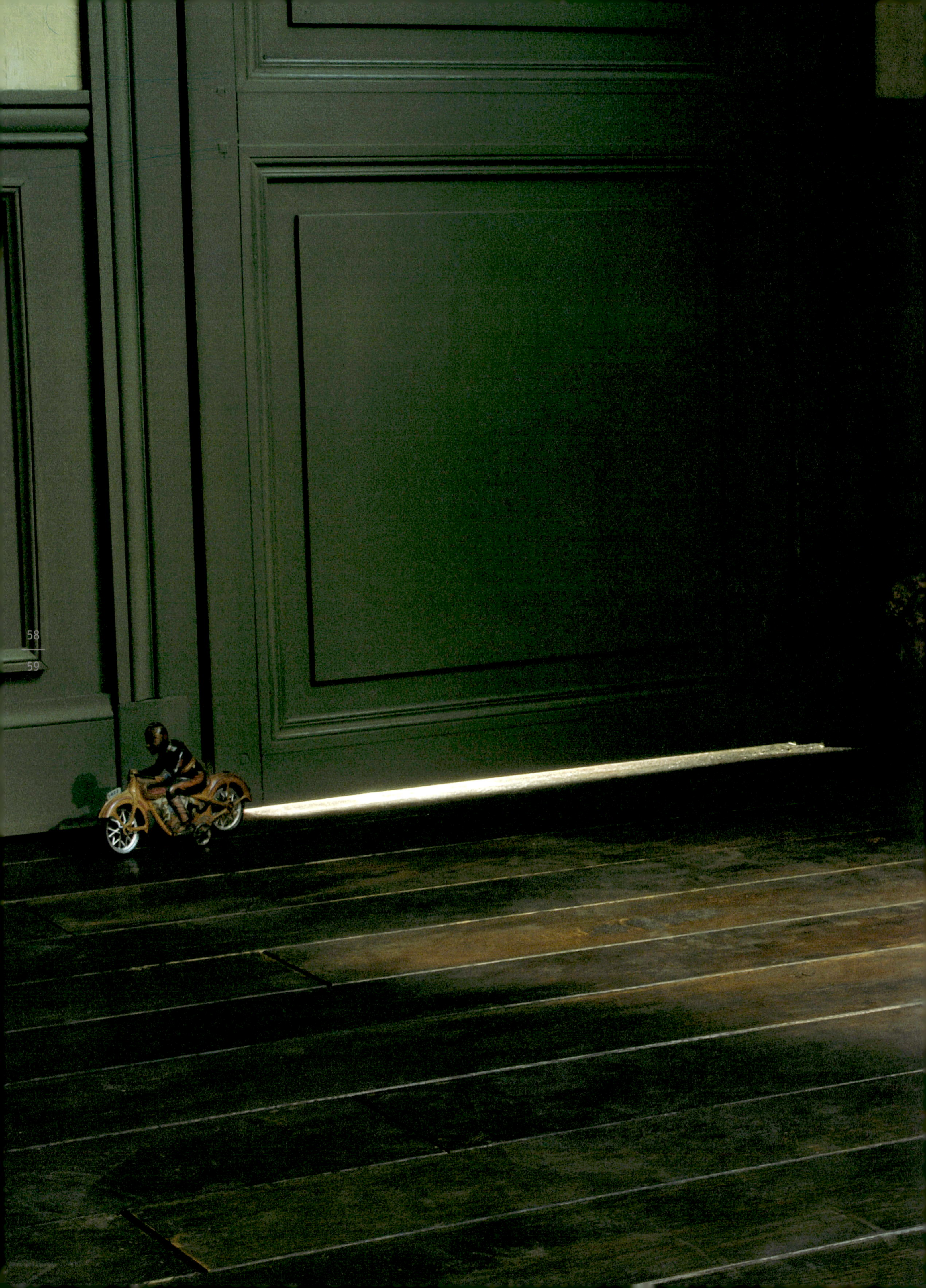
58
59

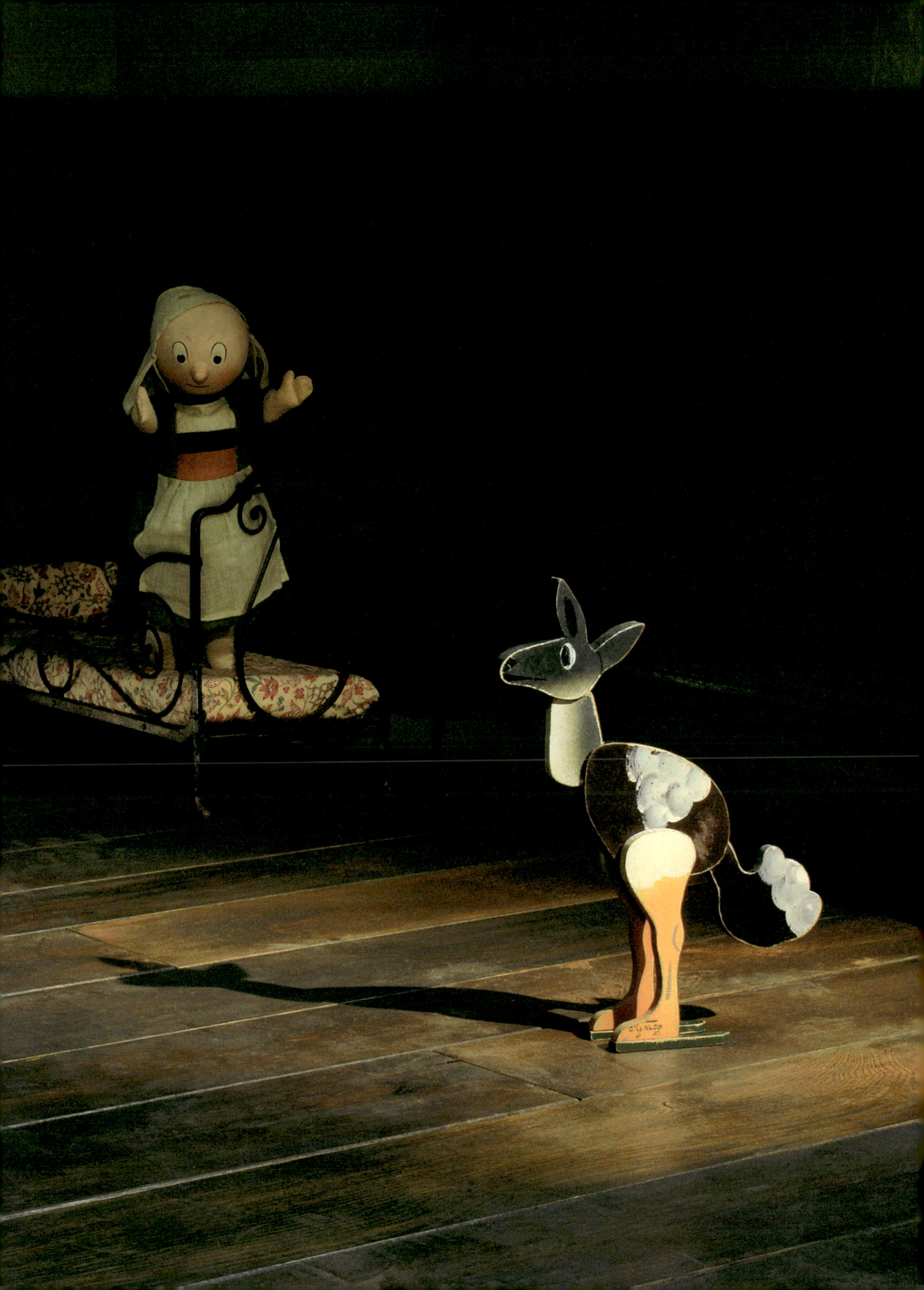

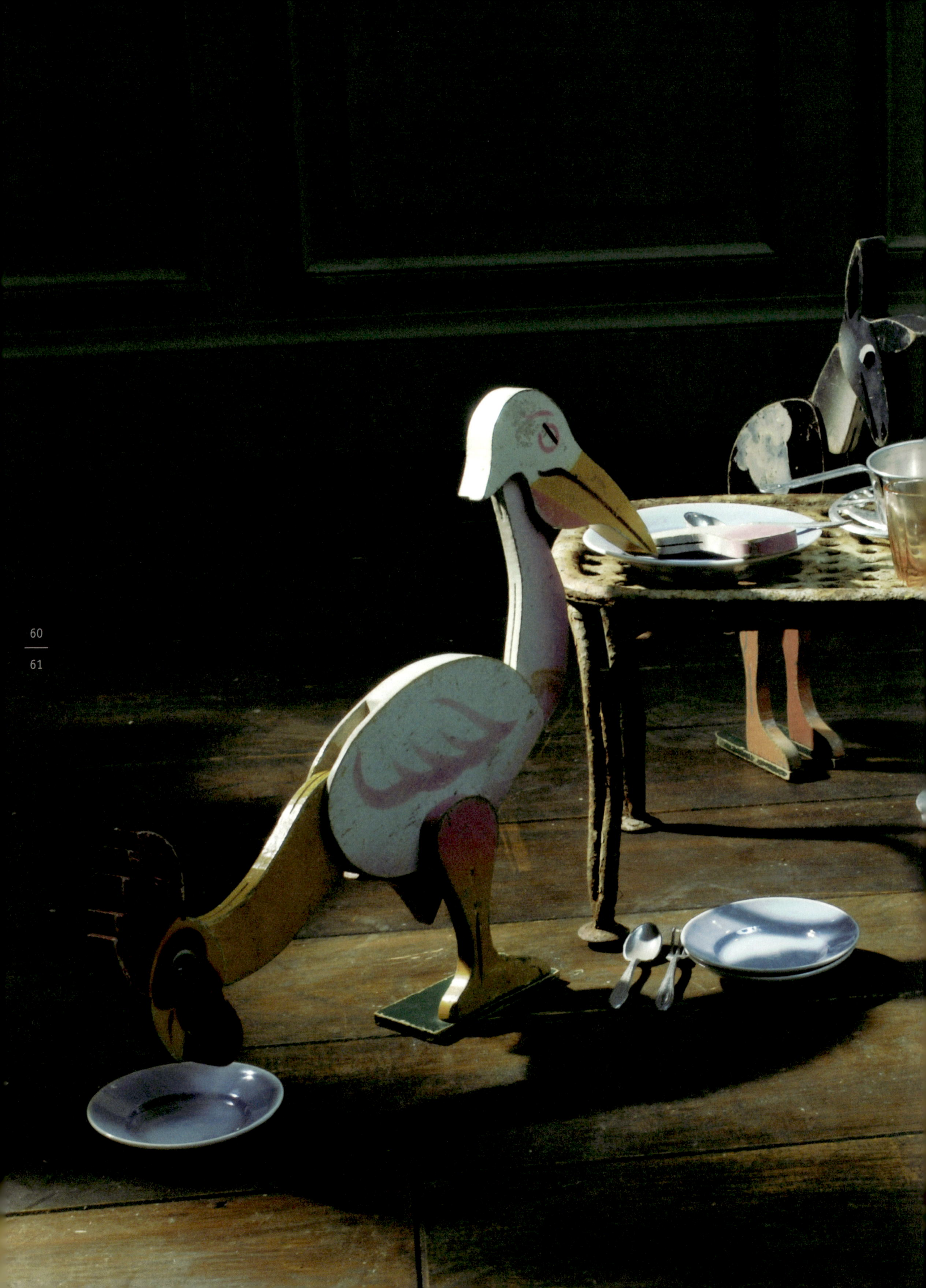

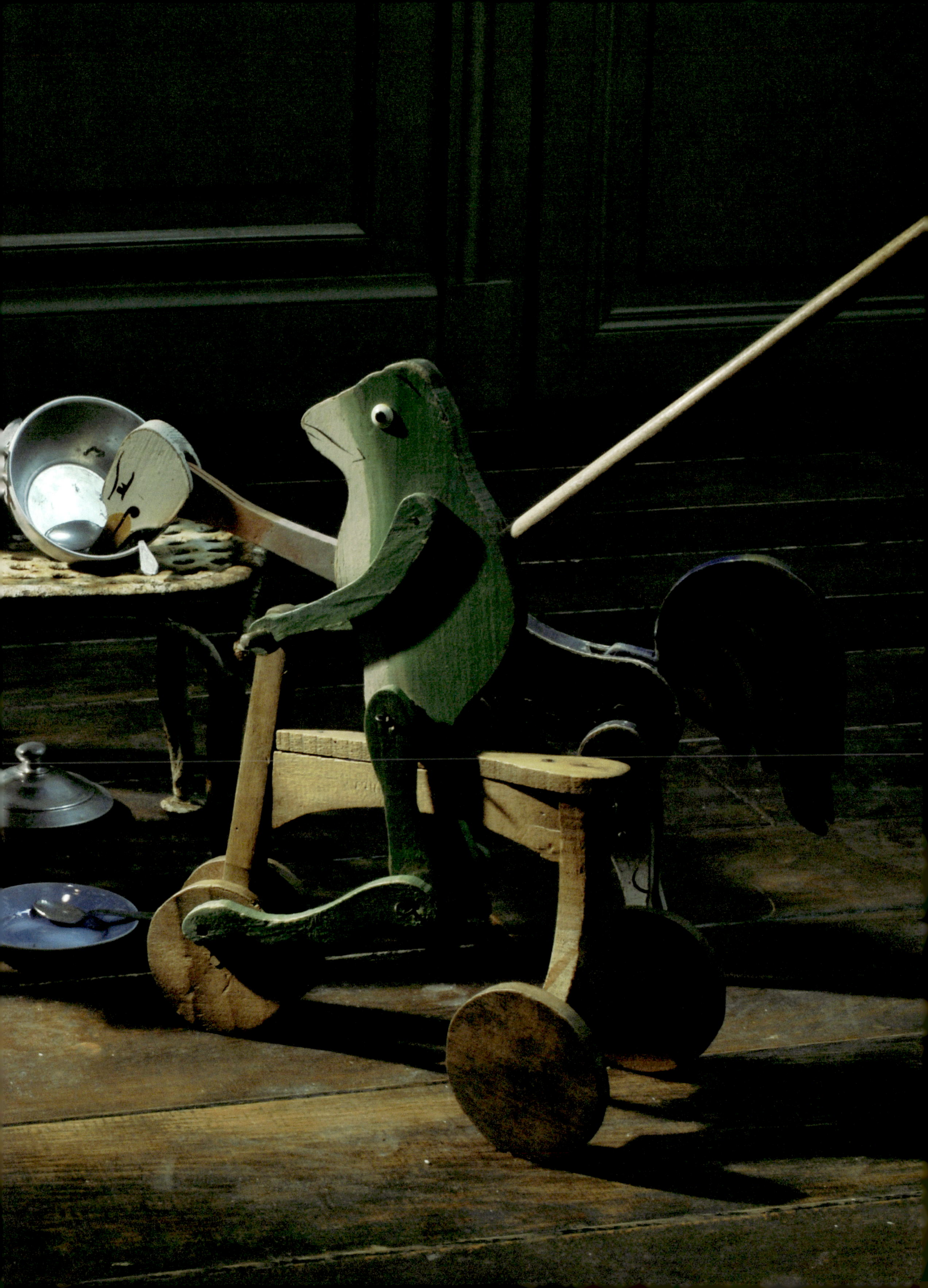

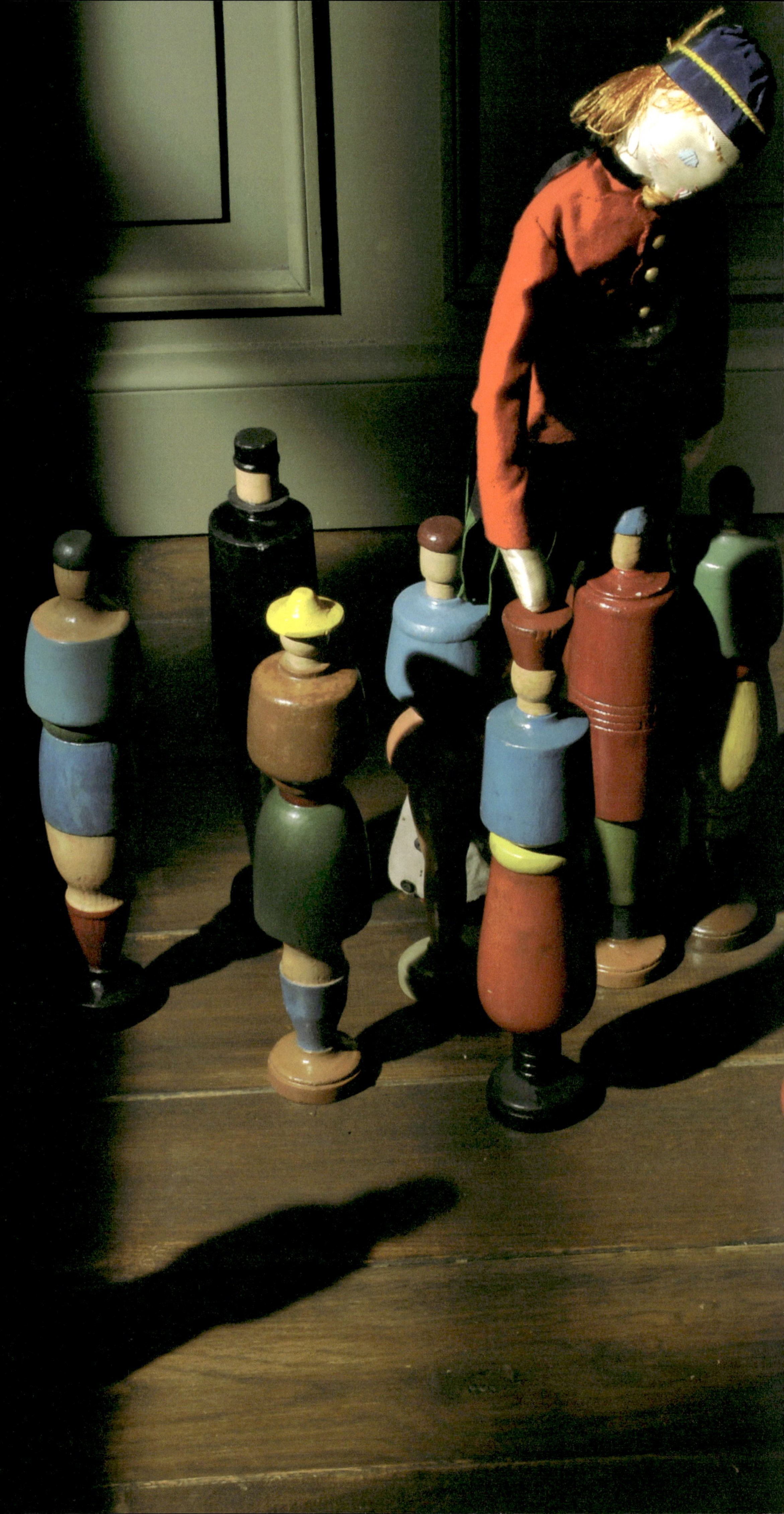

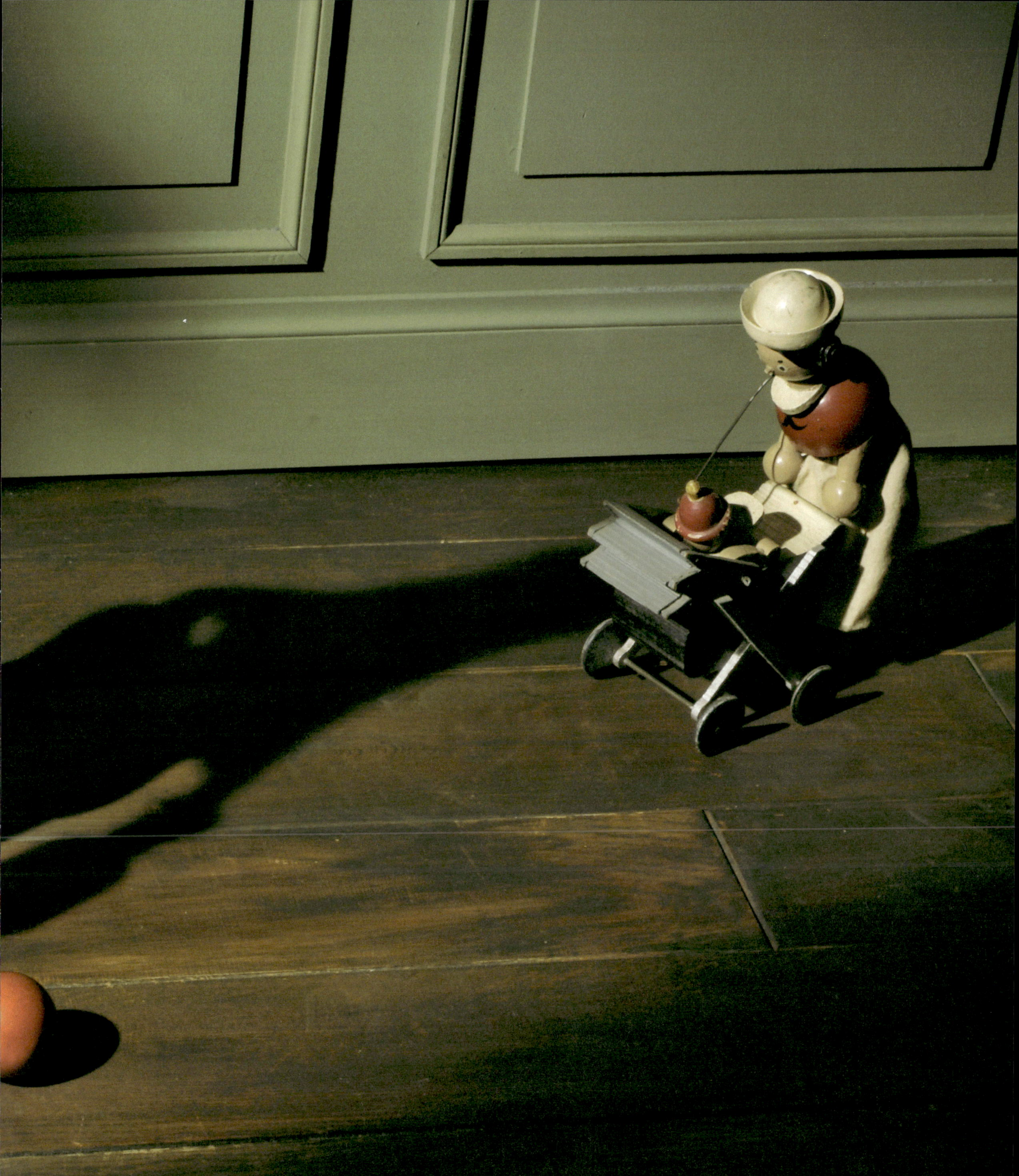

oys are our attempt to grasp the world. We come into a place too large for us, too complicated for our intelligence. We cannot hold the world because we are too much in it: that which we see excludes us. We are born into a kaleidoscope of shapes and a cacophony of sounds too overwhelming to disentangle, in which borders are blurred and contours are vague. Psychologists tell us that we are born with a primordial self-awareness, knowing that our bodies are ours from the start. We learn who we already know we are by learning what we experience – this finger that touches, this foot that I grasp, this mouth with which I suck – and from that place we call 'I', we begin to separate the strands of the world. Like Adam in the Garden, we are given the task of naming what we see and, in order to bring the world into our reach, we are given transitional models of the world that we can hold and keep: a doll, a bear, a rabbit, a castle.

What fits in our grasp is the measure of our understanding. For a child, a bird in the hand is worth two in the bush.

here is always one toy above all that governs our childhood. A particular doll, rabbit, train or teddy bear acquired long ago, for reasons inscrutable, the quality of the best-beloved. Separation from it was anguish; its presence lent comfort and security. Its smell and its touch rooted us in the world, beyond which our senses became lost and frightened us. It had a history of accidents and triumphs: forgotten in the garden, stolen by the dog, left on top of a bedside lamp so that the hot bulb burnt a hole in its bottom, hidden away by an evil cousin, and then found, rescued, restored.

There is a love relationship established with that one toy that, sometimes, outlasts all others. The special toy is the perfect lover, the one that is everything the child wants it to be, incarnating every fantasy and every desire. Love transforms it, beyond all explanation or reason. It is the one solid, unmovable, everpresent, faithful point of the universe on which the child can depend, no matter what.

The special toy is our first lesson in consolation.

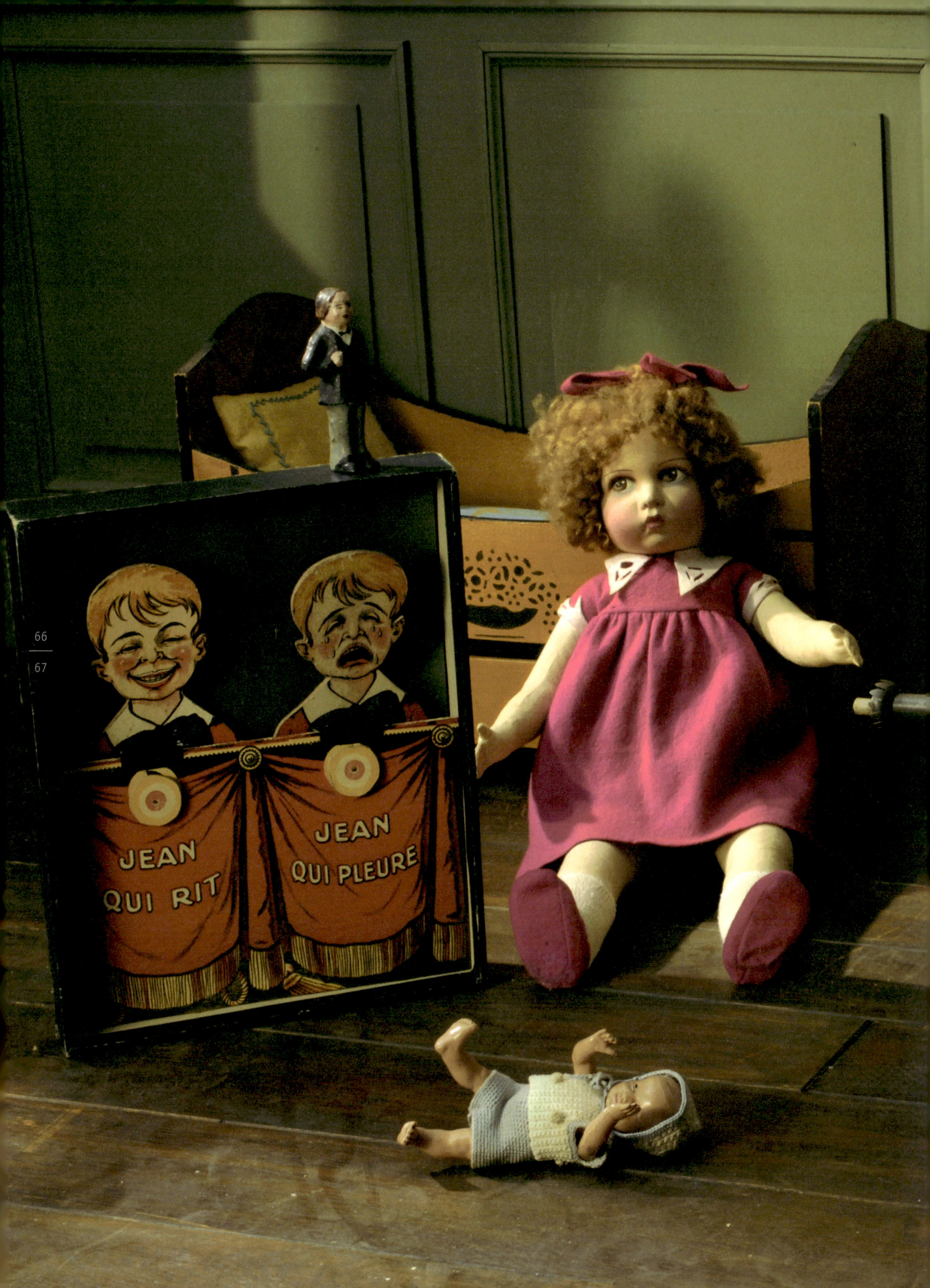

JEAN QUI RIT
JEAN QUI PLEURE

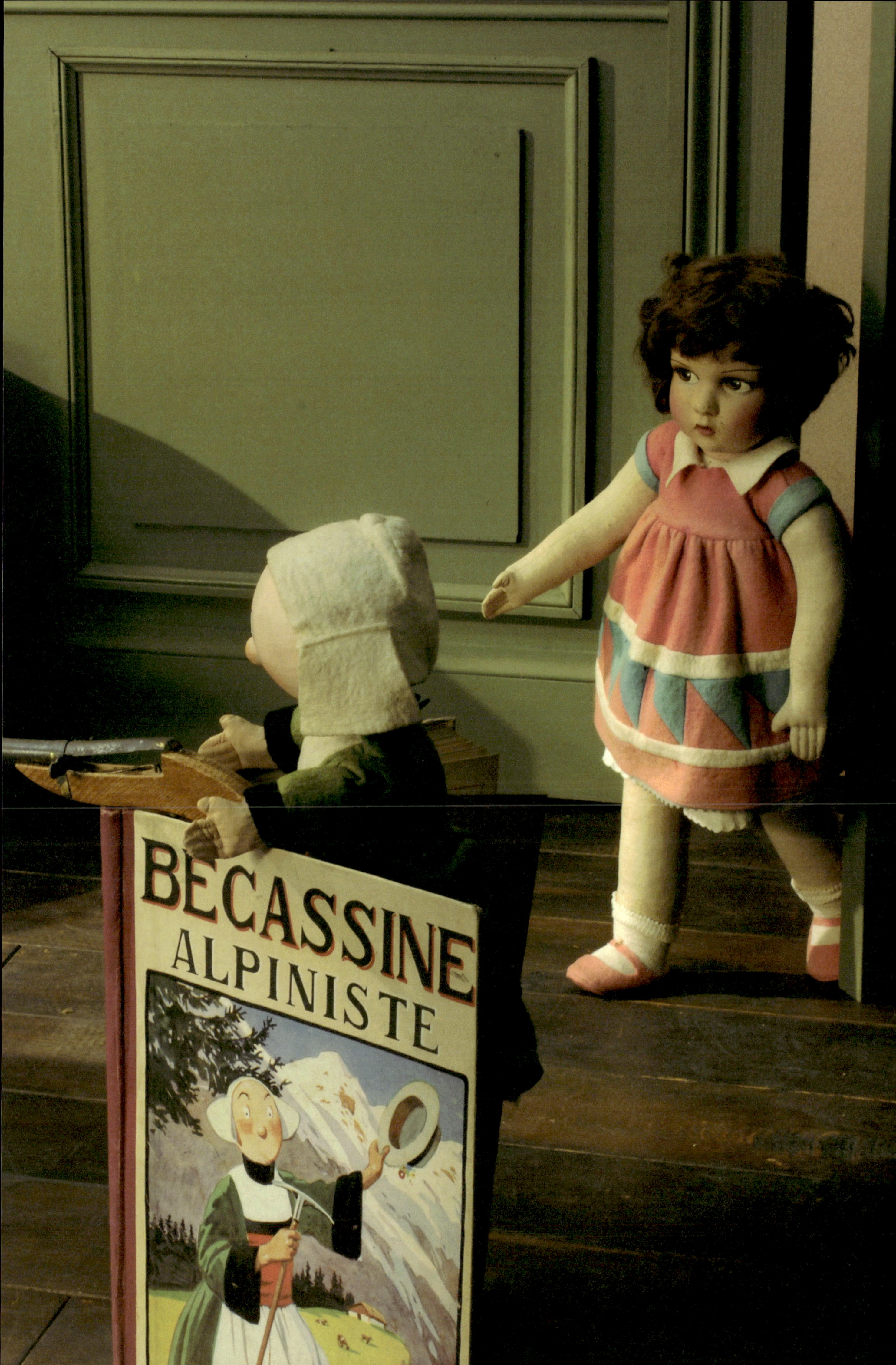

BECASSINE
ALPINISTE

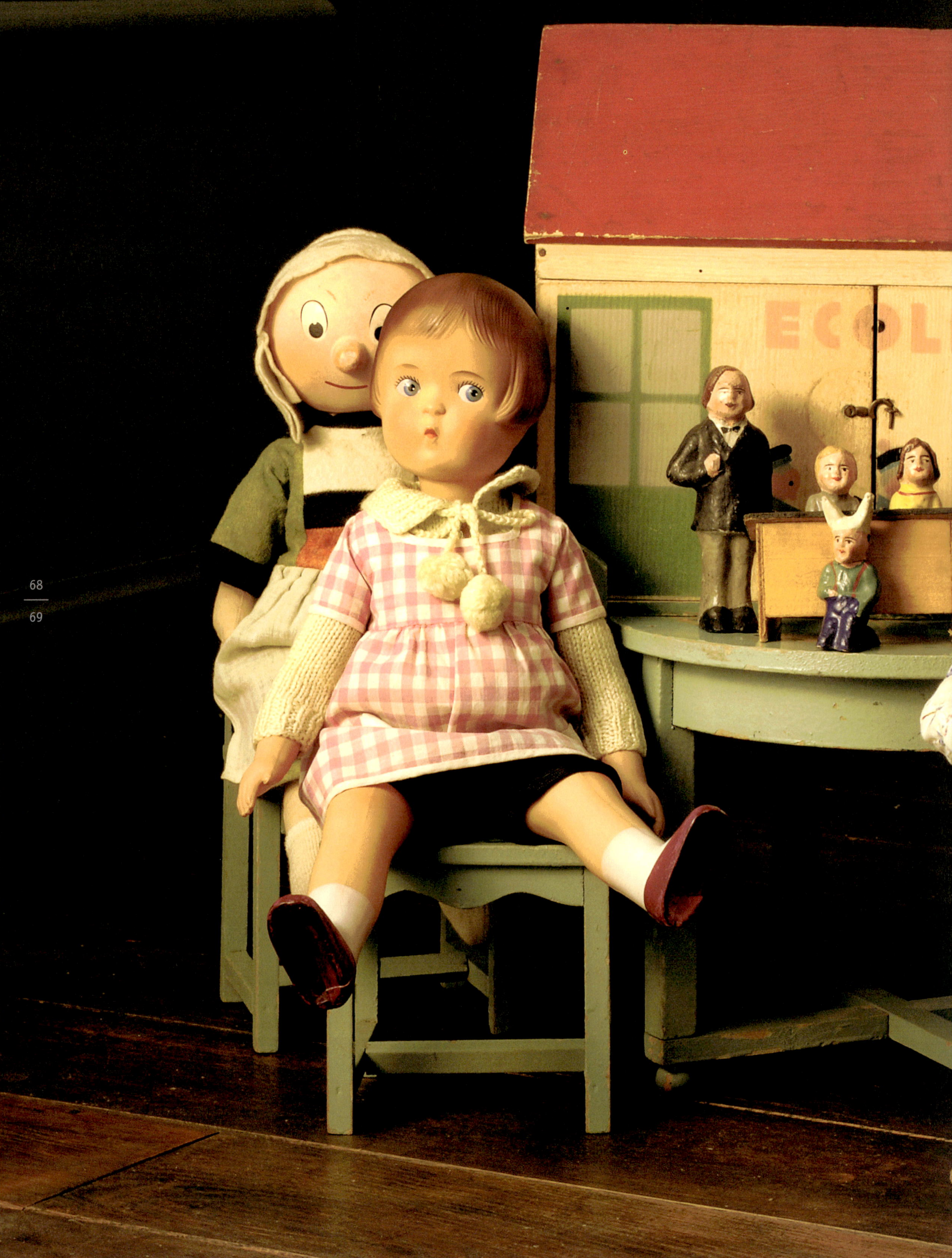
ECOL

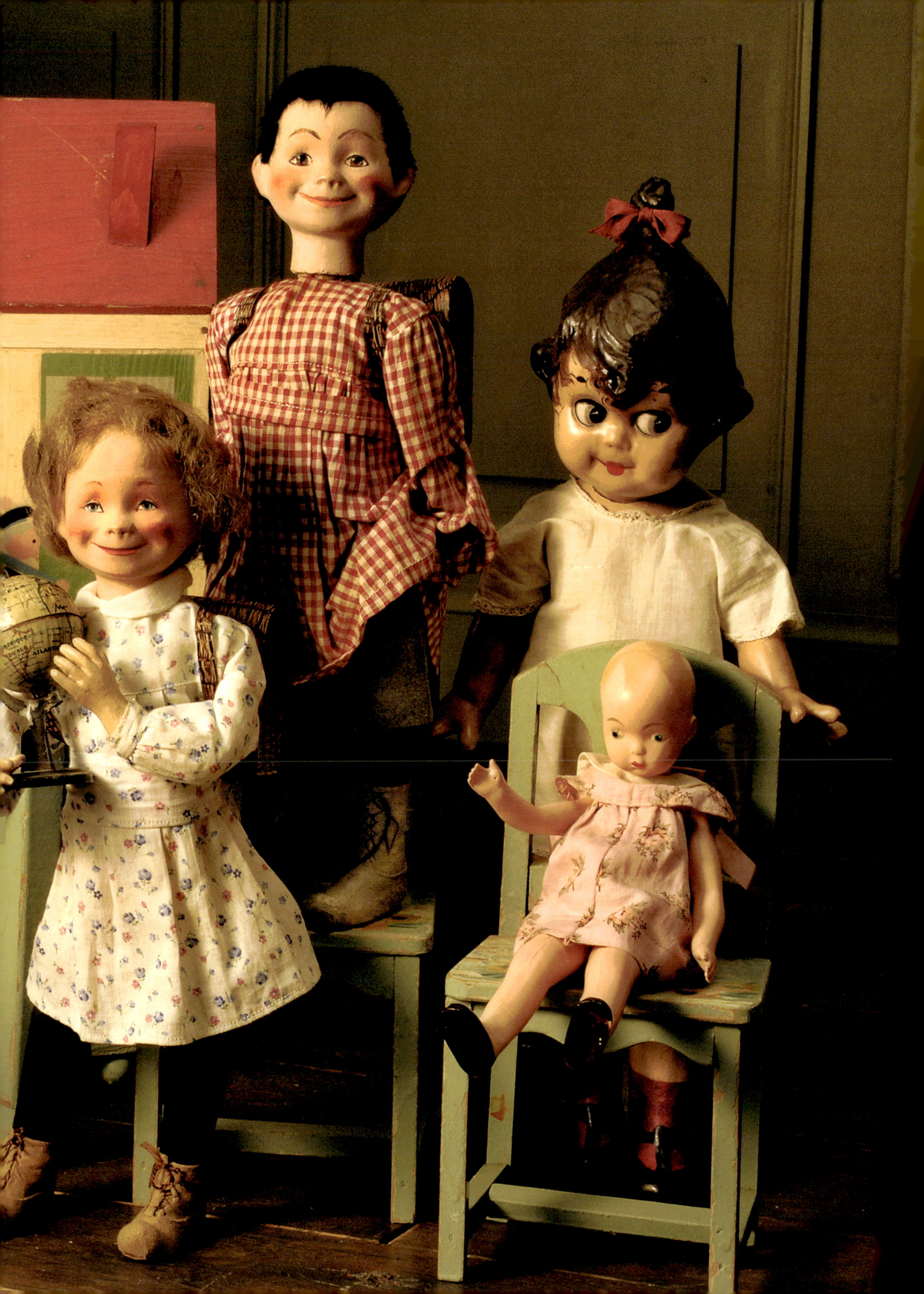

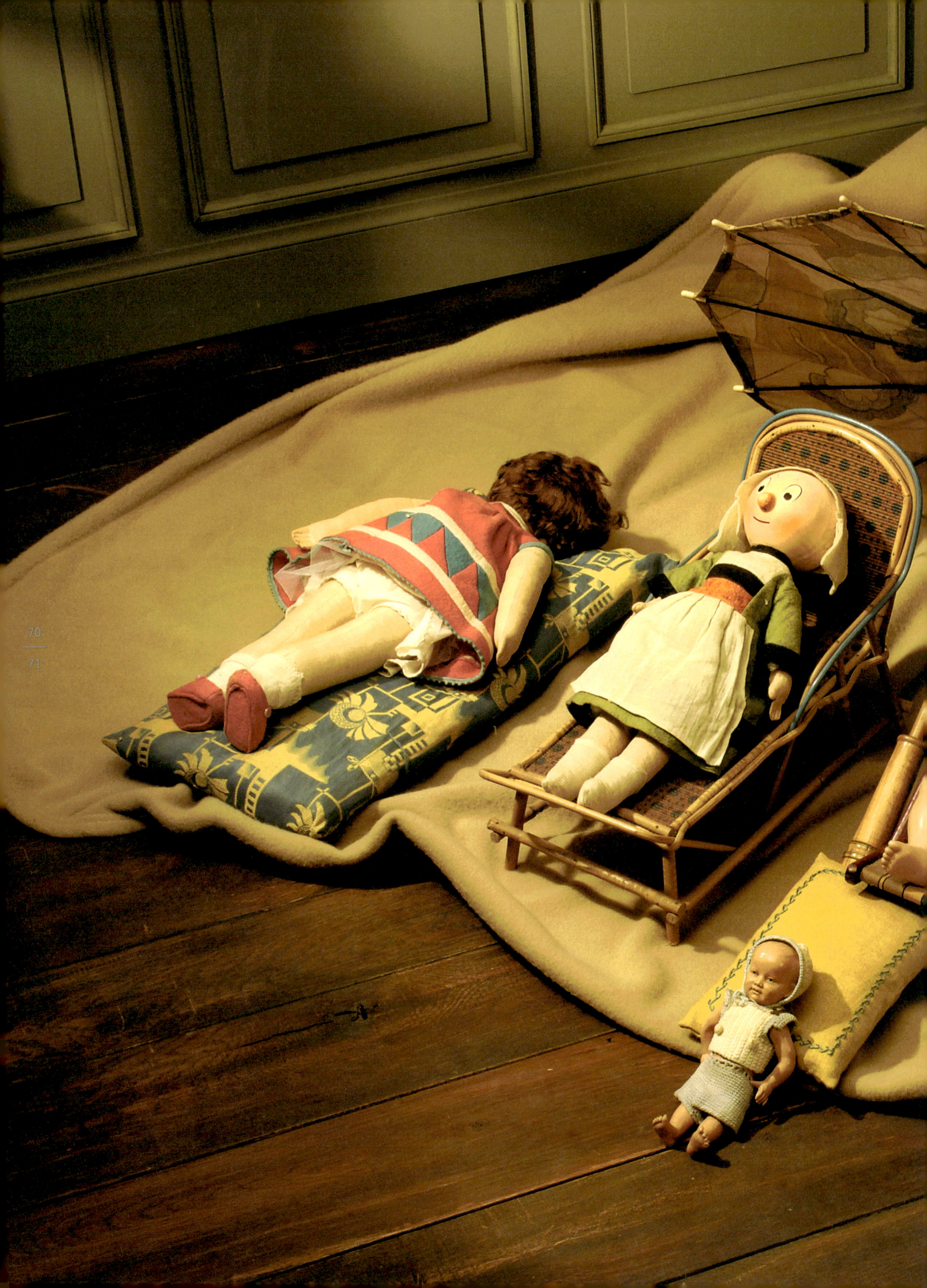

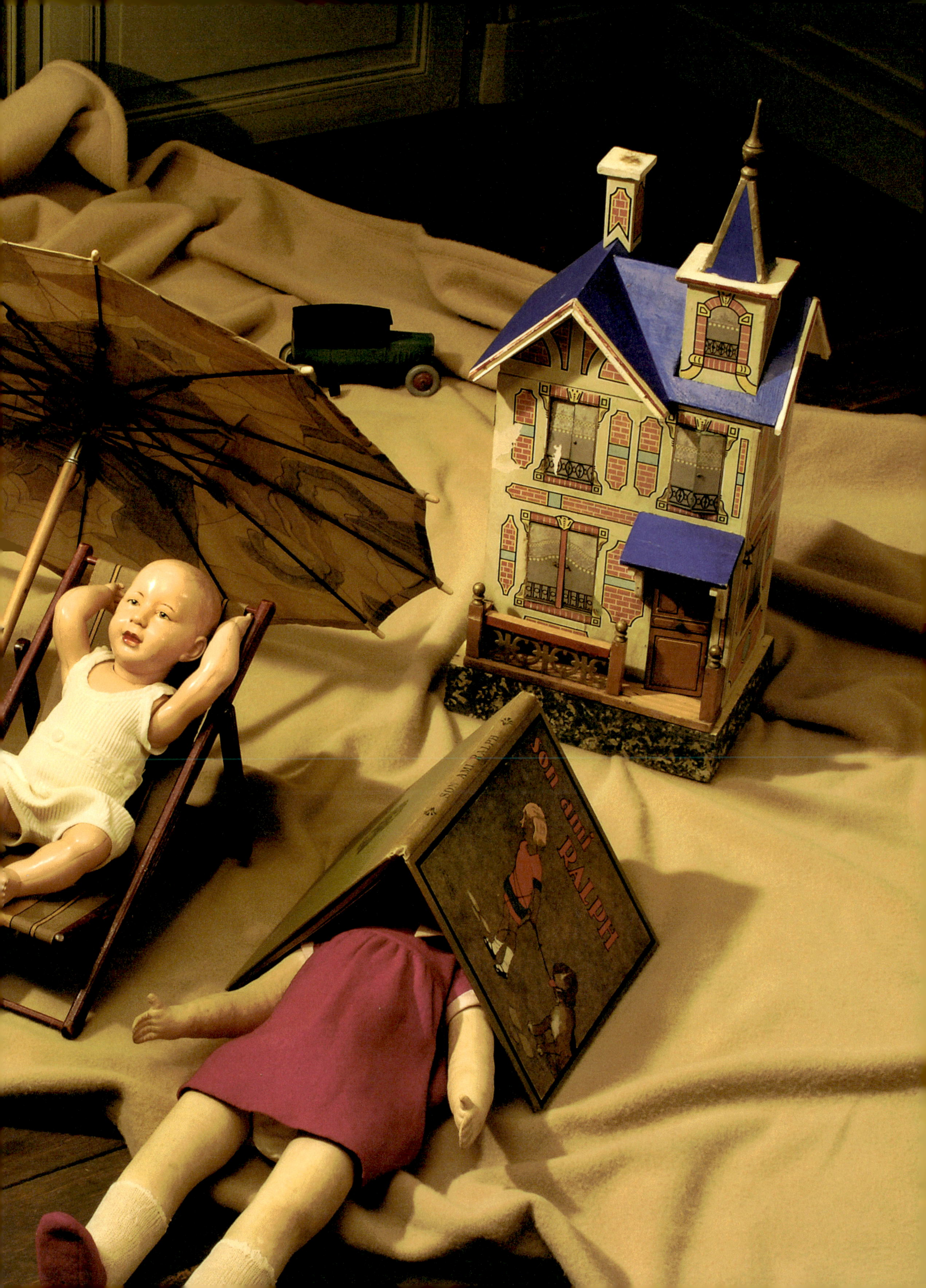

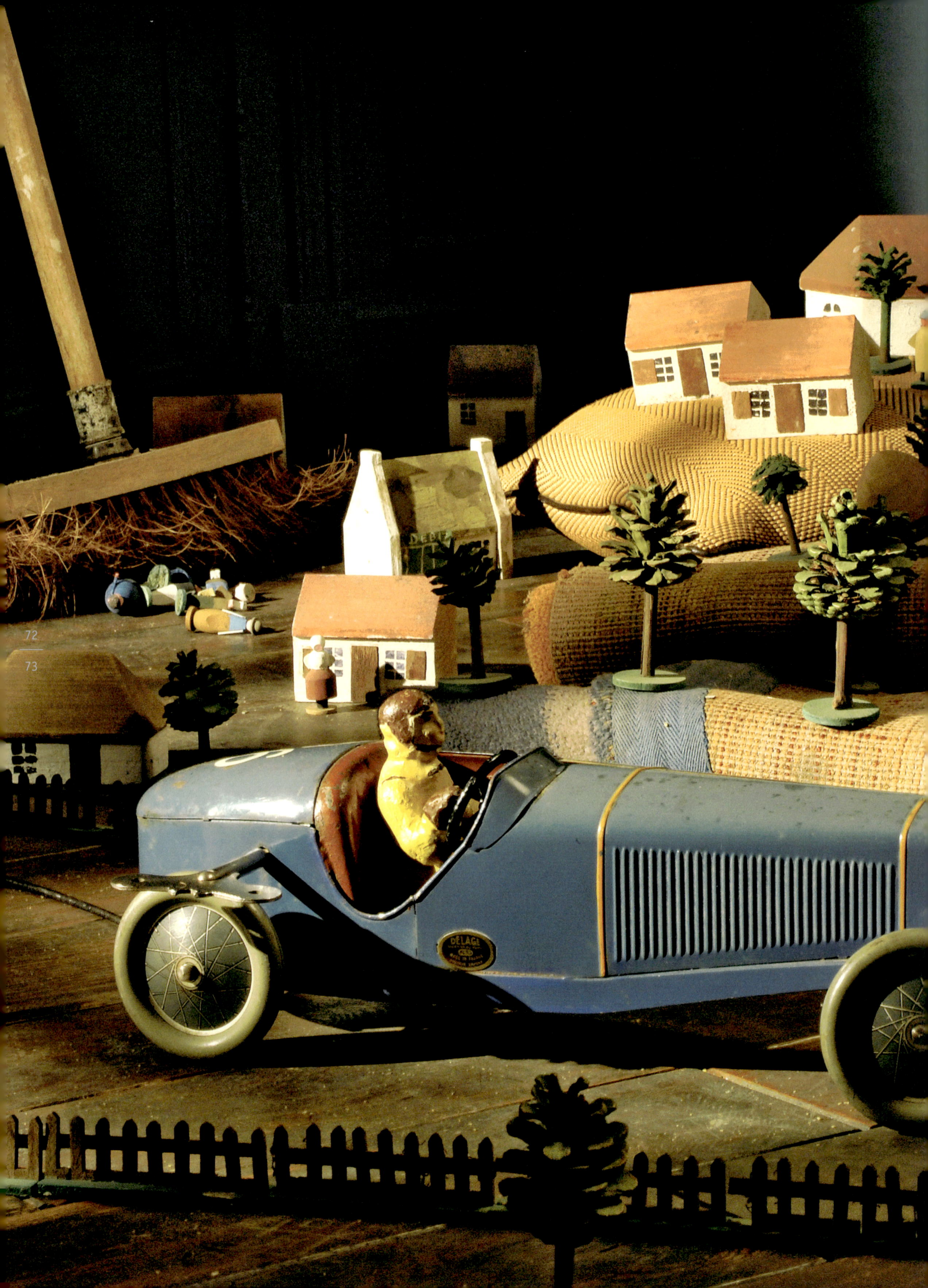

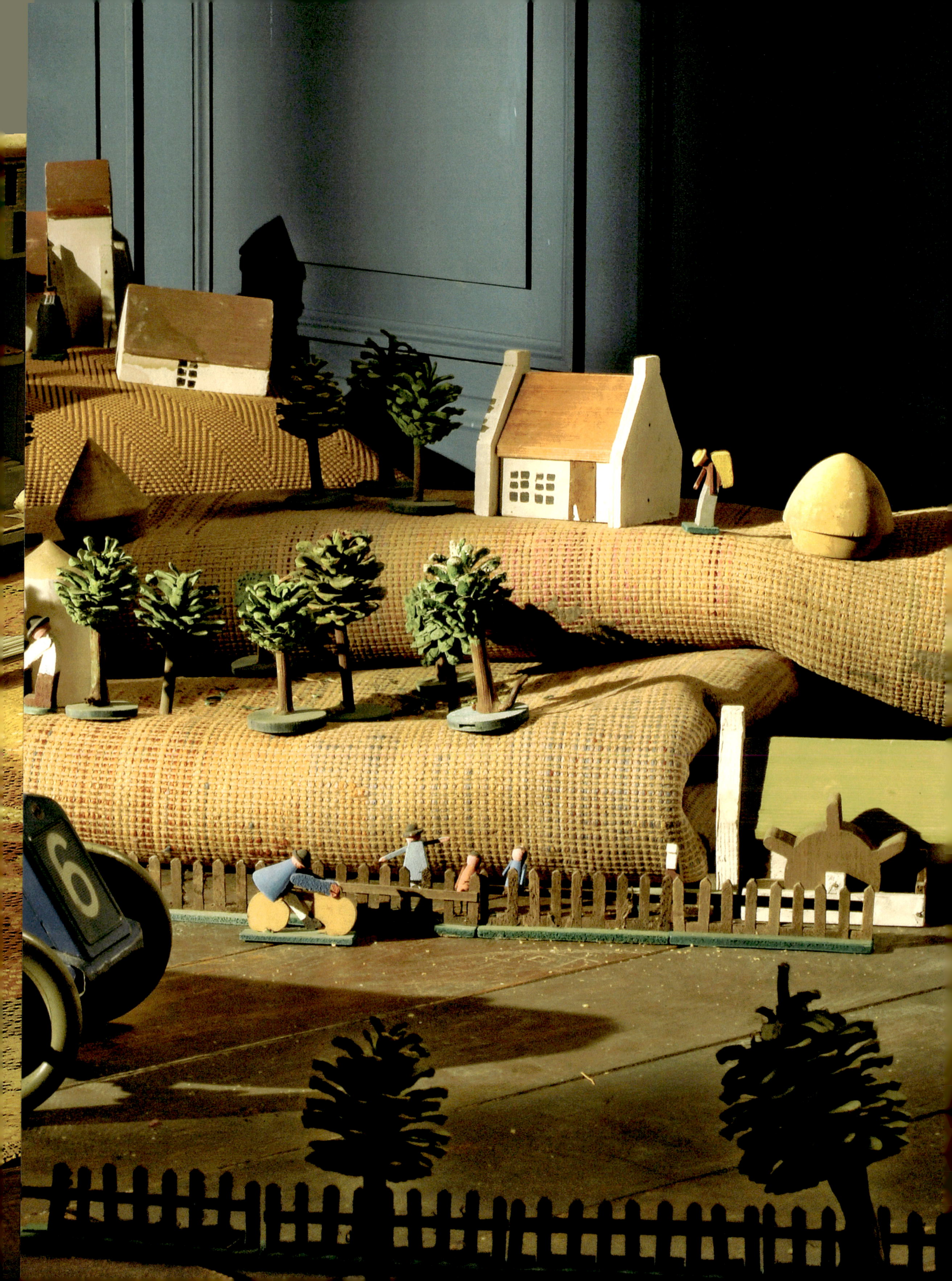

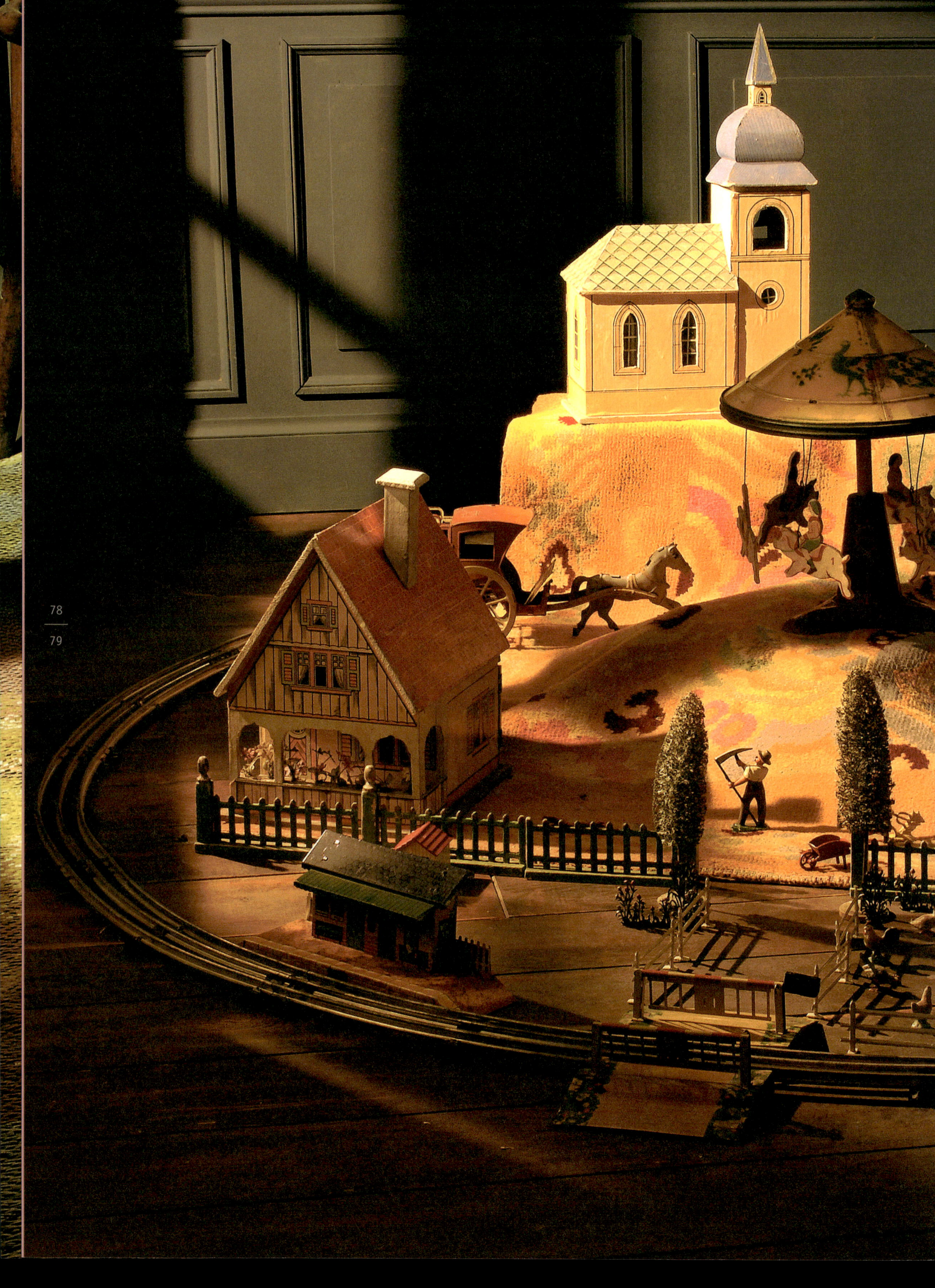

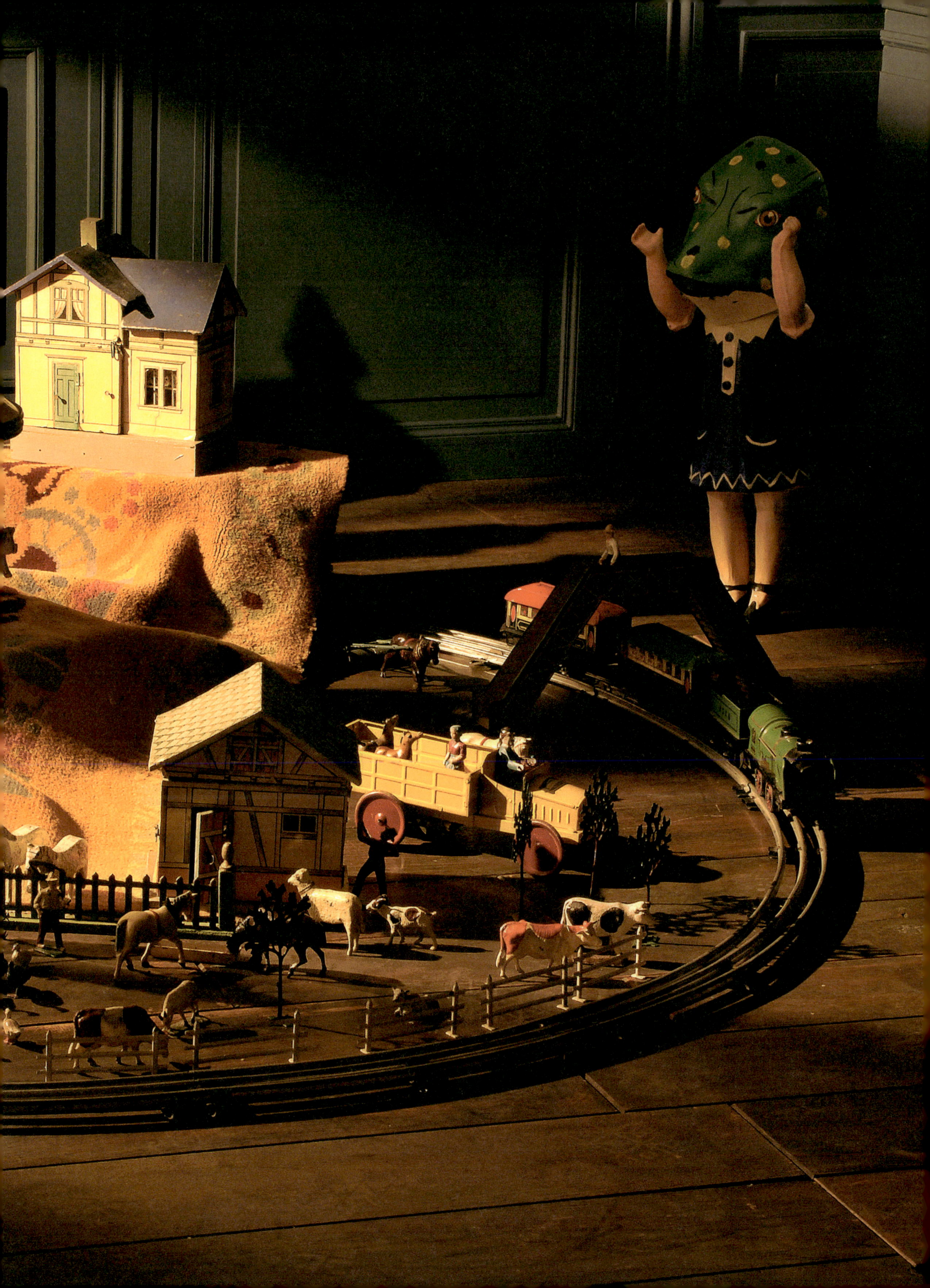

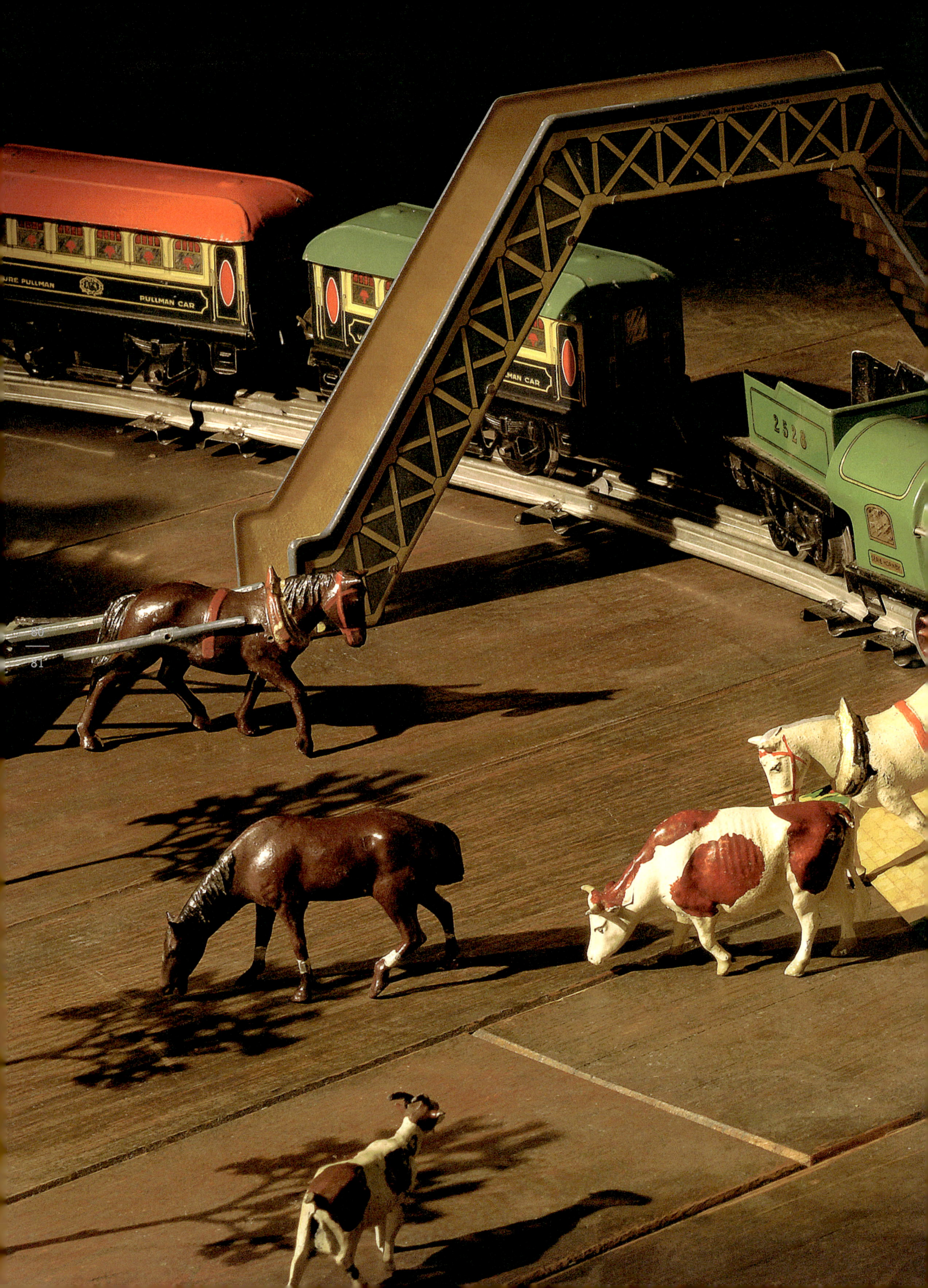
PULLMAN CAR
2525

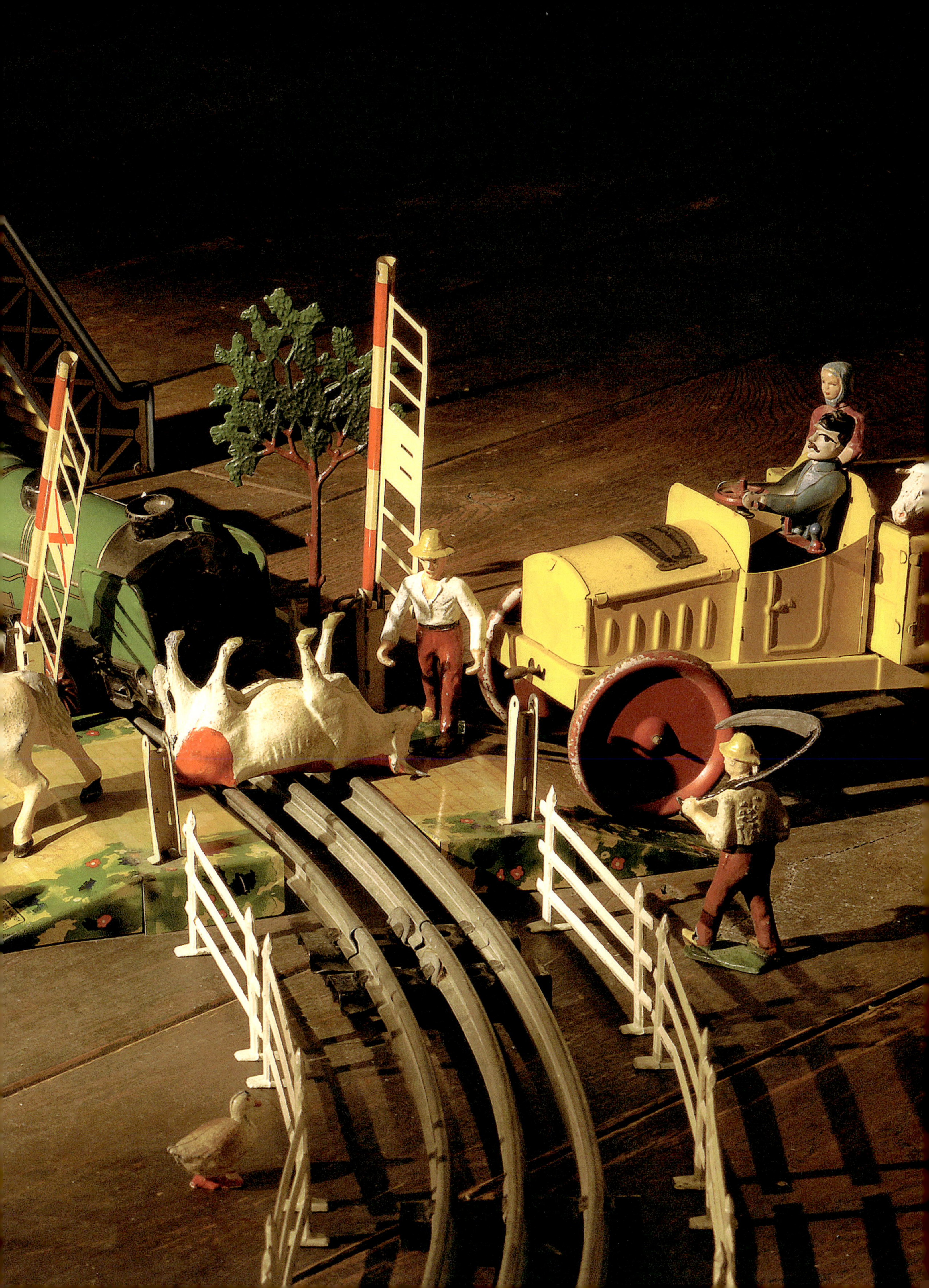

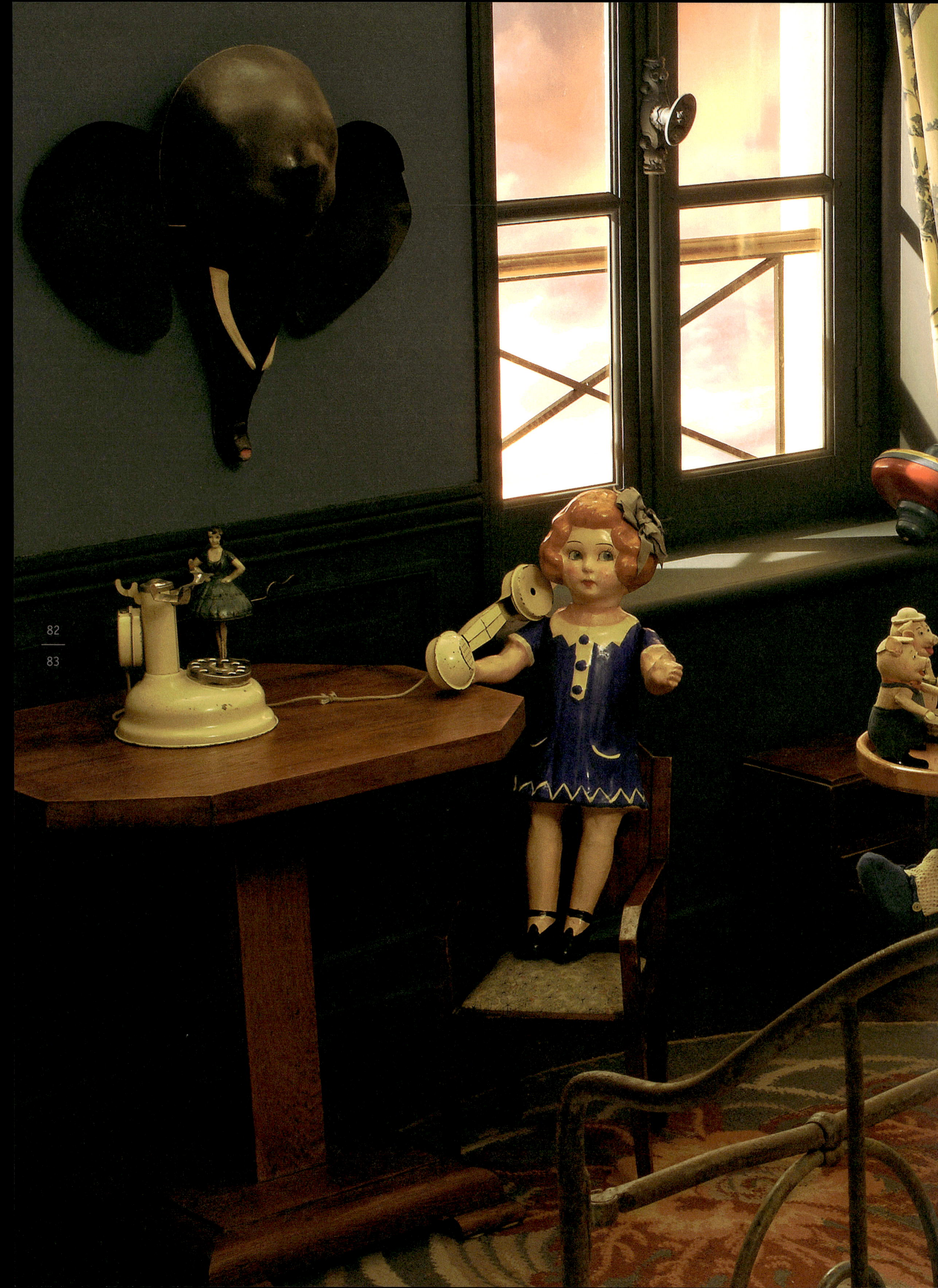

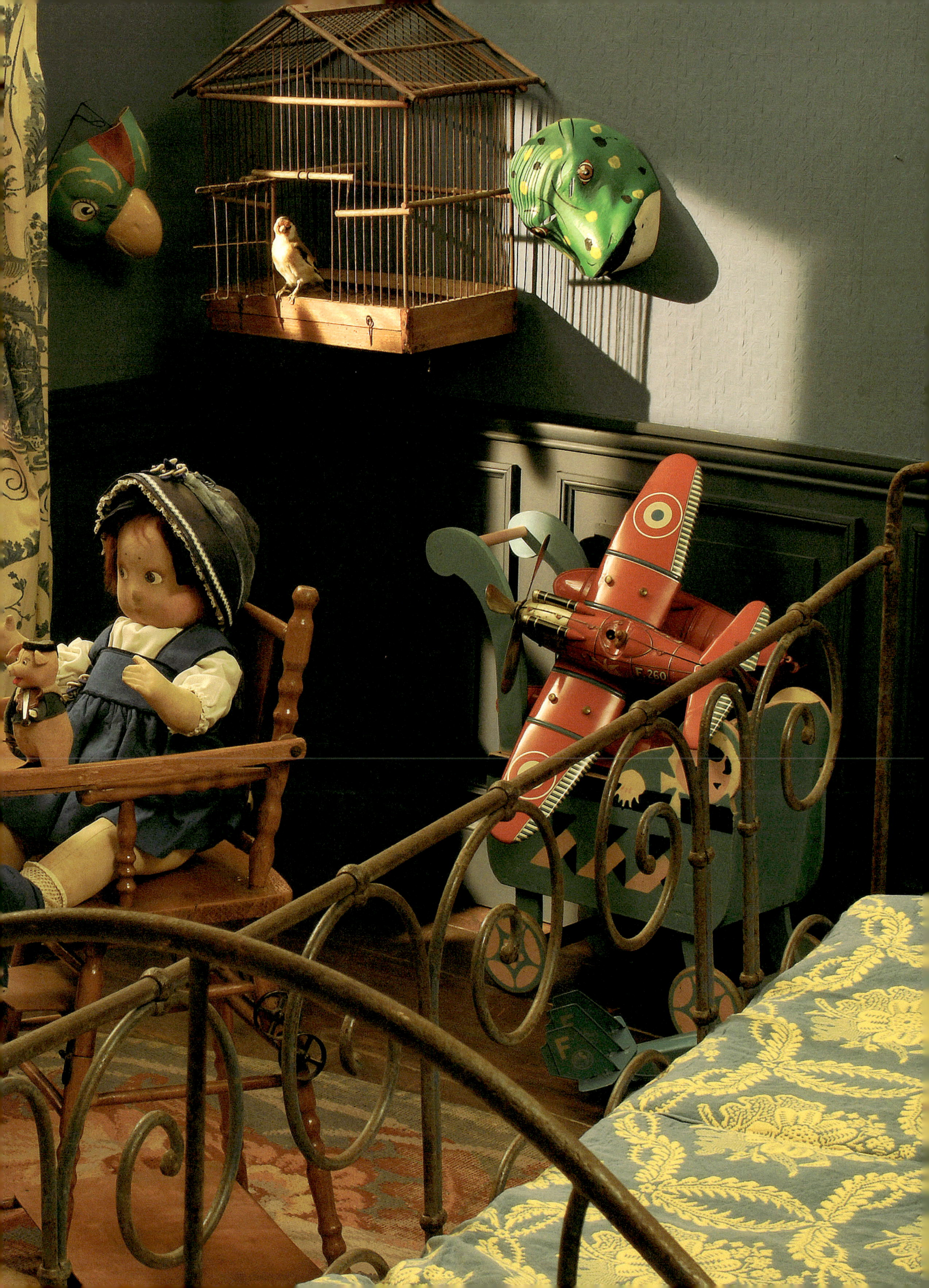

hat does the child play with when he plays with a doll?

The body of a doll is always slightly disturbing. A doll's body is not our own and yet it possesses the same landscape. Its nakedness is ours: to strip it of its clothes is to perform something forbidden on ourselves. Especially with the hyperrealist dolls made out of lifelike plastic. The pink, shiny skin reveals its inner secrets but we know that there is more. Small breasts heave on the torso, the modest belly delicately swells, but something is missing. Arms, legs and head fit into sockets, obscenely, and when we pull them out, the holes reveal the grey, dead stuffing or else a puzzling emptiness. This is not how we are put together, this is not how we become whole. Someone is telling a lie.

These are games of assembling and taking apart. Like Dr Frankenstein at work, the child creates impossible creatures out of a variety of pieces. There are conventional procedures to follow: Mr Potatohead or the Transformers, for instance, programmed metamorphoses. Pin on a nose, twist the body round and, hey presto, a new being emerges.

Or else there are unscripted, disturbing ones. The child undresses the dolls, then takes them apart. The sections of the body are displayed as in a butcher shop or a murder scene. Heads are transposed, limbs inverted. Cruelty is an acquired skill.

ar is not a game. In 1914, the English humorist H. H. Munro, better known as Saki, copied out a paragraph from a London morning paper. 'In view of the National Peace Council, there are grave objections to presenting our boys with regiments of fighting men, batteries of guns, and squadrons of "Dreadnoughts". Boys, the Council admits, naturally love fighting and all the panoply of war ... but that is no reason for encouraging, and perhaps giving permanent form to, their primitive instincts. At the Children's Welfare Exhibition, which opens at Olympia in three weeks' time, the Peace Council will make an alternative suggestion to parents in the shape of an exhibition of "peace toys". In front of a specially painted representation of the Peace Palace at The Hague will be grouped, not miniature soldiers but miniature civilians, not guns but ploughs and the tools of industry... It is hoped that manufacturers may take a hint from the exhibit, which will bear fruit in the toy shops.'

The experiment, of course, fails. Playing with the 'civilian' toys, the children act out a slaughter: the doll representing Louis the Fourteenth 'orders his troops to surround the Young Women's Christian Association and seize the lot of them'. One of the female dolls refuses to be taken and stabs the Marshal Saxe doll 'to the heart'. 'He bleeds dreadfully,' says one of the children, splashing red ink all over the YWCA building. 'The soldiers rush in and avenge his death with the utmost savagery. A hundred girls are killed,' explains the child, pouring the remainder of the red ink over the building, 'and the surviving five hundred are dragged off to the French ships. "I have lost a Marshal," says Louis, "but I do not go back empty-handed."'

Saki's story is called 'The Toys of Peace'.

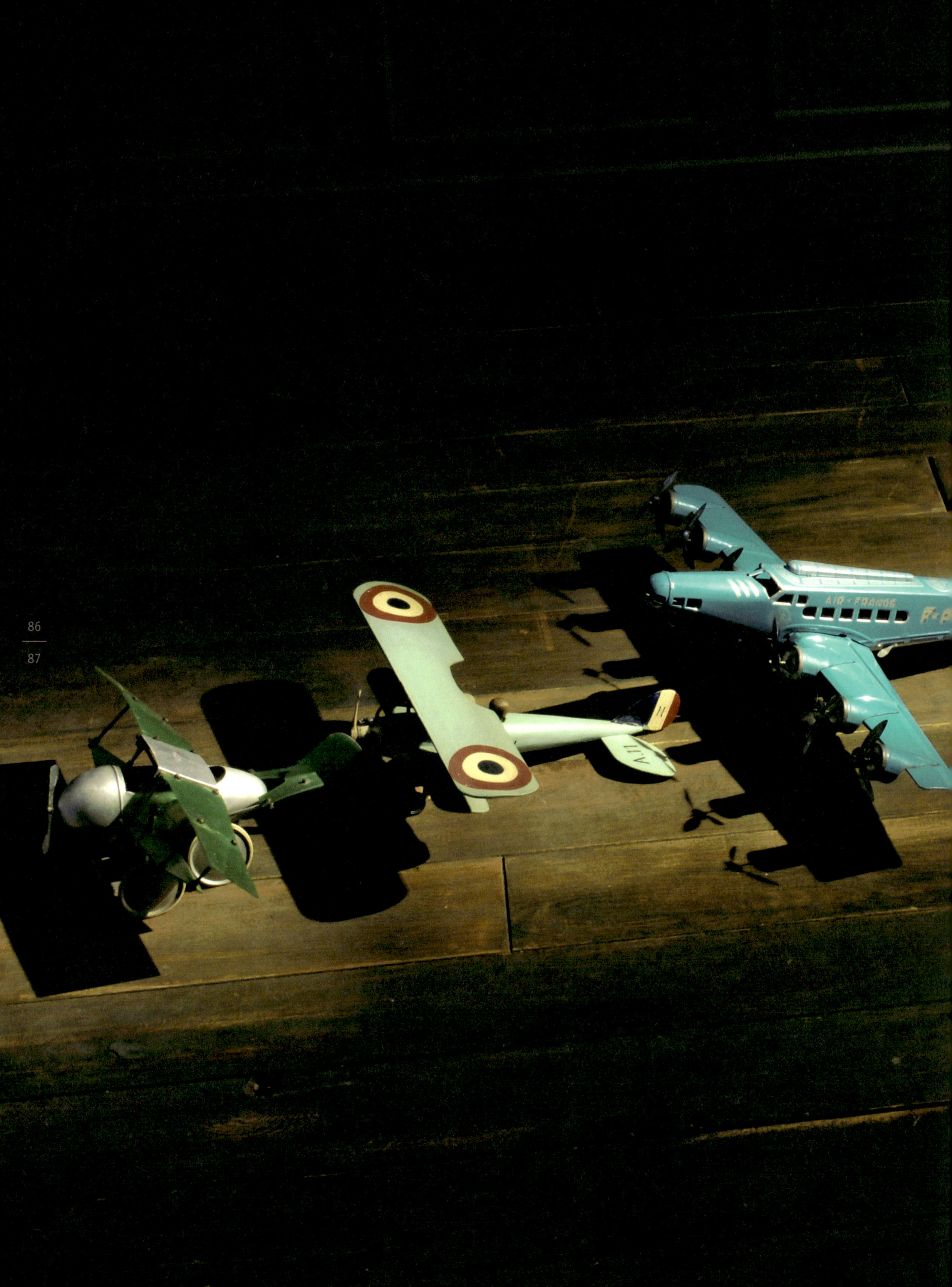

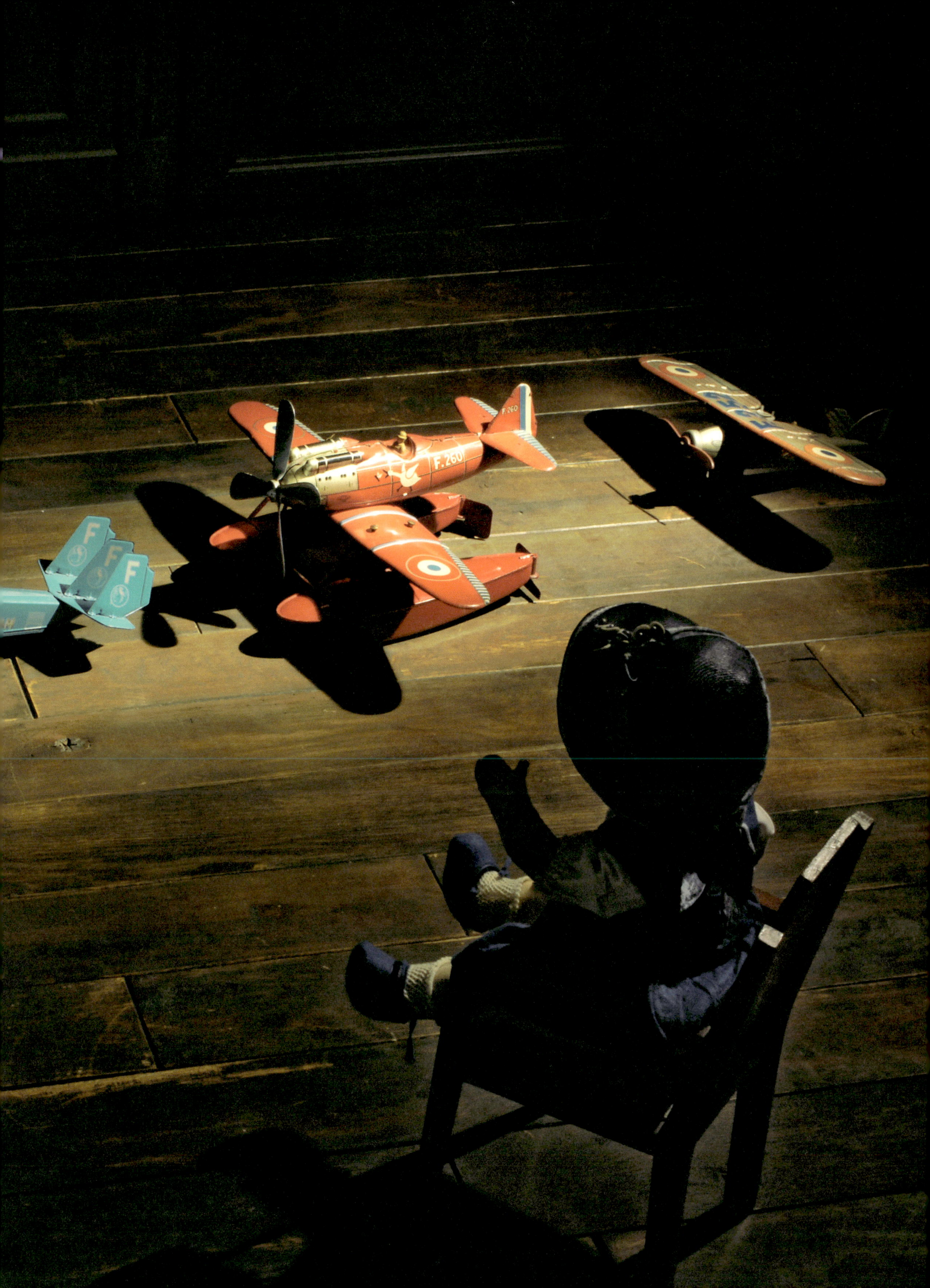

F. 260
F. 260
F. 260
F
F
F

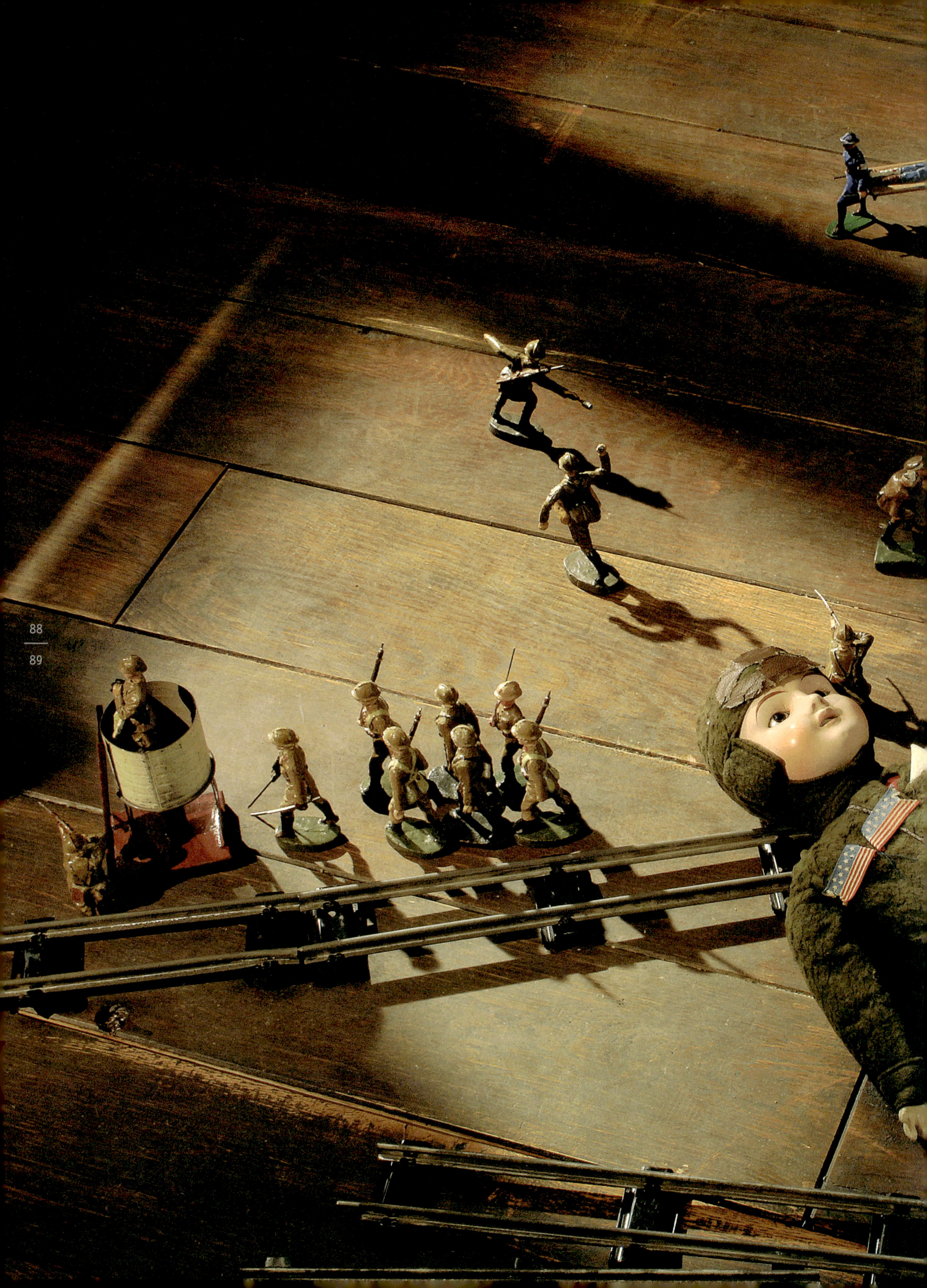

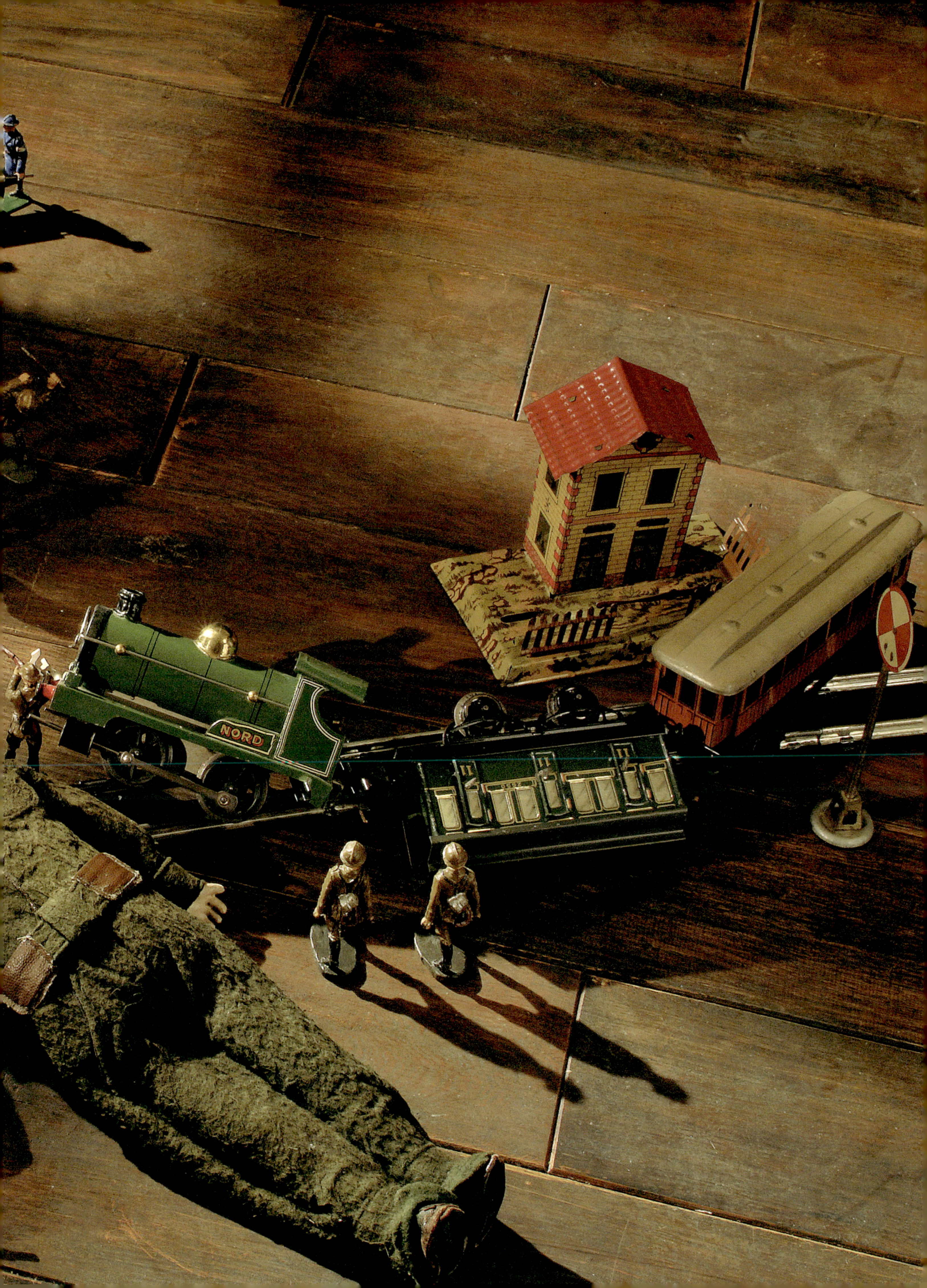

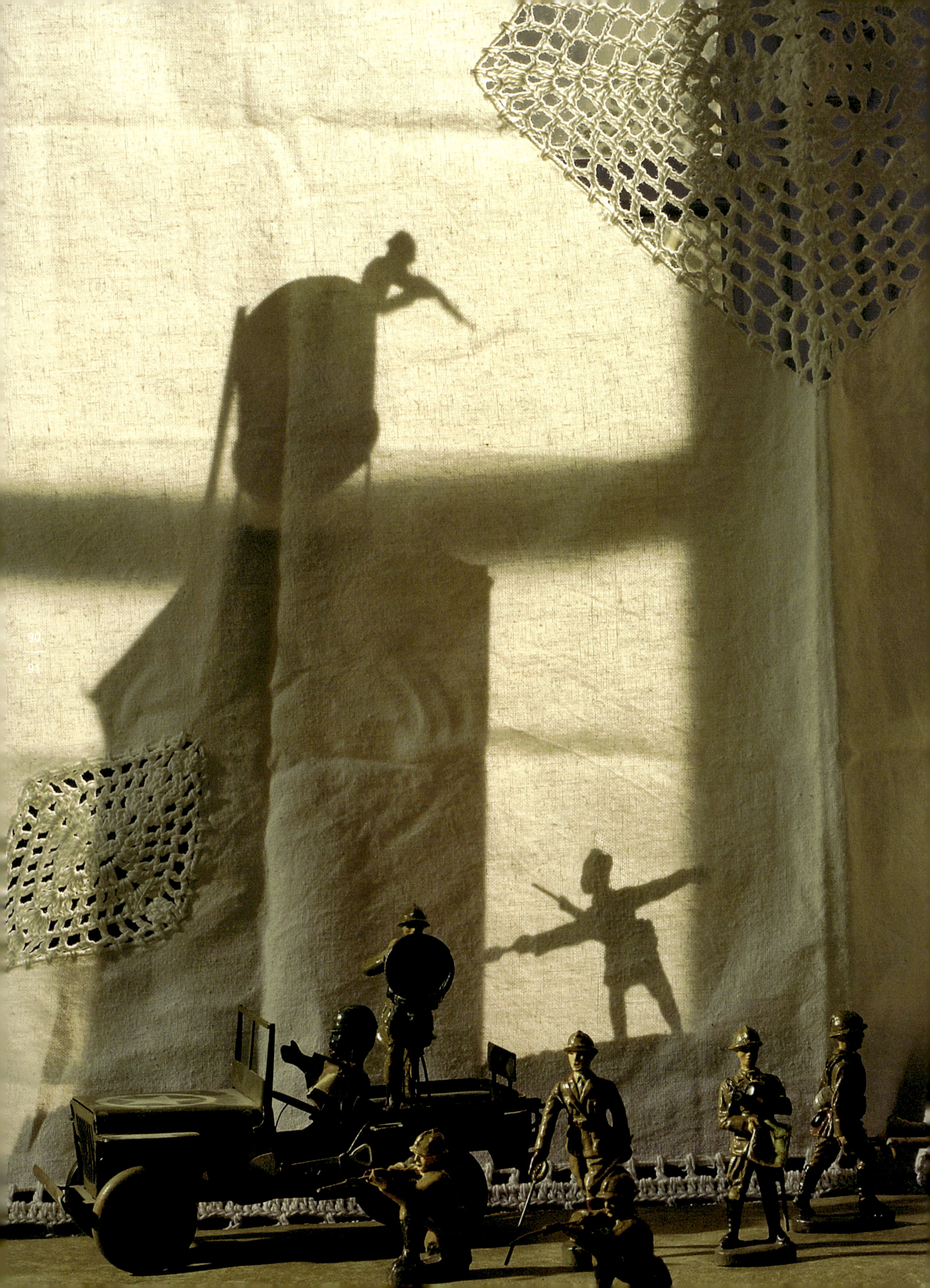

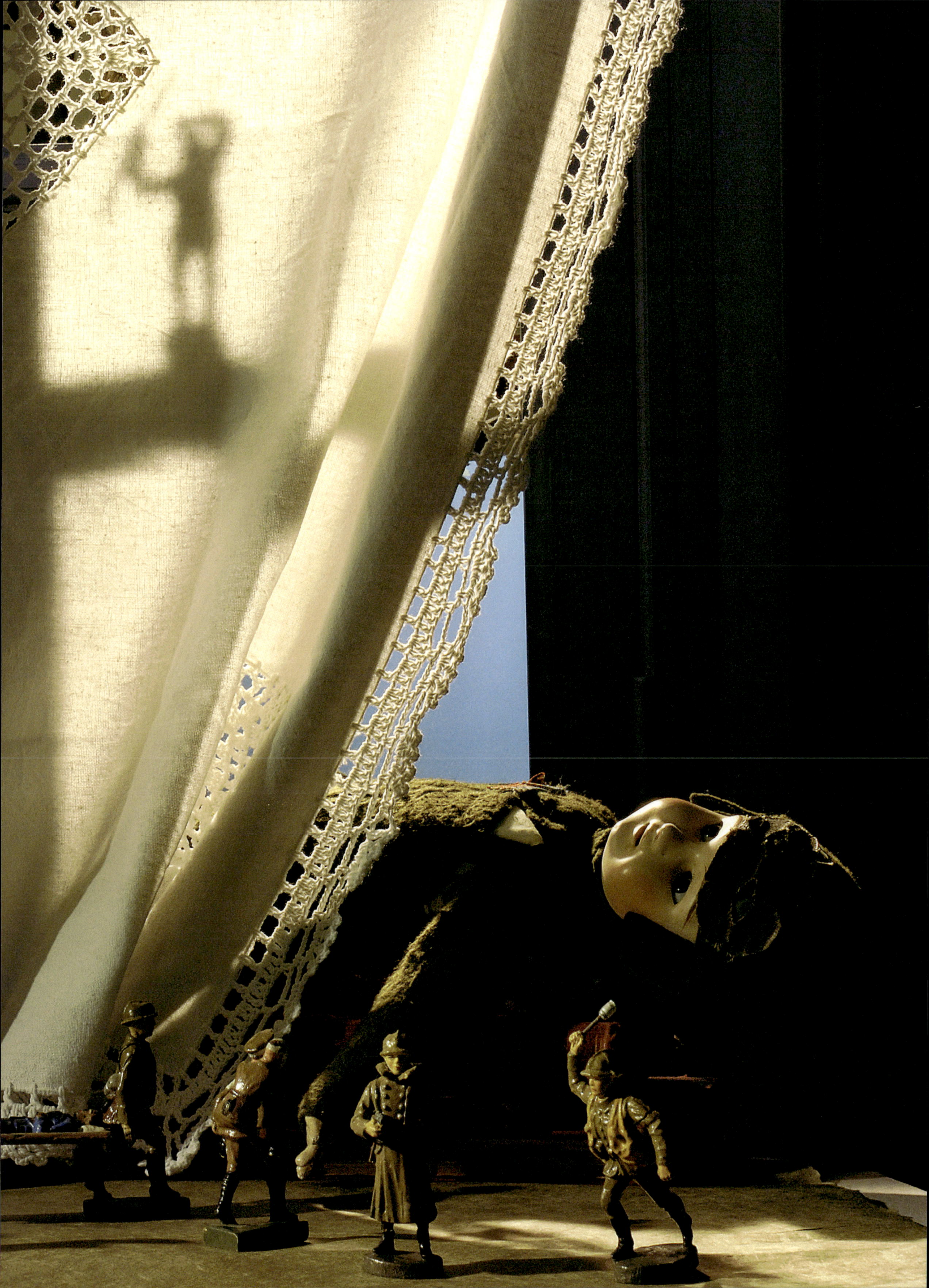

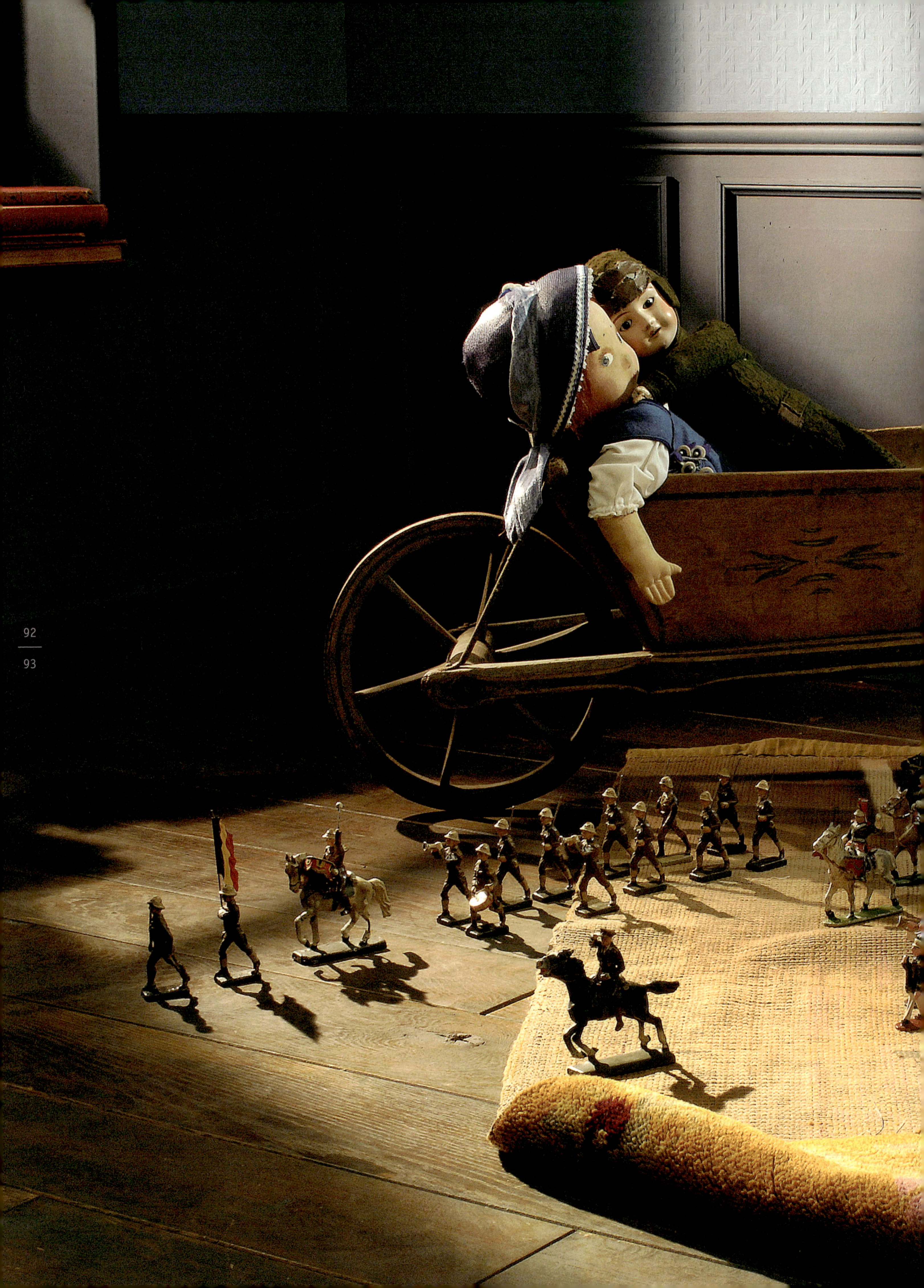

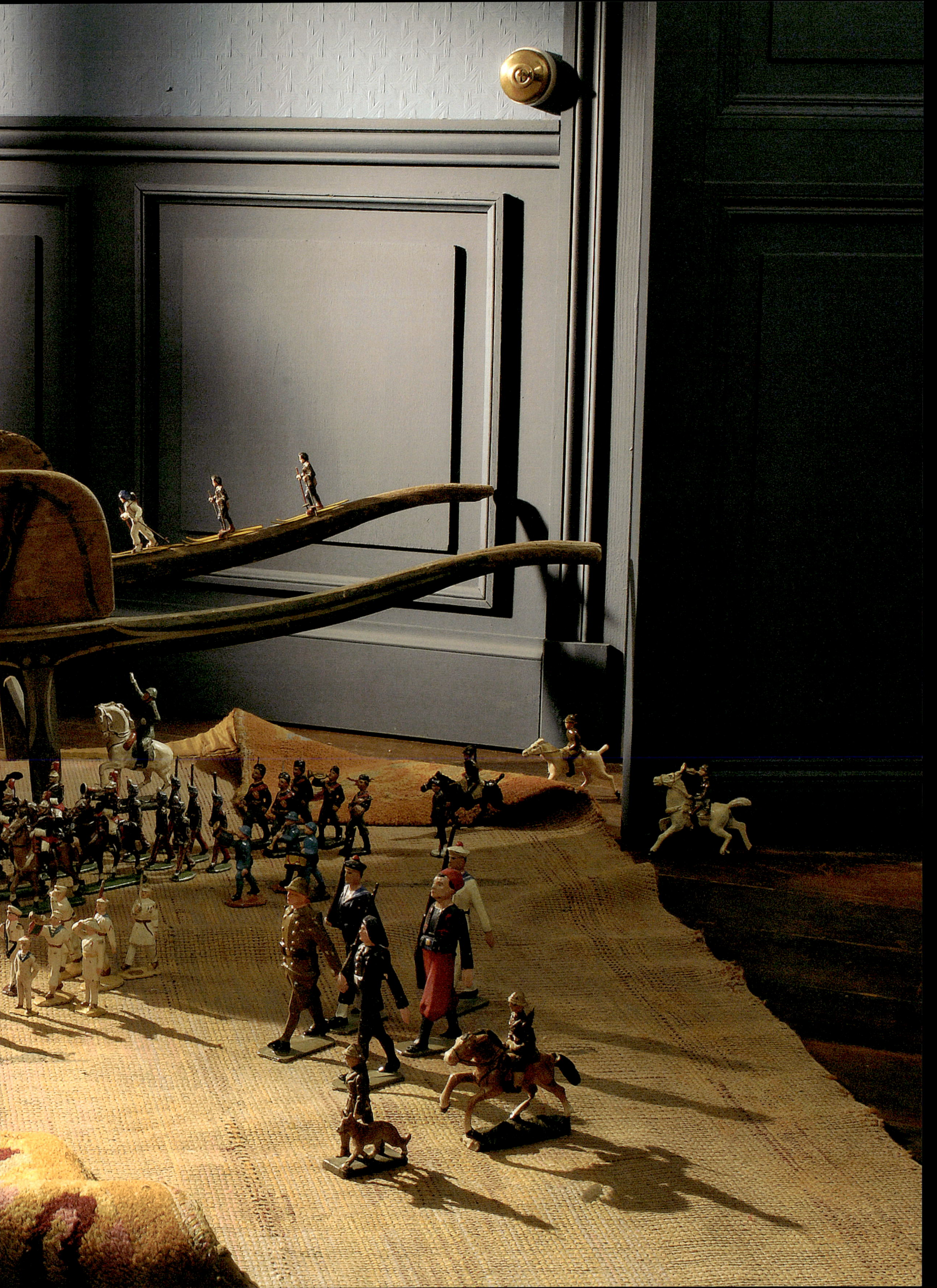

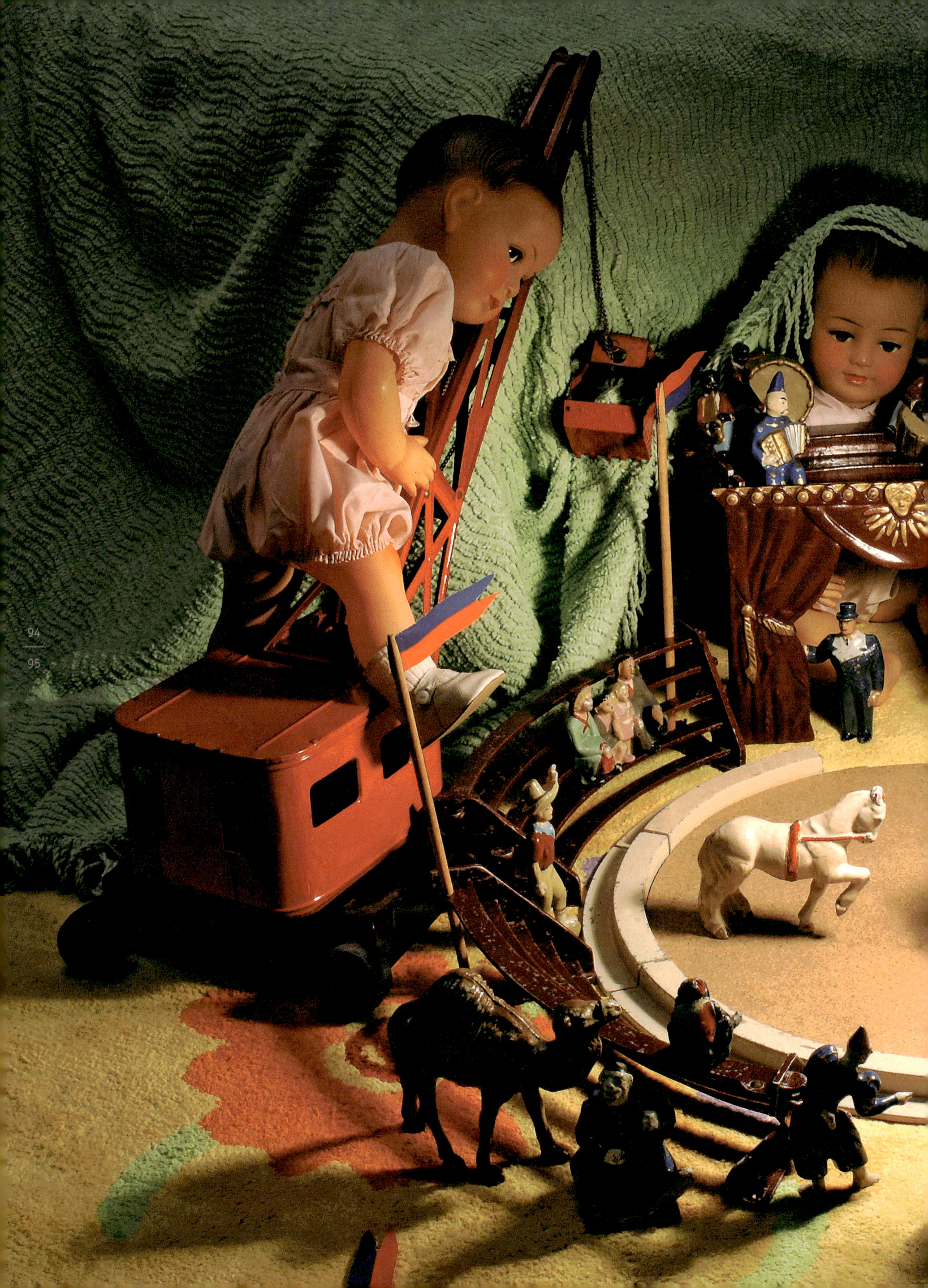

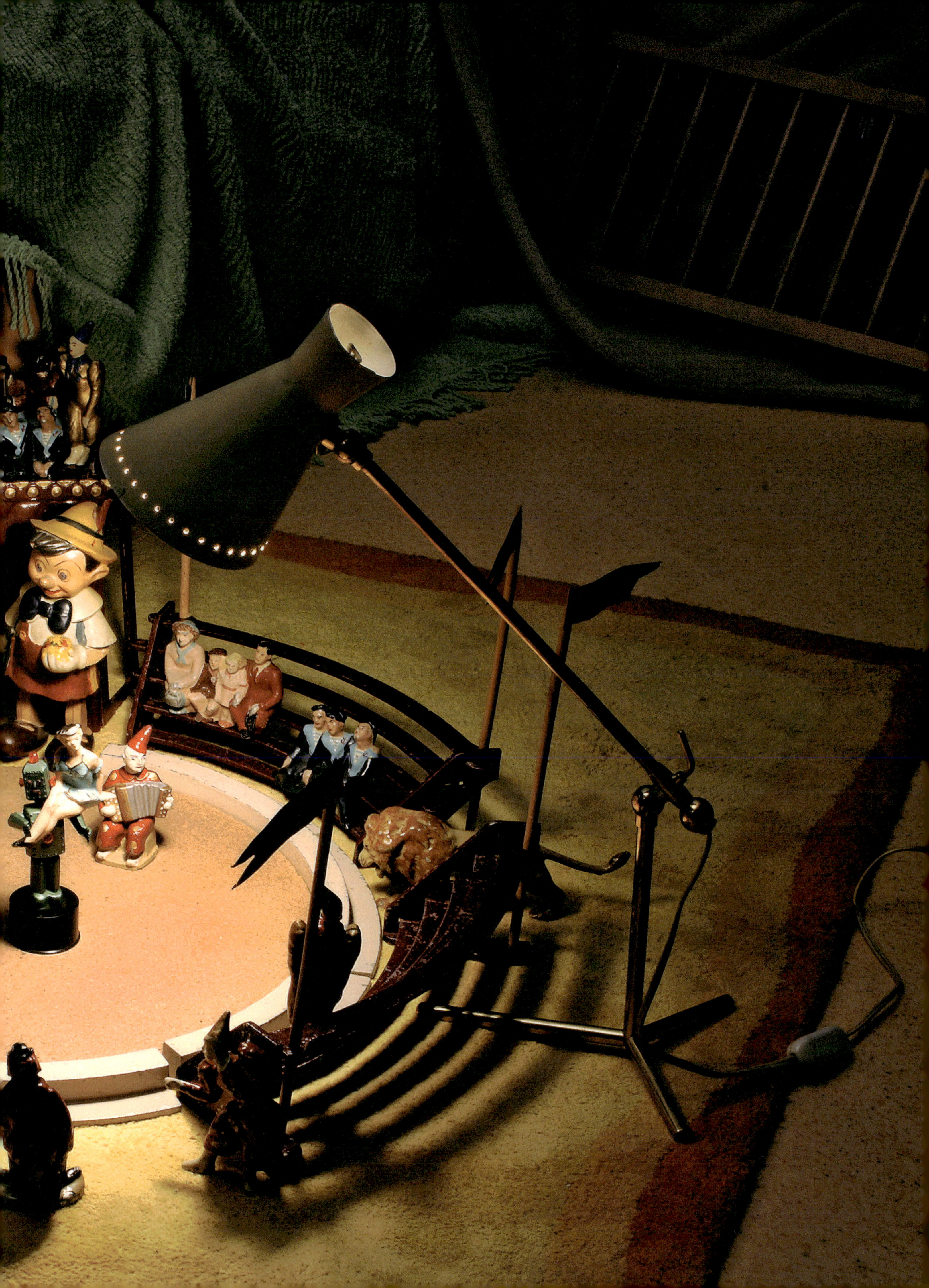

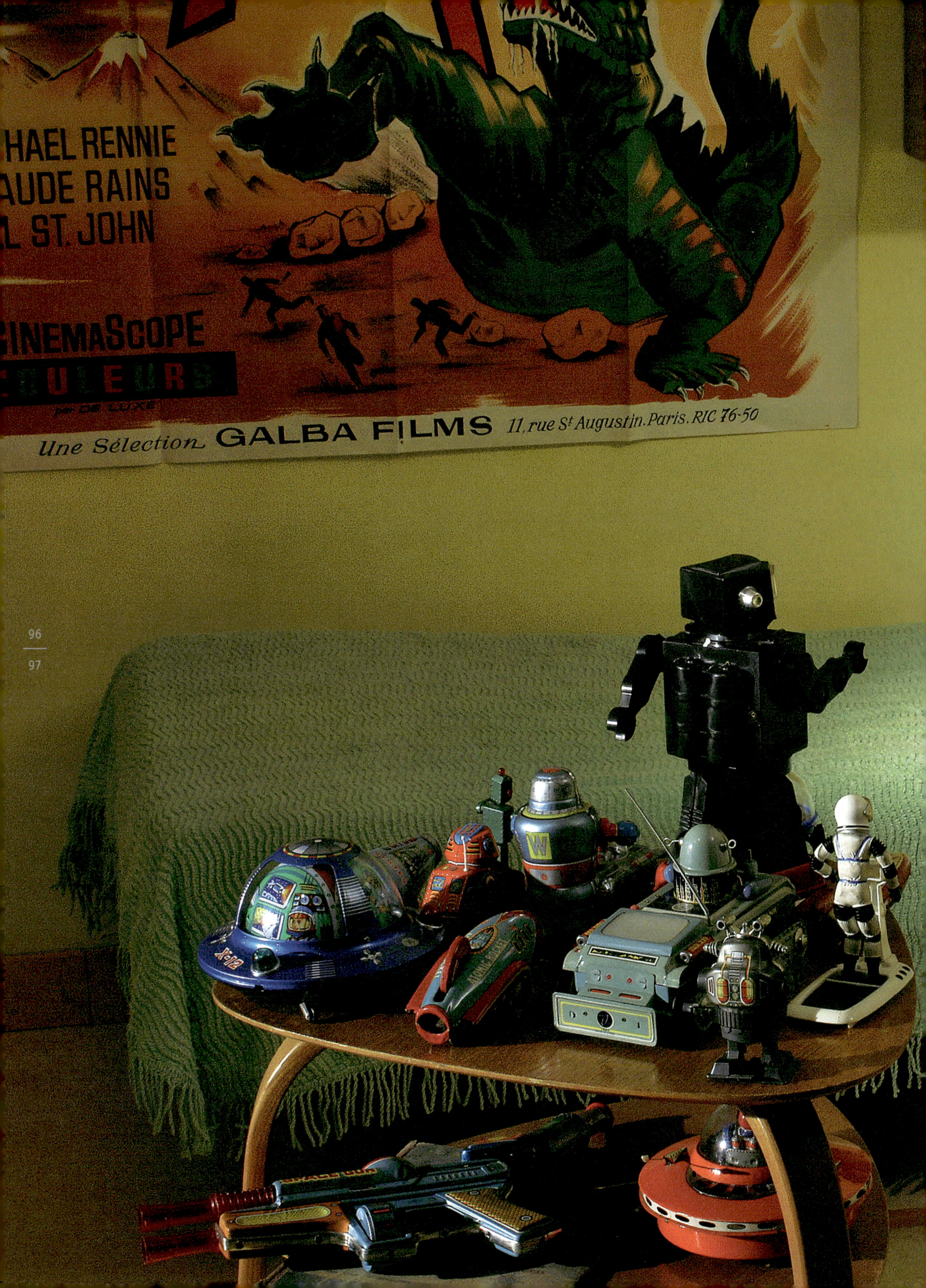

HAEL RENNIE
AUDE RAINS
L ST. JOHN
GINEMASCOPE
OULEURS
par DE LUXE
Une Sélection GALBA FILMS 11, rue St Augustin. Paris. RIC 76-50

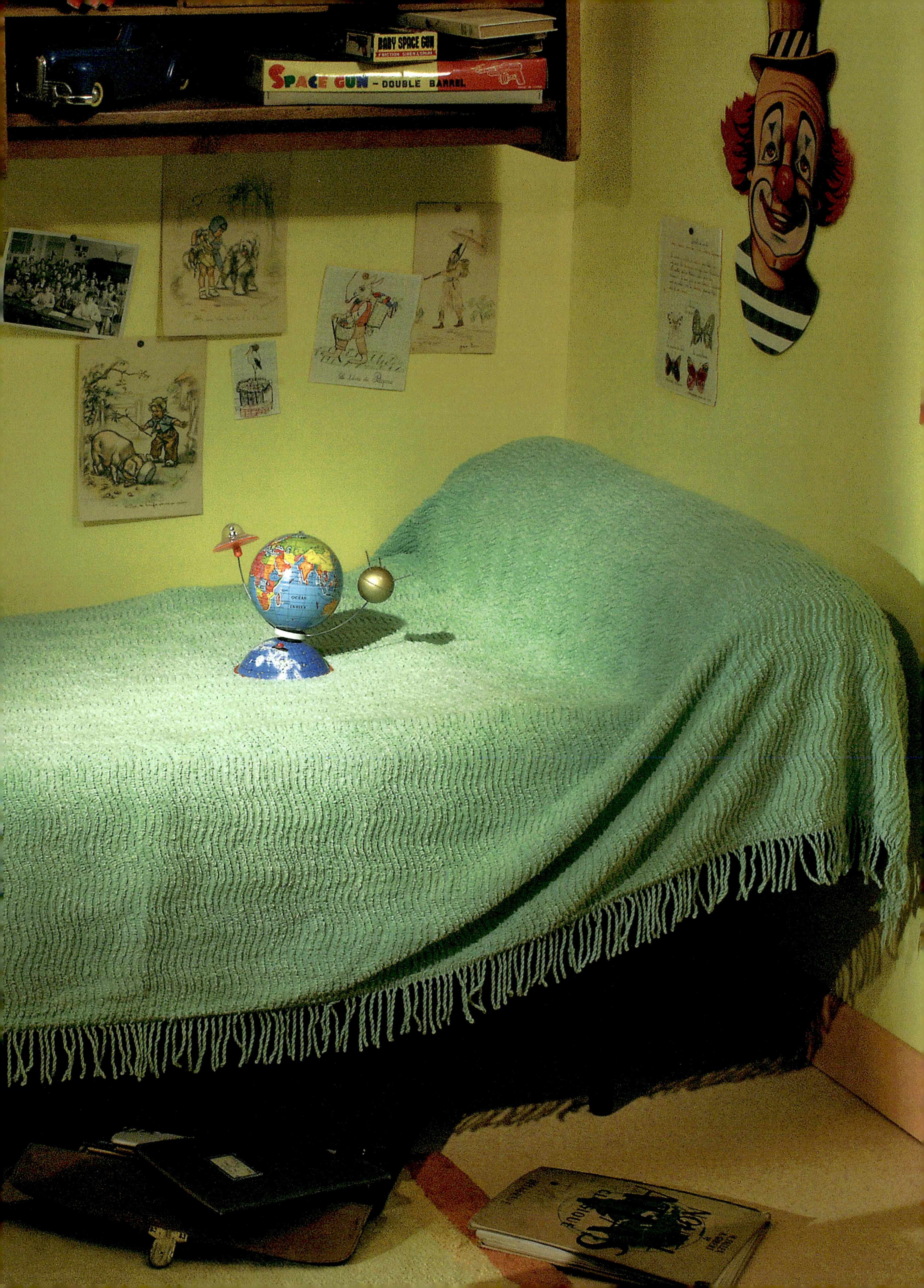

BABY SPACE GUN
FRICTION SIREN LIGHT
SPACE GUN - DOUBLE BARREL
OCEAN
INDIEN

or the child, a toy is both an inanimate and a living thing, both identical and dissimilar to the creatures in the world around him. In believing that his toys have a life, the child senses that he is crossing a dangerous, unmarked frontier. The second Commandment, as if aware of this attraction, forbids us 'to make unto thee graven images' – forbids us to be, in effect, like a small god and create life out of inanimate matter. (Iconoclasts take this to mean that we are not allowed to represent any living thing, be it a dog, a fish or a man.)

Everywhere, however, children make toys out of discarded objects: a piece of wood, a tin, a rope. For the child, this rag has a name, this stone a face, this box is a fortress, these bones live. Elaborate bought toys have complex lives and secret, unavowable defects. Toys that the child makes for himself are perfect, beyond reproach in the eyes of its maker, unaffected by the limits of human magic, possessors of a soul.

According to the Talmudists, any representation of a living thing will turn to its human creator on the Day of Judgment and demand that he grant it a soul. Since he will find himself incapable of accomplishing this, the transgressor will be flung into the everlasting fire.

ur desire to make objects come to life overrides all fear of supernatural punishment. Every child dreams that, during the night, his toys will move by their own will, lead secret lives of which the adults know nothing. The child has named them, taught them how to walk, explained how they should behave. But what exactly do they do when he's not there to watch them? Where do they go when all is dark?

In the eighteenth century, Rabbi Loewe of Prague (legend has it) created a golem, a man made out of mud, 'to sweep the floor of his synagogue.' The experiment failed. Shortly afterwards, the rabbi was obliged to return his golem to the dust after the creature ran amok in the ghetto. Our creations always exceed us.

Like Rabbi Loewe, every child creates golems out the toys he loves and the secret suspicion that they might one day turn against him darkly feeds the thrill of play. Horror films like *Child's Play* and *Gremlins*, or cautionary tales of evil robots (what are robots but adult toys?) such as *A.I.: Artificial Intelligence* and *Robocop* touch upon these ancient fears of the toy who turns against its master, the toy that keeps deep inside its core a secret and terrible self. The ancestors of these cautionary tales lurk in old mythological stories: that of the Trojan Horse, hiding within itself its destructive secret, that of the marble doll Galatea who comes to life in the arms of her sculptor Pygmalion. Toy horses on wheels and statuettes of dolls are among the oldest toys we know.

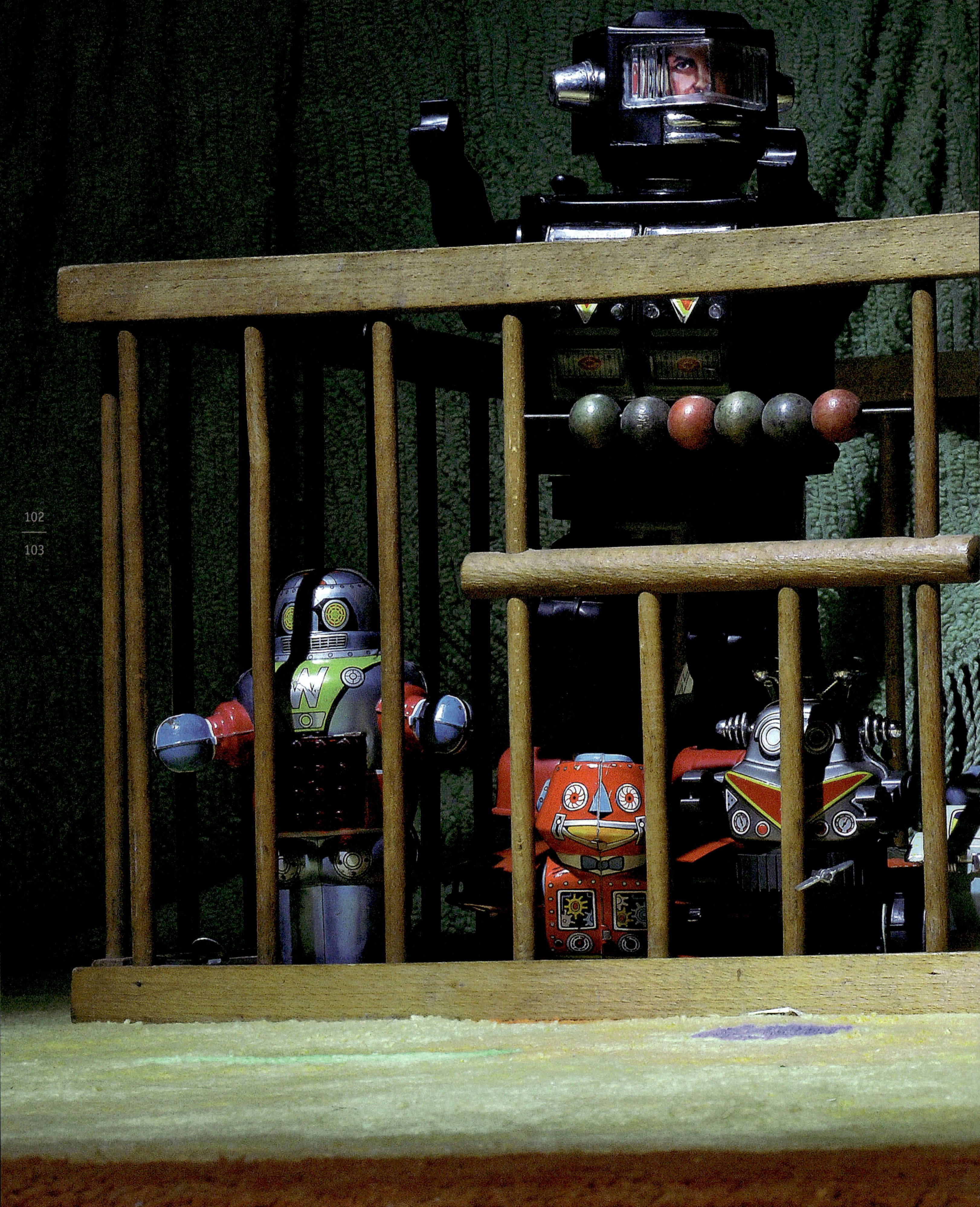

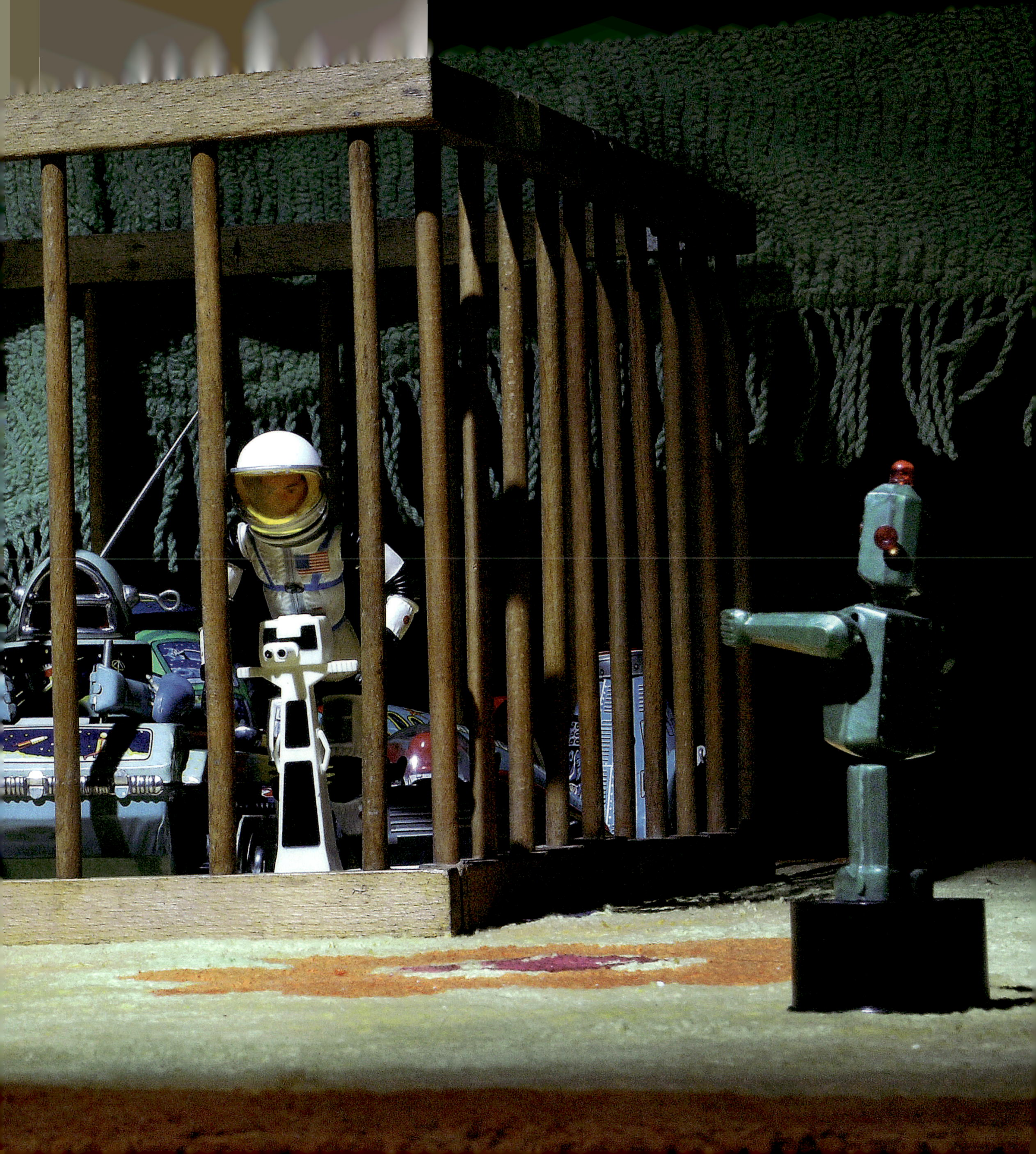

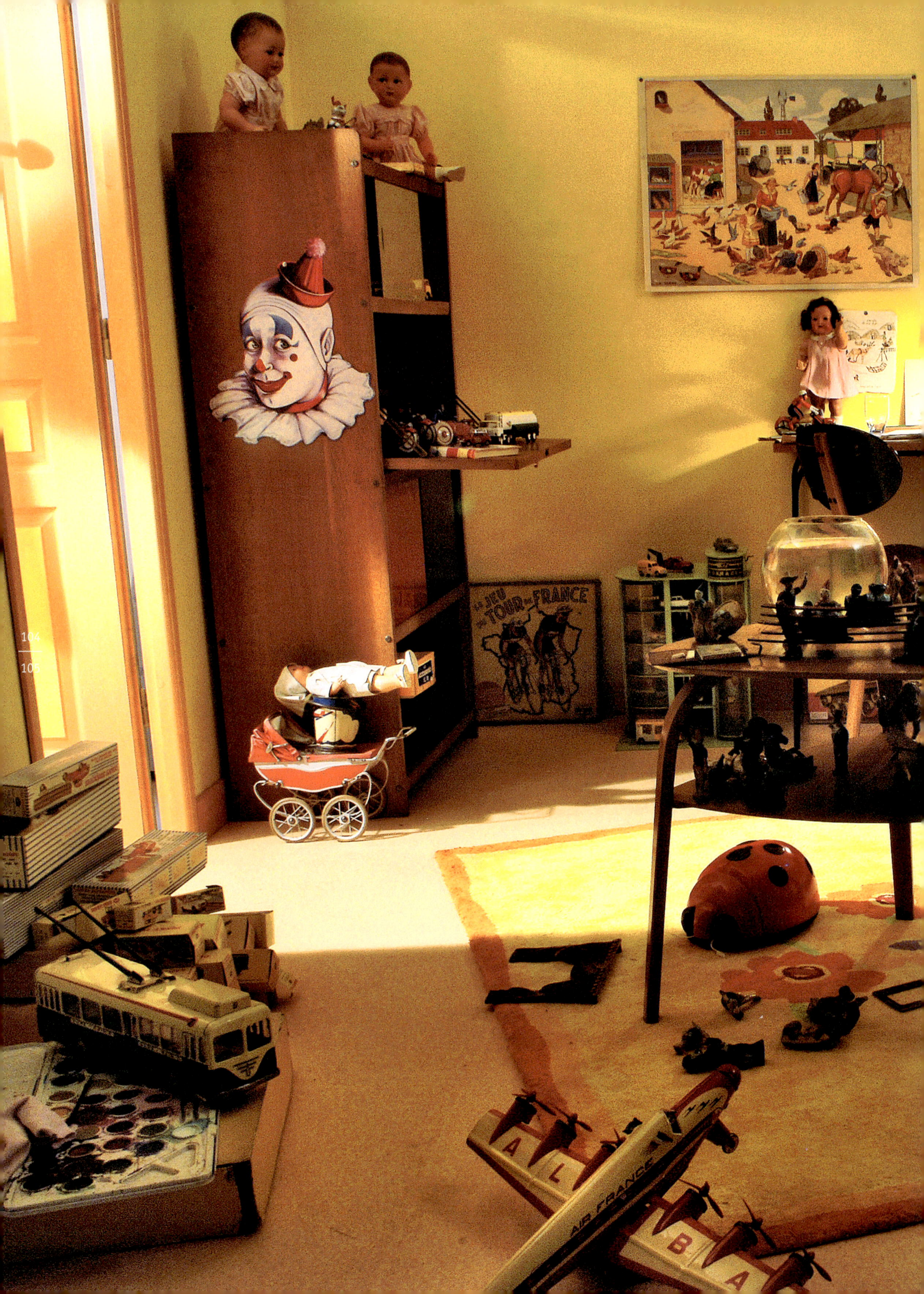

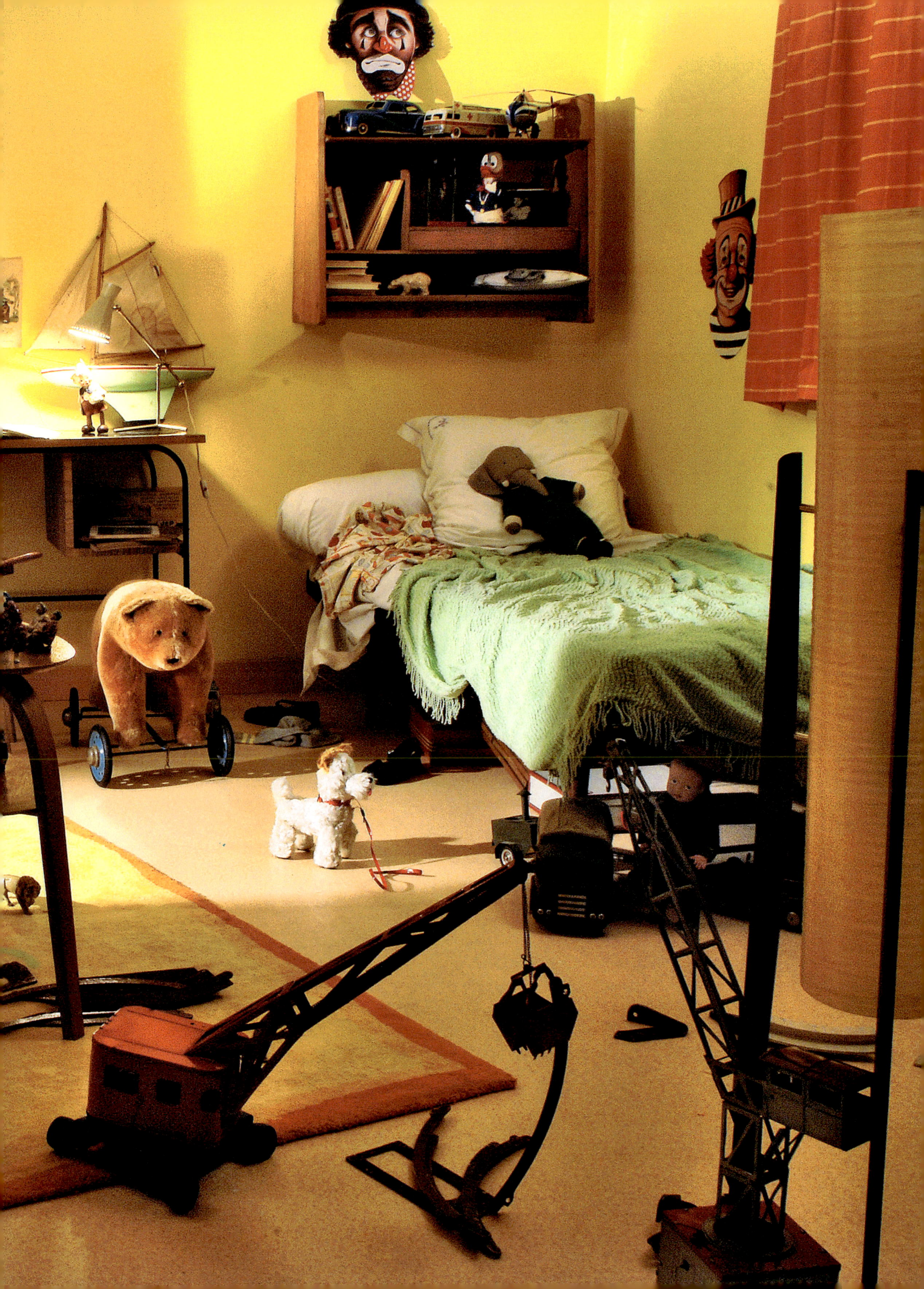

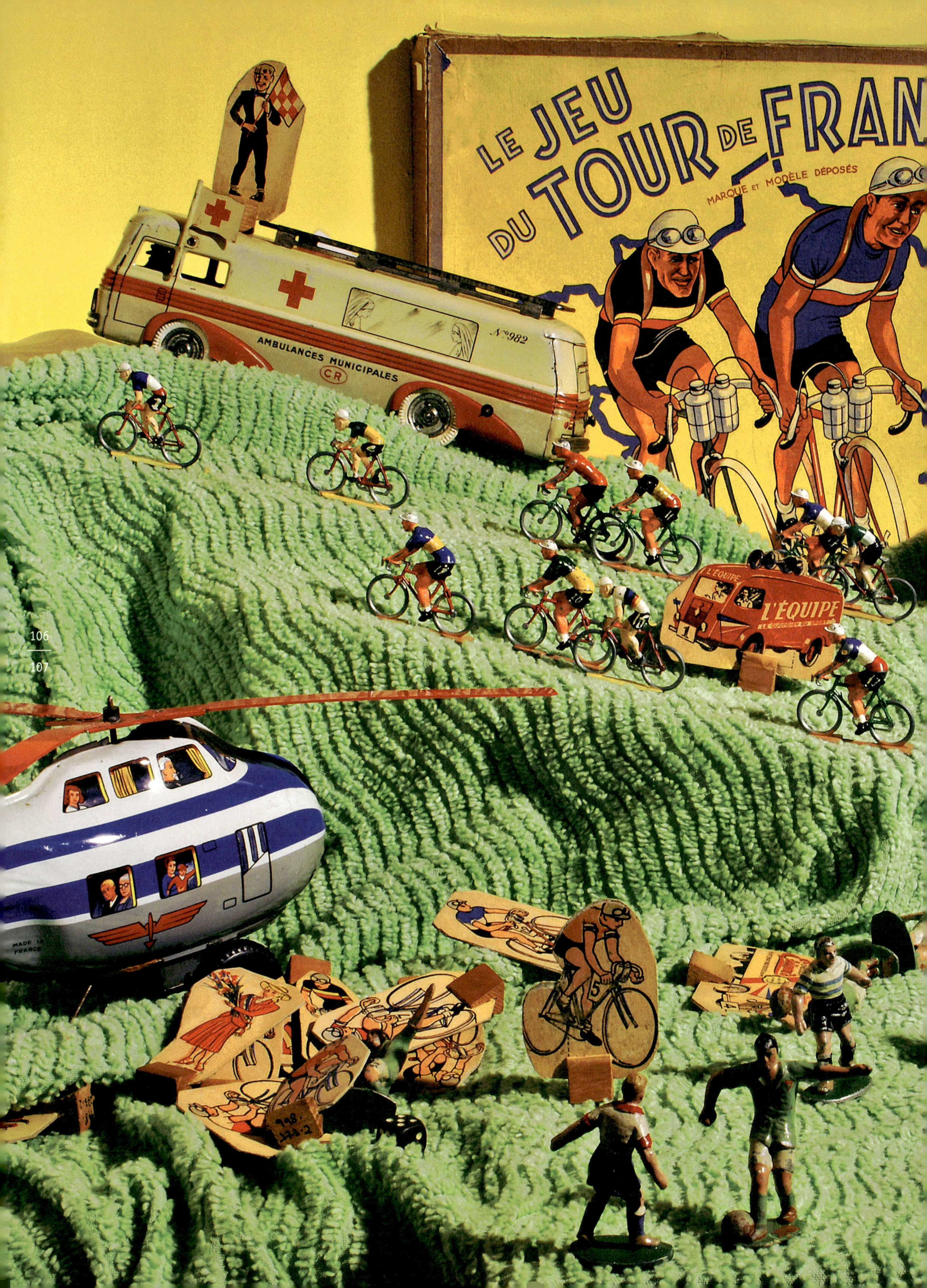

LE JEU
DU TOUR DE FRAN
MARQUE ET MODÈLE DÉPOSÉS
AMBULANCES MUNICIPALES
N° 982
CR
L'ÉQUIPE
MADE IN FRANCE

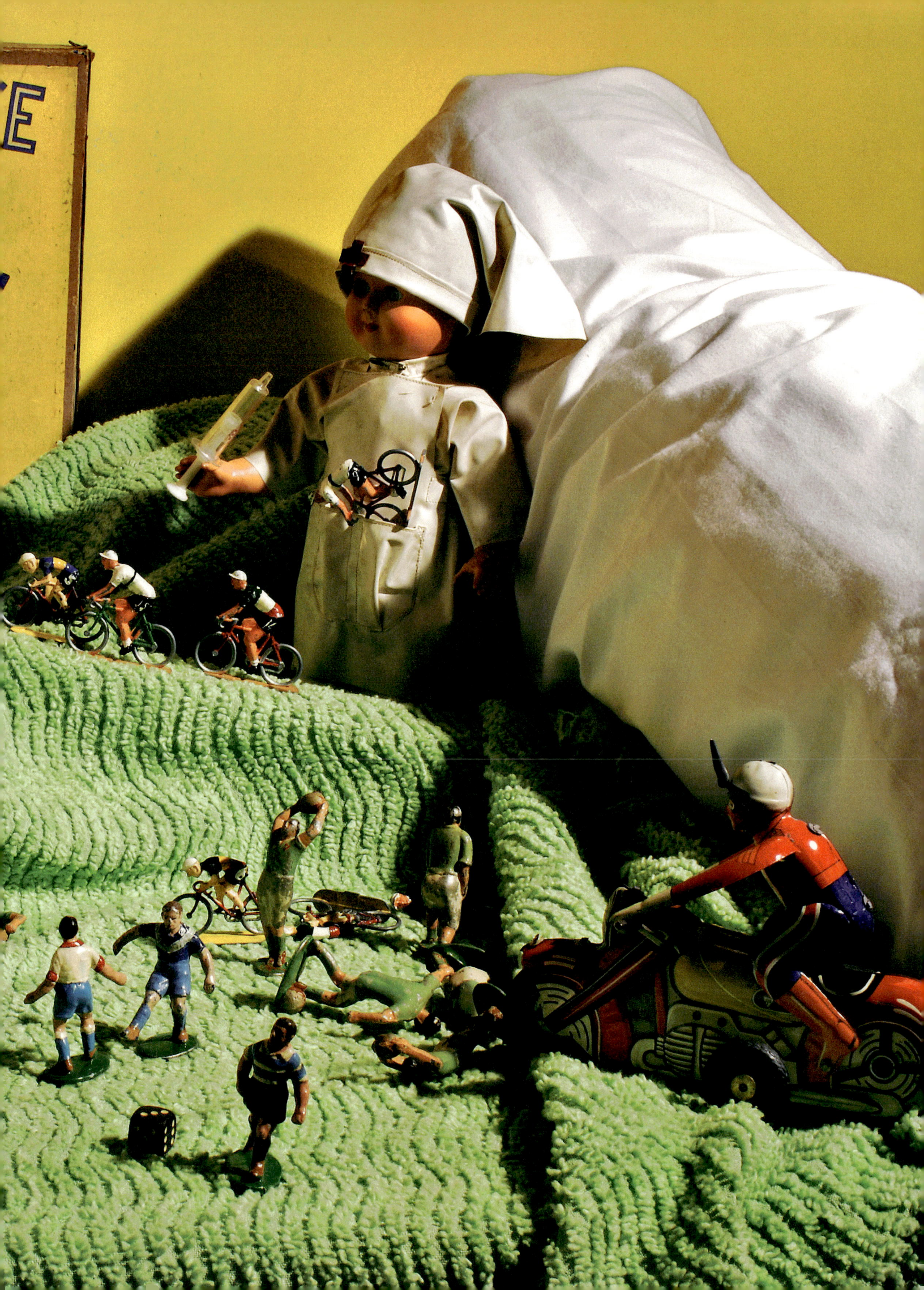

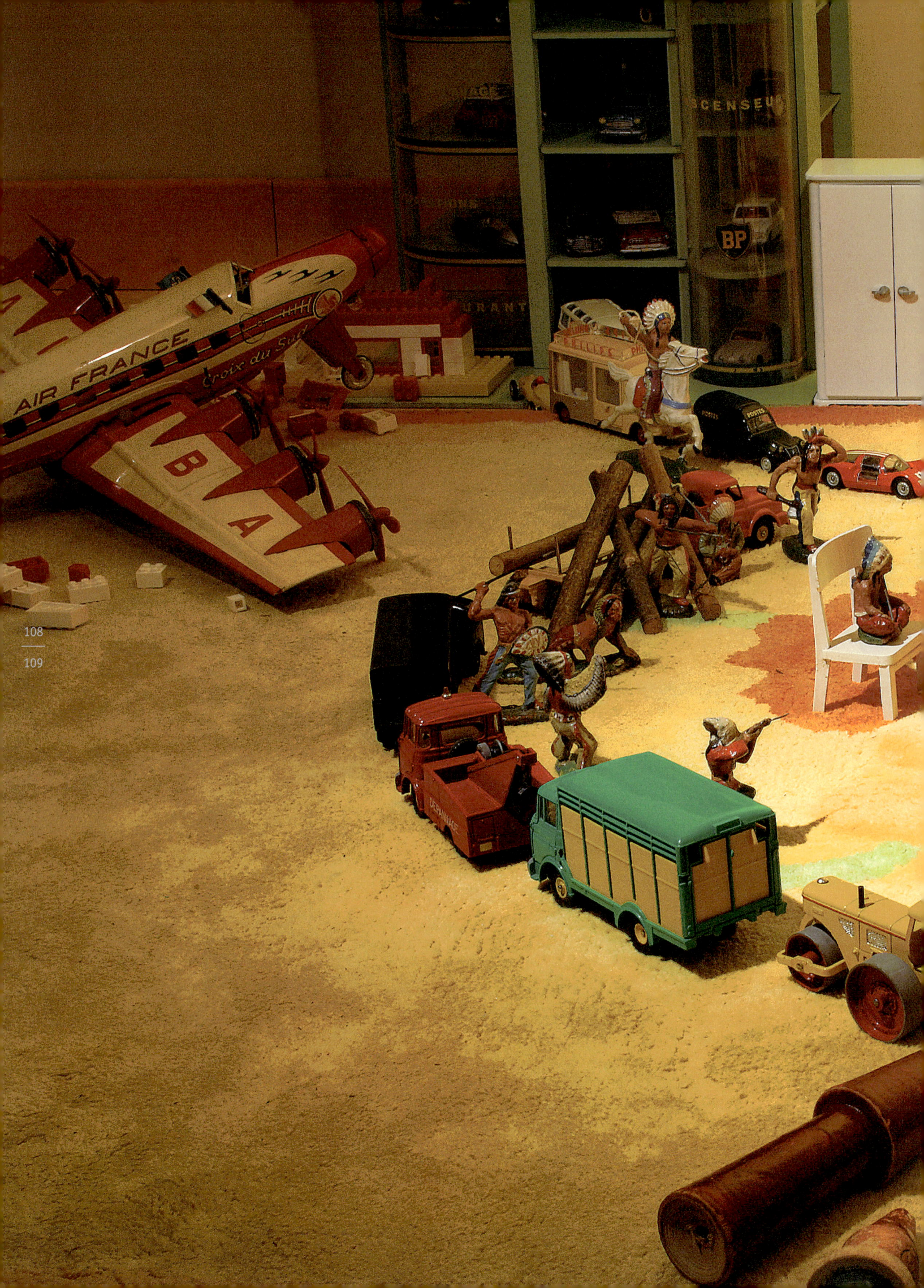
AIR FRANCE
Croix du Sud
VBA

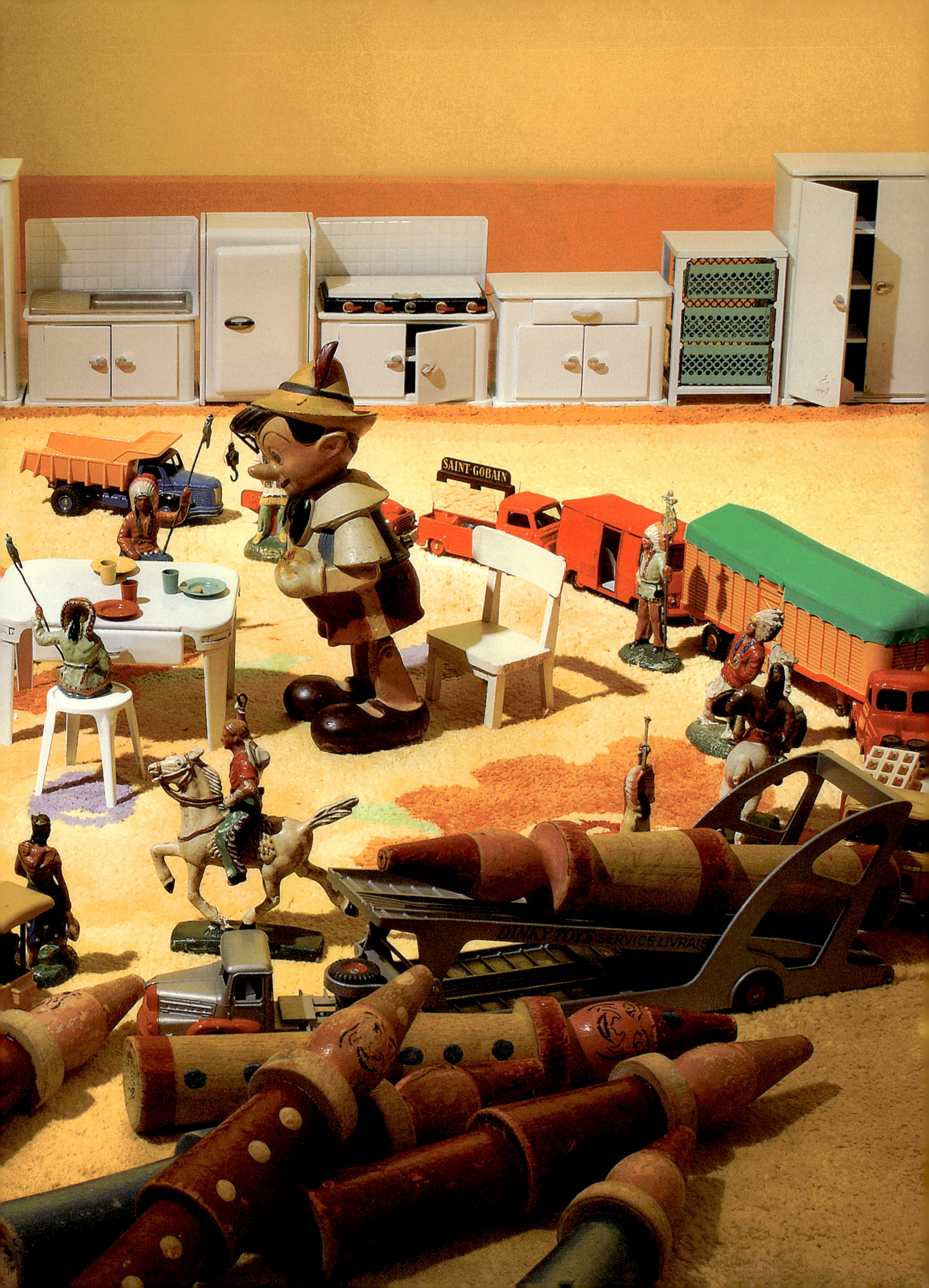

SAINT-GOBAIN
DINKY TOYS SERVICE LIVRAISON

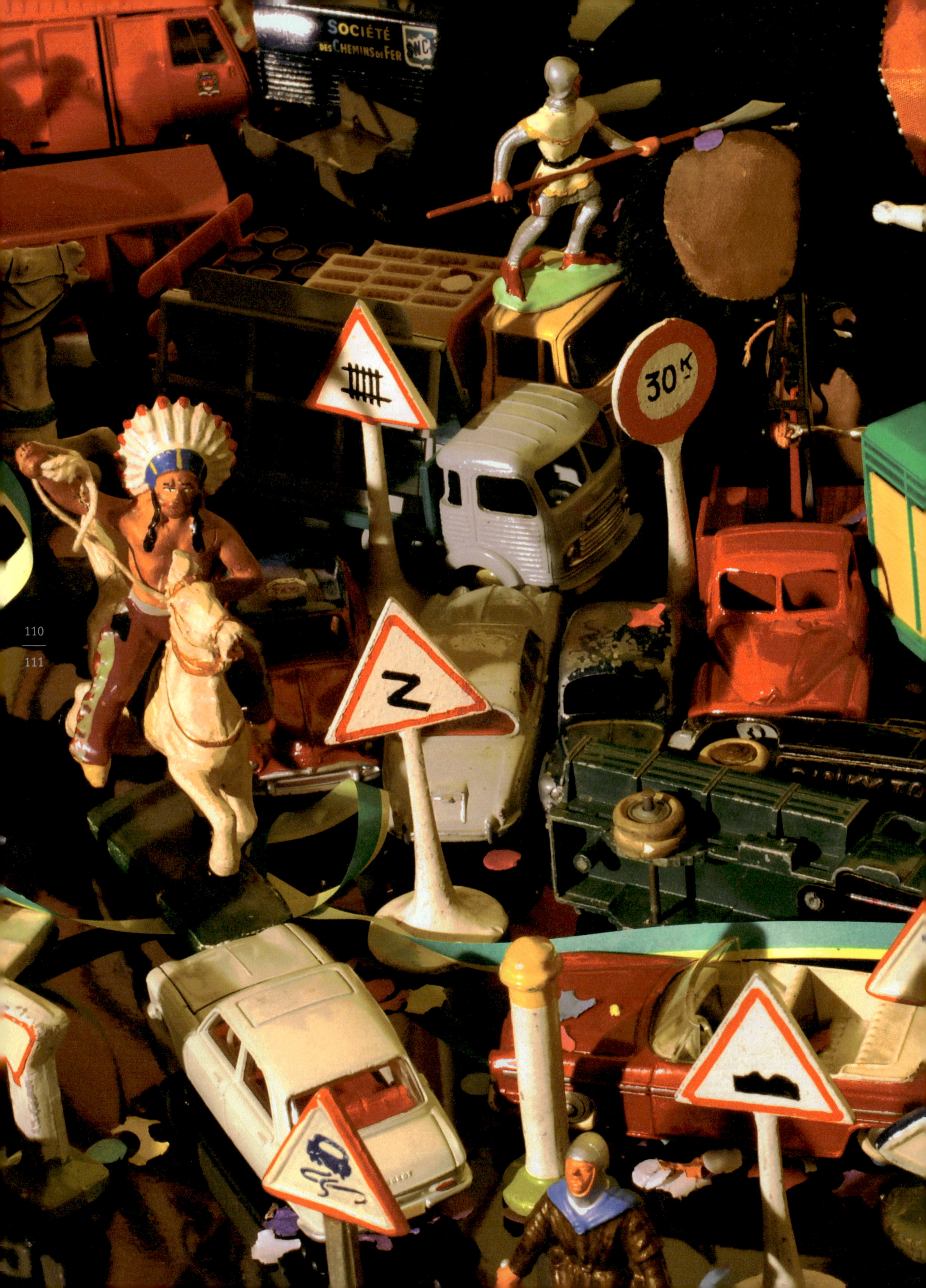

SOCIÉTÉ
DES CHEMINS DE FER
SNCF
30 K

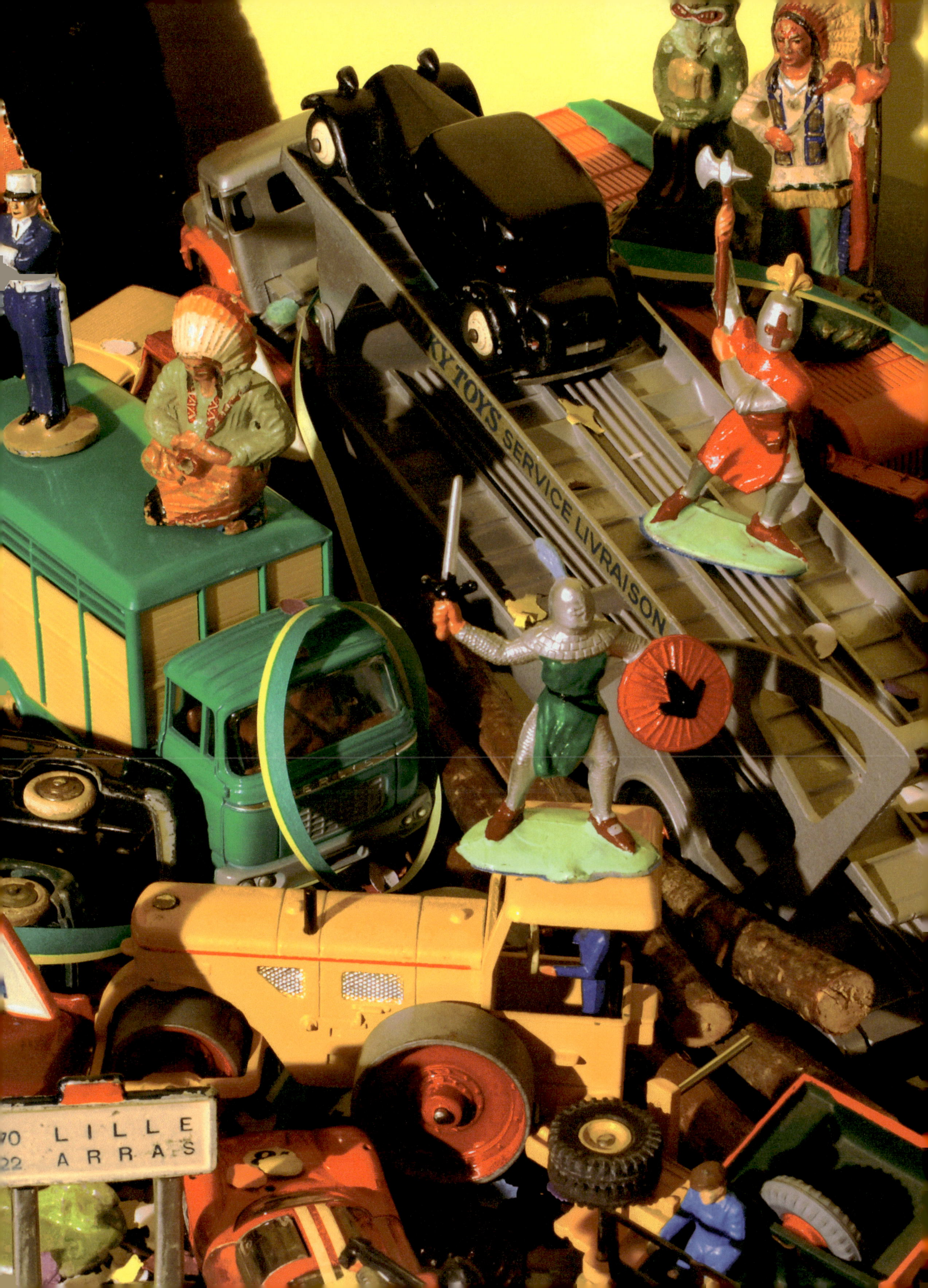
KY TOYS SERVICE LIVRAISON
LILLE
ARRAS

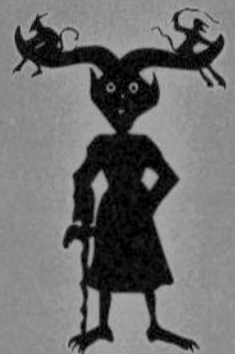

oys are the tools of memory: they remind us of the world and recall us to the world. Every toy is, in a sense, both Goody-Two-Shoes and Dennis the Menace.

Toys say: this is how things are done outside, these are the creatures that exist beyond the playroom walls, this is the way in which they go about their business and dress and party and fight, this is their secret craft of building cities, of baking cakes, of riding horses. But also, later: here there were children like you, here they learned and laughed, here they were frightened, here they sat and played and quarrelled, here they stood up and left the room.

Curiously, the models of the world left by the ancients in the tombs of their dead are identical to the toys they gave to their living children. In the Etruscan Museum in Cortona are displayed, side by side, miniature pots and basins, horses, dolls and weapons found both in a necropolis and in the ruins of a family home. It is as if the Etruscans (like the Egyptians, the Sumerians, the Romans) believed that the soul requires for its final journey the comfort of the toys that accompanied it in its childhood.

Or perhaps it is the other way round. Perhaps through toys the child is taught that the world is made of ephemeral things, and he will not feel despoiled when crossing over into the world to come.

hat happens to the toys we lose?

At the turn of a corner, in a house to which we were taken or in a park where it suddenly grew too dark to go on playing, we lost a soldier, a few marbles or a ball. We thought we'd find them again the following day, the coming week, the next time we played there. Toys have infinite patience, we thought. They'll wait.

Some were replaced but, of course, no toy is ever identical to another. Some we forgot. Some we grieved for. A certain website offers to find any toy we want, for the sake of nostalgia. But it isn't nostalgia. Regret, perhaps. And guilt.

It is said that the afterworld was invented not so much for the sake of some ponderous idea of justice, but in order to console us with the hope that any loss may not be eternal. The toys we've lost (like the friends we've lost) remain somewhere in the past, uncorrupted and incorruptible. Memory betters them, restores a lost button, a faulty wheel. Fixed in time, in a place we can no longer name, they wait unchanged, healthy and whole, without further fear of crack or tear.

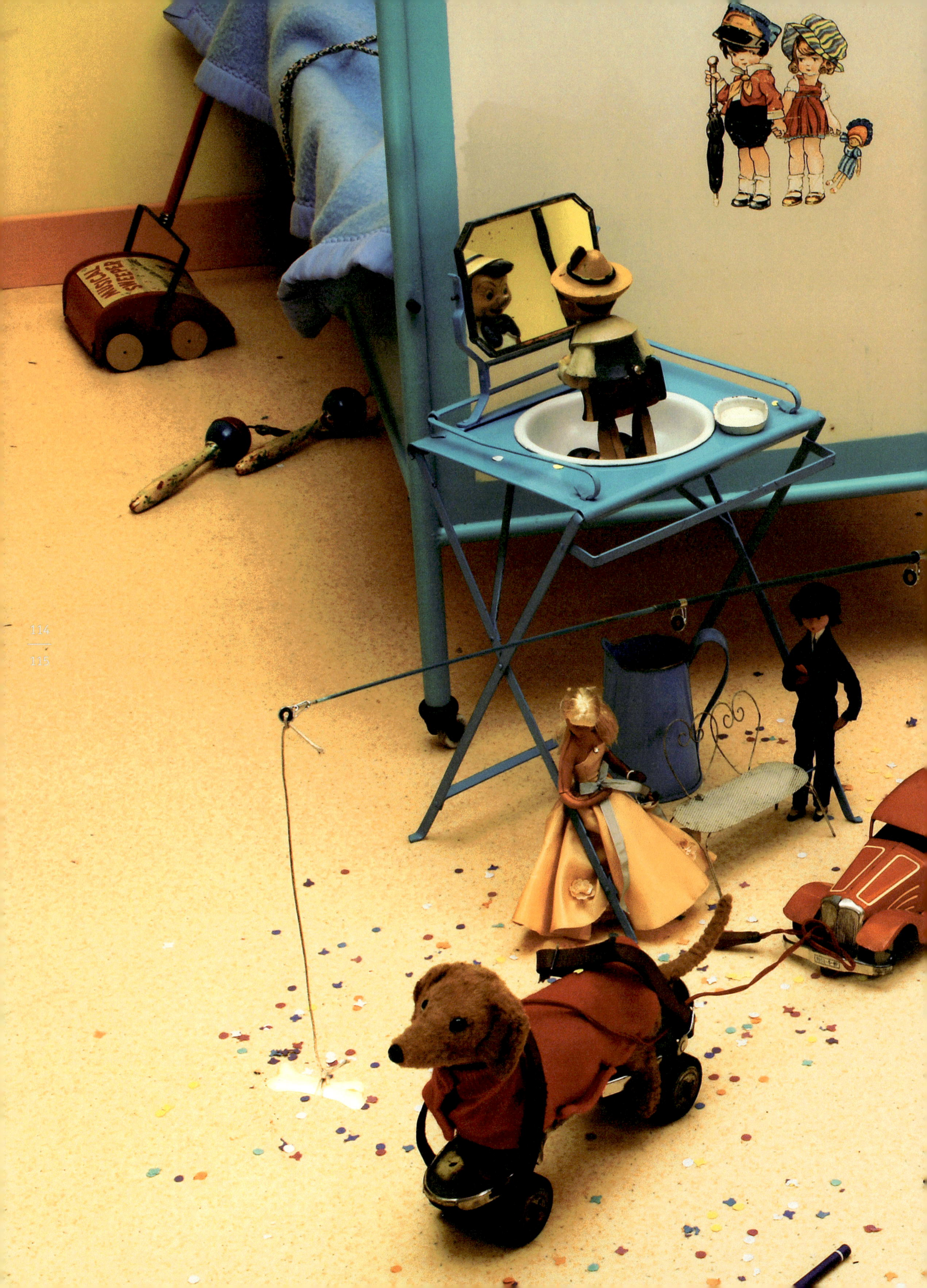
MUSICAL SWEEPER

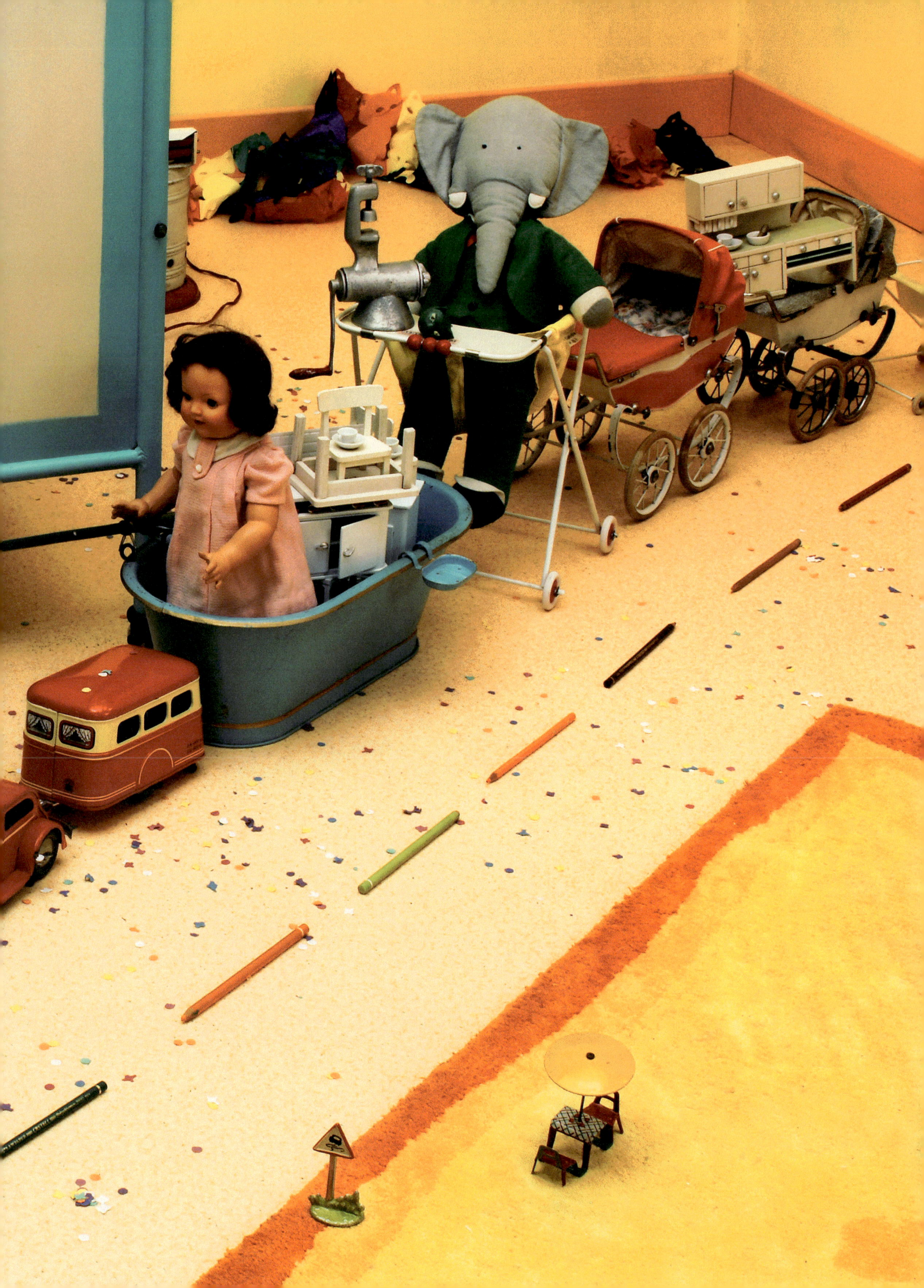

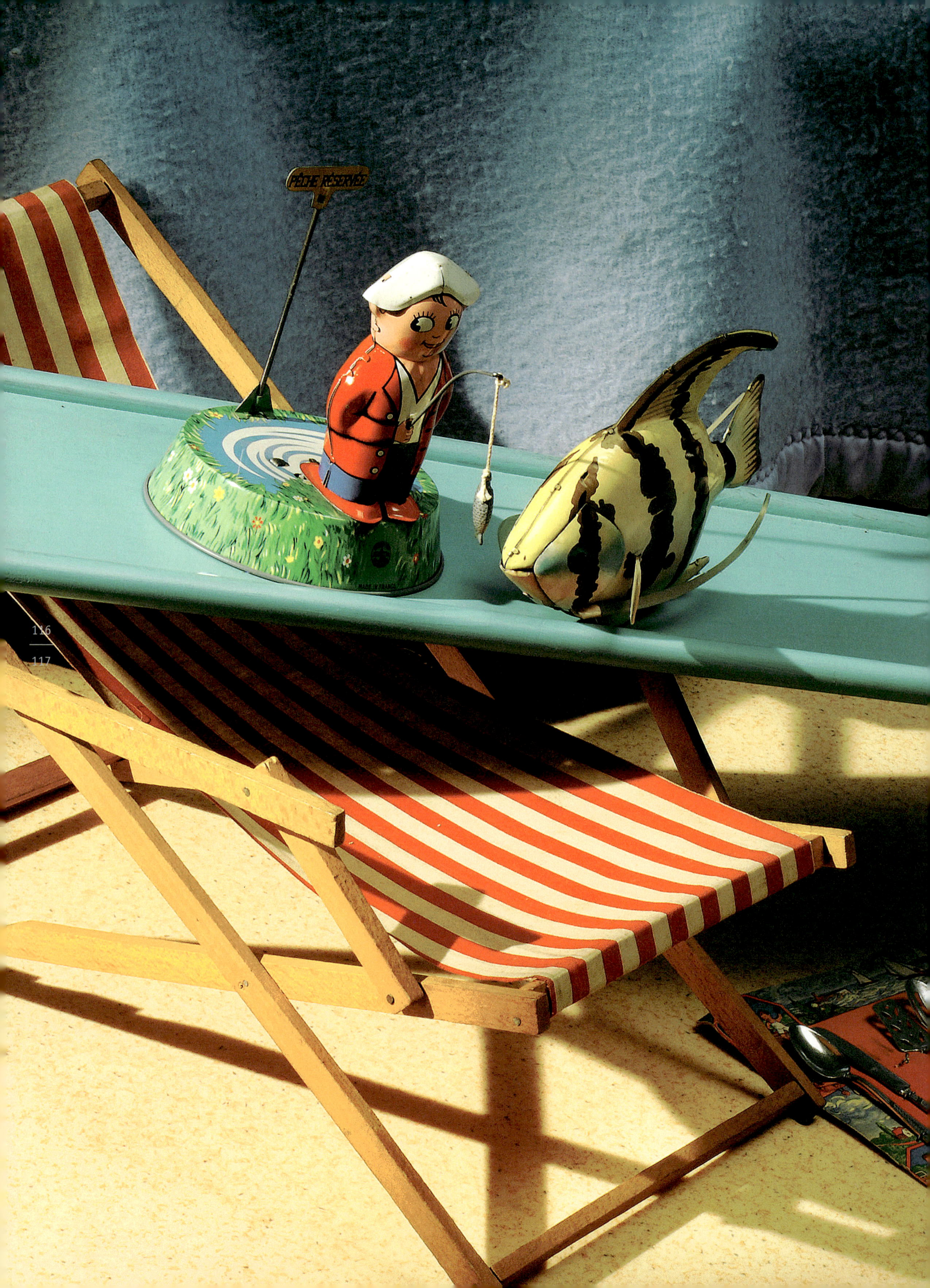
PÊCHE RÉSERVÉE

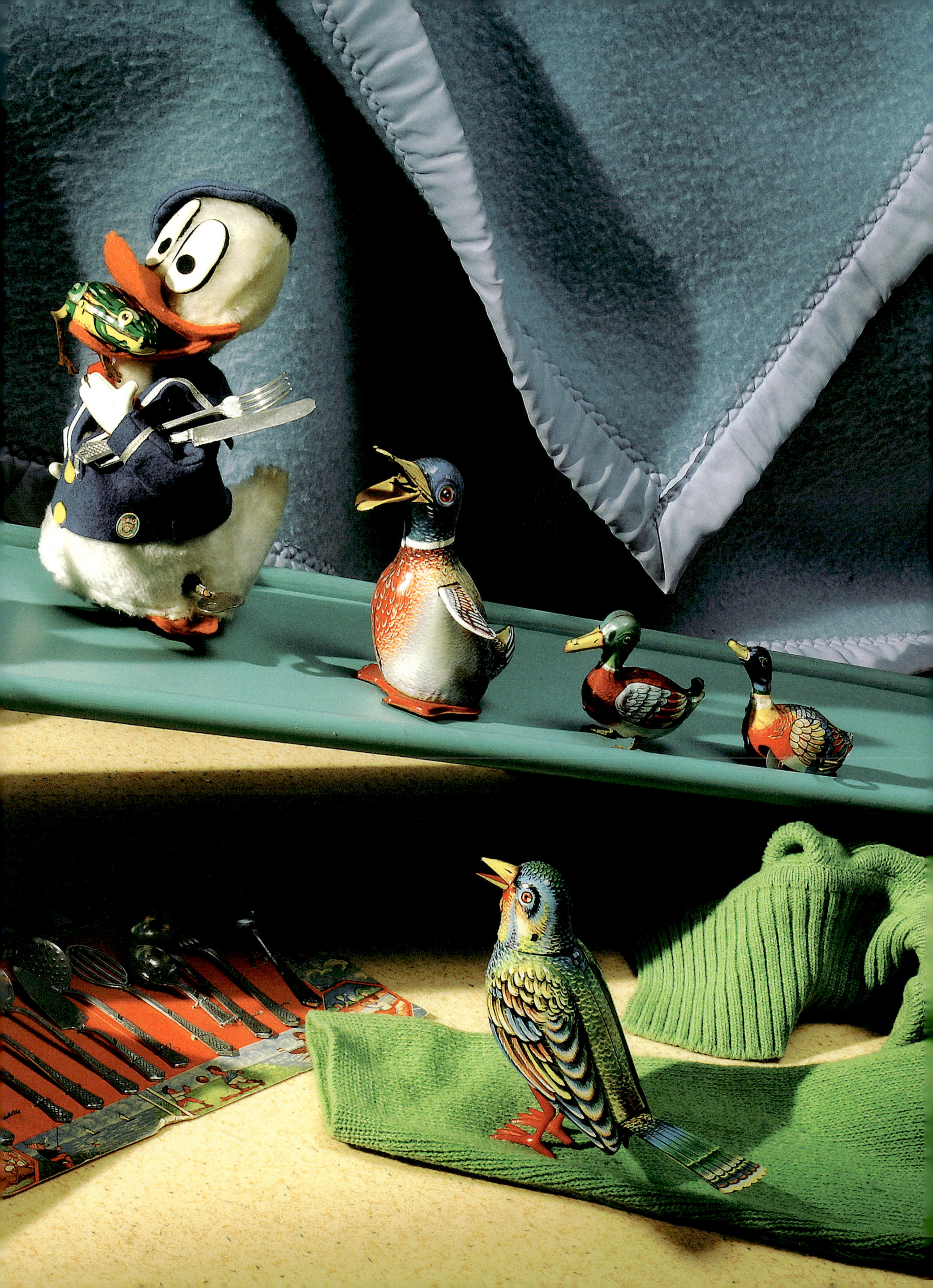

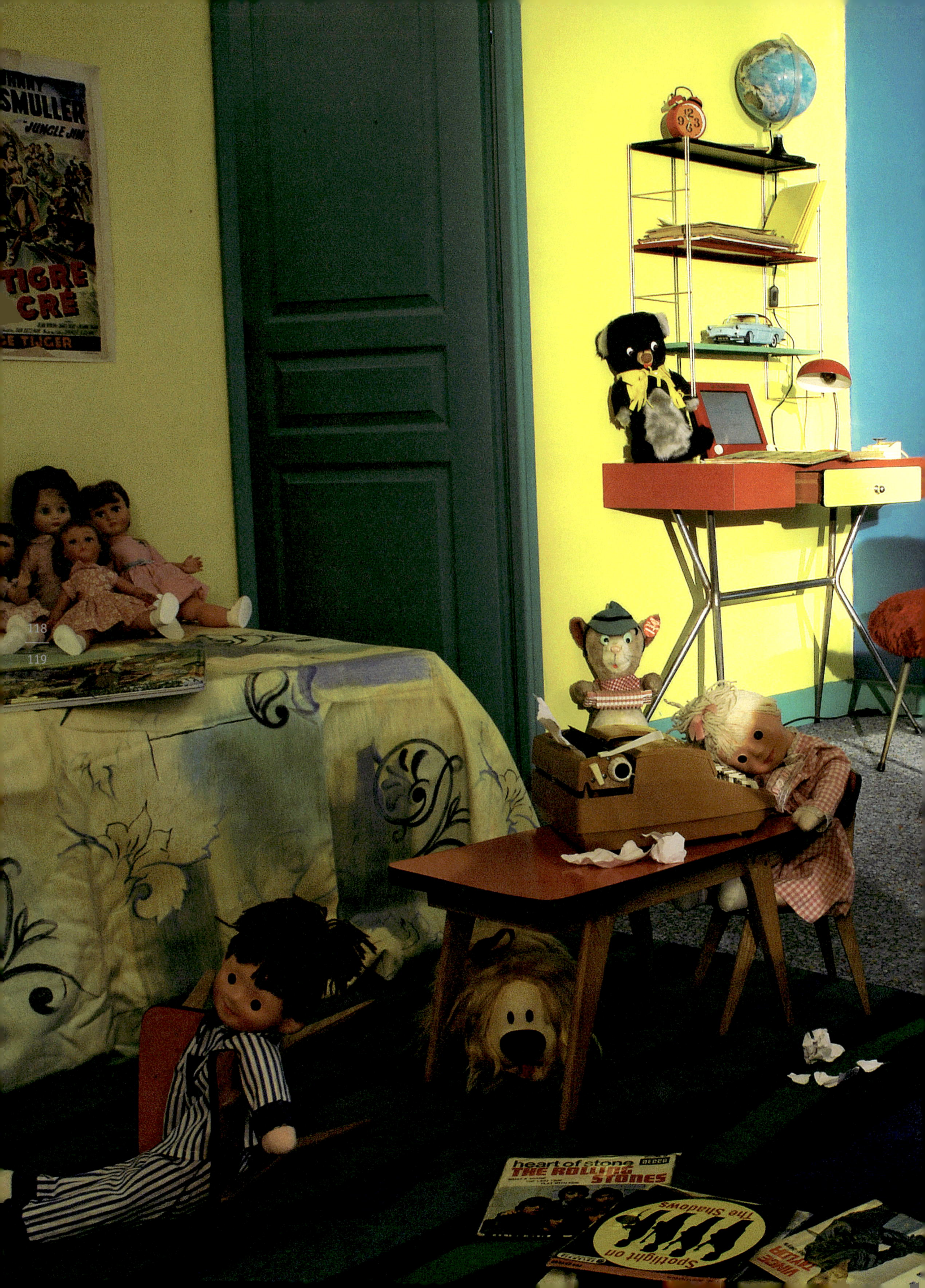

SMULLER
"JUNGLE JIM"
TIGRE
CRE
CE TIGER
heart of stone
THE ROLLING STONES
DECCA
The Shadows
Spotlight on

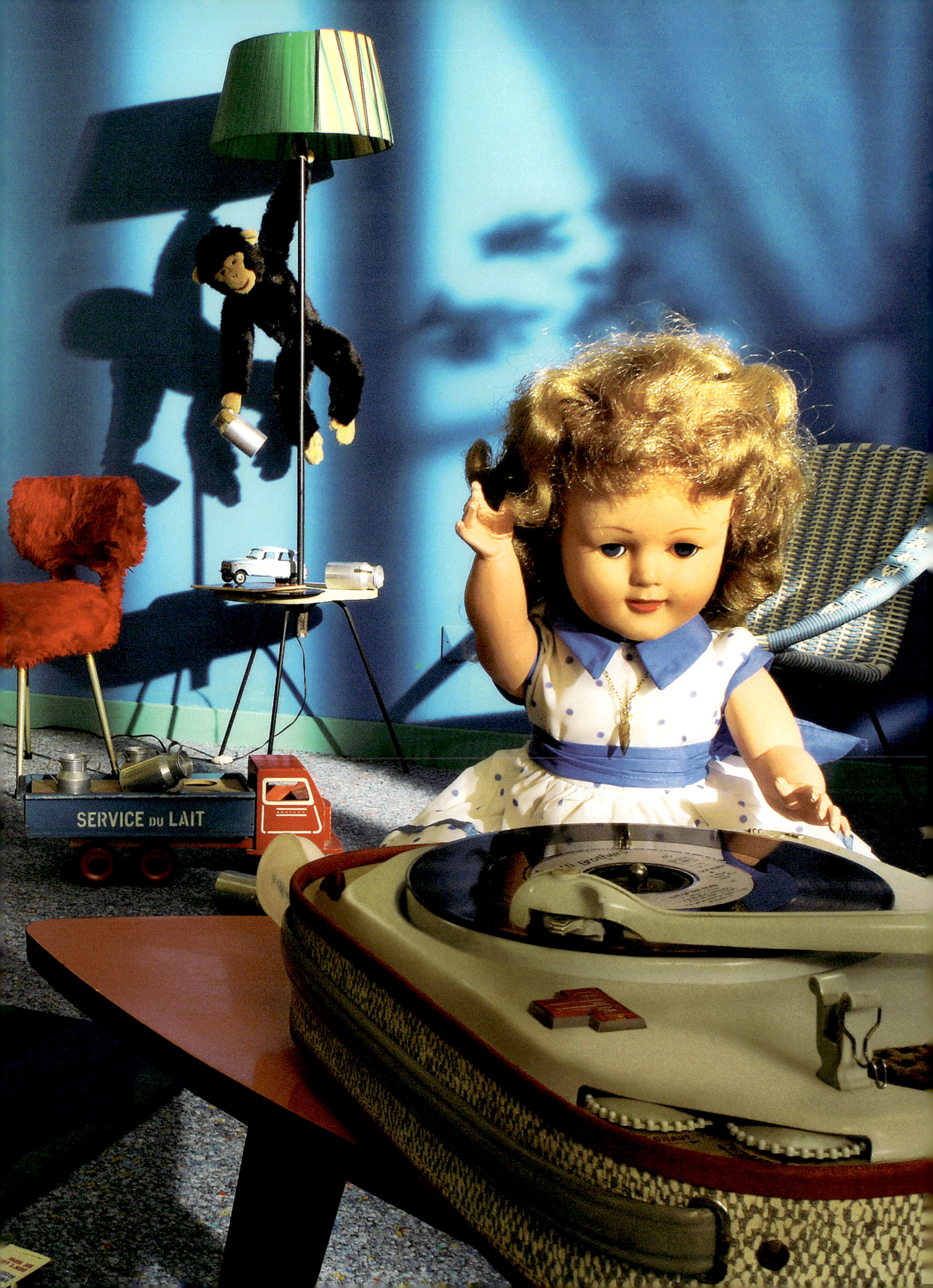
SERVICE DU LAIT

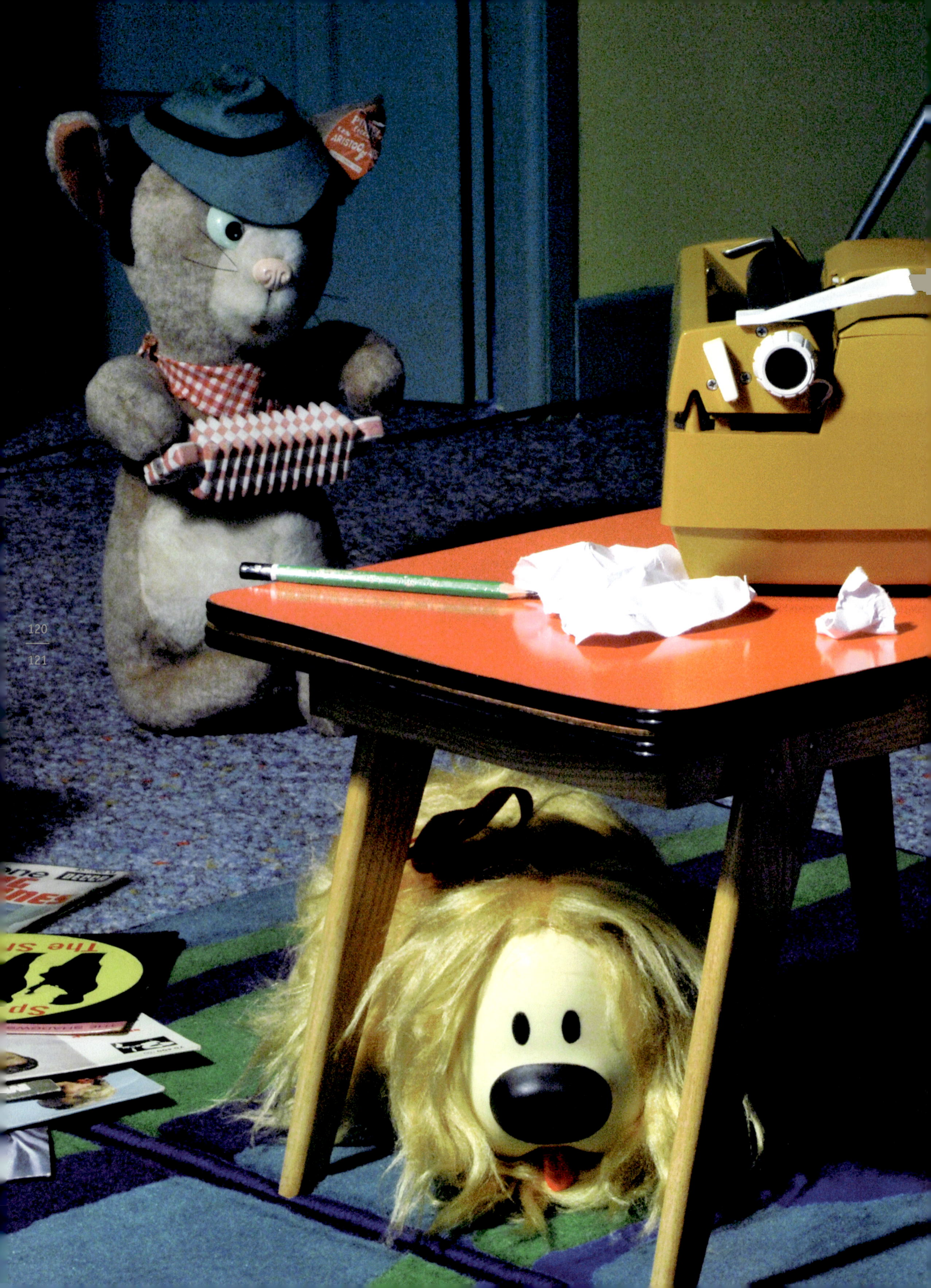

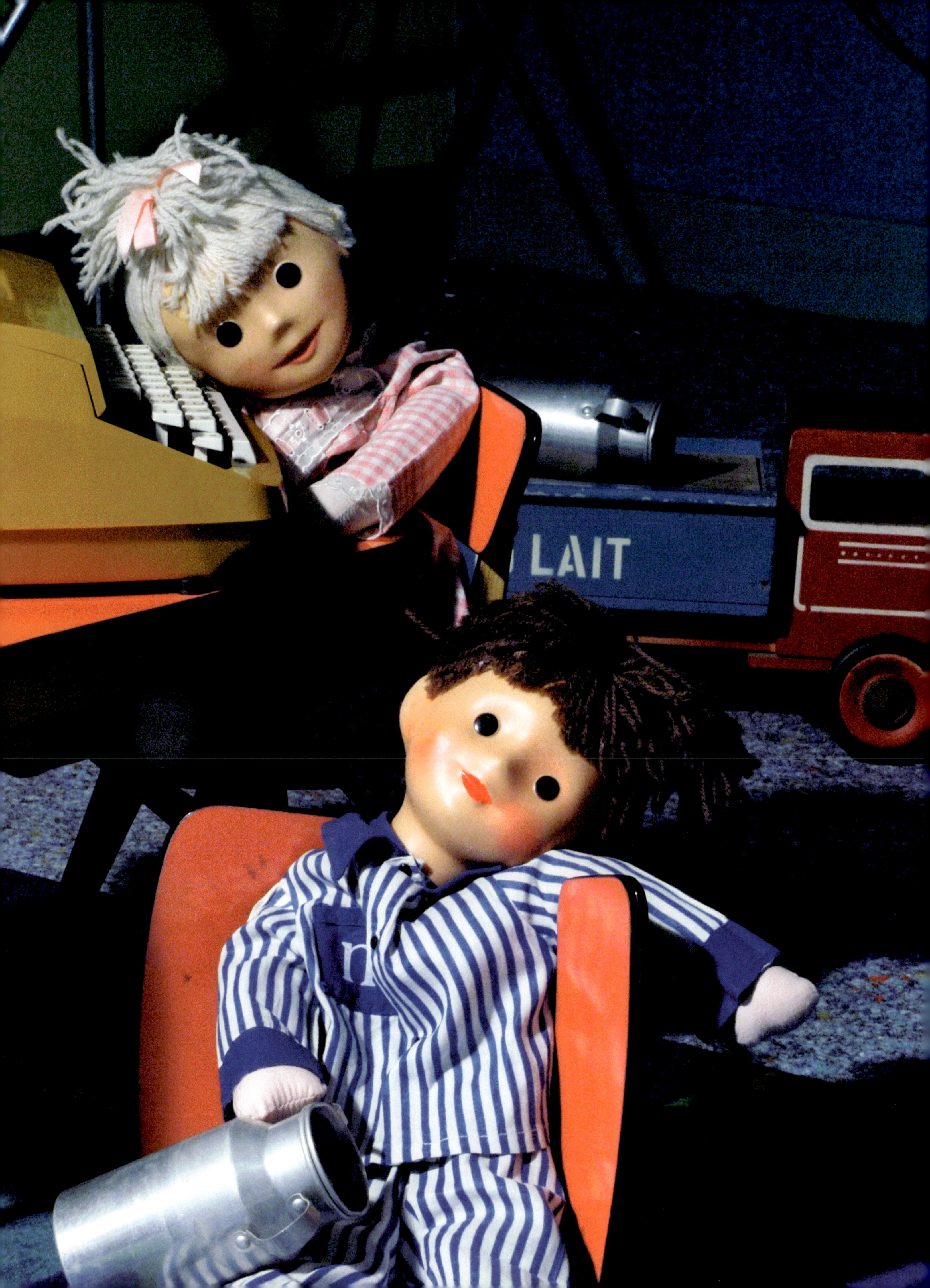

LAIT

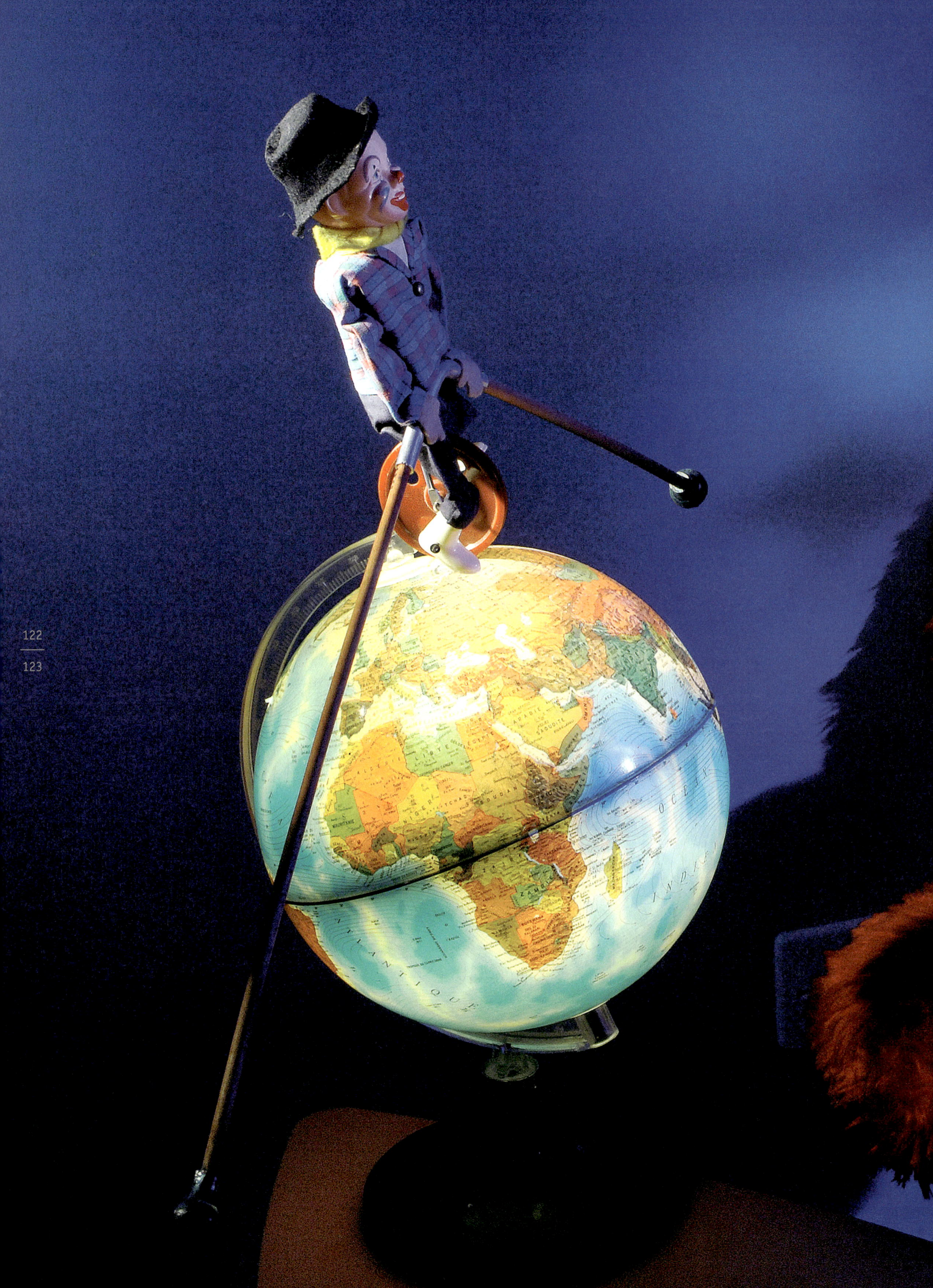

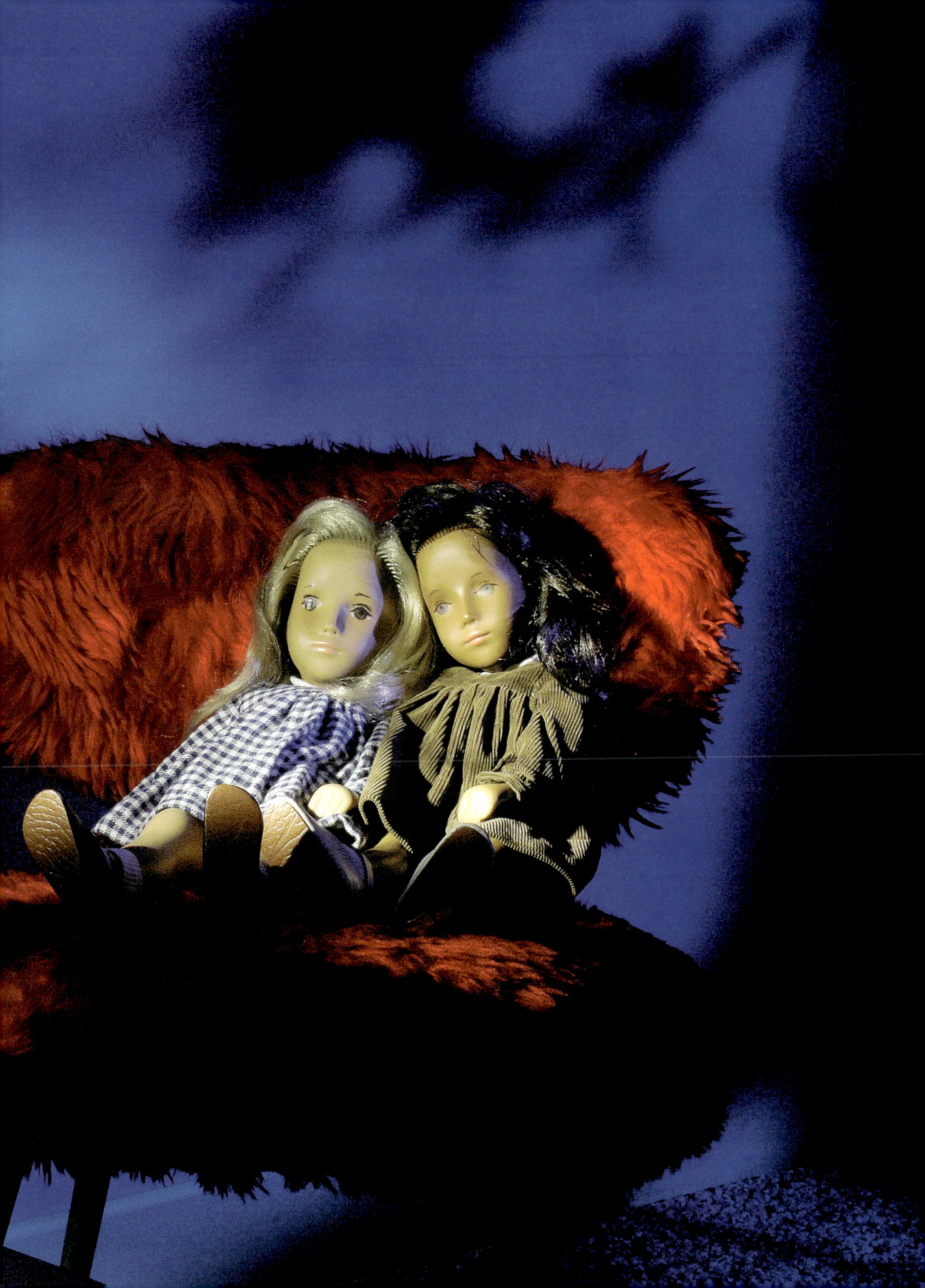

oys inhabit two worlds simultaneously: the concrete world of the child's house, the world of animate and inanimate beings; and the world of make-believe. Neither plane of existence supersedes the other. Adult life requires a distinction and values one above the other; in the world of the child, both realities coalesce. For the child, the toy bear (train, horse, soldier, lion) is real and is not real, as in the comic strip *Calvin and Hobbes*, where Hobbes the tiger comes to life when alone with Calvin and assumes a toy-like state in the presence of others.

The procedure is the exact reverse of the one told in the apocryphal *History of the Childhood of Jesus*, written sometime before the mid-fourth century. One Sabbath day, when Jesus was five years old, he was discovered playing on the banks of a stream, making toy birds out of clay. Joseph scolded him for not obeying the Sabbath laws. Instead of answering, Jesus clapped his hands. In an instant, the toy birds flapped their wings and, chirping loudly, flew off into the heavens.

n the shelf, in the trunk, by the bedside table, the collection of toys displays no obvious hierarchies. Their place in the bedroom's society isn't marked by age, size, species, retail price, chronology of acquisition, standards of beauty – only by the whim of their owner. This bear or that doll, this engine or that dinosaur have been chosen from among their peers because of reasons that are indefinable and that carry no justification. We can get rid of this toy or that, but never of certain others that are as essential to our world as our name or our own features.

The collection of toys tells who we are. Like the layout of our garden or the books in our library, our toys display a secret portrait that grows as we grow and changes as we change, and eventually disintegrates or is reduced to a single, timeworn survivor. In the meantime, they betray us to the world. Orderly or haphazard, neat or unkempt, pristine or maimed, they proclaim our love. They are our earliest autobiography.

But these passionate affections are not steadfast. One morning, the best-beloved are best-beloved no longer. 'What has happened?' asks Chateaubriand in a memorable passage. 'Is it a new attachment that begins or an old attachment that ends? No matter: it is love that dies before the object of love itself. We are forced to acknowledge that man's feelings are exposed to a secret labour: to the fever of time that breeds lassitude, dissipates illusion, undermines our passions and changes our hearts, as it changes our hair and our years.'

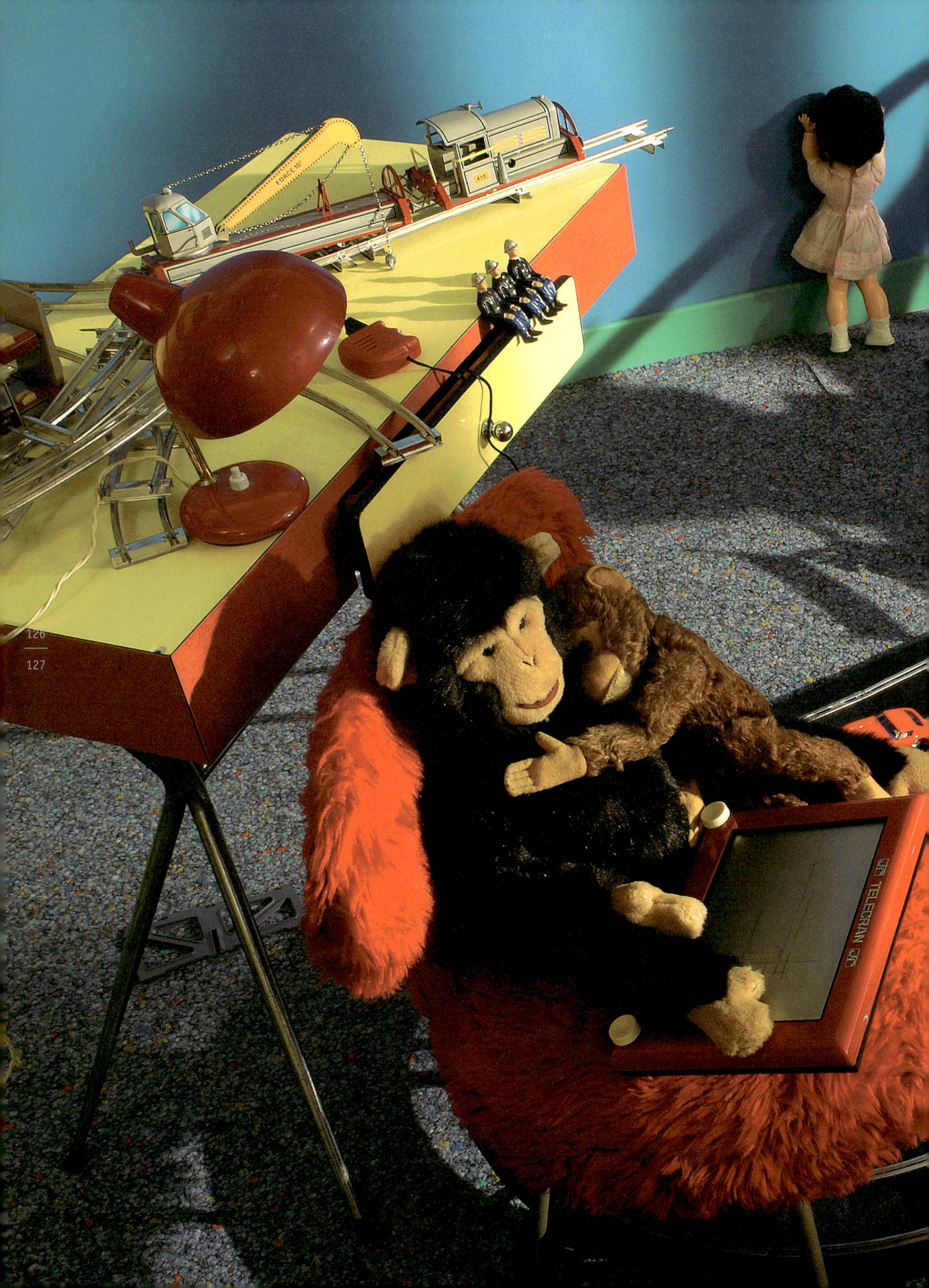
FORCE 10
TELECRAN JL

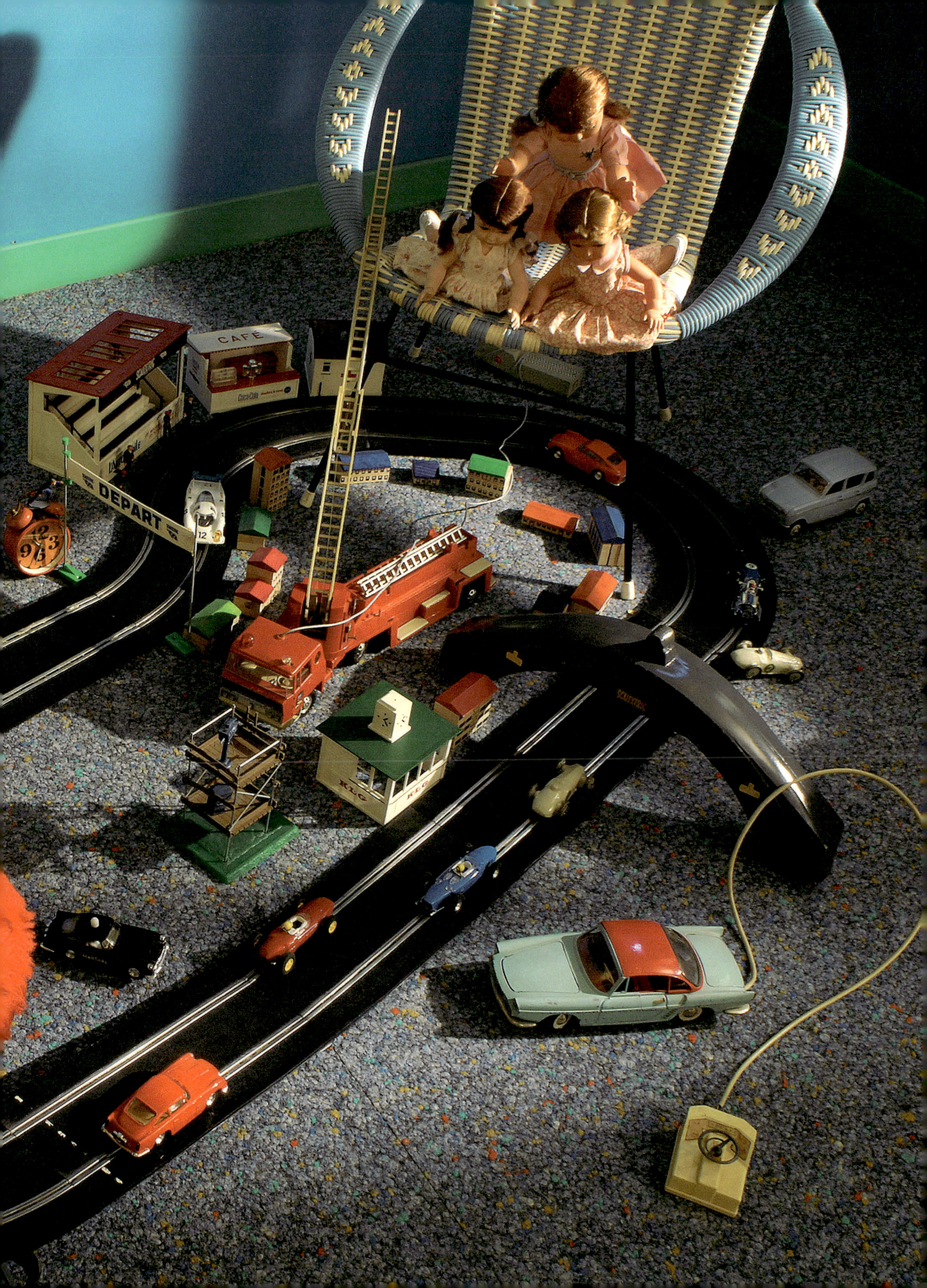

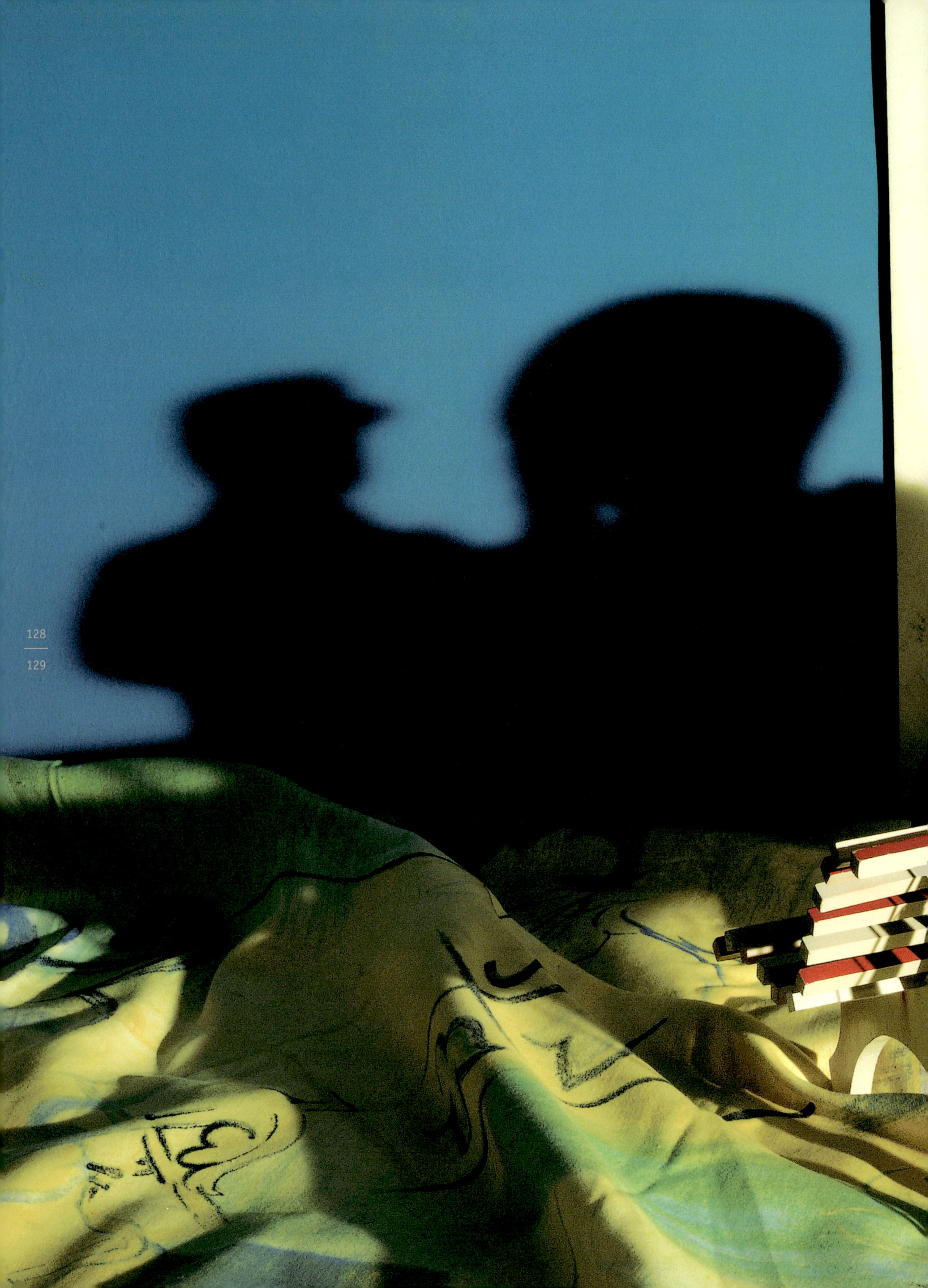

128
129

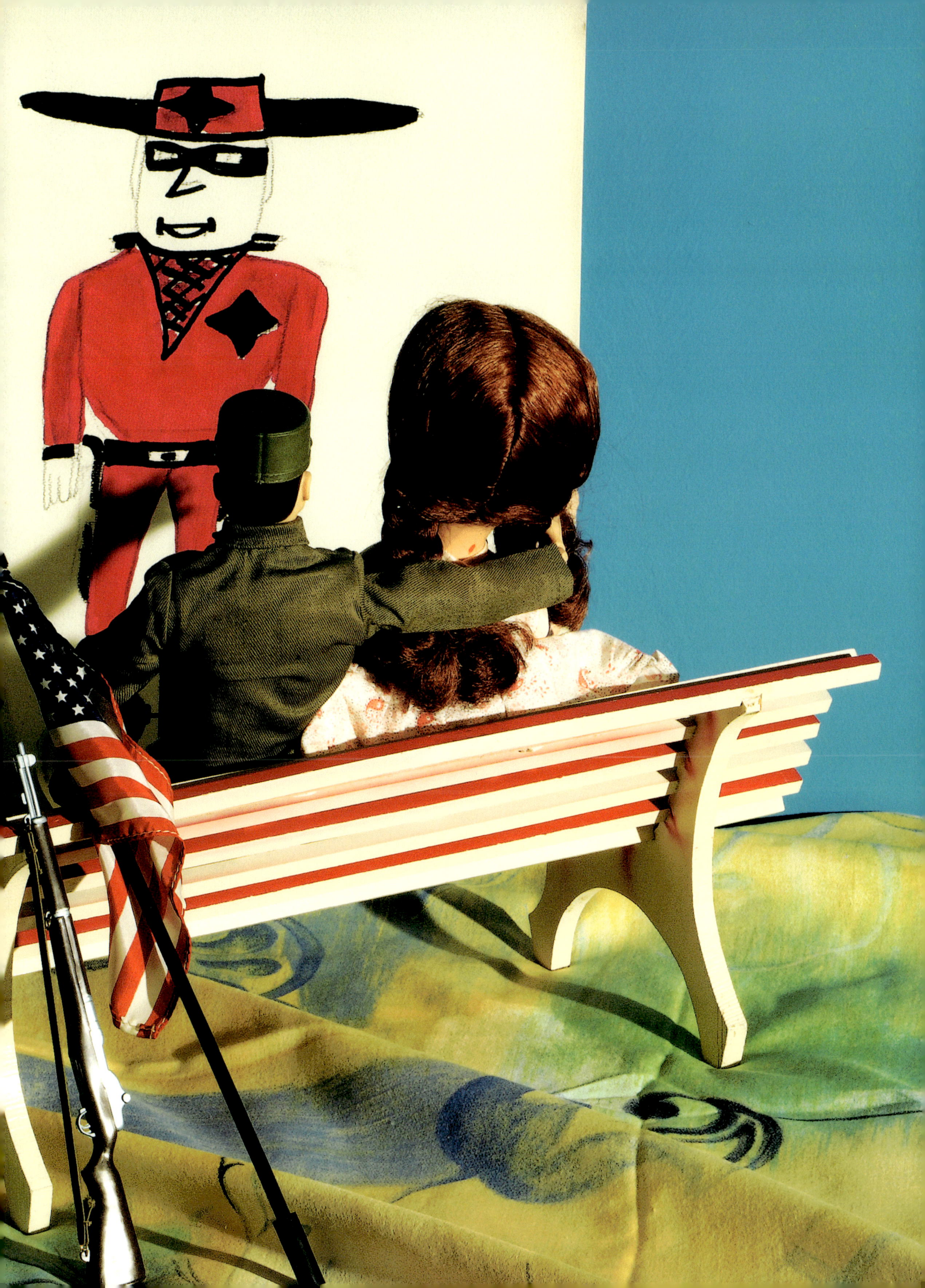

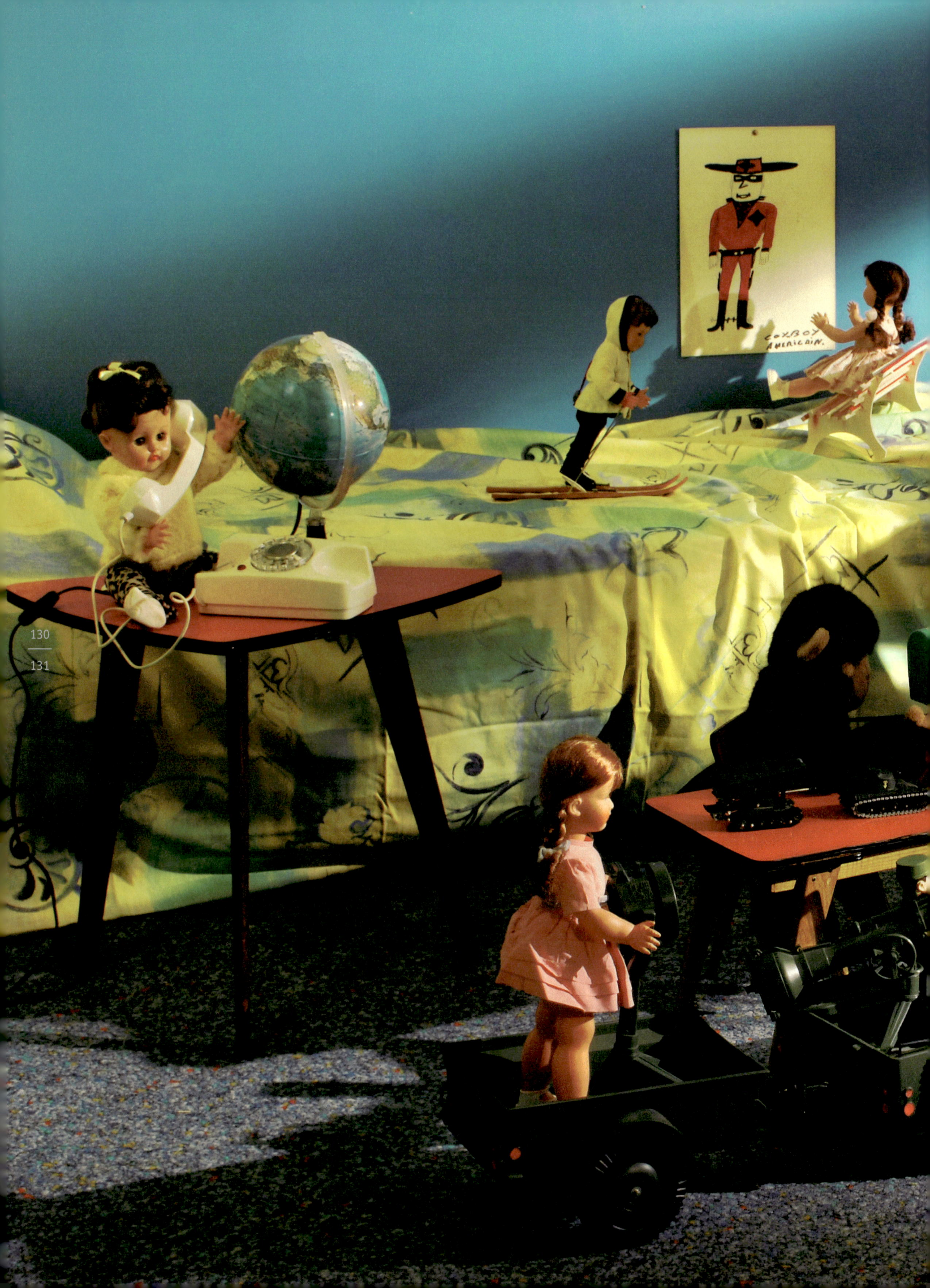

COXBOY
AMERICAIN.

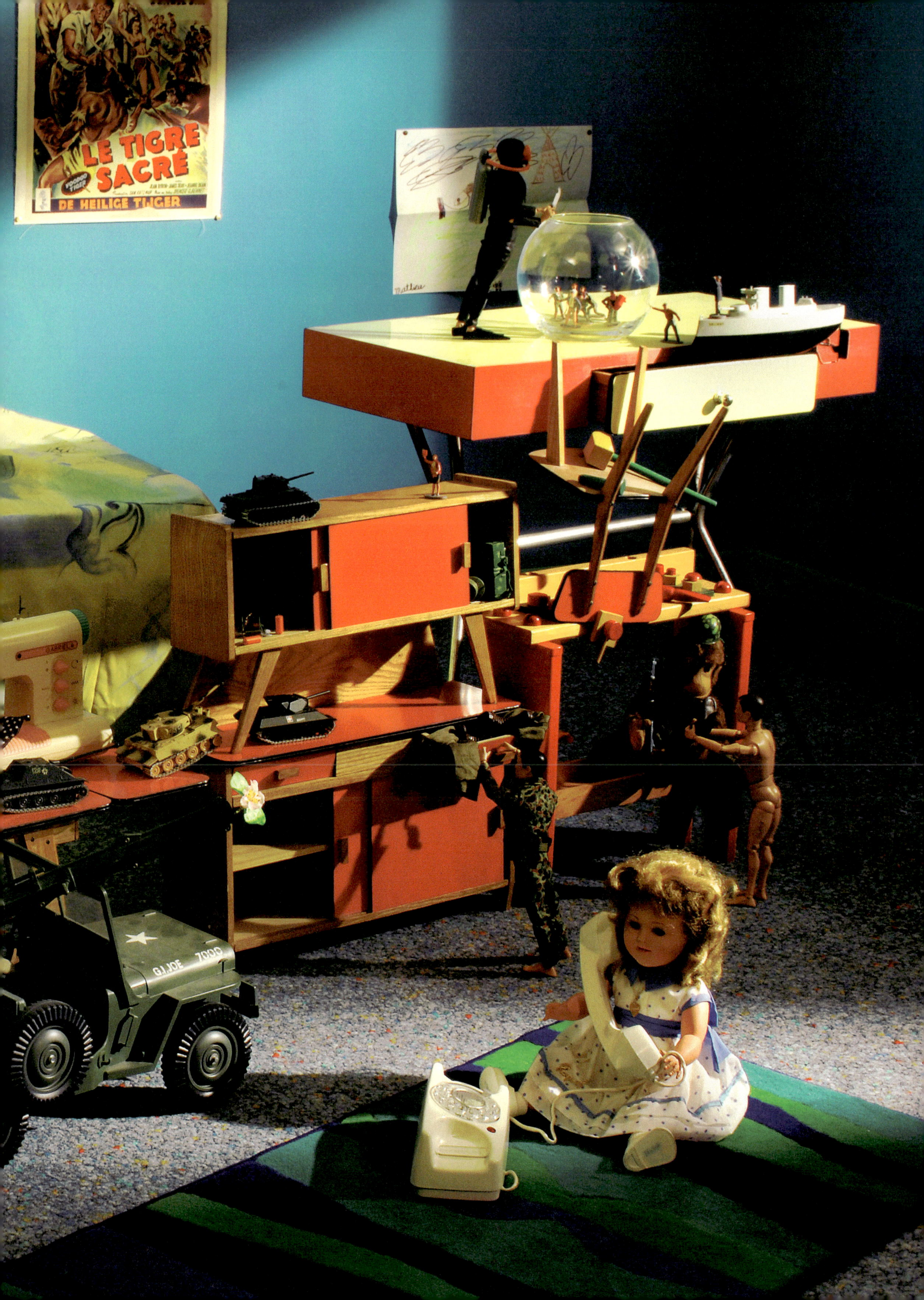
VOODOO TIGER
LE TIGRE SACRÉ
DE HEILIGE TIJGER
GA.JOE 7000

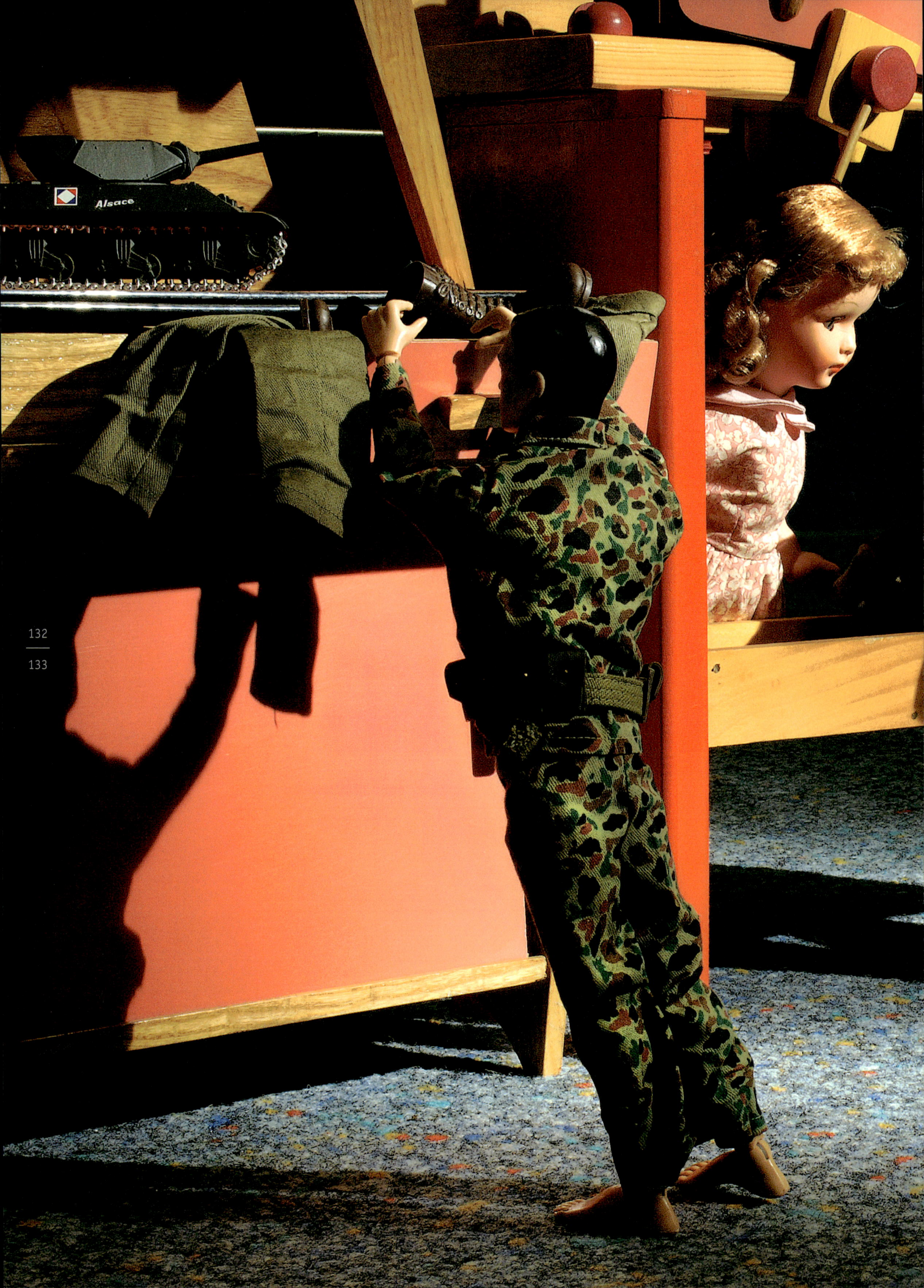
Alsace

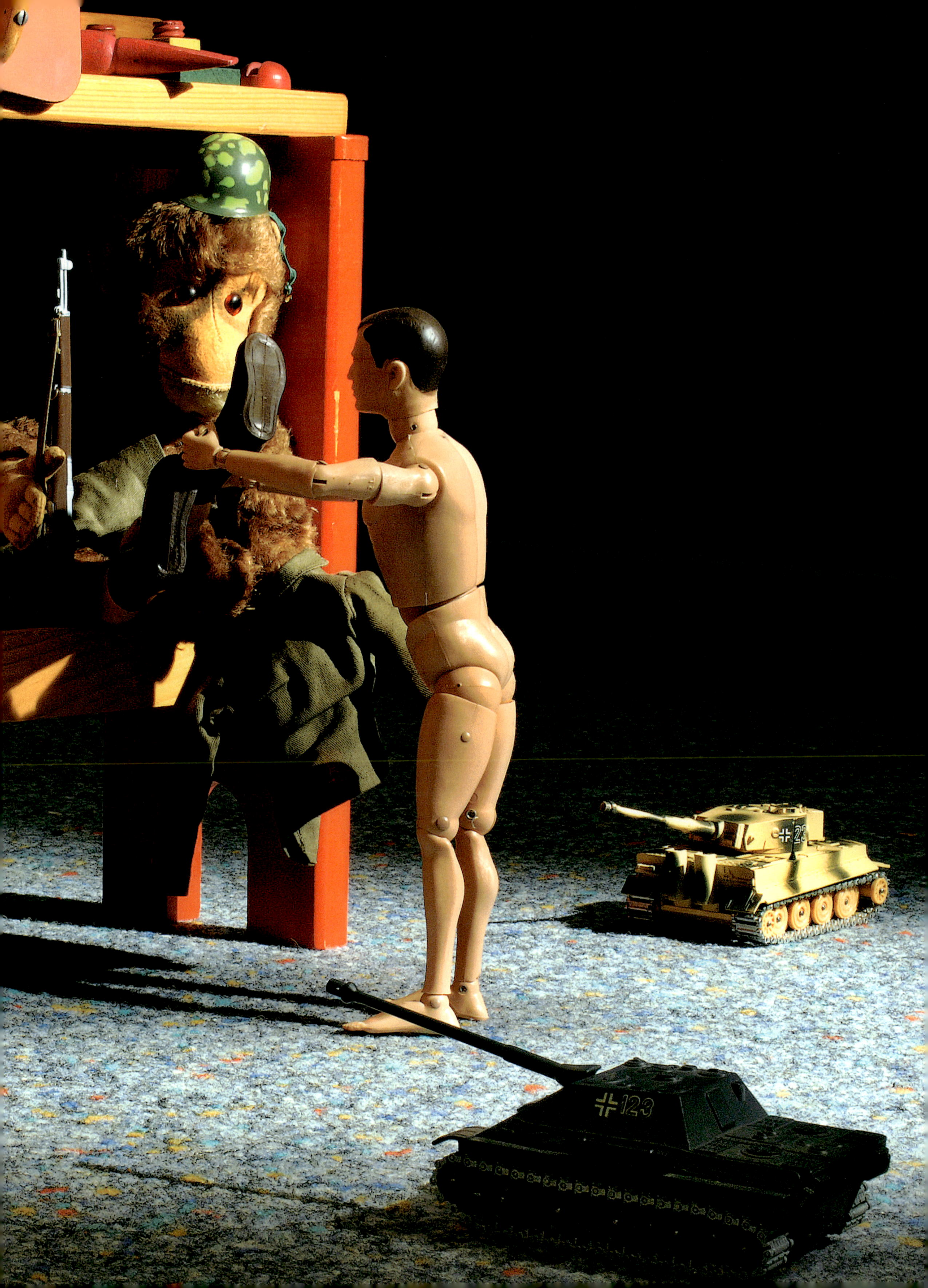

The time of play is its own time. It is neither the time of the clock nor that of the story, nor is it fixed by the conventions of commercially-ruled television slots. It is determined by the plot of the game, by the quality of the weather, by the bursts of energy of the player, by the nature of the toy itself. Unmeasured time dictates the setting-up of a stage for miniature animals; centuries parade by as one toy army attacks the fortress of another; a long hour is given over to a dolls' tea party; seconds tick along the train tracks; a quasi-eternity is occupied by the progression of a video game.

Every playtime is unique. Attempts to continue an interrupted game result merely in patchwork. Everything that happens happens in a given frame of time. Then it ends. Then it begins again.

The history of the world unfolds during the afternoon of play. Everything that can happen happens now. The child begins the game at a certain age and ends it at another. Something has taken place in the interval: he is no longer the same. The toys look on unchanged, like statues, but the player has grown, advanced in a time of his own making. He tries to recapture the moment of play, but fails, again and again. He keeps trying and will not accept Heraclitus's truth: You never go down to the same playroom twice.

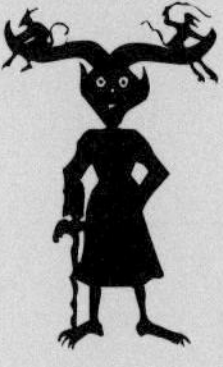he playroom has its rules to which toys must submit. These rules are both arbitrary and strict, immemorial and created on the spot, universal and individual, part superstition and part icy logic. For example:

Four toys of the same kind may not sit on the same shelf at once.

At least one doll must always face the window.

No toy that is red must ever be placed on the bed.

If a toy falls on the floor, it must be kissed three times before being put back in its place.

Stuffed animals must never be shut in their box or they'll stifle.

A doll must not be left naked overnight.

Certain toys must not be kept in close proximity: a ballerina and a clown, an elephant and a cat, a rag doll and one with a porcelain head.

Before beginning a game of soldiers, you must close your eyes and count up to twenty-five.

No two toys must bear the same name.

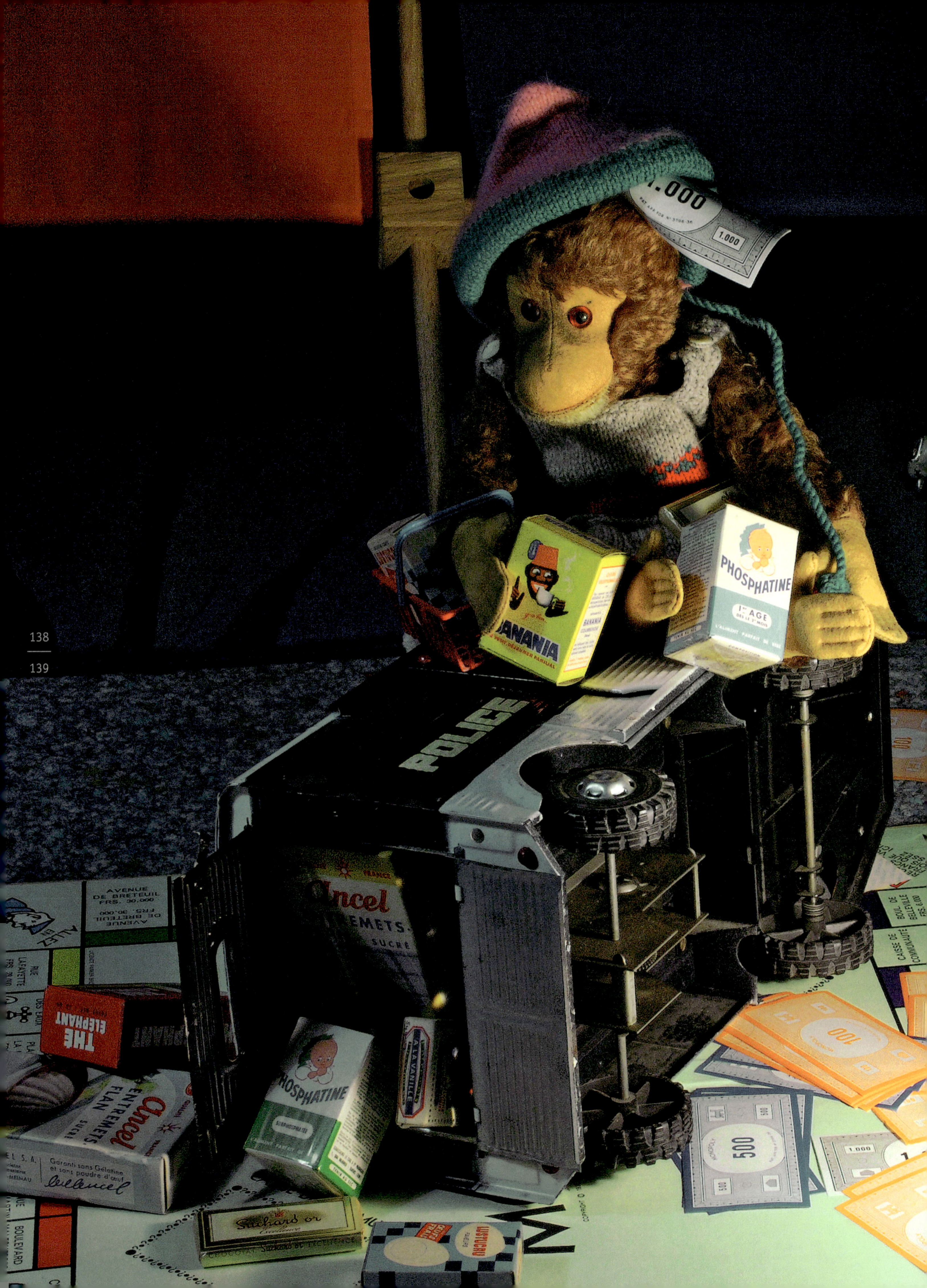
1.000
1.000
BANANIA
PHOSPHATINE
1er AGE
POLICE
AVENUE DE BRETEUIL
FRS. 30.000
Ancel
ENTREMETS
SUCRÉ
THE ELEPHANT
PHOSPHATINE
A LA VANILLE
Ancel
ENTREMETS
FLAN
SUCRÉ
Suchard or
100
500
1.000

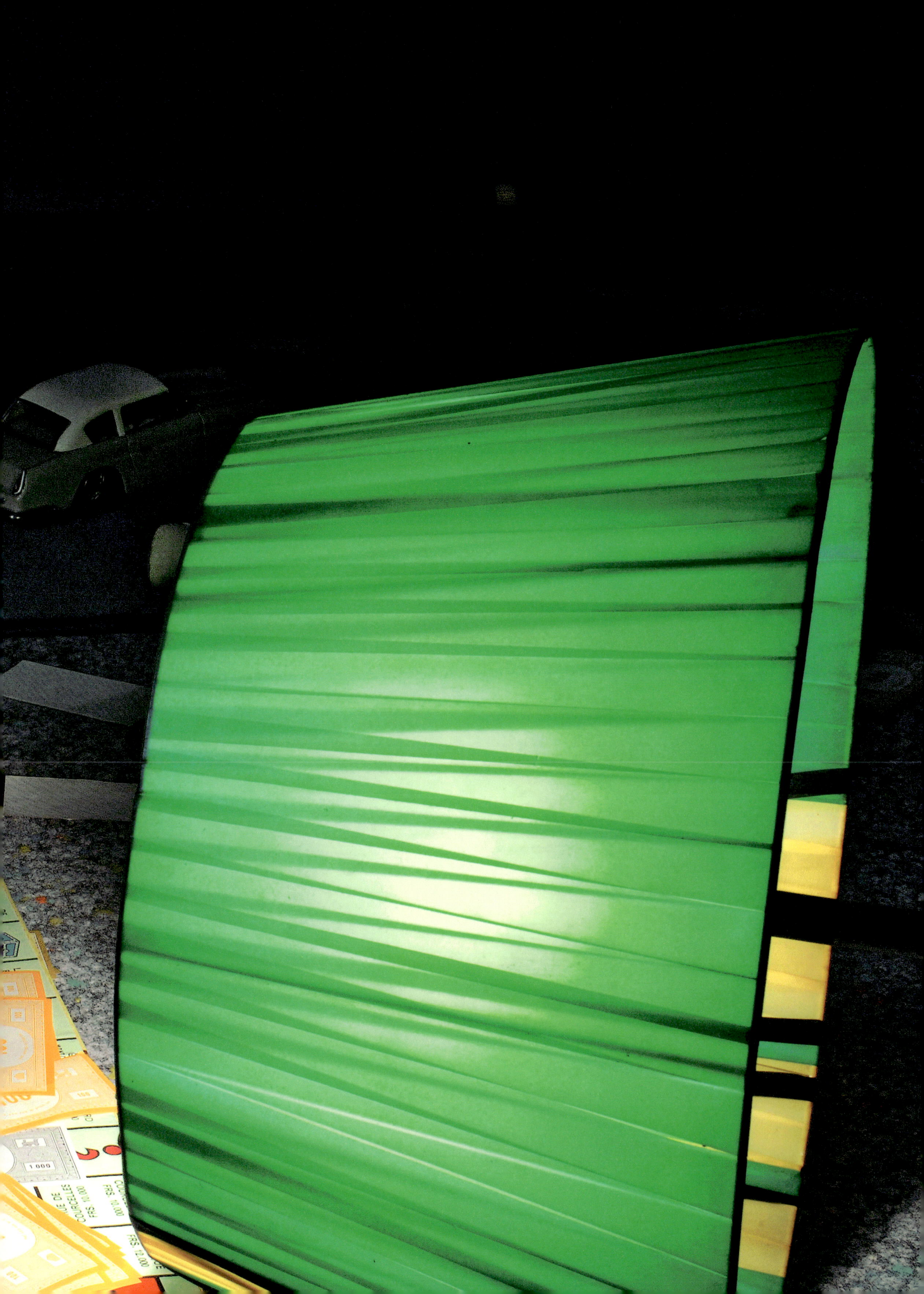

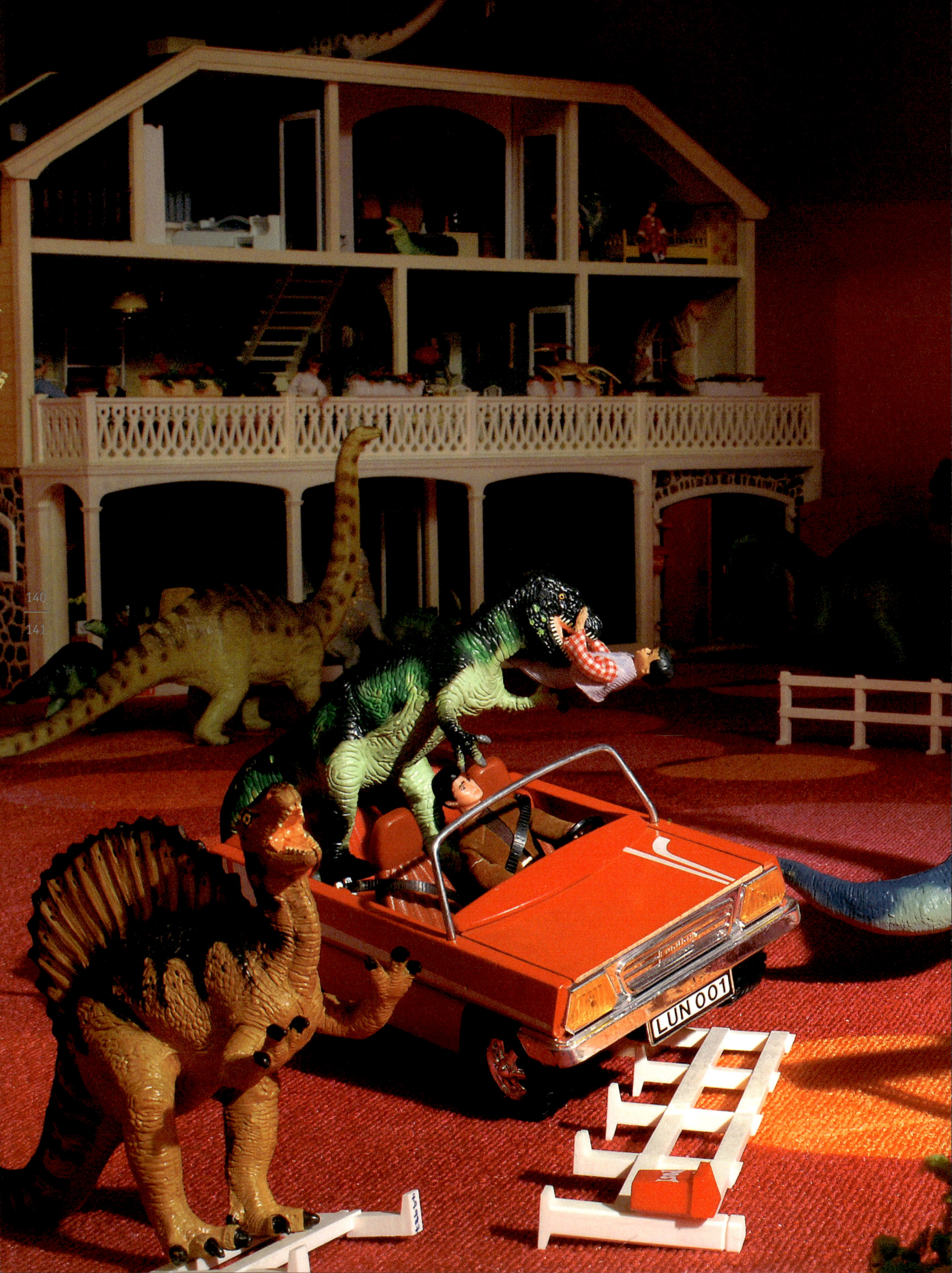

140
141
LUN 001

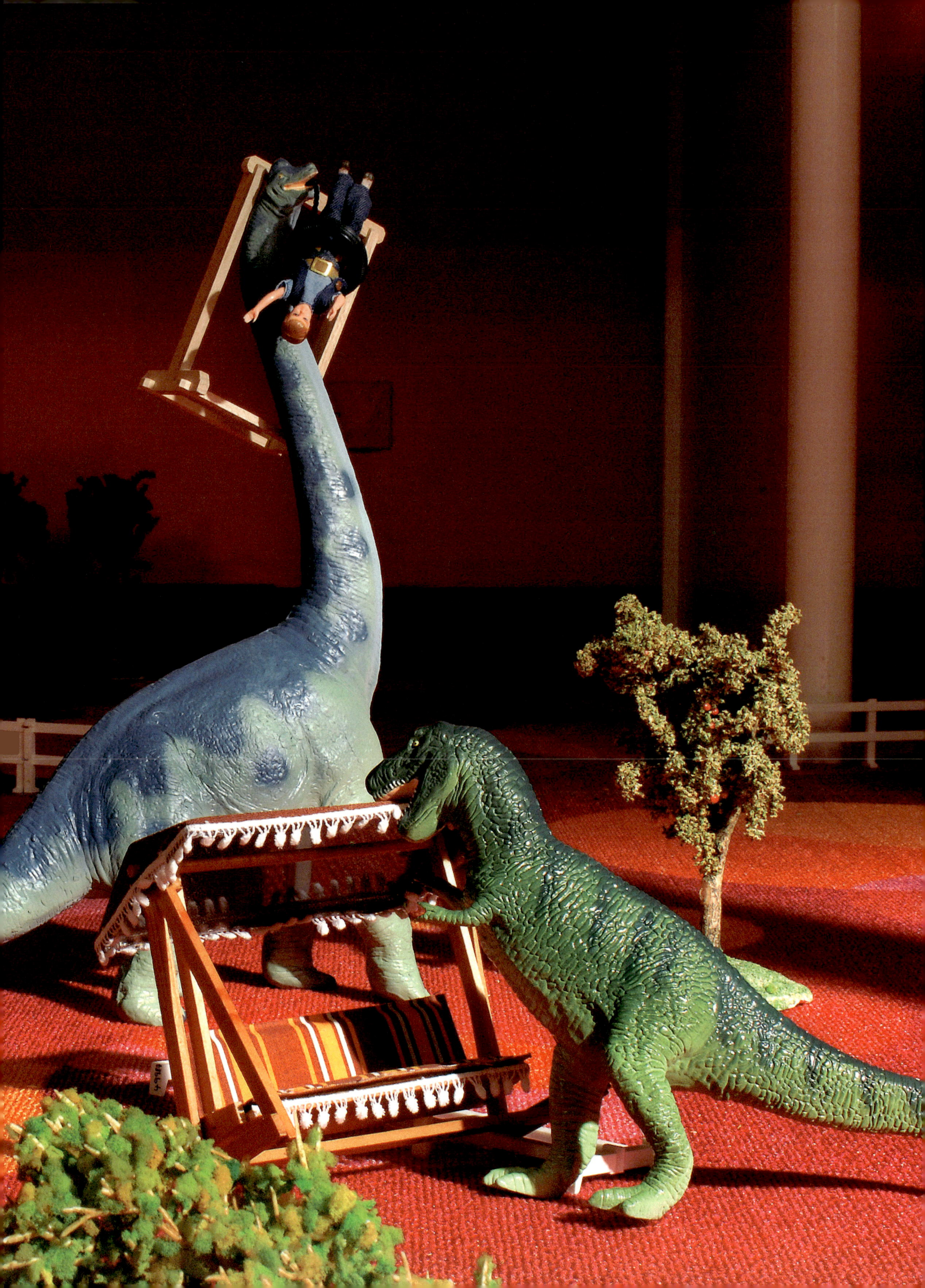

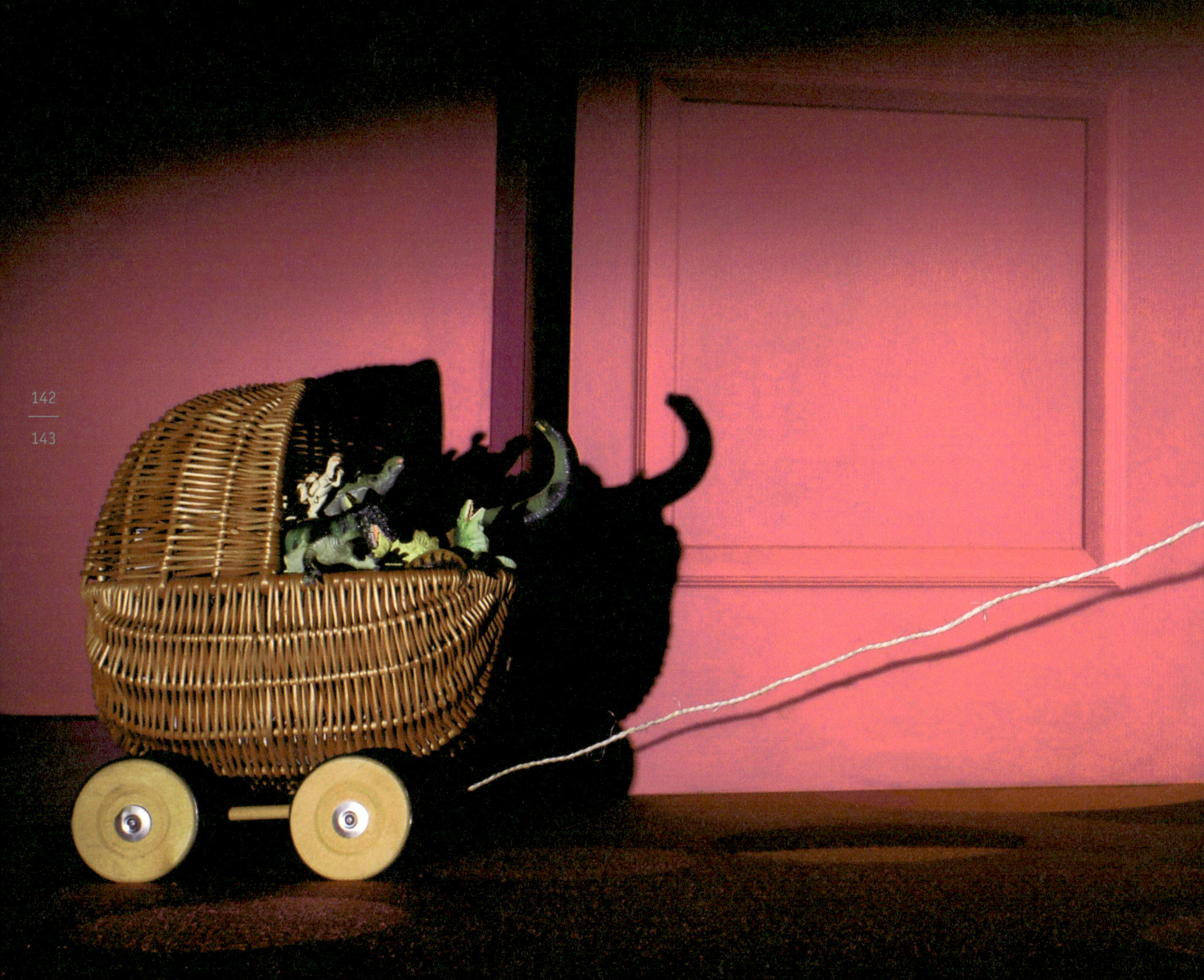

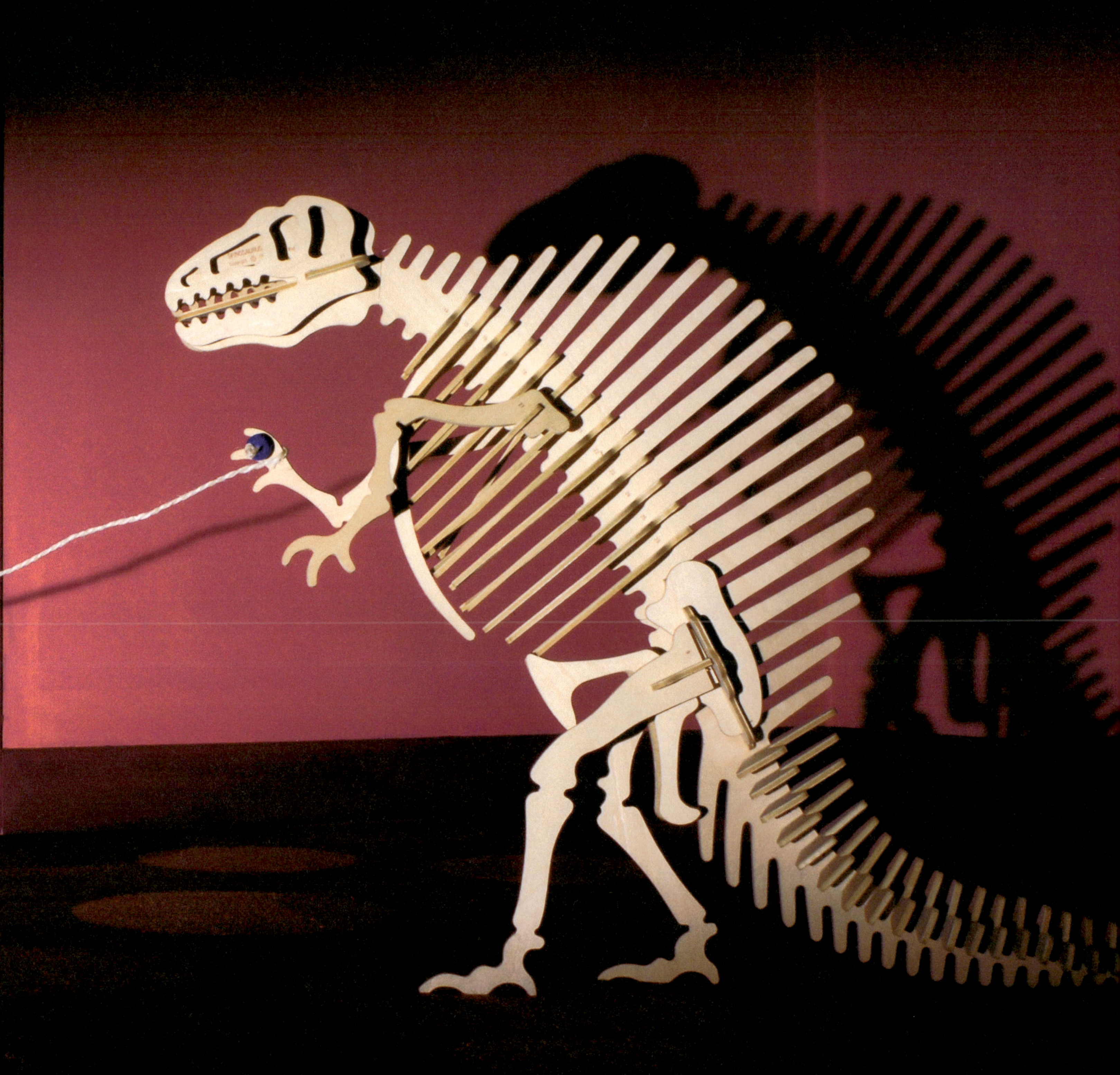

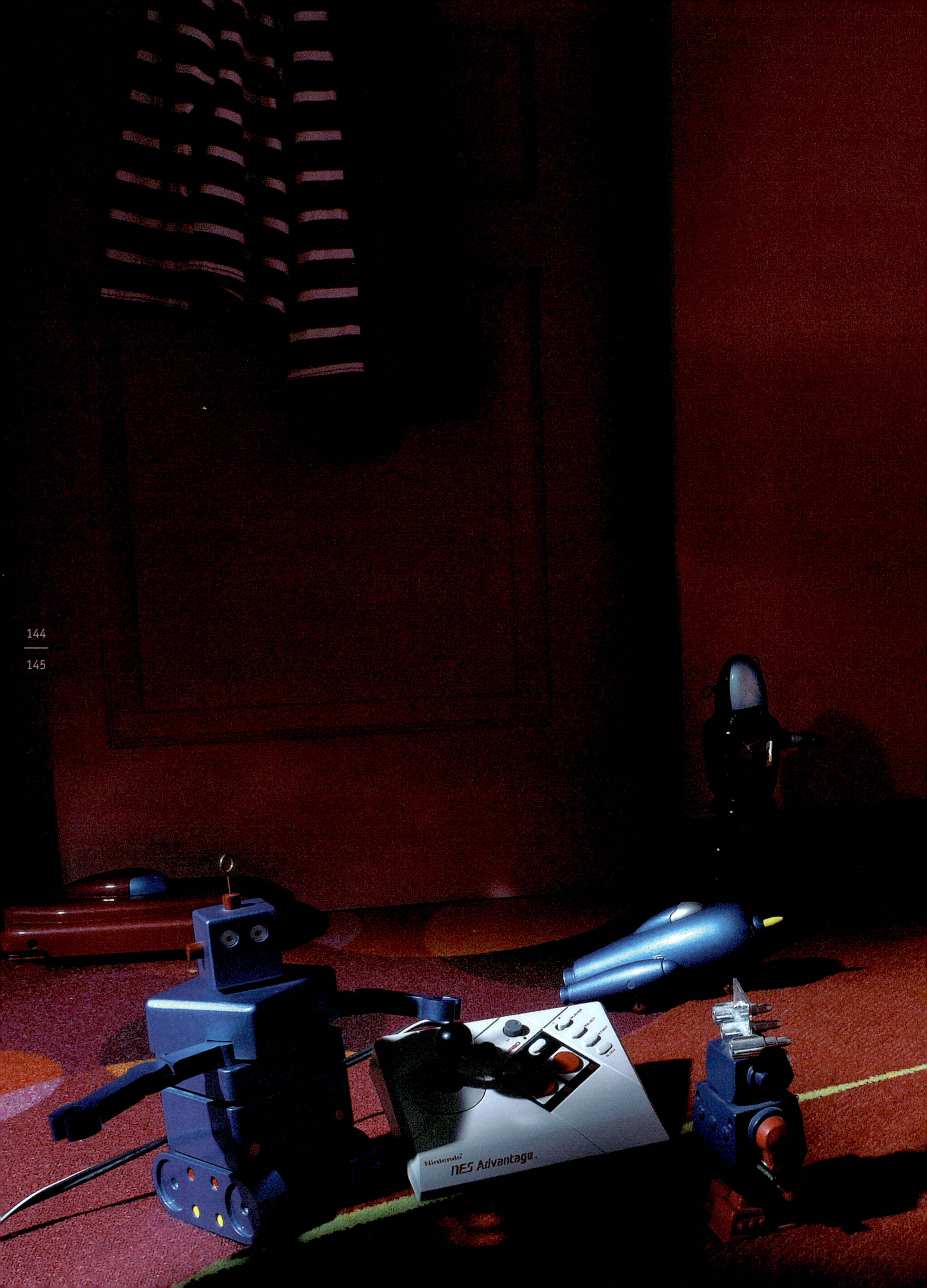
Nintendo
NES Advantage

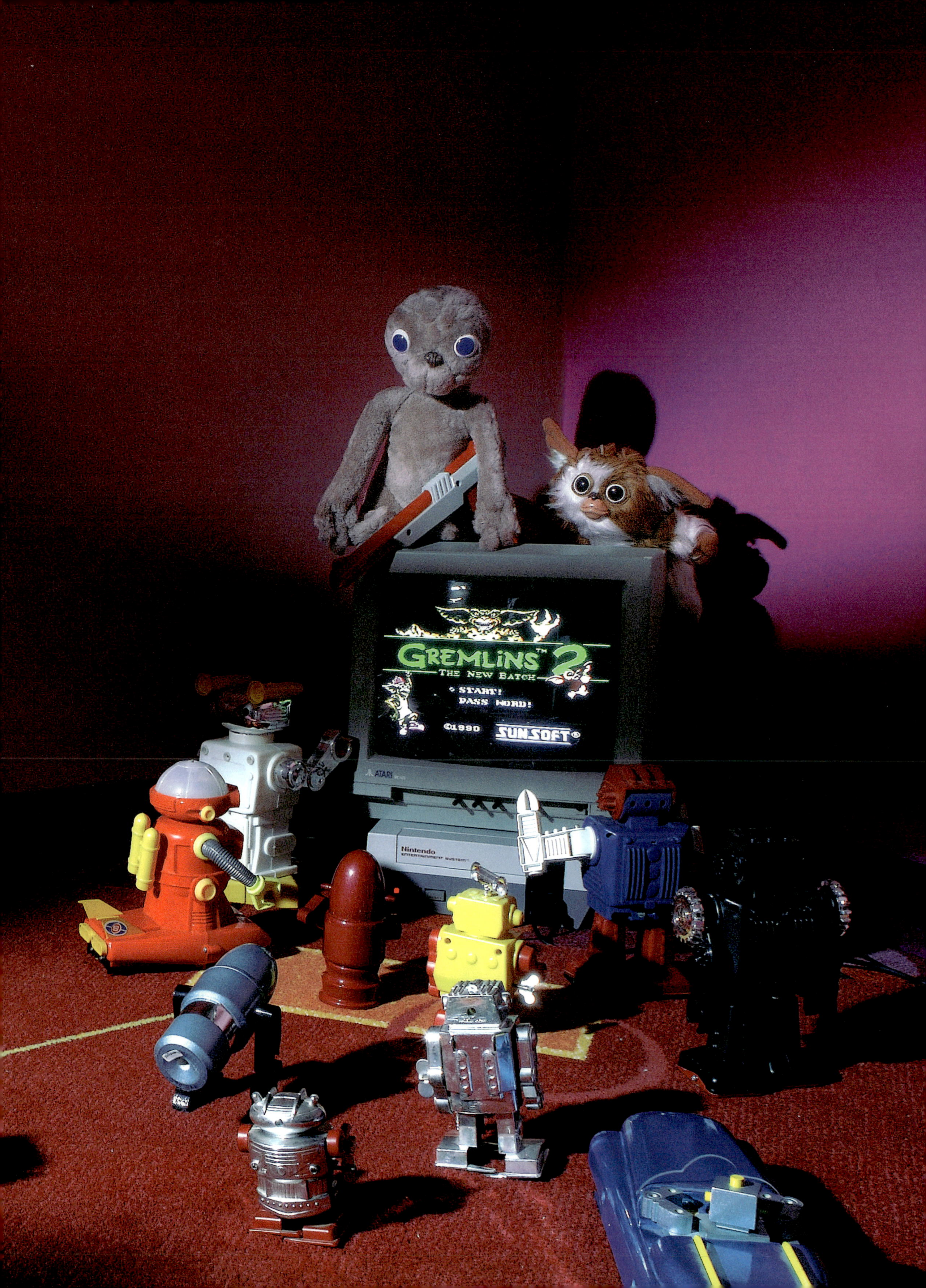
GREMLiNS 2
THE NEW BATCH
START!
PASS WORD!
©1990 SUNSOFT

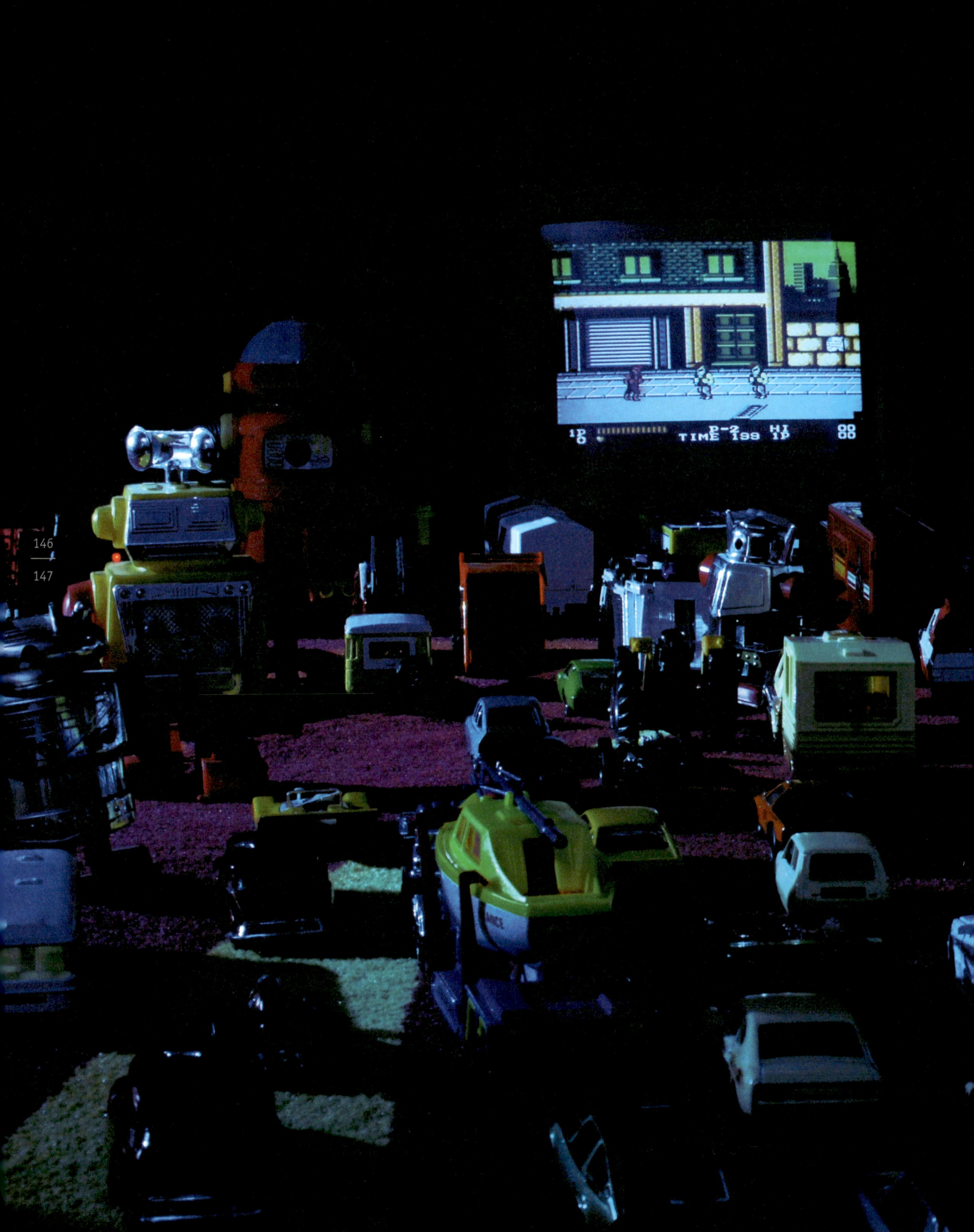
1P
00
P-2   HI
TIME 199 1P   00

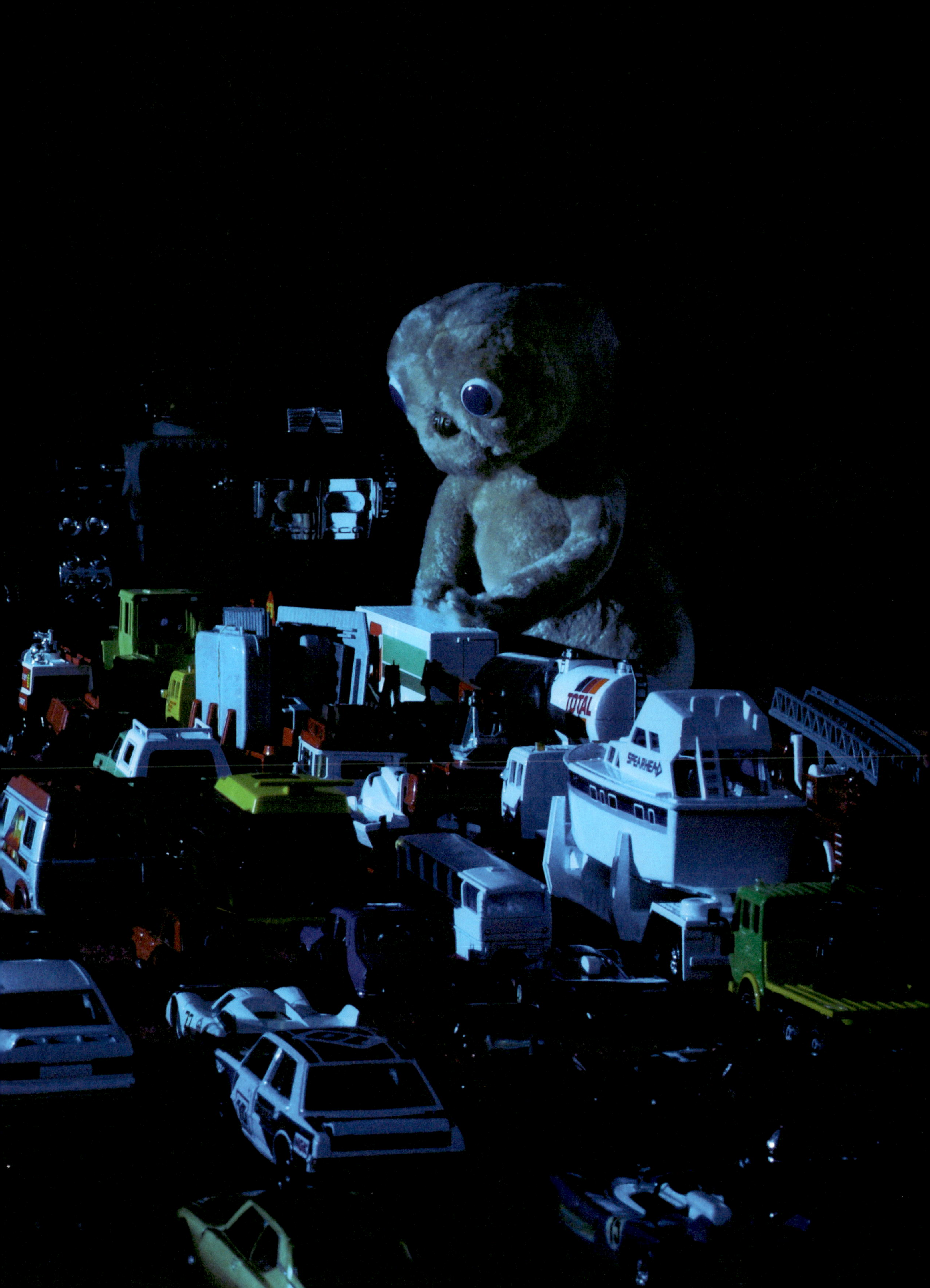

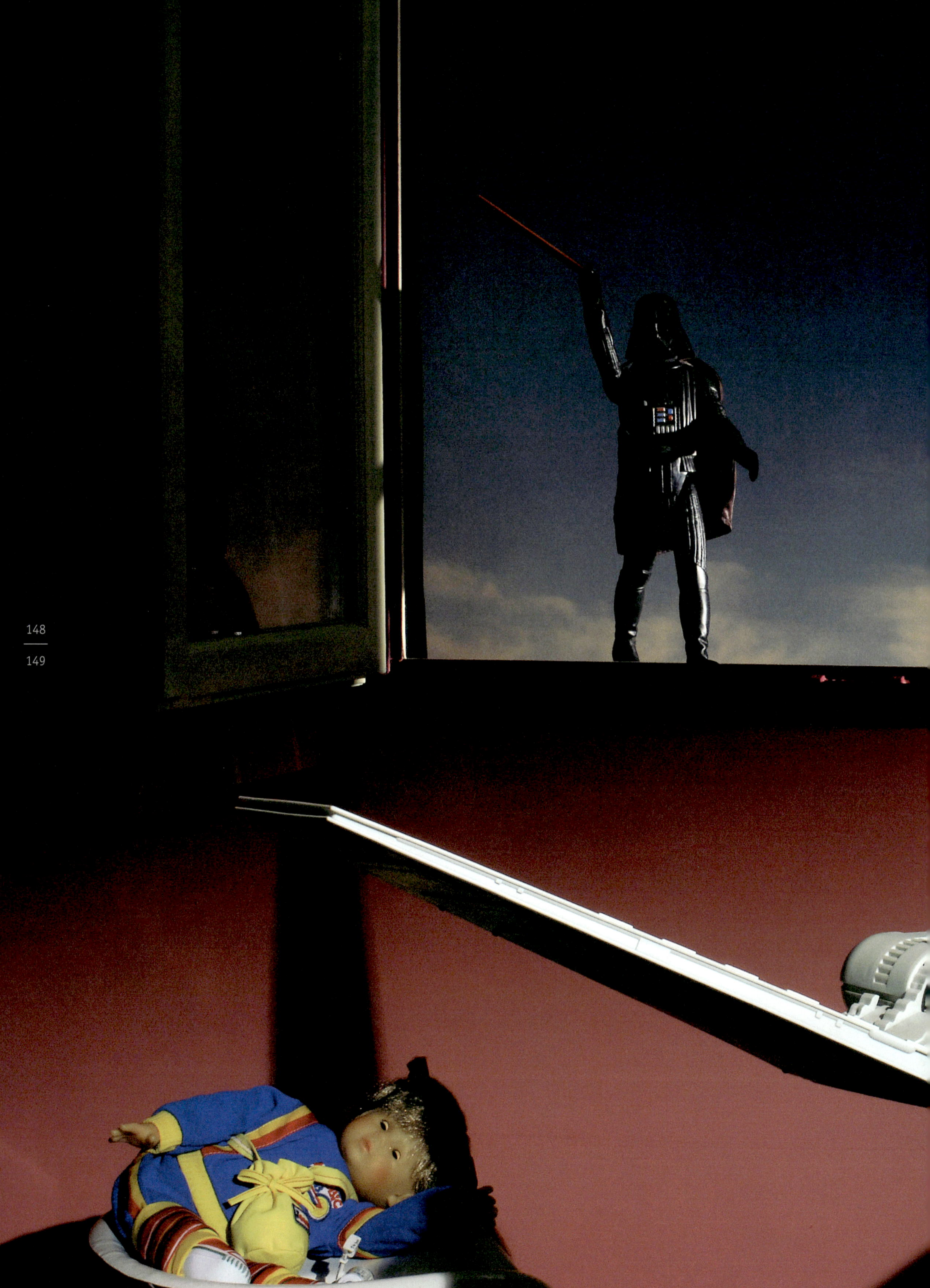

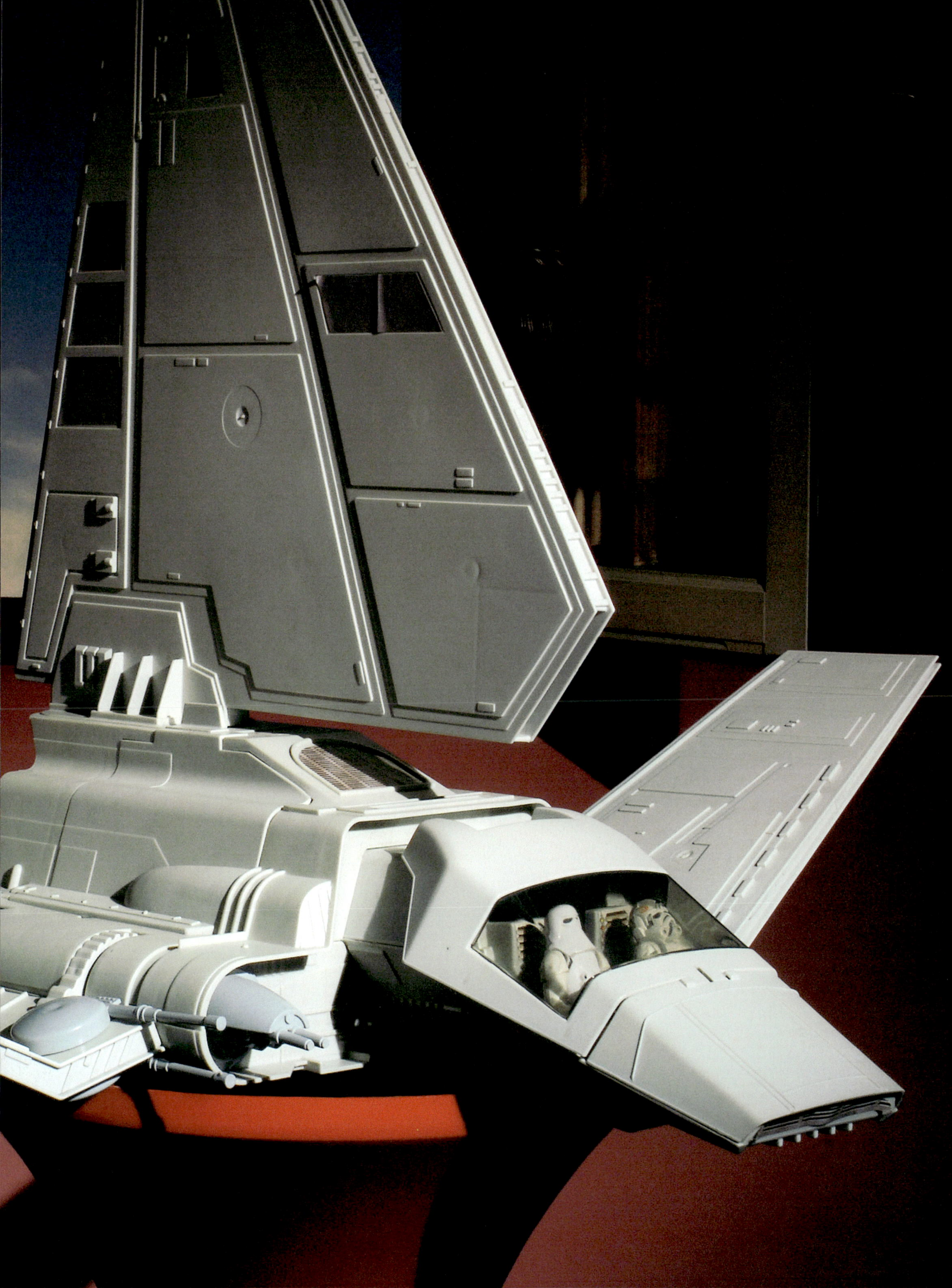

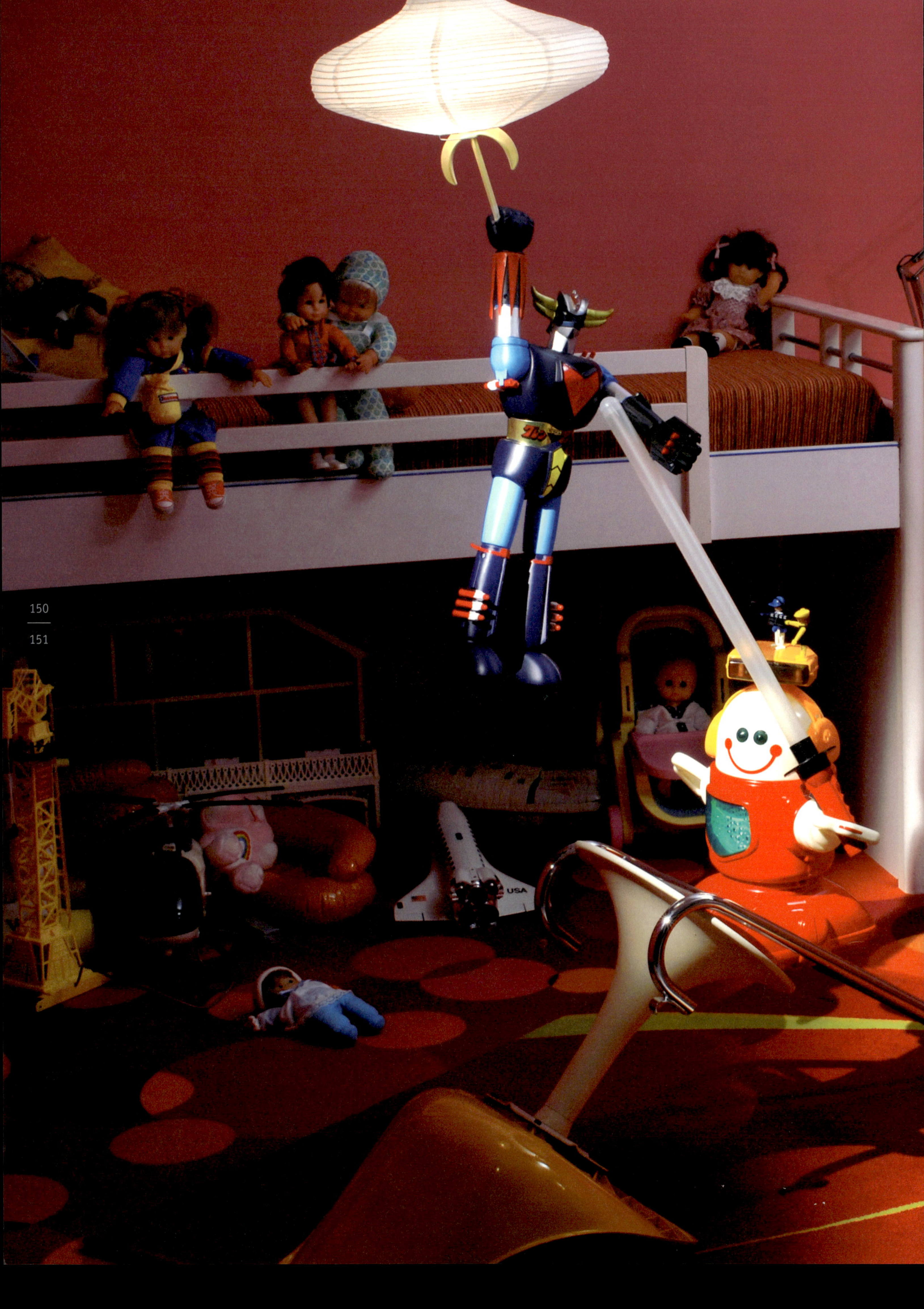

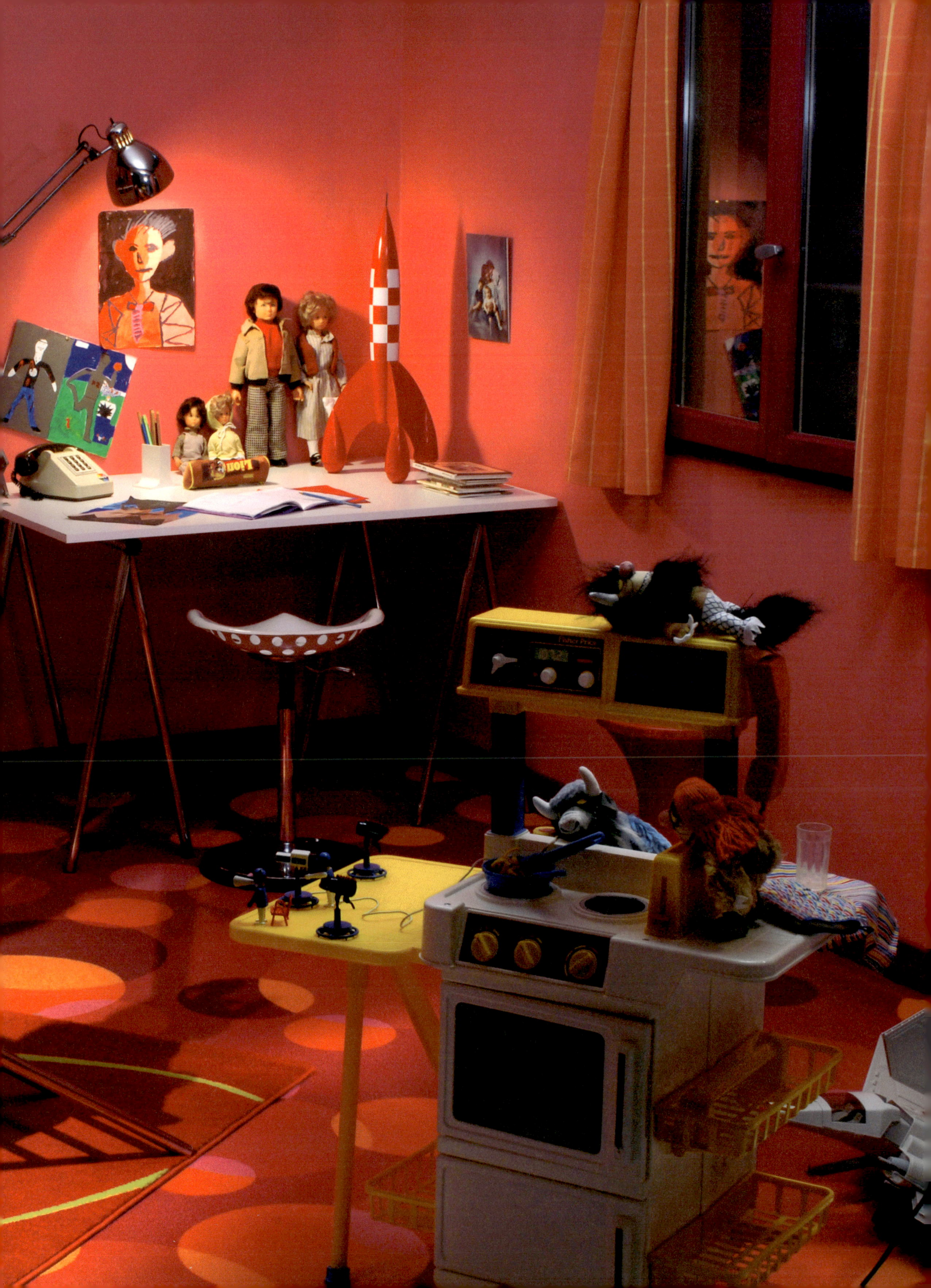

e reduce the world to the space in which we play, and here we build a pygmy realm that we decree is a mirror of the one around us. What takes place on the floor of our playroom, we say, takes place in the world. What we invent, we believe in; the walls of our space are the limits of our universe. King, queen, magician, sorceress, overlord, the child constructs the history and geography of the land of toys and imagines that this is how and where things truly happen. His hand moves the soldiers over the mountainous carpet, hides the animals in the crevices and wrinkles of a sheet, places the dolls in their house and their hospital and their school; in a secret way (which he cannot articulate) he knows that these actions govern the ebb and flow of real wars and migrations and societies. The game the child plays mirrors the world, but is also mirrored in the world.

According to the *Mabinogion*, a collection of medieval Welsh tales, two kings sit at a game of chess while their armies fight in the plains around them. In the evening, one of the kings is placed in checkmate and, furious, overturns the chessboard. At this point, a messenger announces: 'Your army is in flight, you have lost your kingdom.'

ar is a game. The armies of tin or plastic soldiers displayed over the floor, whether the carefully copied figures of historical battles or the imaginary creatures of *Star Wars* and Bionic Men, engage in a entertainment that is also a performance. The stage is set in a leisurely way, the pieces put in position; the preparation usually takes longer than the war itself. In the war game, the toys have little or no individuality. They exist *en masse*, their function is to attack or be defeated but for no personal reason. The soldiers are nameless, storyless. Only later, on the video screen, do the actors acquire a personality, a name, become individual heroes. Playing with toy armies has more of competition than of battle, winning or losing; a video game is more about killing, about force and survival of the strongest. Both play deadly games but for one, the accent is on play, for the other, on death.

The notion is ancient. When (according to 2 Samuel) the troops of King David confronted their adversaries at the Pool of Gibeon, one of the enemy commanders ordered: 'Let the young men come out and play', whereupon twelve soldiers stepped forward from each side, met and slaughtered one another. In Greece, wars were sometimes resolved as a game between two armies. In the seventh century BC, two cities of Euboea, Chalcis and Eretria, fought each other. According to the rules of combat laid down in the Temple of Artemis, the place and hour of the fighting were set in advance, and the arms to be used were limited to the sword and the spear (javelins, arrows and slings were forbidden). Perhaps for that reason the headquarters of an army's commanders-in-chief, with its laid-out maps showing the advance and retreat of troops, resembles nothing as much as the nursery floor.

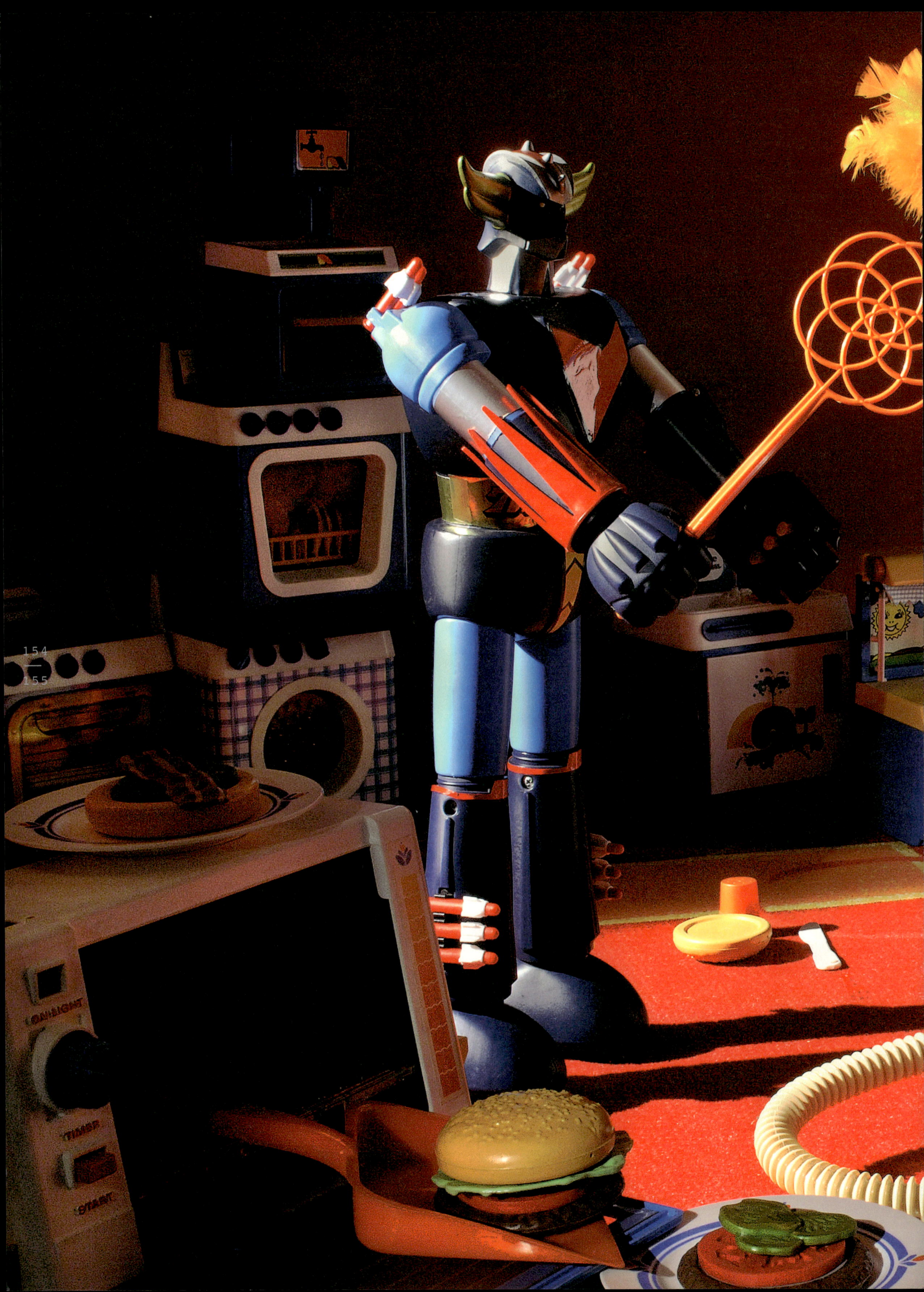

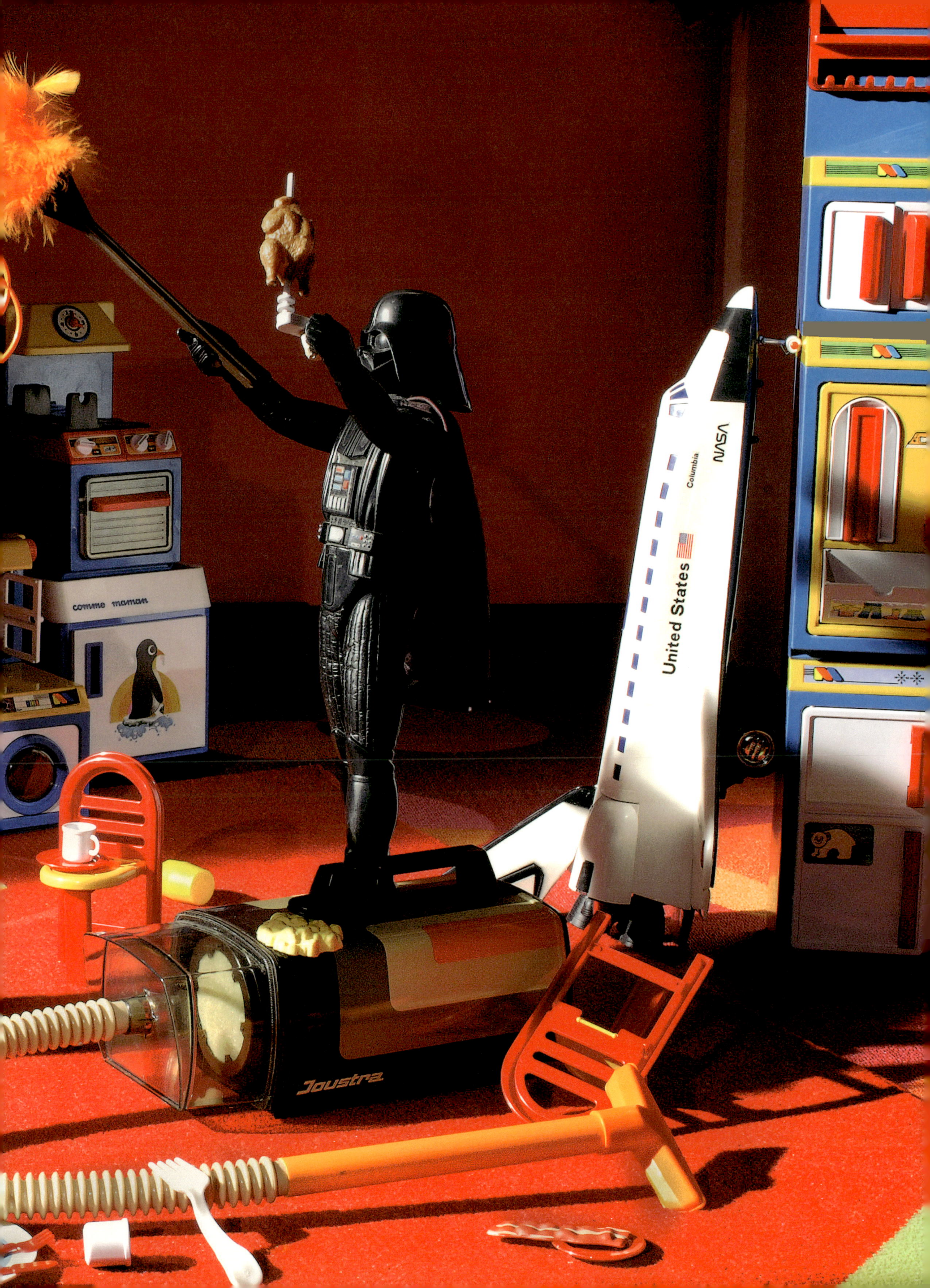

United States
Columbia
NASA
comme maman
Joustra

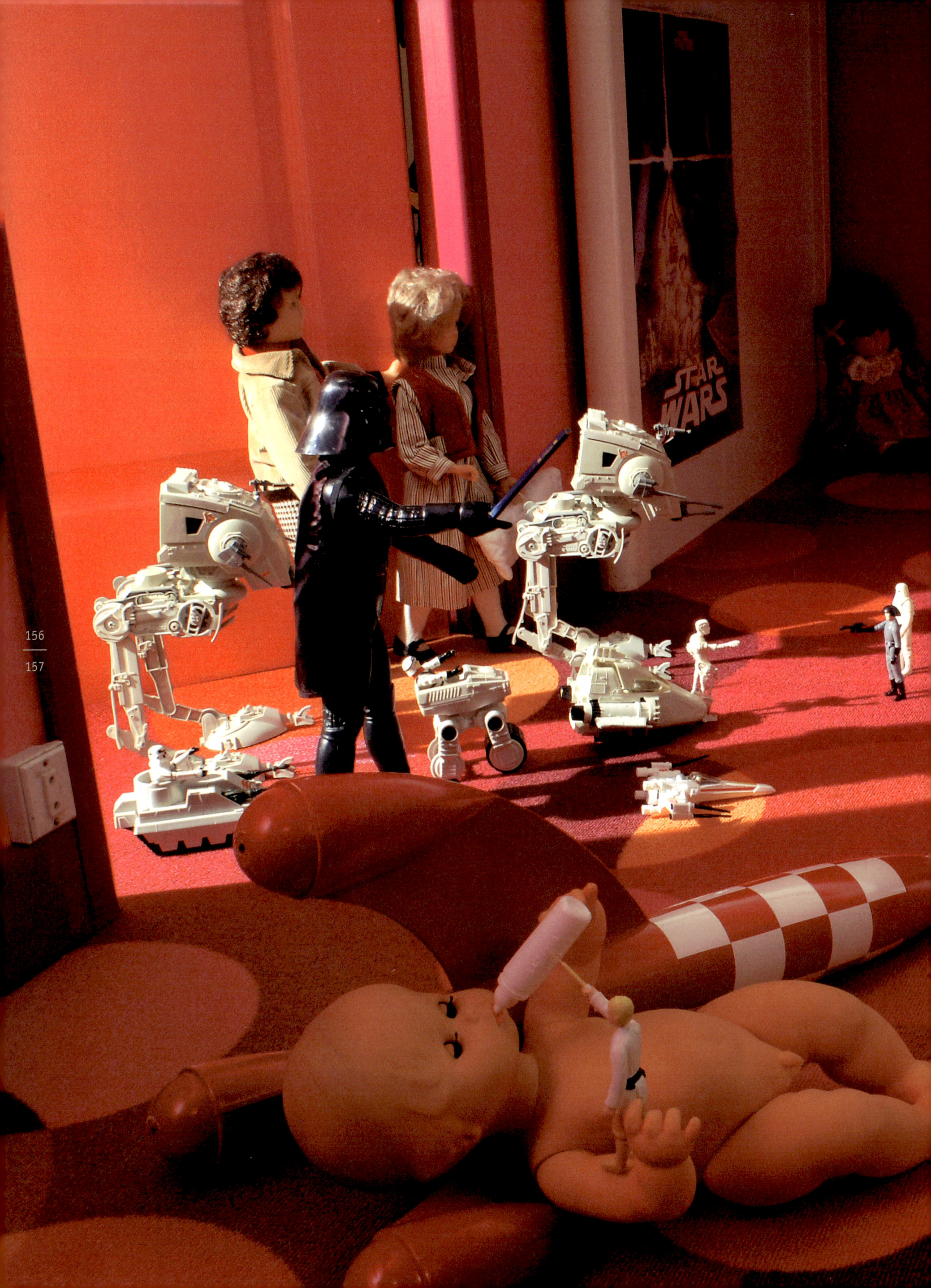

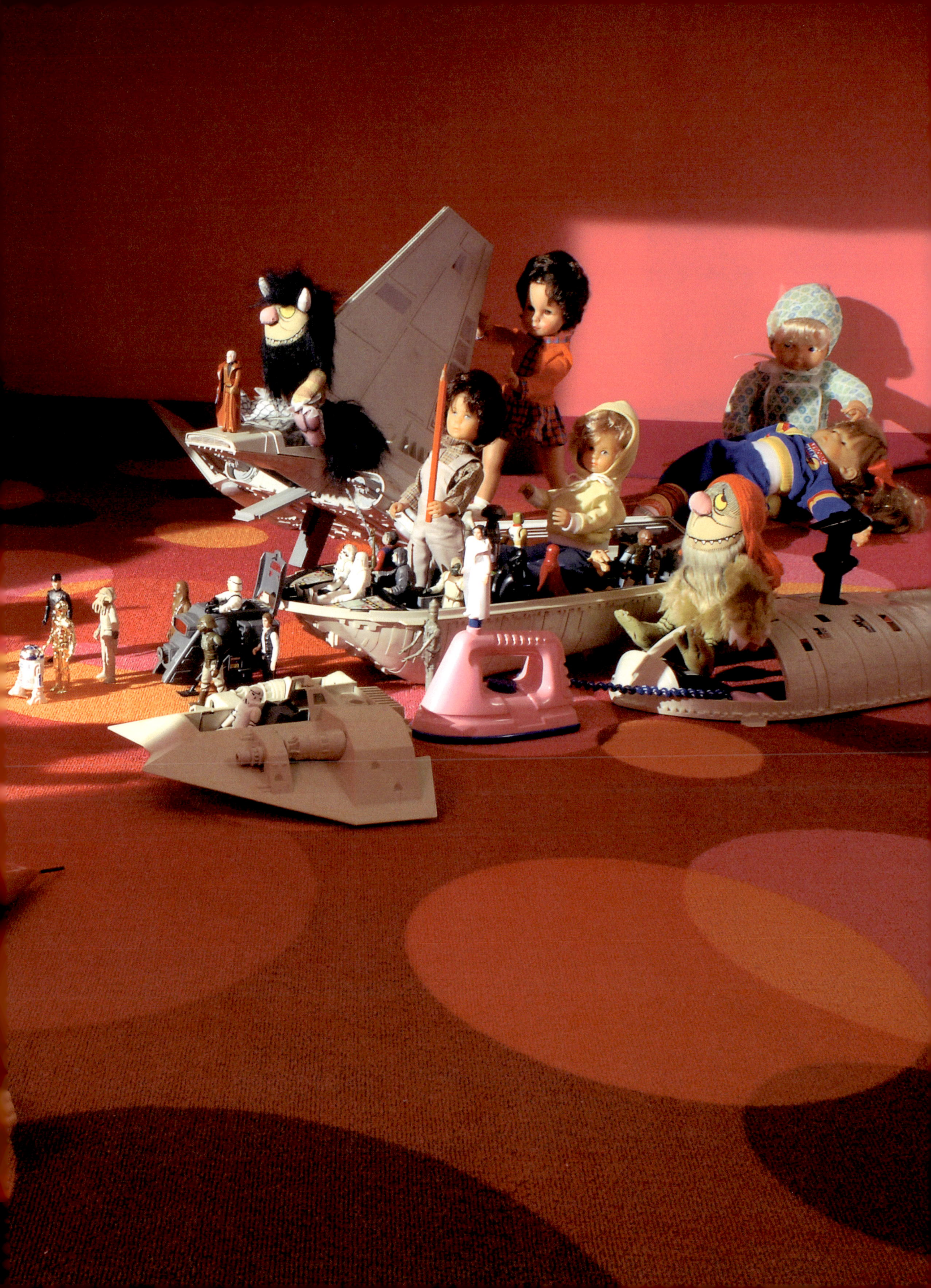

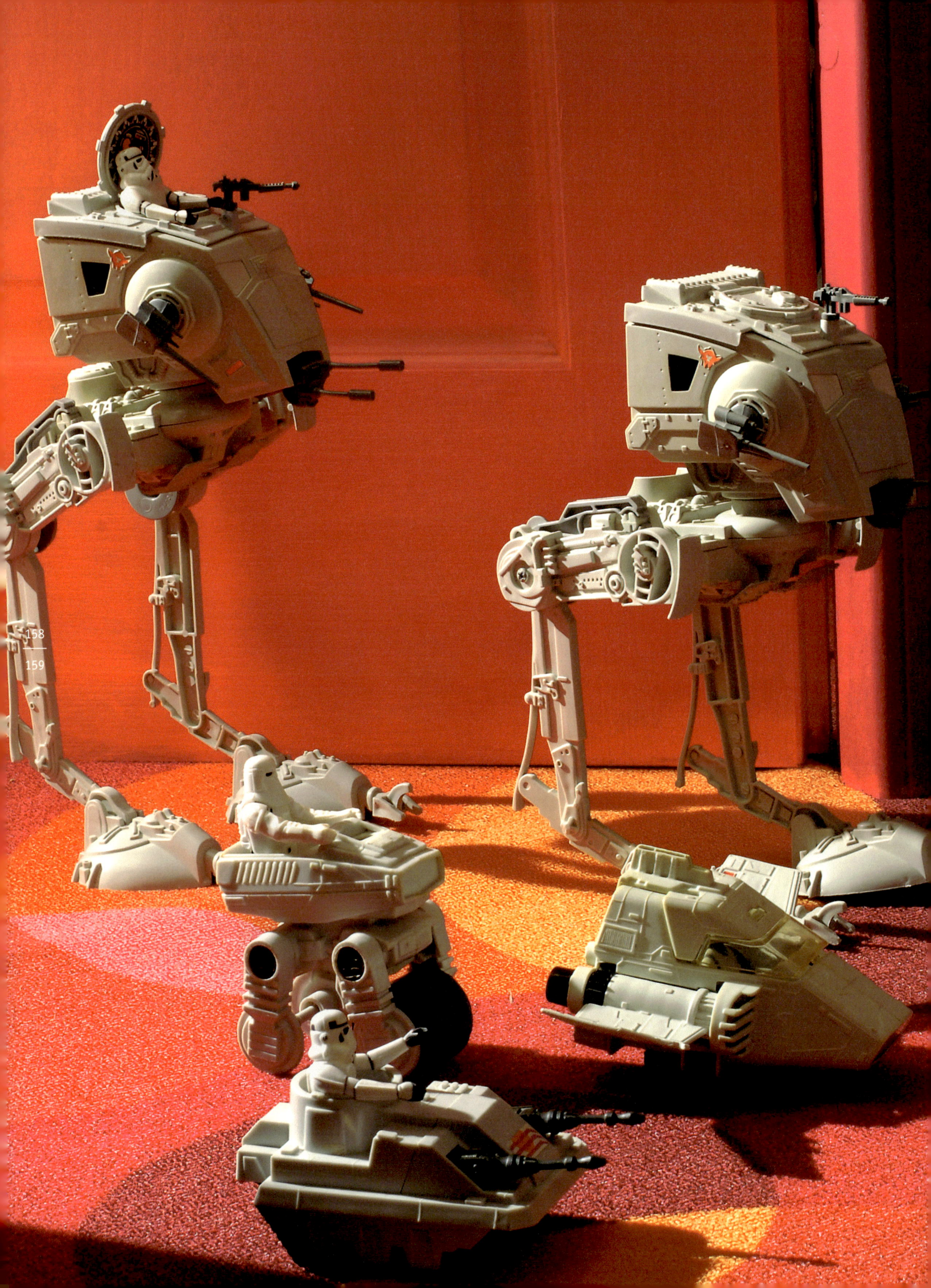
158
159

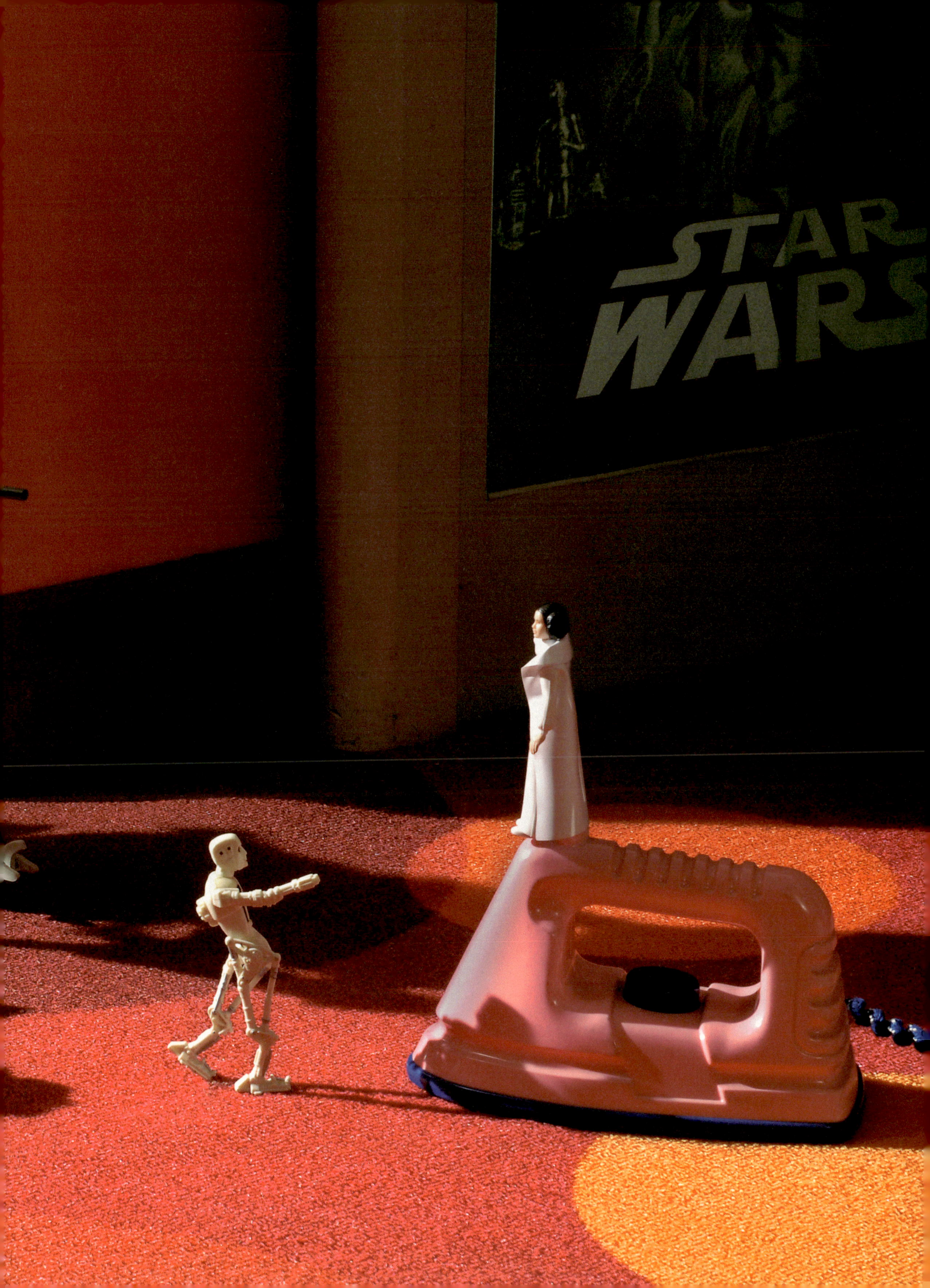

STAR
WARS

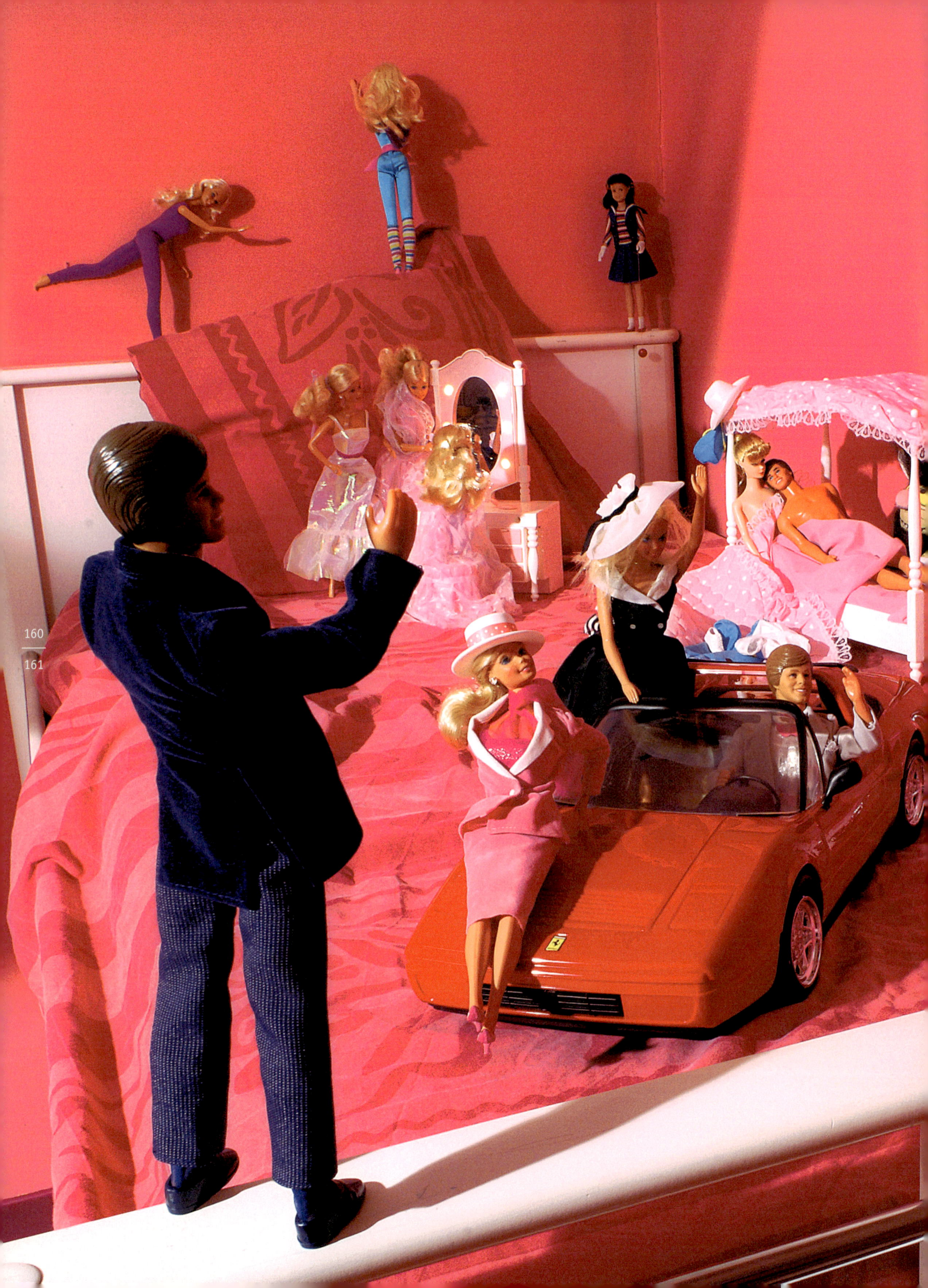

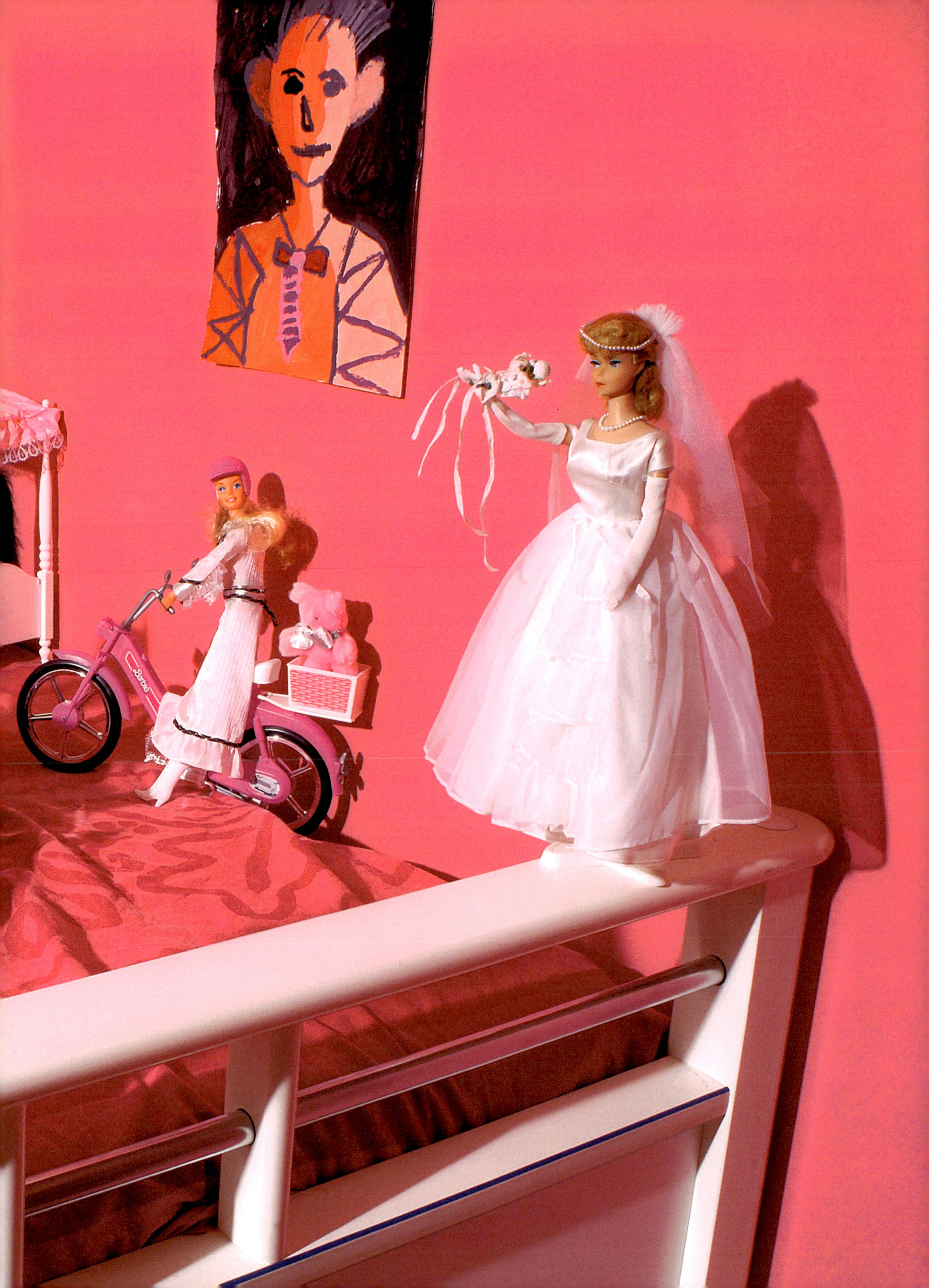

olls owe their existence to the child who plays with them. A doll in a box has something of an Egyptian mummy, a captive slave, a Sleeping Beauty. It demands to be lifted, to be handled, to be brought back to life. The French word *poupée* (like the English 'poppet' and the German *Puppe*) derives from the Latin *pupa* meaning 'a girl' and, by extension, used to designate any small image like a trinket or a votive offering. Pupa is also the name given to the passive developmental stage of an insect, between the larva and the imago state; that is to say, a being in suspension, a latent presence, a life implicit, something about to be.

The simple, schematic dolls of antiquity were for every child: fashion rendered them aristocratic. In the Middle Ages, dressed according to the latest styles, they became the property of the rich and noble. Appearance overrode function and, in the hands of the powerful, dolls became emblems rather than playthings, and instead of being confined to the nursery, crossed borders as ambassadors of good will. Among royalty, men offered swords; women, dolls. Isabeau of Bavaria sent several dolls to the Queen of England in 1391 and, in 1497, Anne of Brittany had a large doll delivered to Isabel of Spain.

What came first? The doll-like figures used for religious rituals, or the dolls made for the rituals of children? No game with dolls is innocent. The building of the doll's house, the setting-up of a toy classroom, the tea parties and the bottle feeding, the wardrobe and fashion shows, the ceremonies of the bedroom, obviously play out stories perceived in the adult world but also spring from deeper places that teach children who they are and how they are supposed to behave. Playing at being adults allows them to learn to be children, seeing themselves from outside themselves, as if on a stage on which they are actors, directors and audience. We learn to walk, to eat, to interact with the world not only through imitative play but through awareness of the imitation.

Seeing what we do allows us to become who we are, or to move towards what we are.

doll's tea party is a curious ceremony: it is the archetype of the real thing.

Meals are changing occasions, variable in tone and content. No two meals are the same. Schedules are altered by circumstance, the number of guests varies from week to week, food is better some days than others, the mood at the table clouds over or clears up. Some meals are unremarkable, others are festive, a few are tragic.

The doll's tea party, however, adheres to a routine. To begin with, it is a magical meal. Reduced to the scale of the child, dishes and cutlery assume correct proportions. Food (the plasticine cookies, the invisible tea, the wooden cake) no longer depends on the judgment of the palate but exists *per se*, absolutely. The guests behave exactly as the host wishes them to. If a cross word is said, it is willed; if someone spills the milk, it was not an accident. Not even in dreams do things happen so deliberately.

Much the same takes place in the toy kitchen. Every dish is prepared to the cook's exact wishes, every result is a success. If a dish fails (the chicken burnt to a cinder or the pie underbaked), it is just to lend a little excitement to the ceremony. Perfection can be boring.

Afterwards, the memory of the game becomes a model and, while a waiter hovers over the expensive tablecloth, or a friend generously slices a Black Forest cake, or we bring the steaming Sunday pot roast to the family table, the image of a tiny hand picking up a minuscule knife and pretending to cut a toy sausage will remind us of something we once were capable of, and which we can no longer master.

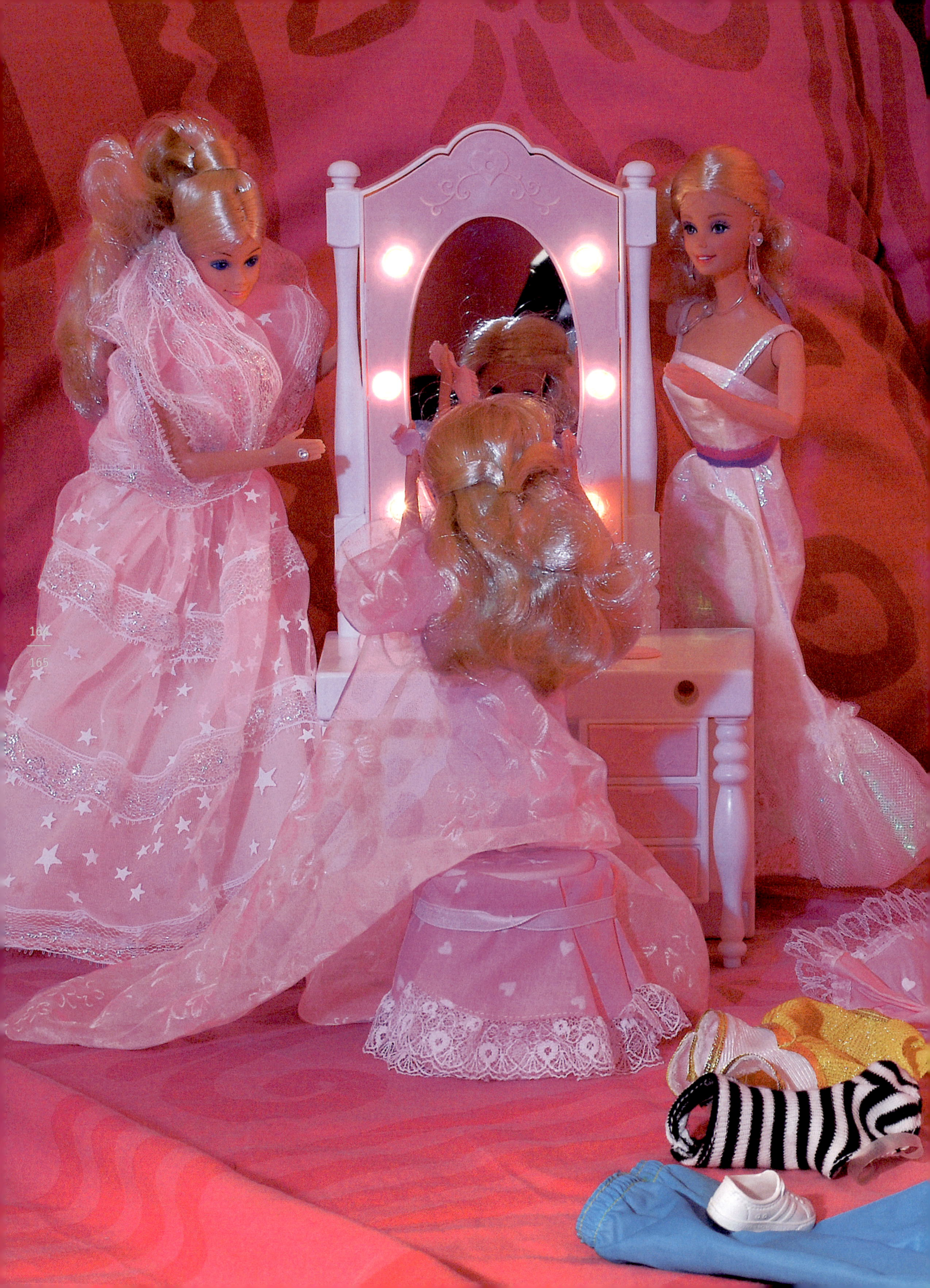

164
165

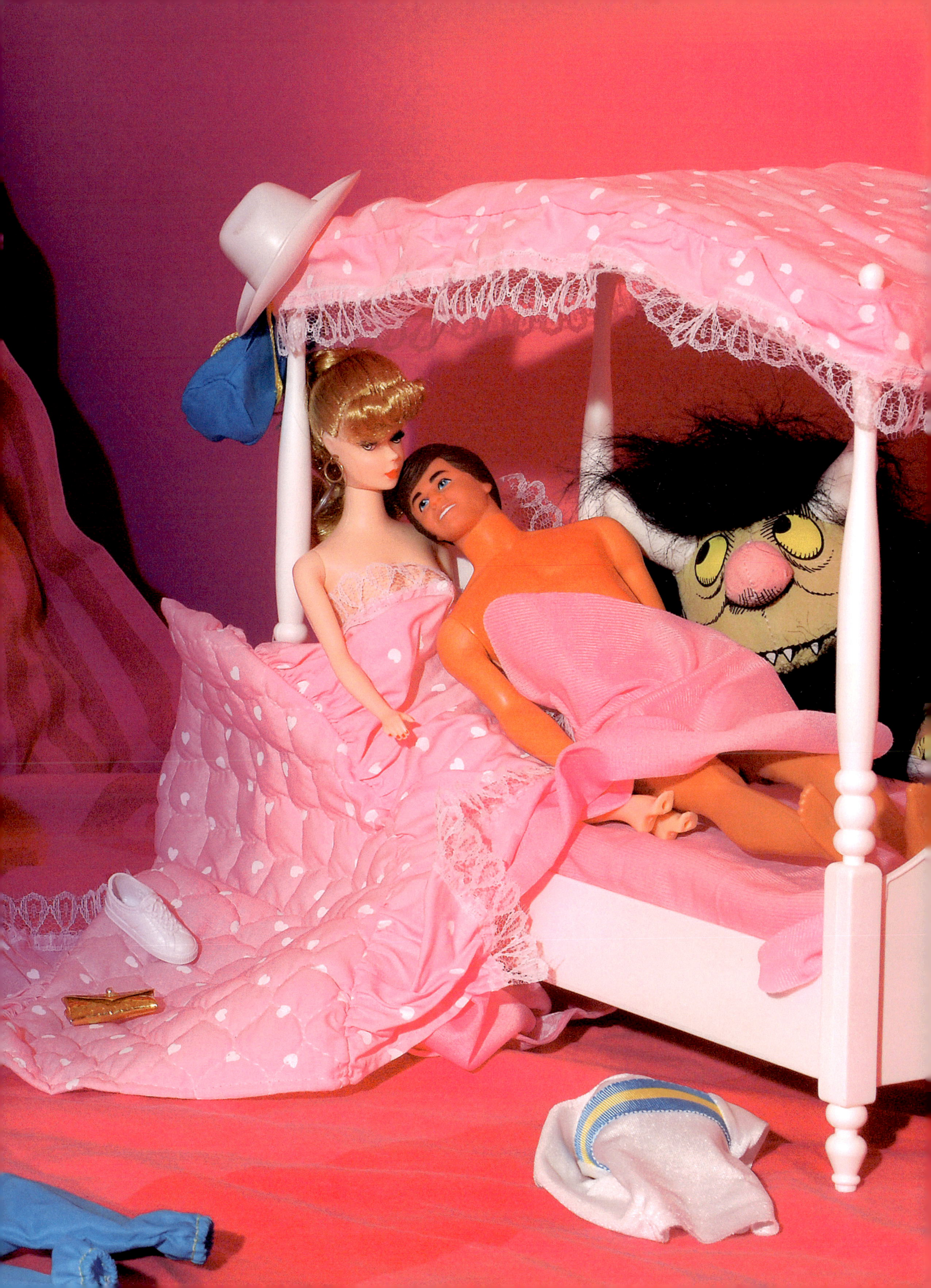

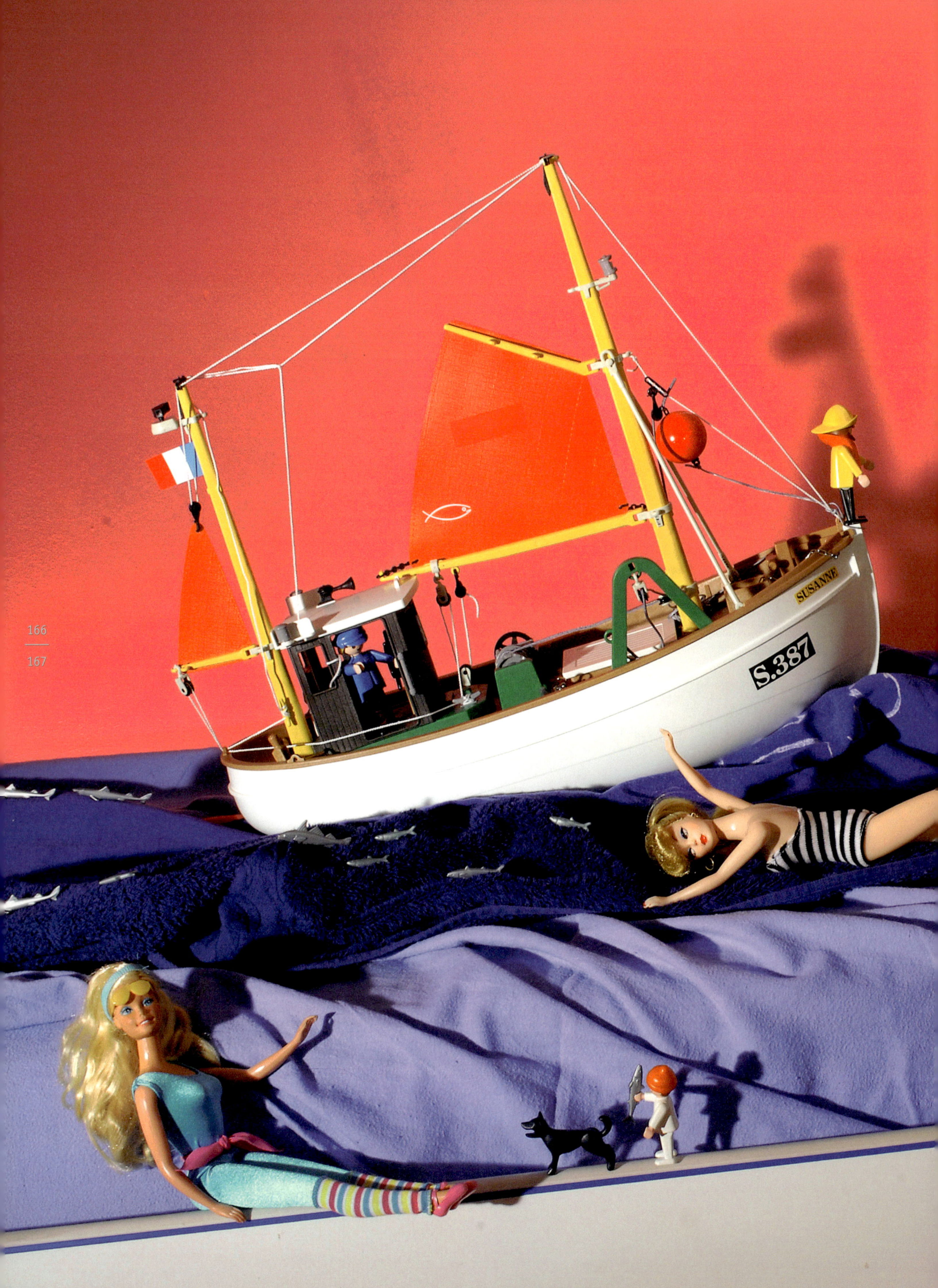
SUSANNE
S.387

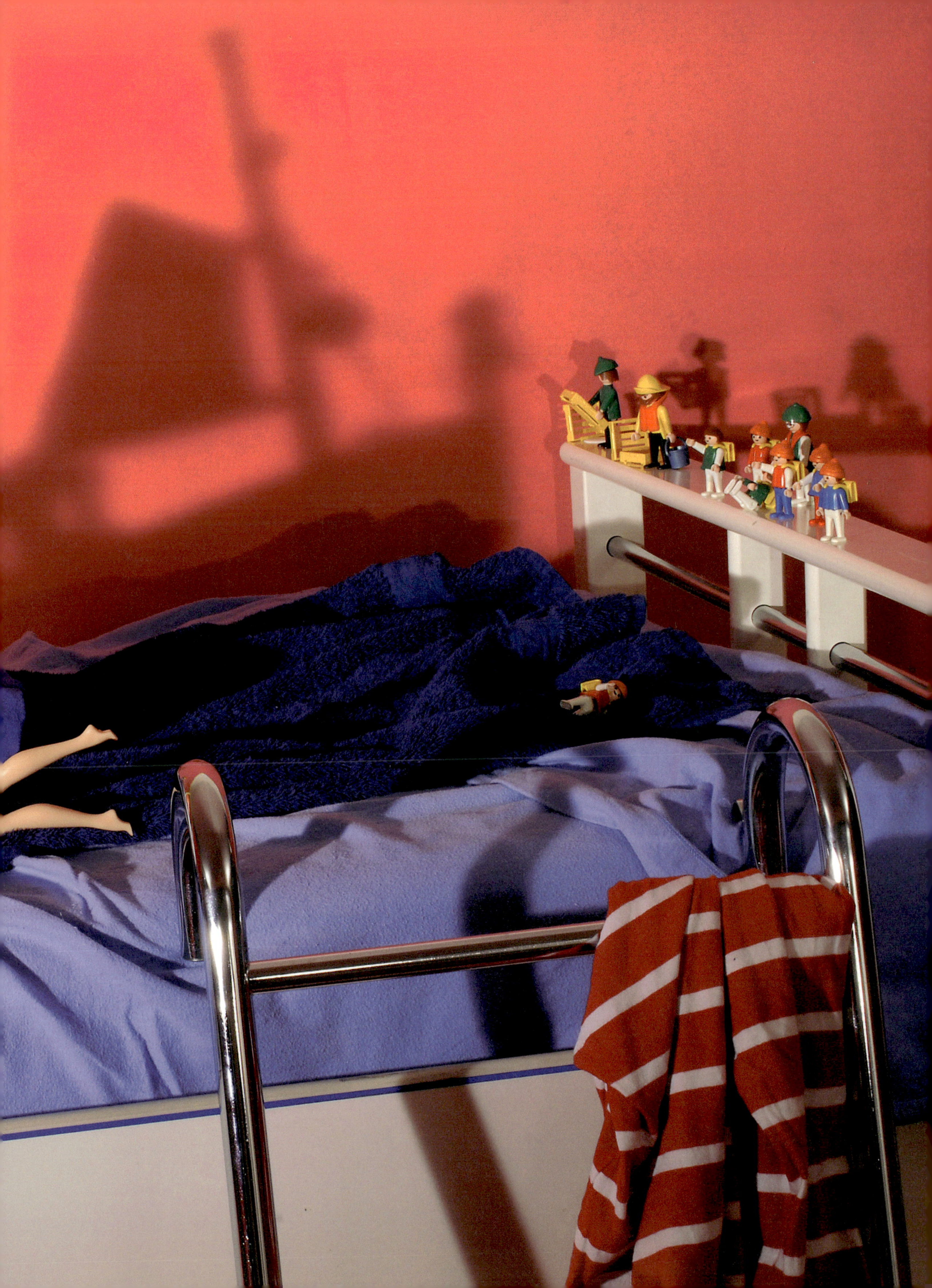

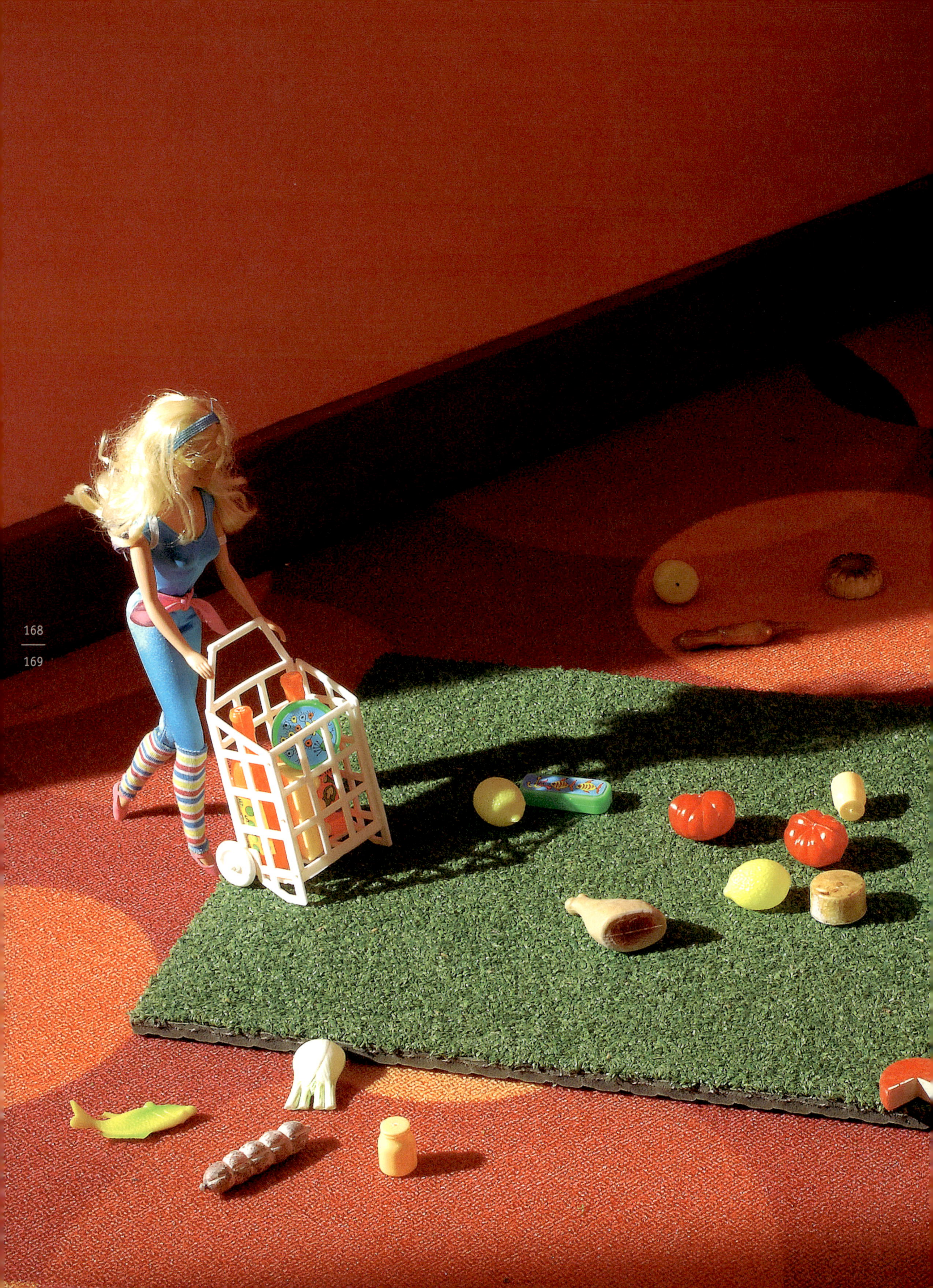

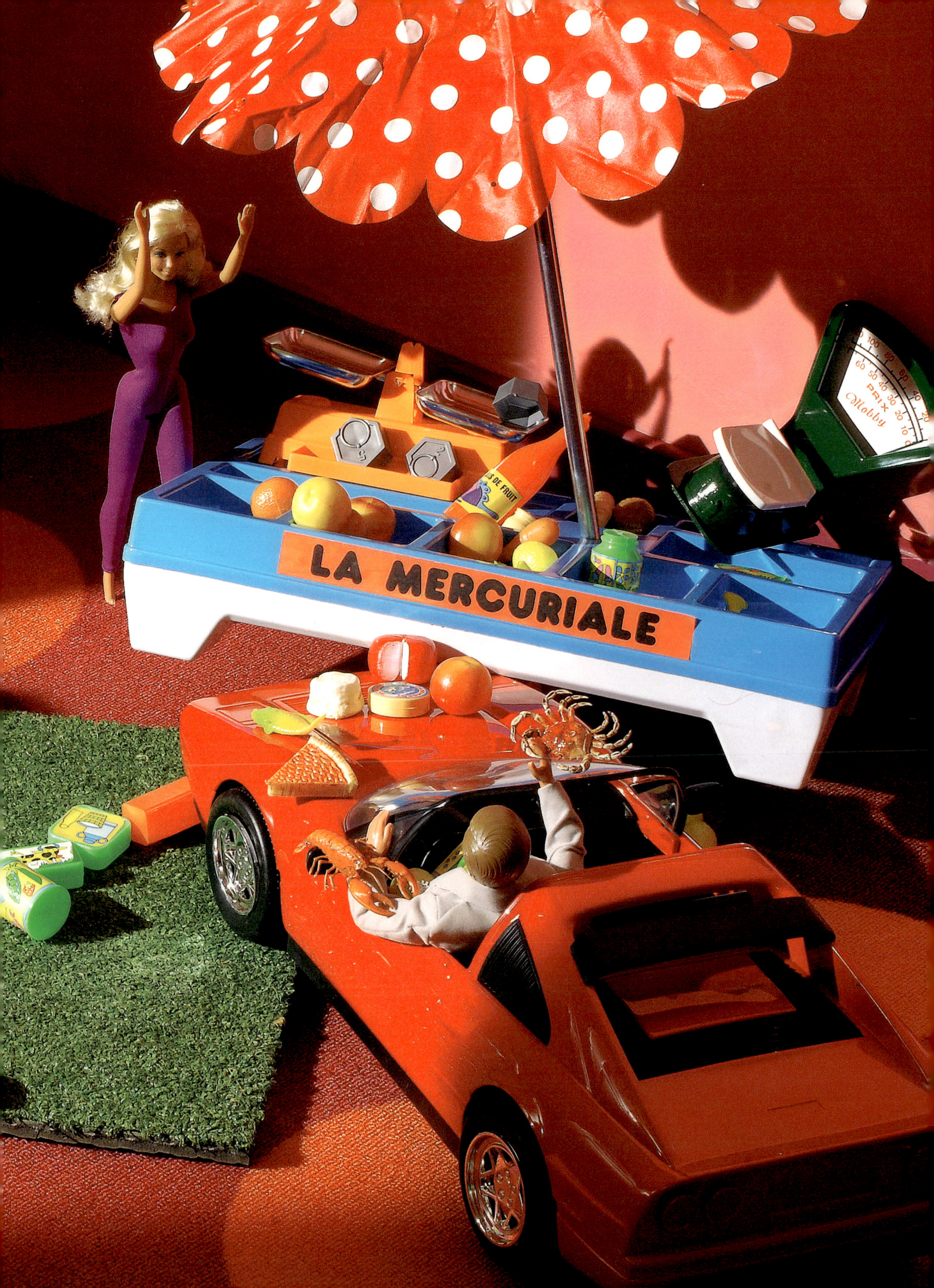

LA MERCURIALE

ike the statue of Diana of Ephesus, which (according to legend) fell from the heavens, Barbie stands in the position of one who is to be adored, arms straight at both sides, hands extended. The statue of Diana was said to be beyond compare; so, we are told, is Barbie. The statue had its trunk and legs encased in an ornamental sheath; Barbie's party dresses encase her in exactly the same manner. The many breasts represented on the statue granted the goddess's female worshippers fertility and strength; Barbie's discreet bosom, slim waist and lovely hair seem to promise her worshippers similar attributes. Diana of Ephesus was thought to fulfil women's secret wishes; there is a Barbie for every fantasy, from princess to country maid.

Diana of Ephesus jealously sought the veneration of her people. Traditionally, she was paired with her brother, Apollo. Through the voice of sibyls and clairvoyants, she would deliver oracles.

Barbie's homepage lists her three principal aims in life:

Get noticed!
Go out with Todd.
Be a news anchor.

e are given toys. For birthdays, holidays, visits, as celebratory offerings, prizes, mementoes, they come into our lives marked by the hand that brought them. The first toys will be explained to us later: 'That rattle was given to you by Aunt Clara,' 'Cousin Charles carried that tiger all the way back from New York.' A certificate of provenance is attached to a given toy; the spirit of the giver hovers implacably over it. Every gift of a toy entails a debt.

Because toys are given, they must appeal to the adult who buys them. They must accord with his standards, expectations, moral codes and aesthetic values. They must tempt him with the fantasy of childhood and the memory, true or false, of happiness. They must tell him that this will redeem him, change the past or bring it back, mend a broken promise, fulfil an unattended need. They must declare: 'The toy you give will be also yours.'

To the child, every gift of a toy must say: 'This is a mirror, this is what I think of you, this is who you are.'

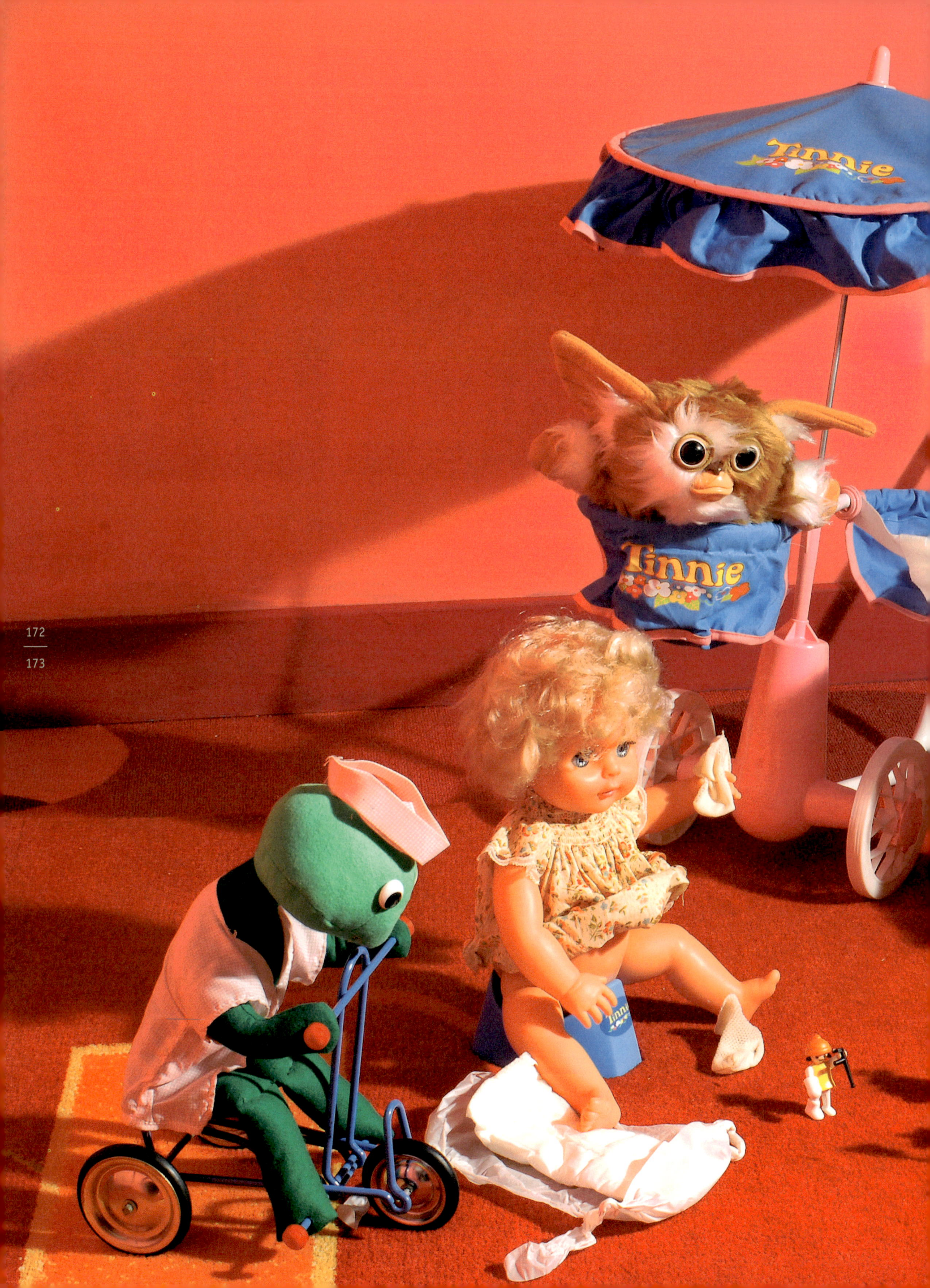
Tinnie
Tinnie
Tinnie

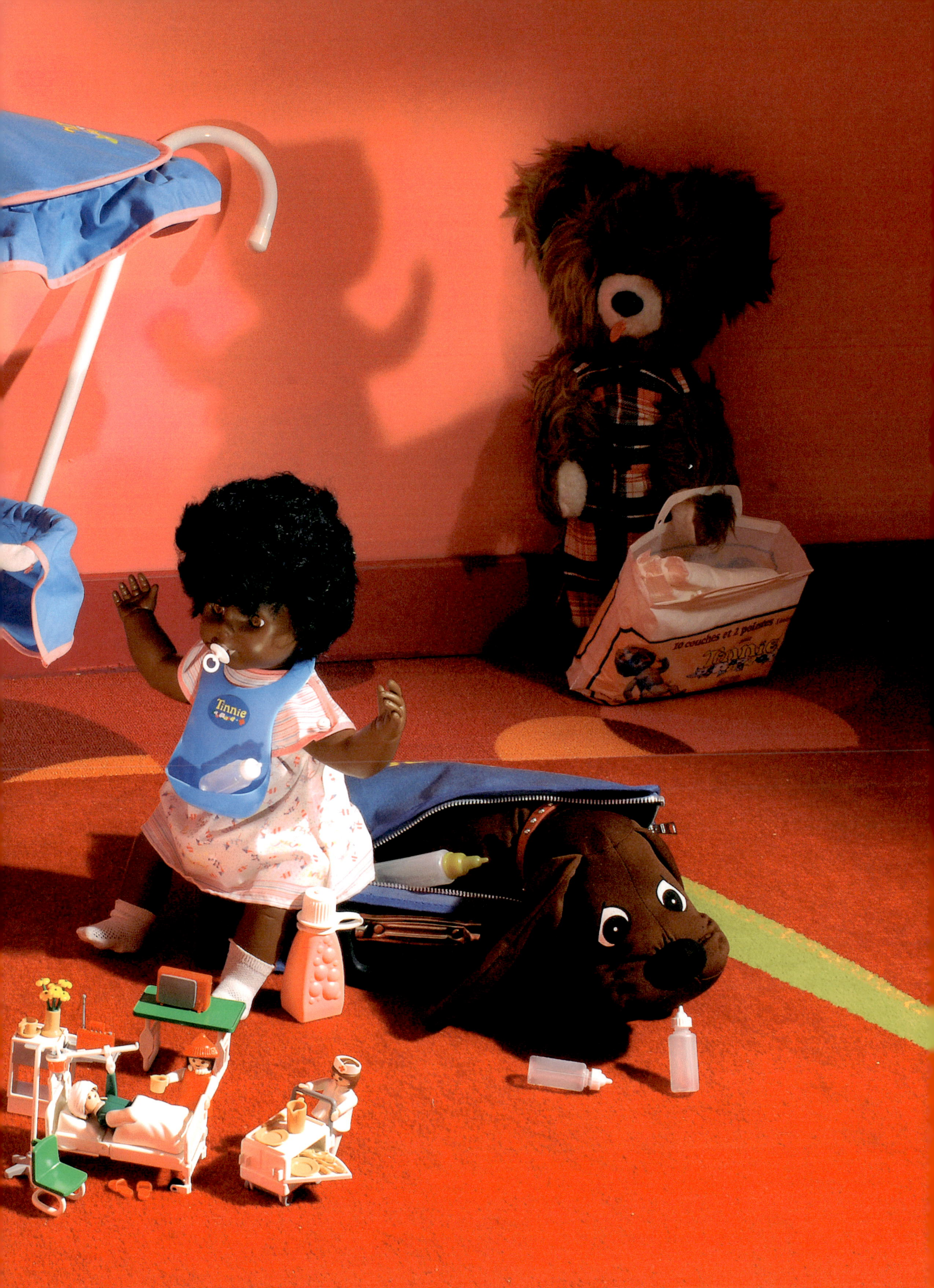
Tinnie
10 couches et 1 poignées
Tinnie

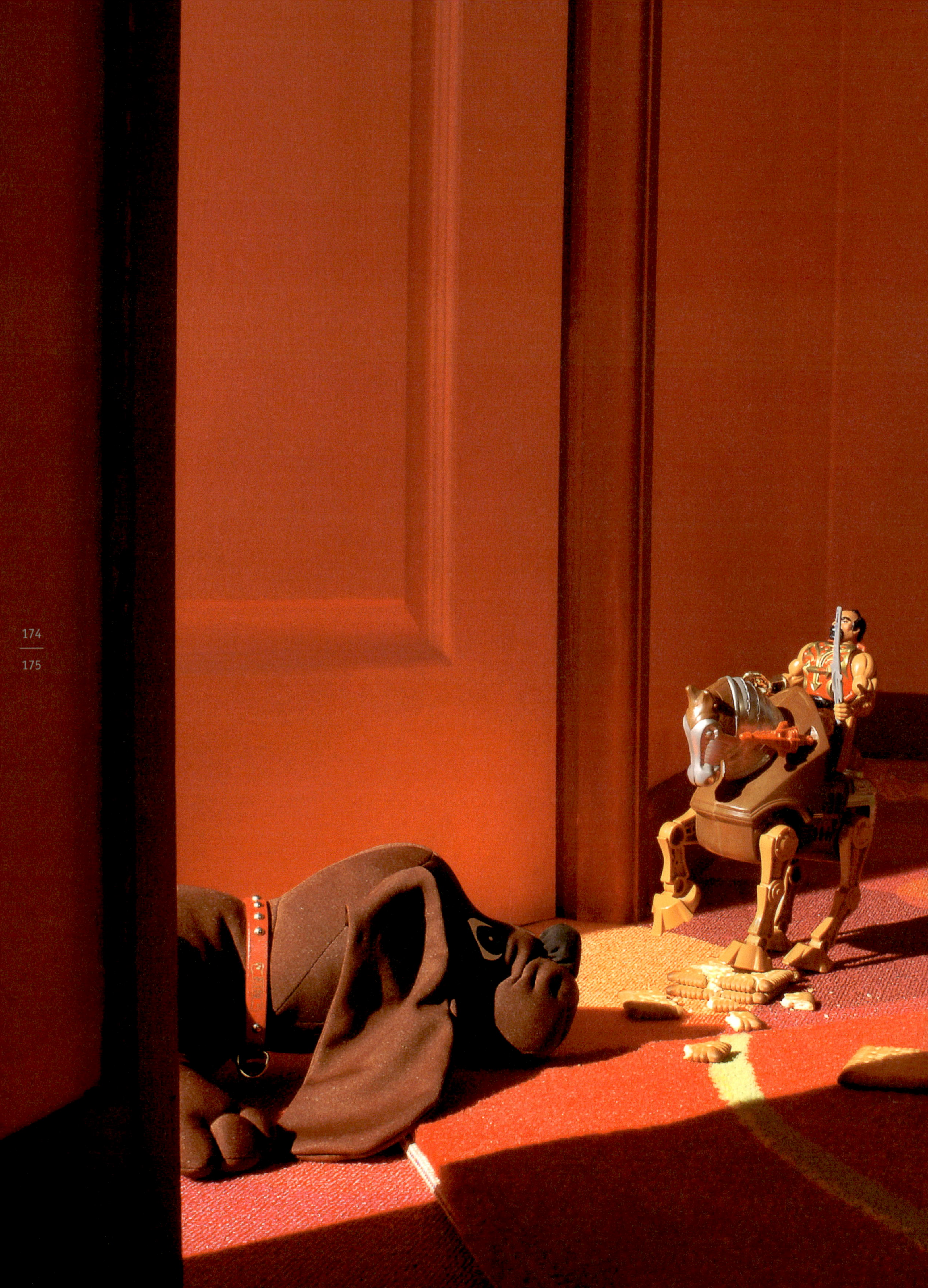

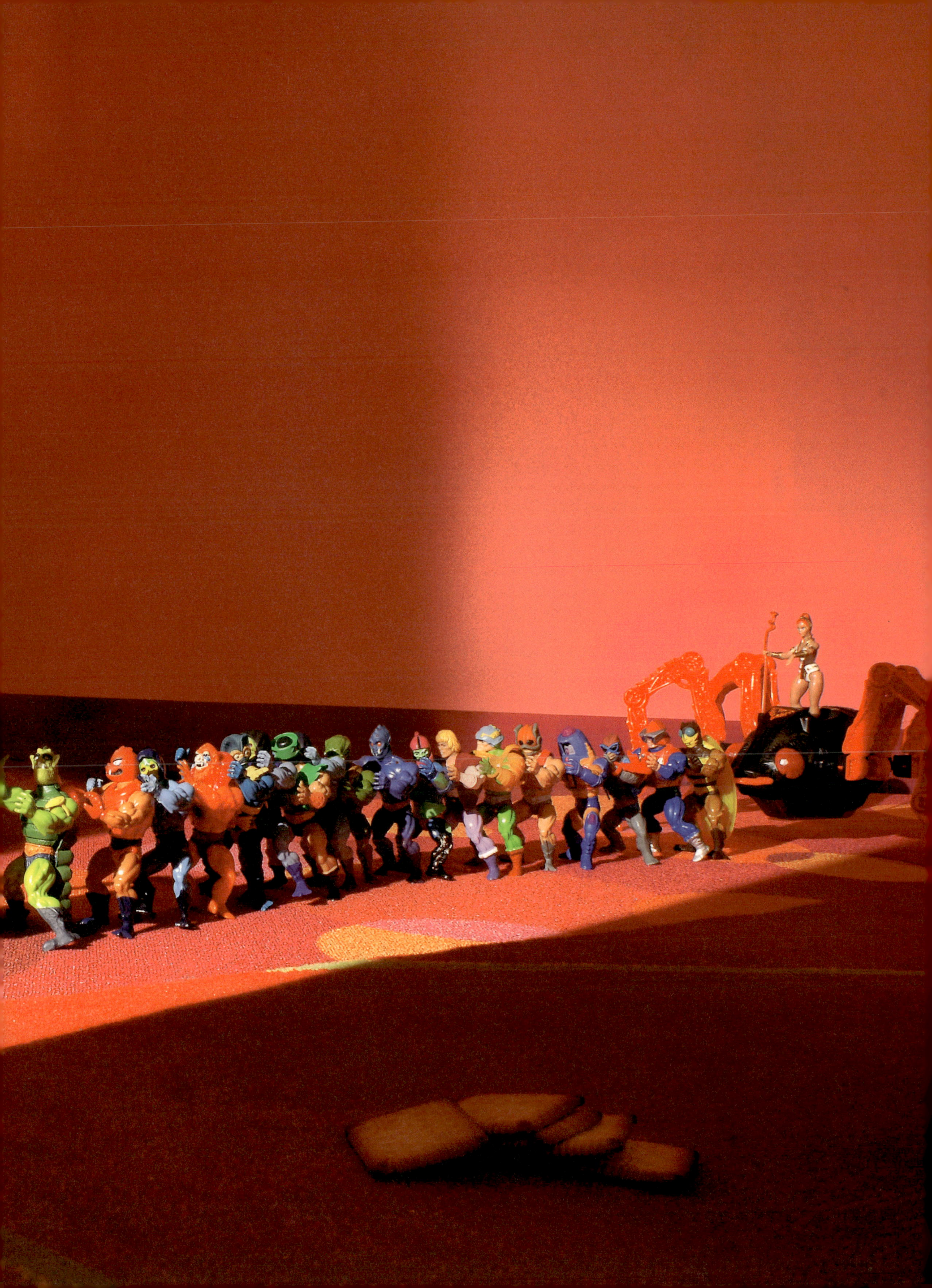

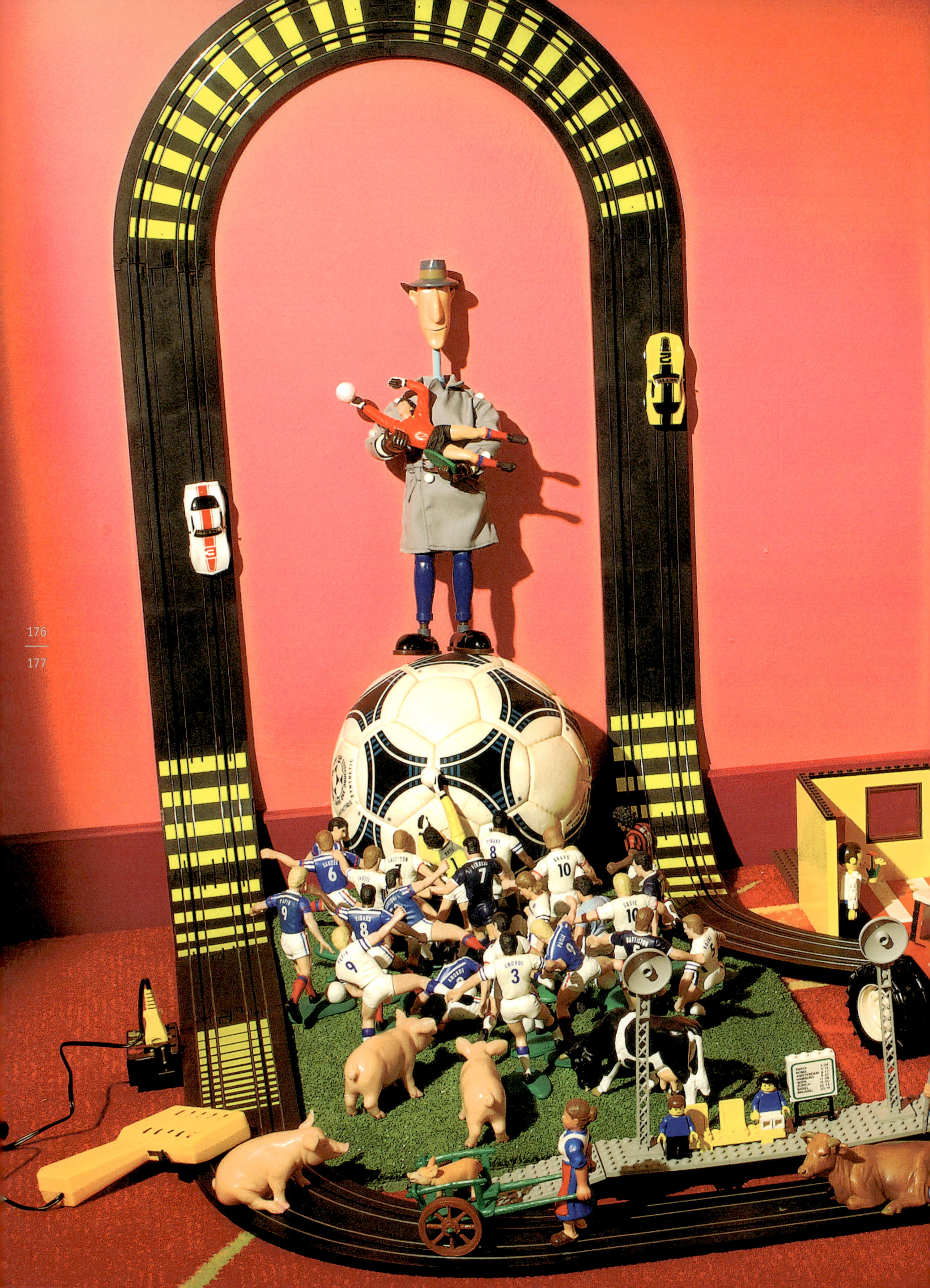

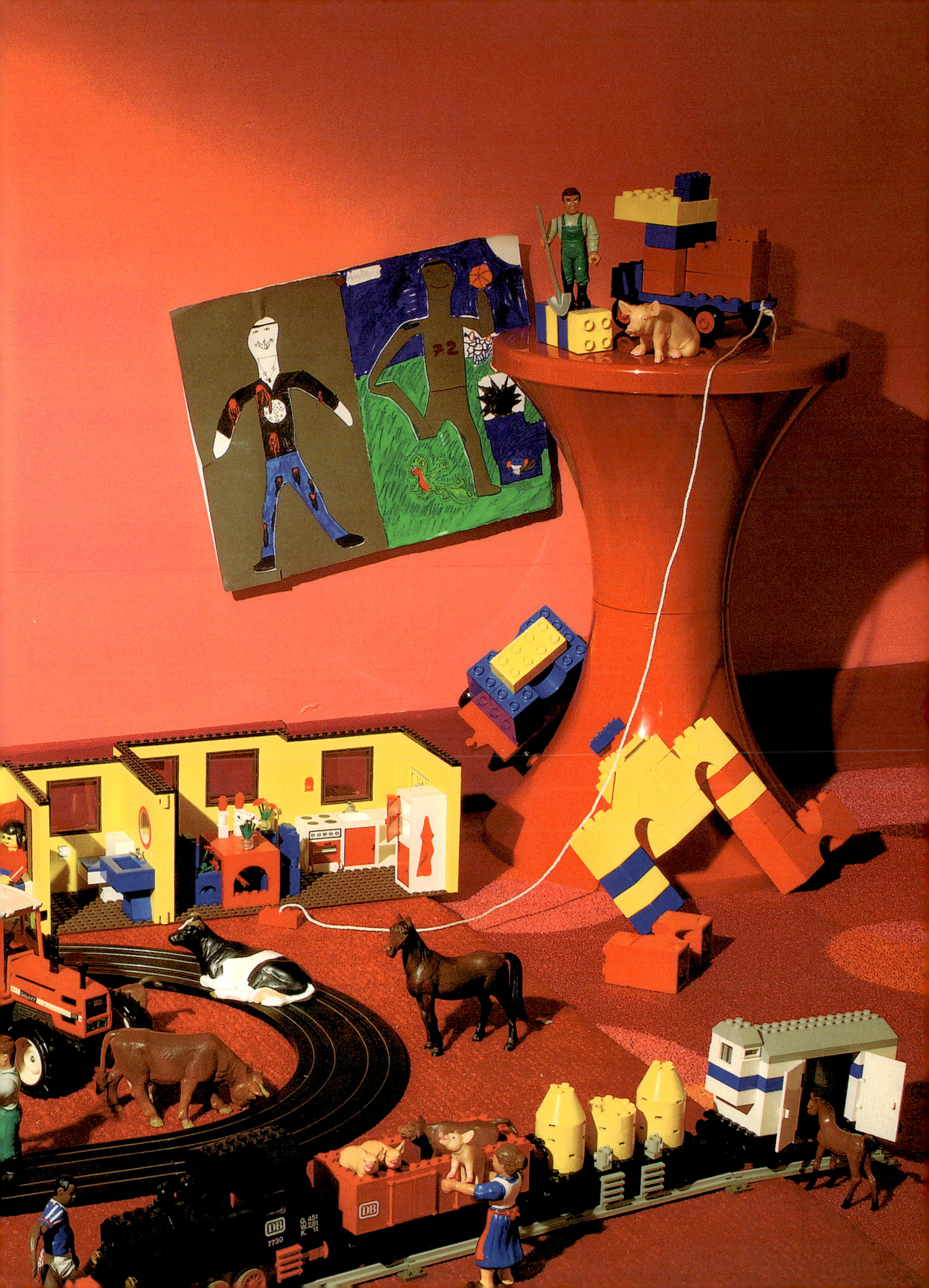

alls, hoops, tops, wheels, objects that spin and turn are emblematic of an essential freedom. To run in circles, to link hands in a ring, to turn around to the point of dizziness is exhilarating, an inkling of perpetual motion, unconsciously imitating the path of the celestial spheres. This sense of freedom elicited by play (not the lack of rules but the creation of one's own rules, not the absence of discipline but a self-imposed discipline) conjures up its contrary: curtailment. The adult watching the child play senses that here, among his toys, the child escapes him. This is uncharted territory, beyond the strictures of conventional behaviour. Even if the child copies adult manners and rituals, it isn't enough: the procedures must be monitored, examined for imperfections, for breaches of morals or respect. The enjoyment itself becomes suspect: to play, the adult opposes labour to entertainment, serious pursuits to frivolous activities, time profitably employed to time wasted in games.

Even when allowed, play must be measured. The humanist Pope Pius II, in his treatise on the education of boys, insists that boys must be allowed their games, 'so long as they are not lewd or indecent. I approve of and praise your playing ball with boys your own age,' he says. 'There is the hoop; there are other perfectly respectable boyish games, which your teachers should sometimes allow you for the sake of relaxation and to stimulate a lively disposition.'

child grants inanimate objects all the life they need. A piece of wood or a corncob suffice to make a doll. But technology, ancient and modern, intrudes upon the primordial imagination. Over the centuries, the object animated only by the child in play was given a painted face, articulated arms and legs, moveable eyes, real hair, perfect skin, a voice, the ability to drink and pee, the talent to walk. For the price in the shop window, a life-like doll could now be yours. To restore the child's magical powers, the Waldorf Schools, following the teachings of Rudolf Steiner, offer only cloth dolls with featureless faces.

Progress. In the eighties, an American toymaker produced a series of dolls, the Cabbage Patch Kids, that could not simply be bought to be played with: they had to be 'adopted'. With every Cabbage Patch Kid came an adoption certificate with a name and date of 'birth'. The child now had full responsibility for the doll: had to feed it, clothe it, make sure it slept and played, keep it from danger. It was even rumoured that, if the doll took sick and died, or suffered from an accident, fell in the fire or was mangled by a dog, the makers would send the child a toy coffin in which the doll could be decently buried, and a death certificate would duly be issued.

If you can grant a doll life, you can also grant it death.

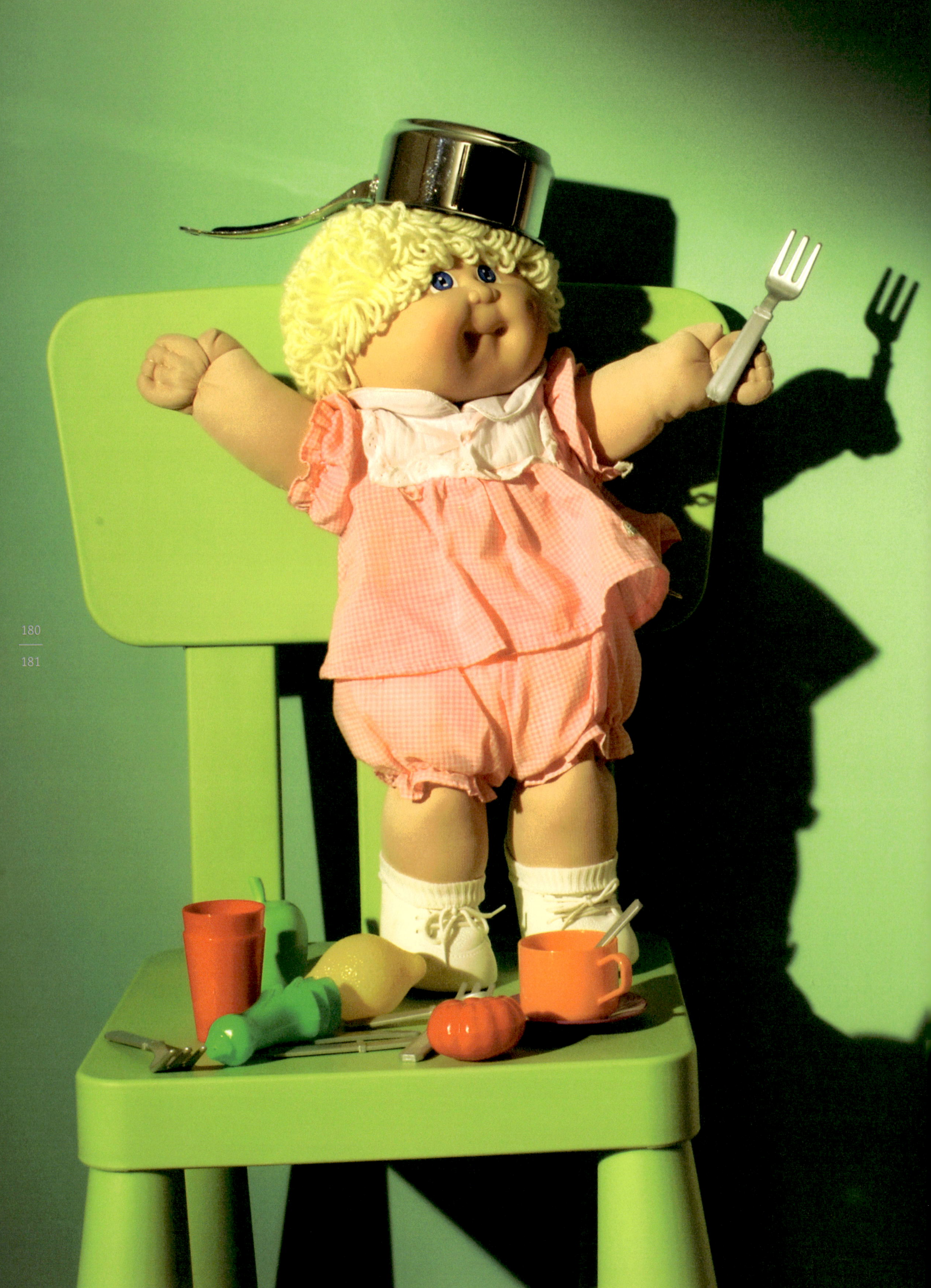
180
181

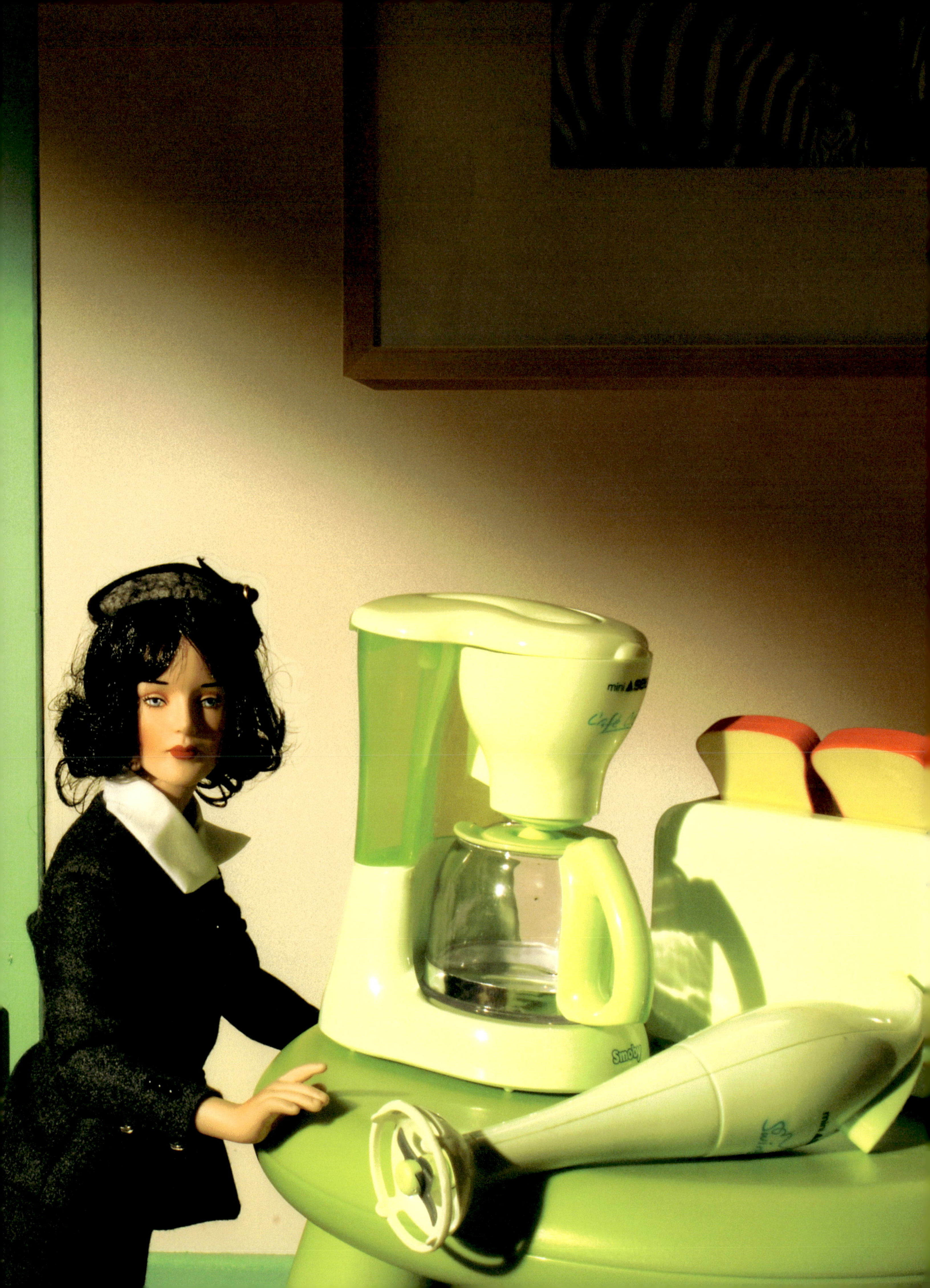

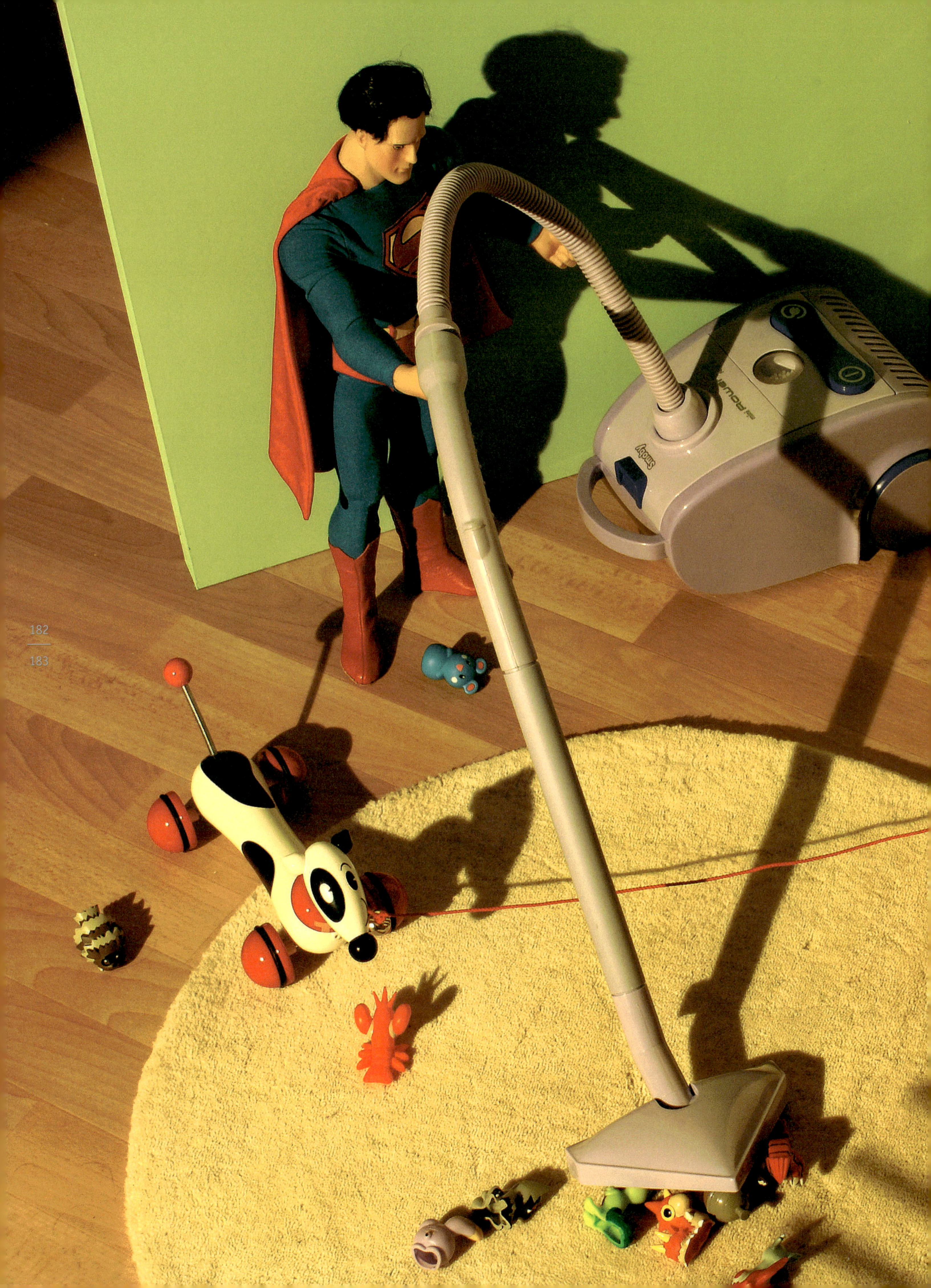

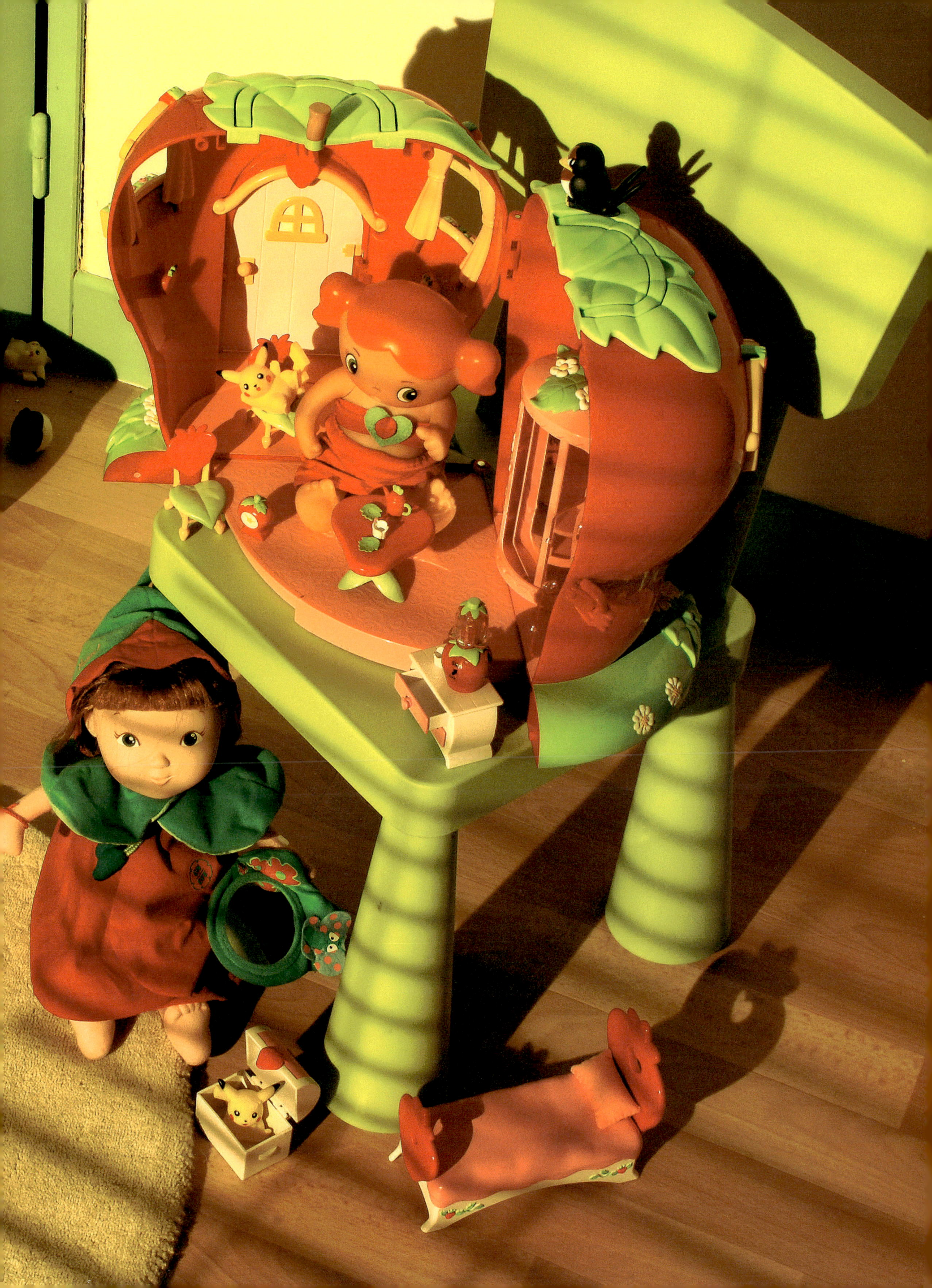

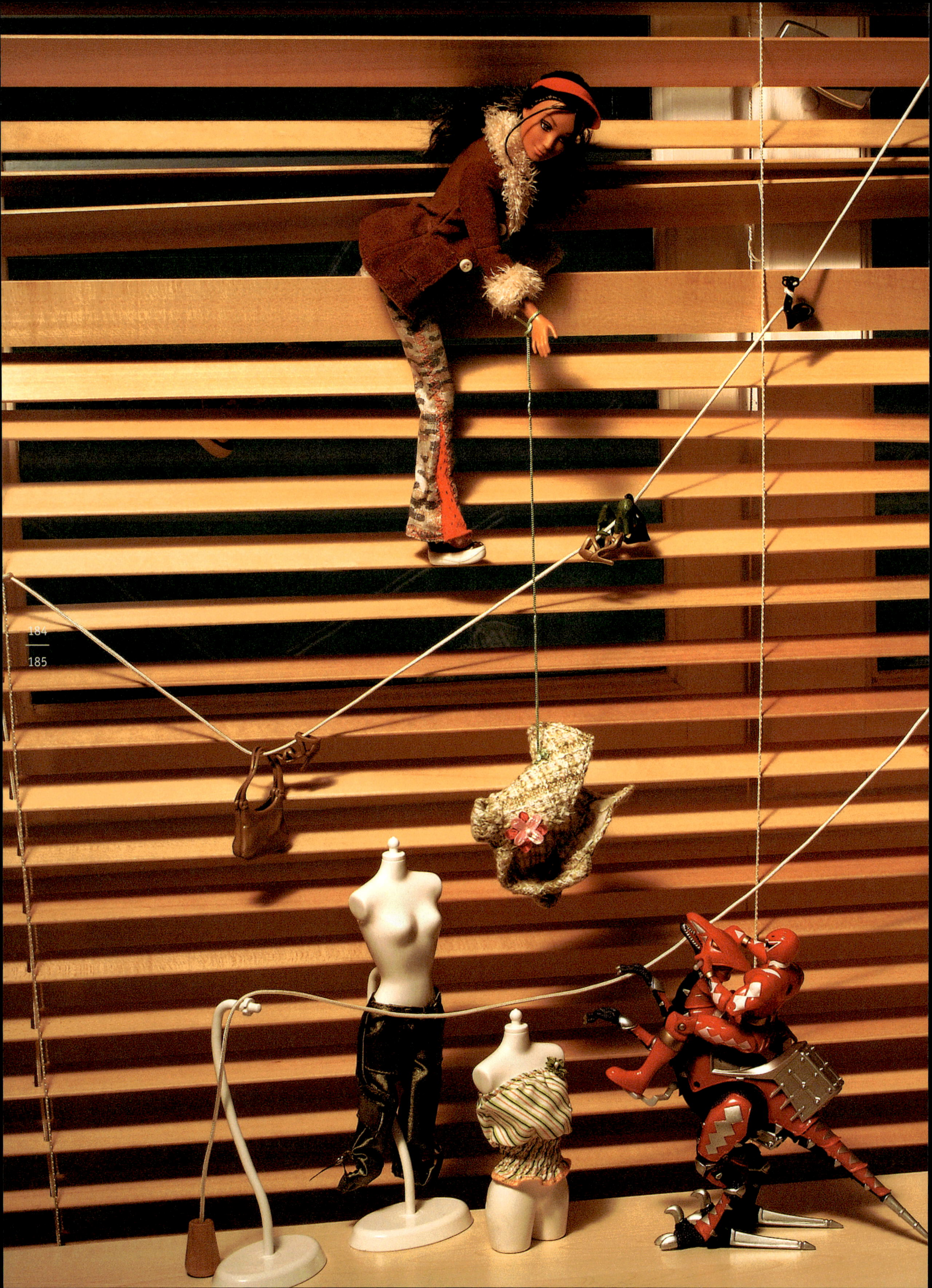
184
185

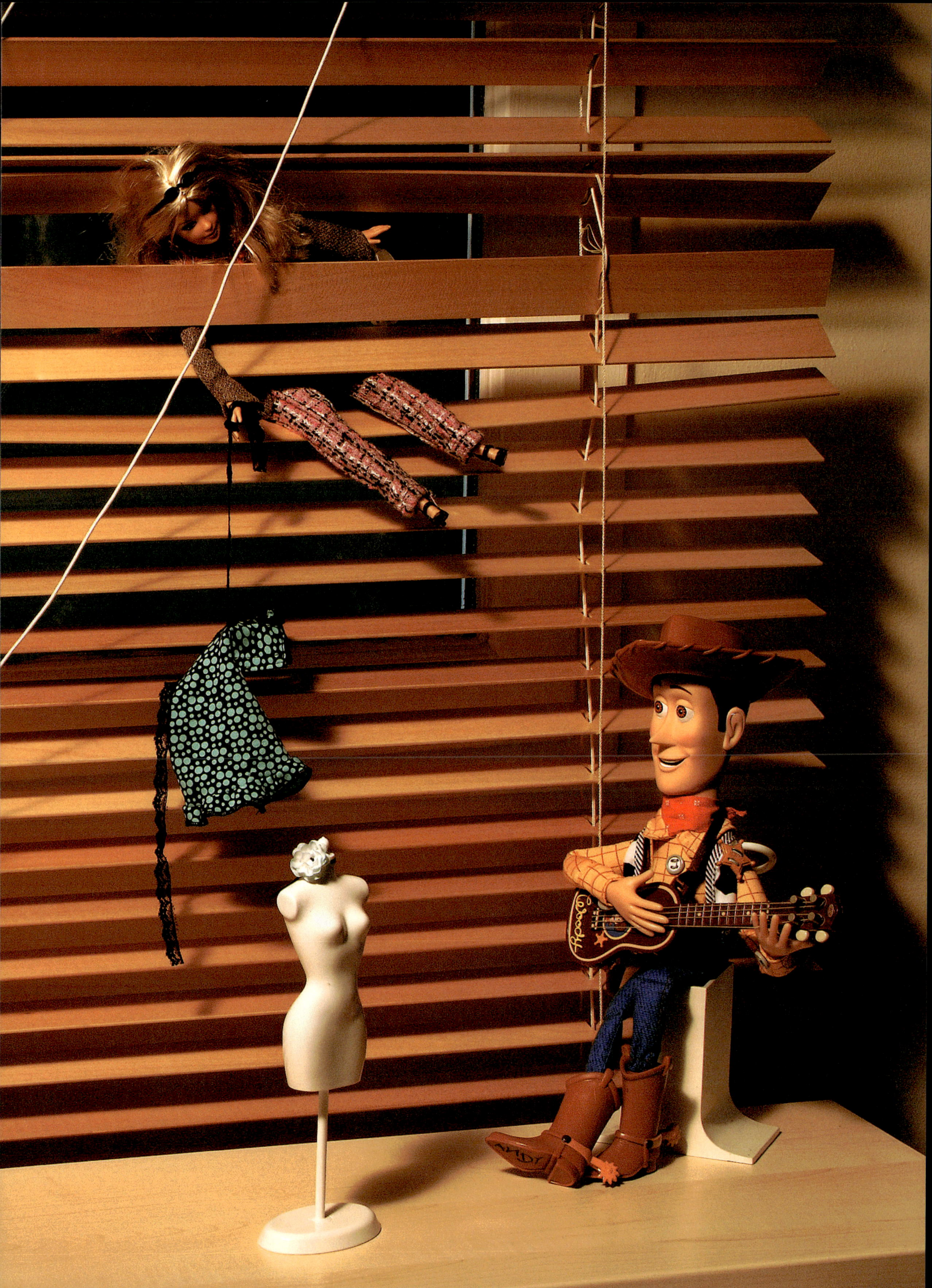

oys have shape, volume, colour. They also have voices. Toys bang, whirr, whistle, clang, sing or talk. The sounds they make fill the world of the child with an oral presence. Not only the parents speak, not only the child cries or gurgles. The things that fill this world have voices also. One of the earliest toys is the rattle, a hollow ball or ring filled with pellets or seeds, that makes a sound when shaken by its handle. Rattles are very ancient toys. Aristotle, in the last book of his *Politics*, praises the rattle as 'an excellent invention to keep children occupied; they cannot be expected to remain still, and playing with this toy keeps them from smashing things about the house. Of course,' Aristotle adds sagely, 'a rattle is only suitable for small children. For older ones, education is their rattle.'

Before audiovisual games and screens that respond out loud to the child's questions, there were musical boxes and talking dolls, dogs that barked and clowns that giggled. Pull a cord, turn a key, and the toy comes to life with sounds that carry meaning. Dolls began by saying 'Hello,' 'Will you play with me?', 'I love you.' Later, toy soldiers too were given their voice: 'Fight with me,' 'You're brave,' 'Attack!'. Toys speak with conventional lines. There are no surprises here.

Sometime in the eighties, a group of feminist activists purchased a number of talking Barbie dolls and G.I. Joes from a well-known toy store, exchanged their sound boxes and returned them a few days later. Customers who then bought the doctored toys found that when their children activated the doll's voices, G.I. Joe would whine in girlish tones, 'I want to go shopping!', while Barbie growled ferociously 'Kill! Kill! Kill!'

t is through use that a child grants toys life. Play gives them movement, motive, personality. Toys become that which they are made to do. A doll can be a nurse, a mother, a fireman, a child. Uniforms help but are not all. Place a teddy bear in a circus ring or at a table, inside a train or in a bed, and his character changes.

Some uses are prescribed; others invented. Trademark toys, for instance, have acquired a life of their own before they come into the child's hands. The Ninja Turtles, E.T. or the Teletubbies belong to the marketplace before they belong to any individual child. The anonymous toy, discovered on the shelf of a shop, is an uncharted space; it begins with the child's seeing it. The trademark toy, on the other hand, has a televised, advertised history that establishes its identity in a story, a film, a video game. It already is before it is the child's.

And yet, in time, a toy tends to lose its trademark identity. A hundred years ago, a Bécassine doll in its Breton costume carried within it all the contradictions of its creation, an emblem of both its prejudiced nature and its rebellious quality, of the conventional view of Brittany as well as its independent spirit. So strong was its symbolic power that, as late as 1940, during the occupation of France, barely forty-eight hours after entering Paris, the German authorities banned its image in public displays. Today Bécassine survives partly as local colour, partly as harmless nostalgia, another doll among the dolls.

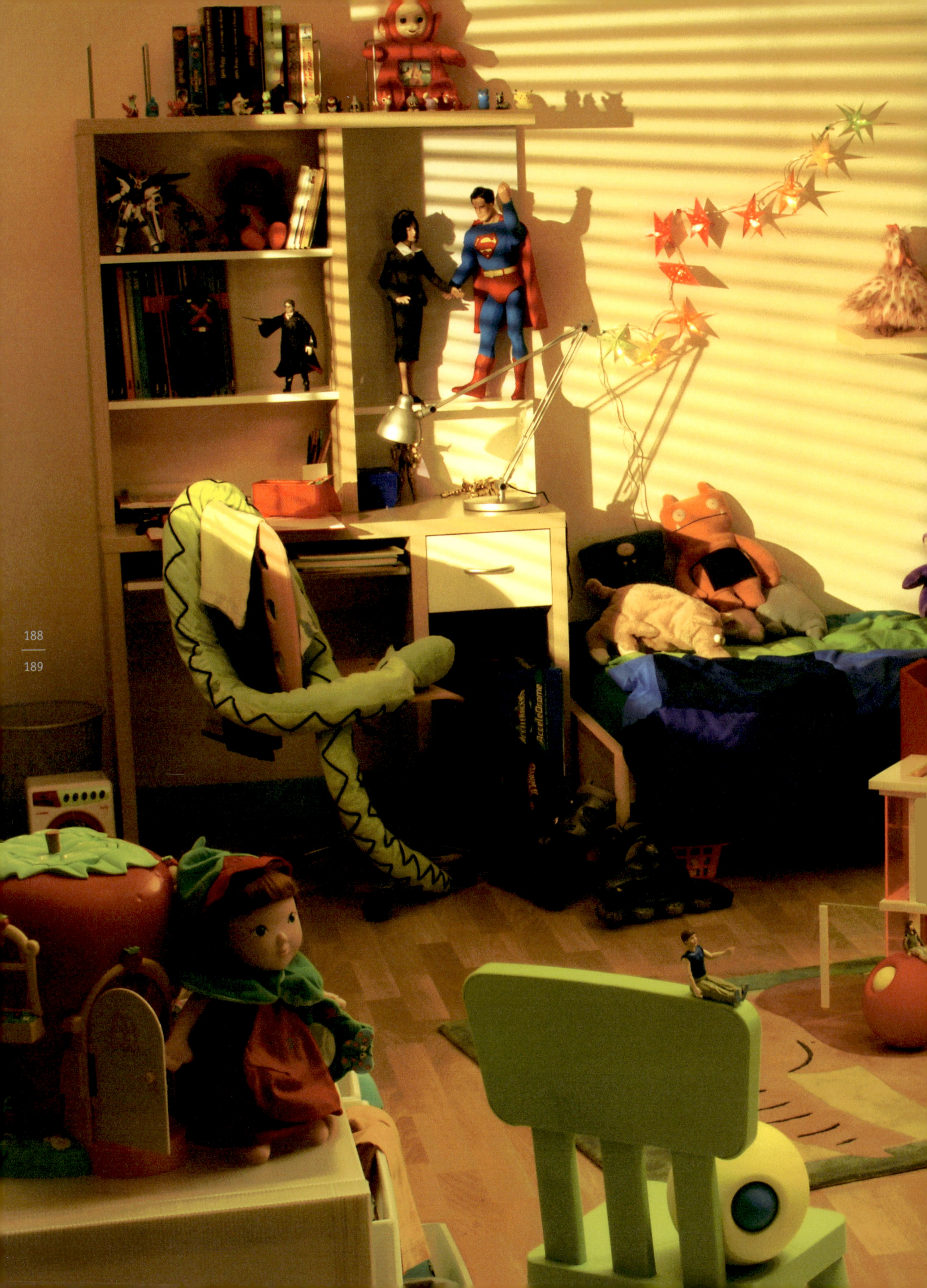

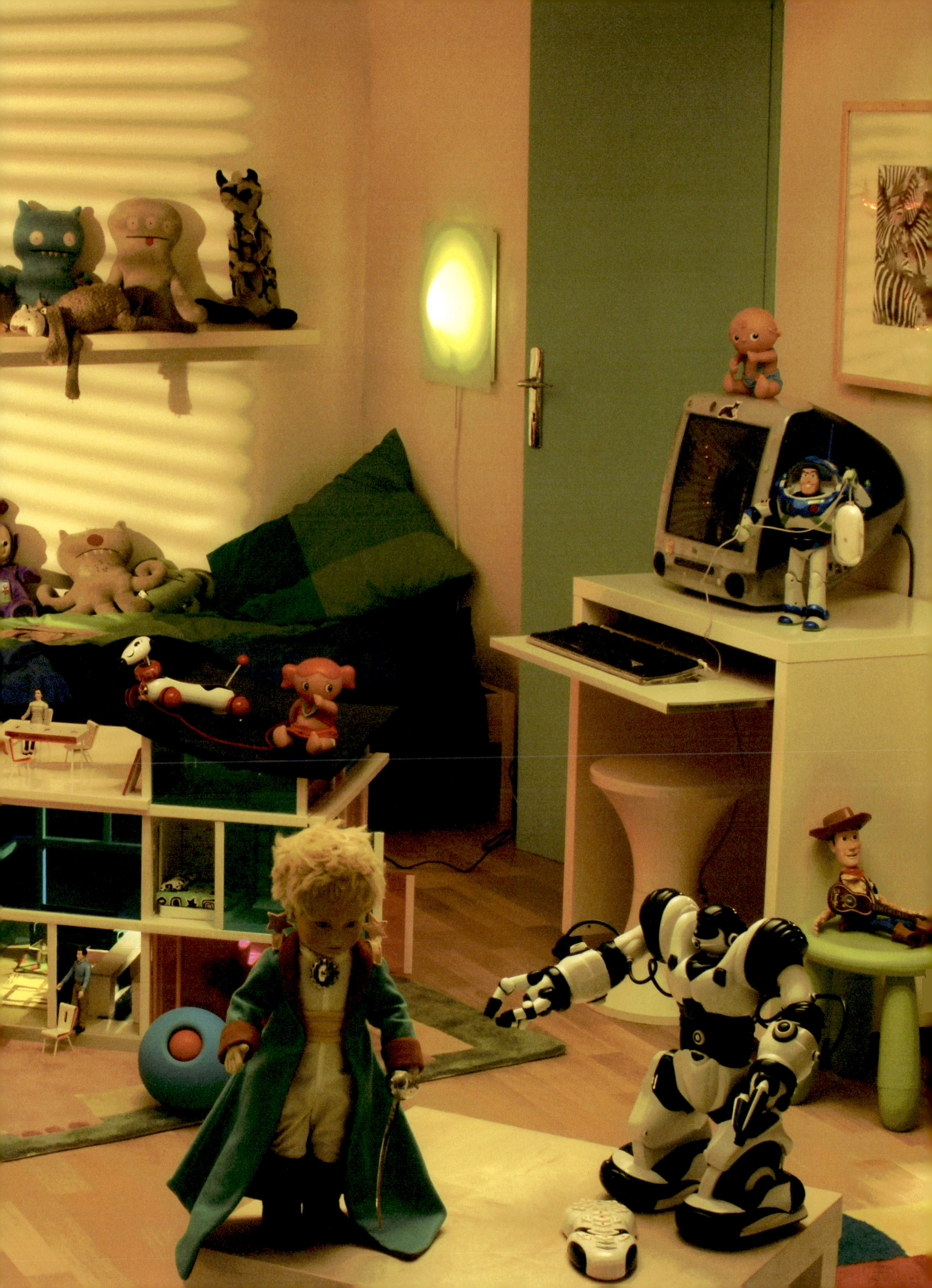

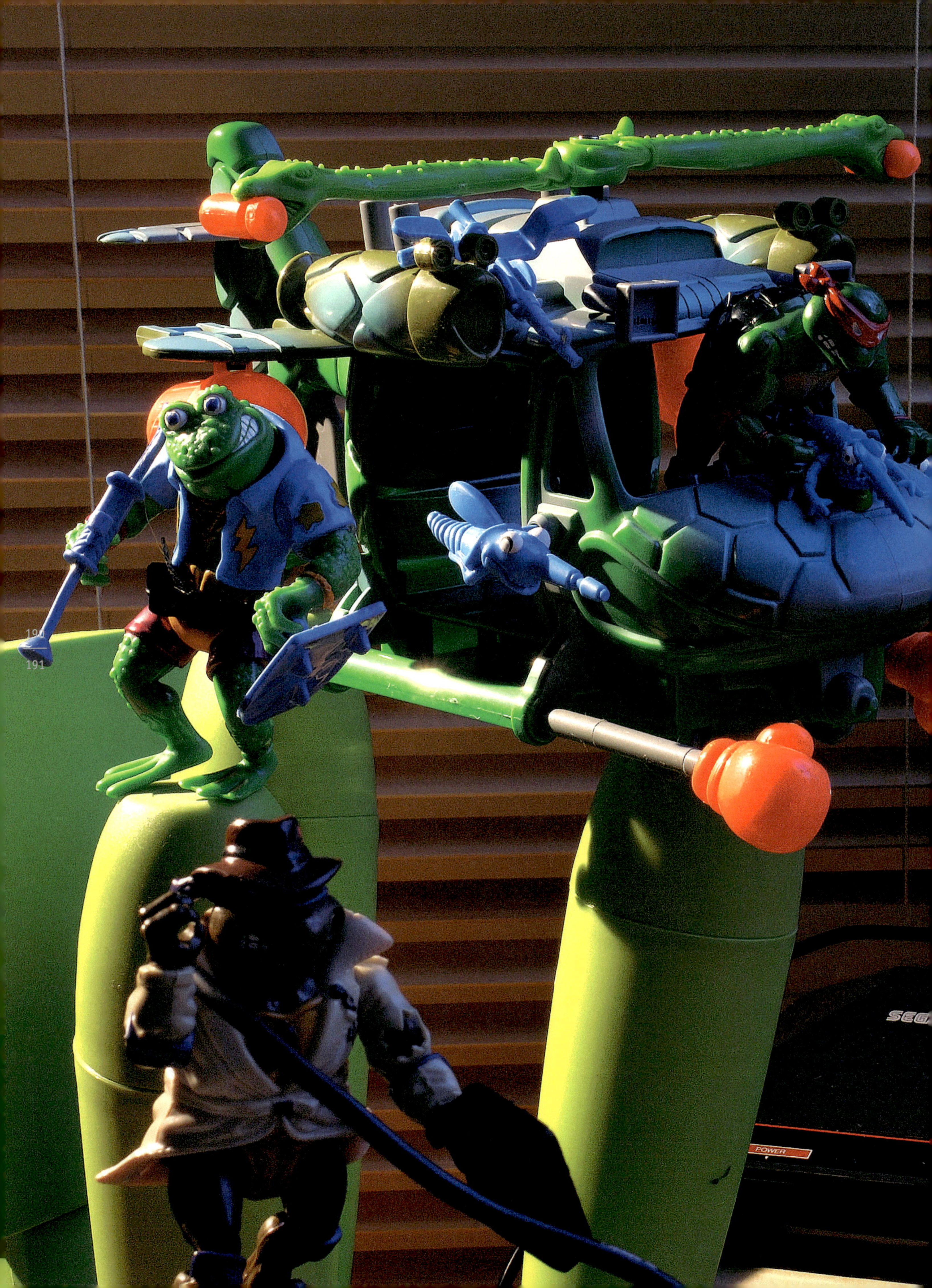
SEGA
POWER

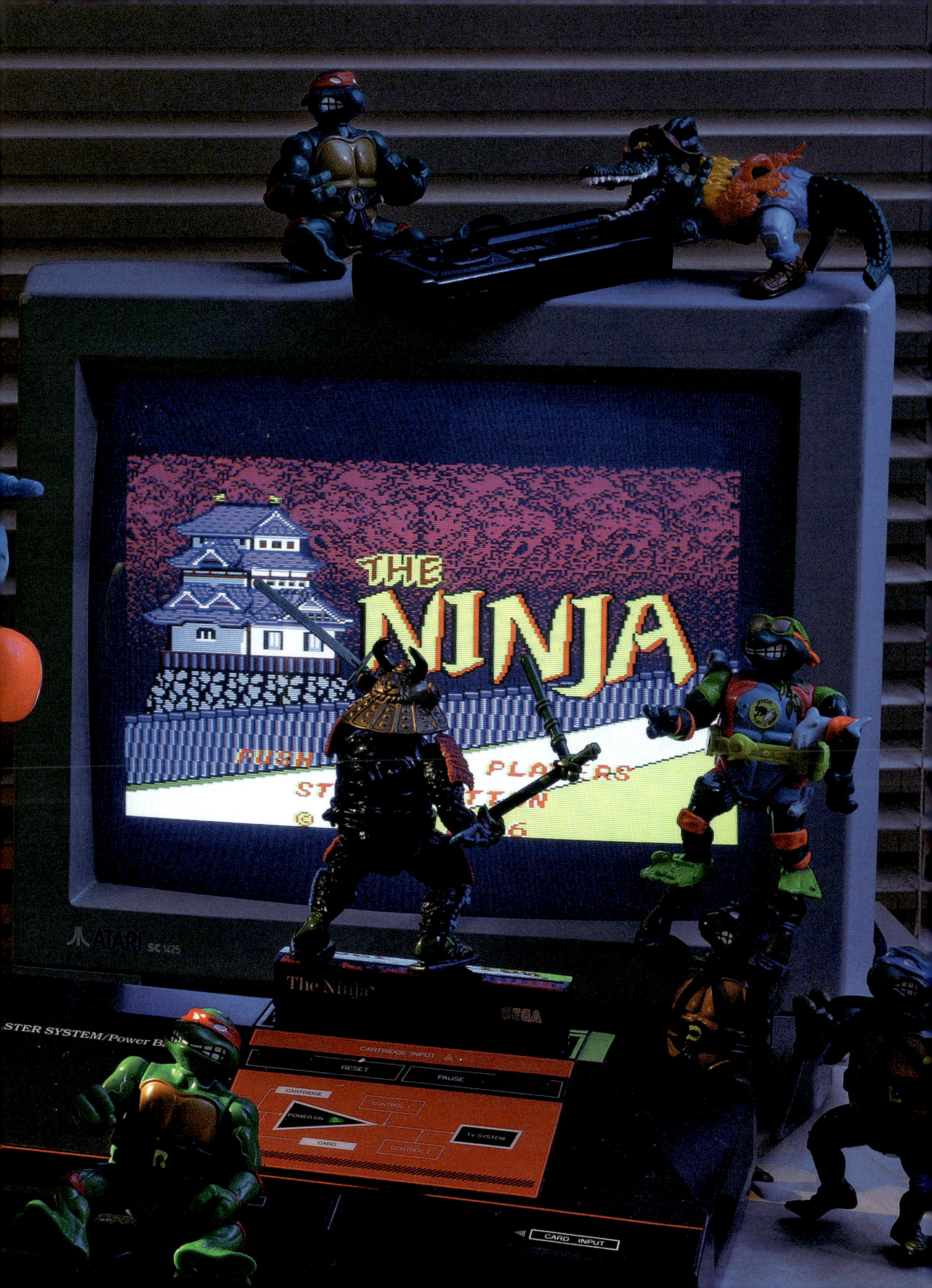

THE NINJA
PUSH   PLAYERS
ST   TT
6
ATARI SC 1425
The Ninja
SEGA
STER SYSTEM/Power B
CARTRIDGE INPUT
RESET   PAUSE
CARTRIDGE
POWER ON   CONTROL 1
CARD   CONTROL 2   TV SYSTEM
CARD INPUT

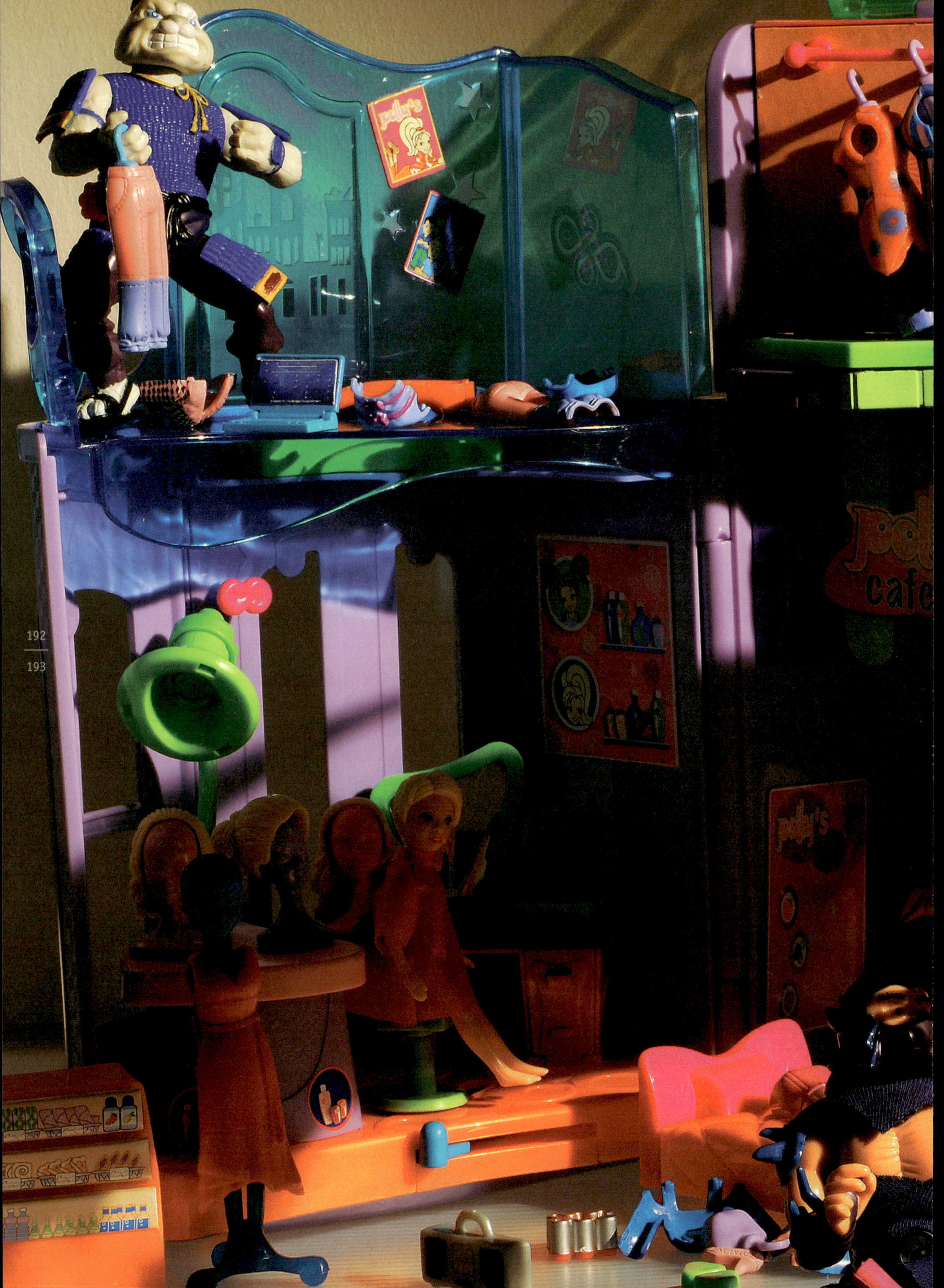

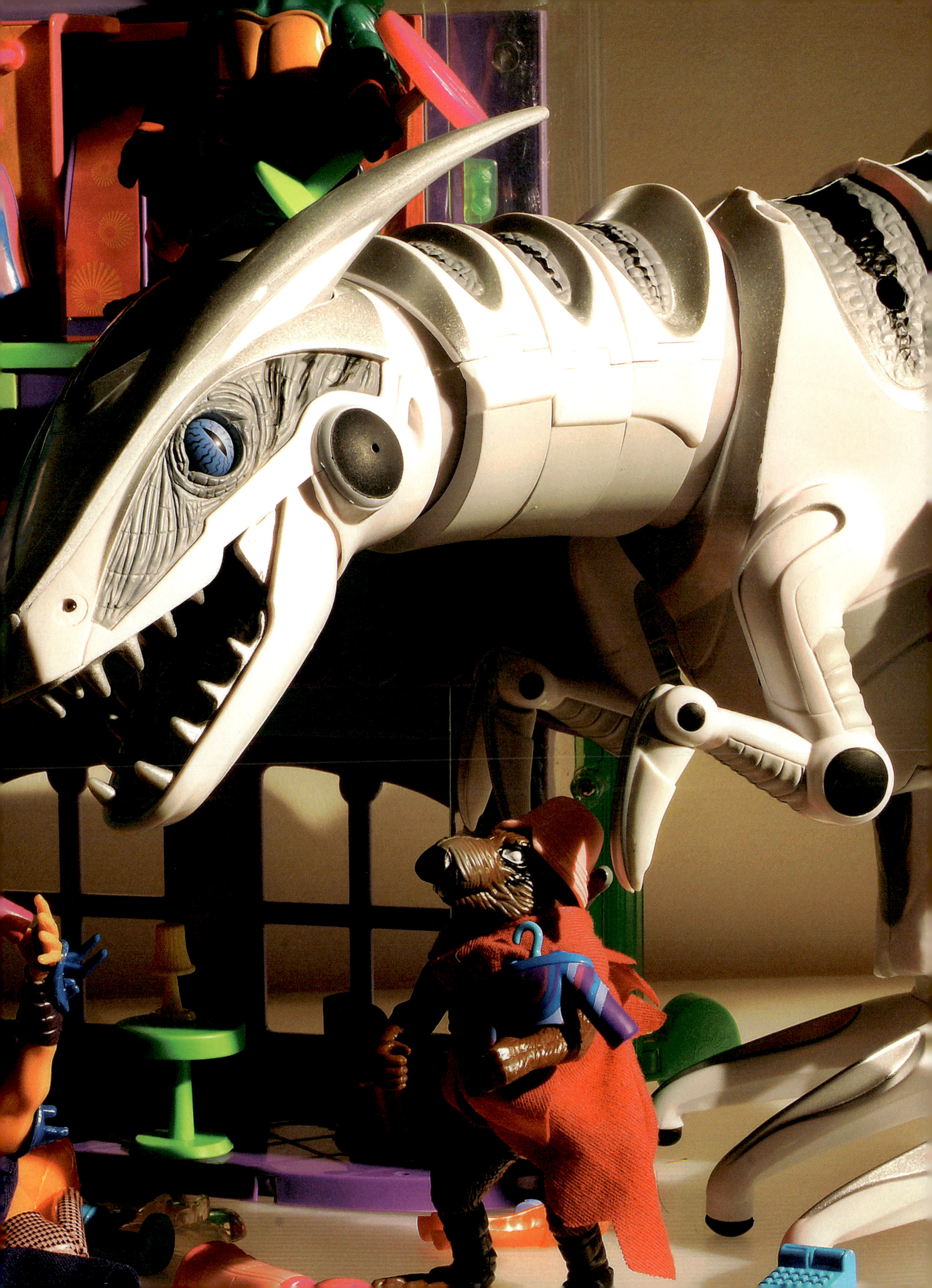

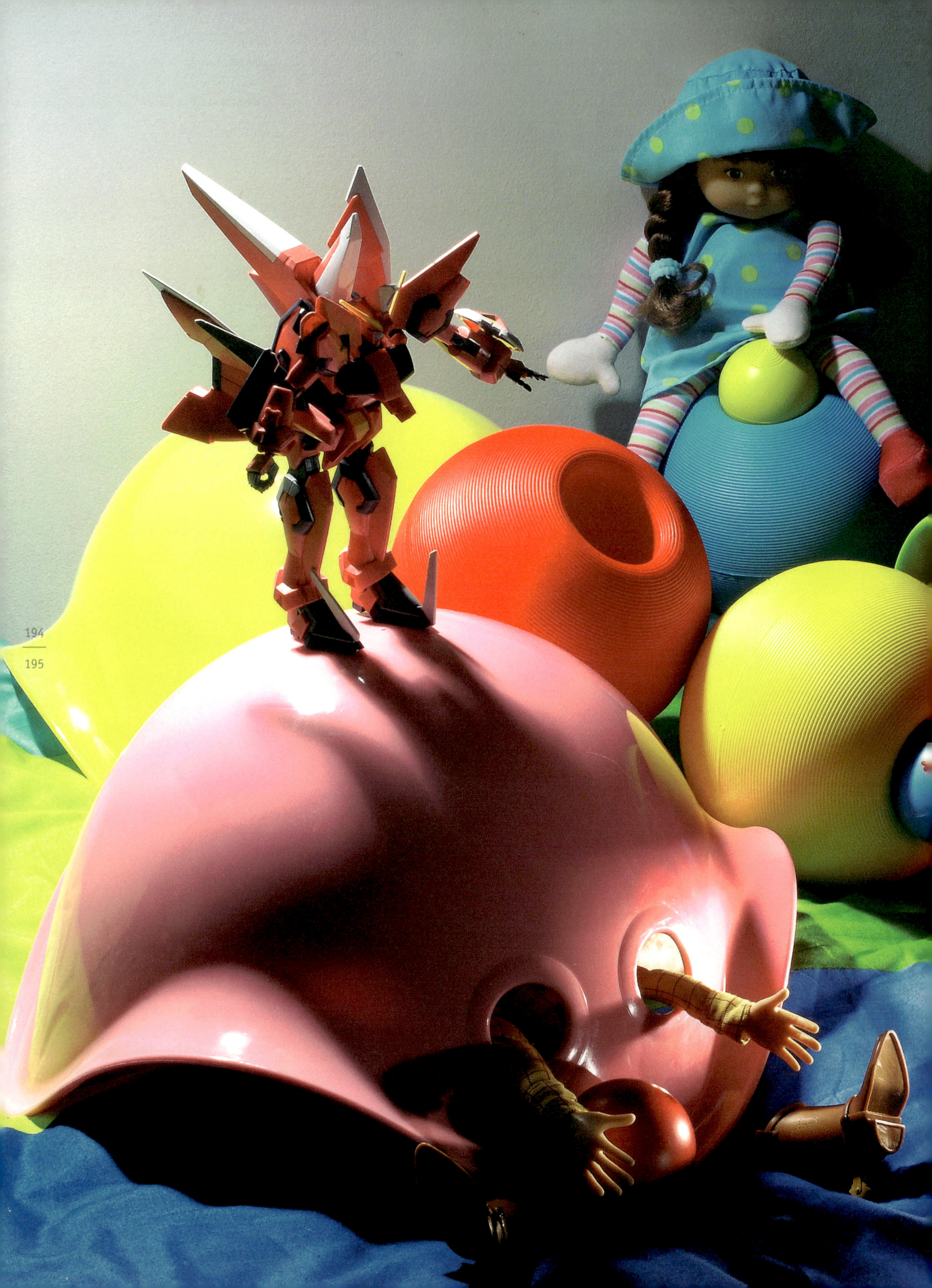

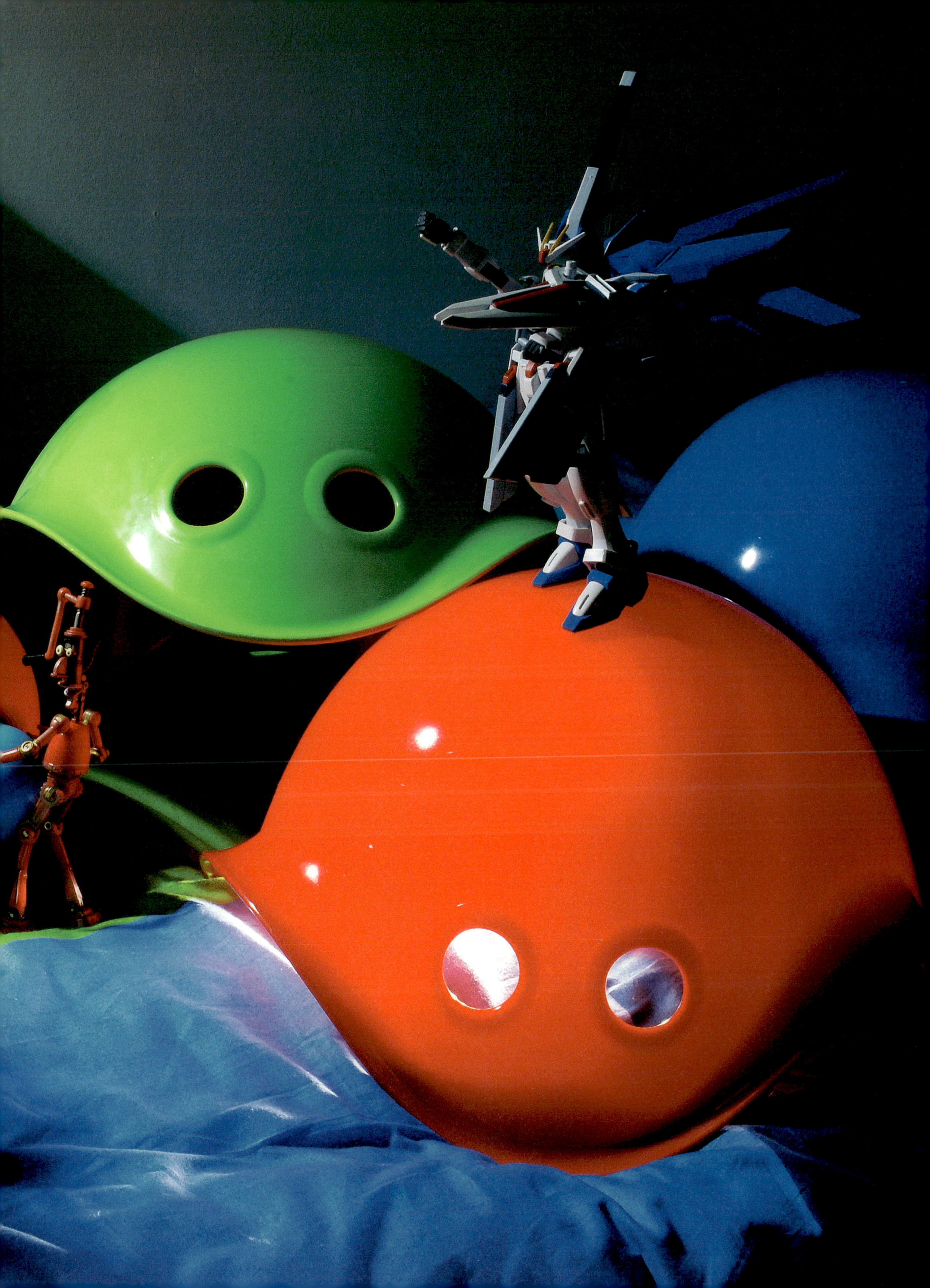

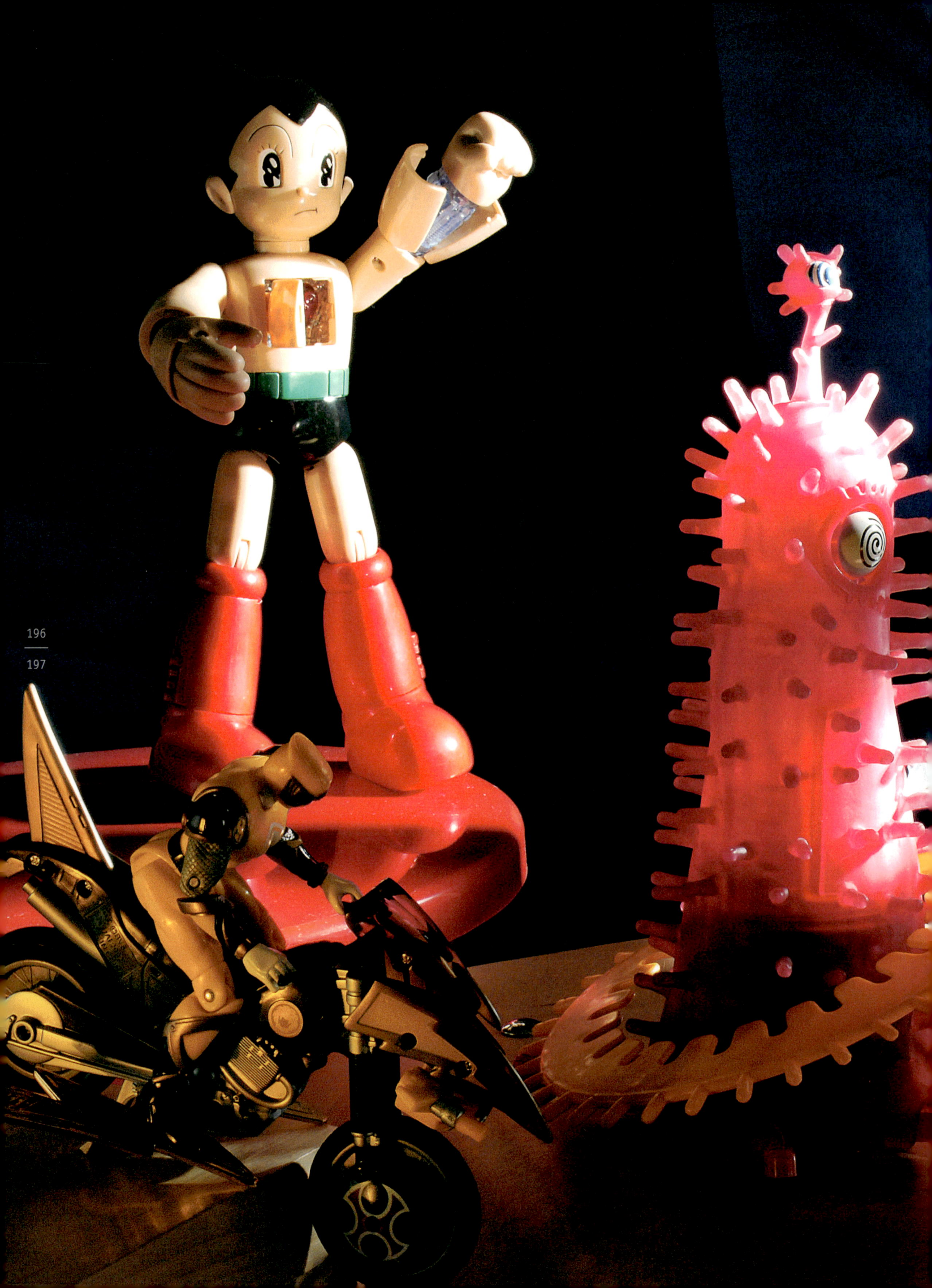
196
197

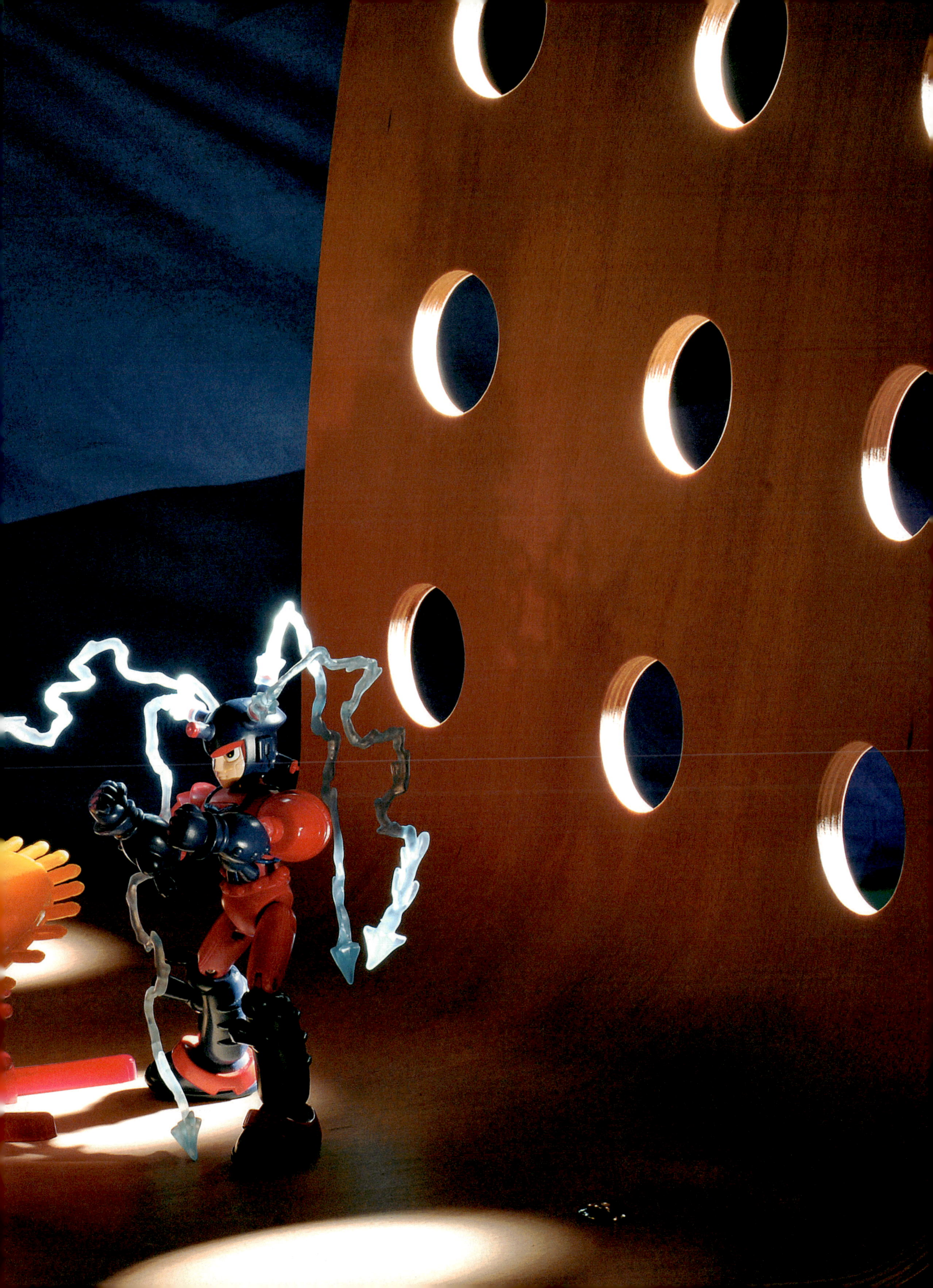

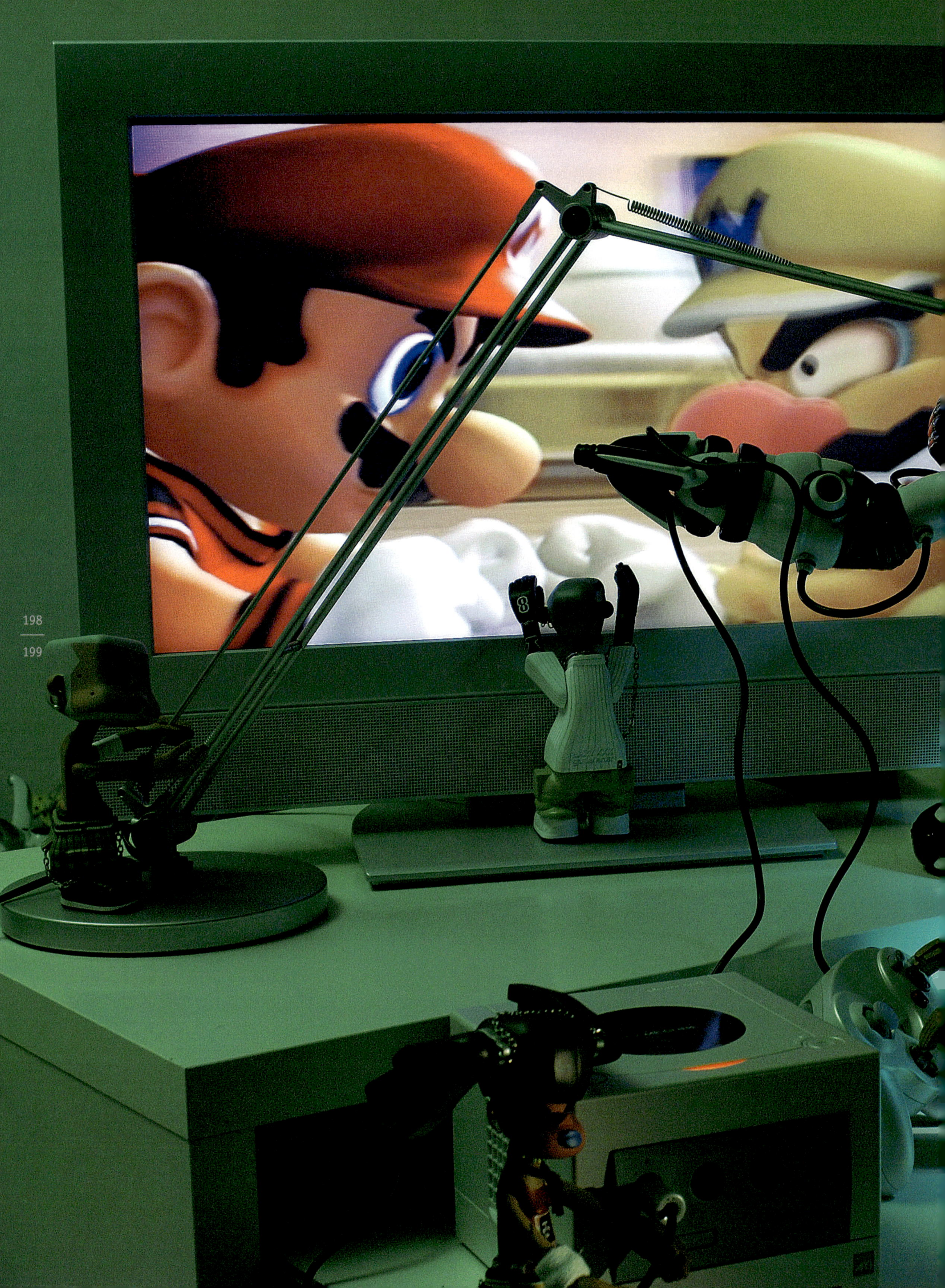

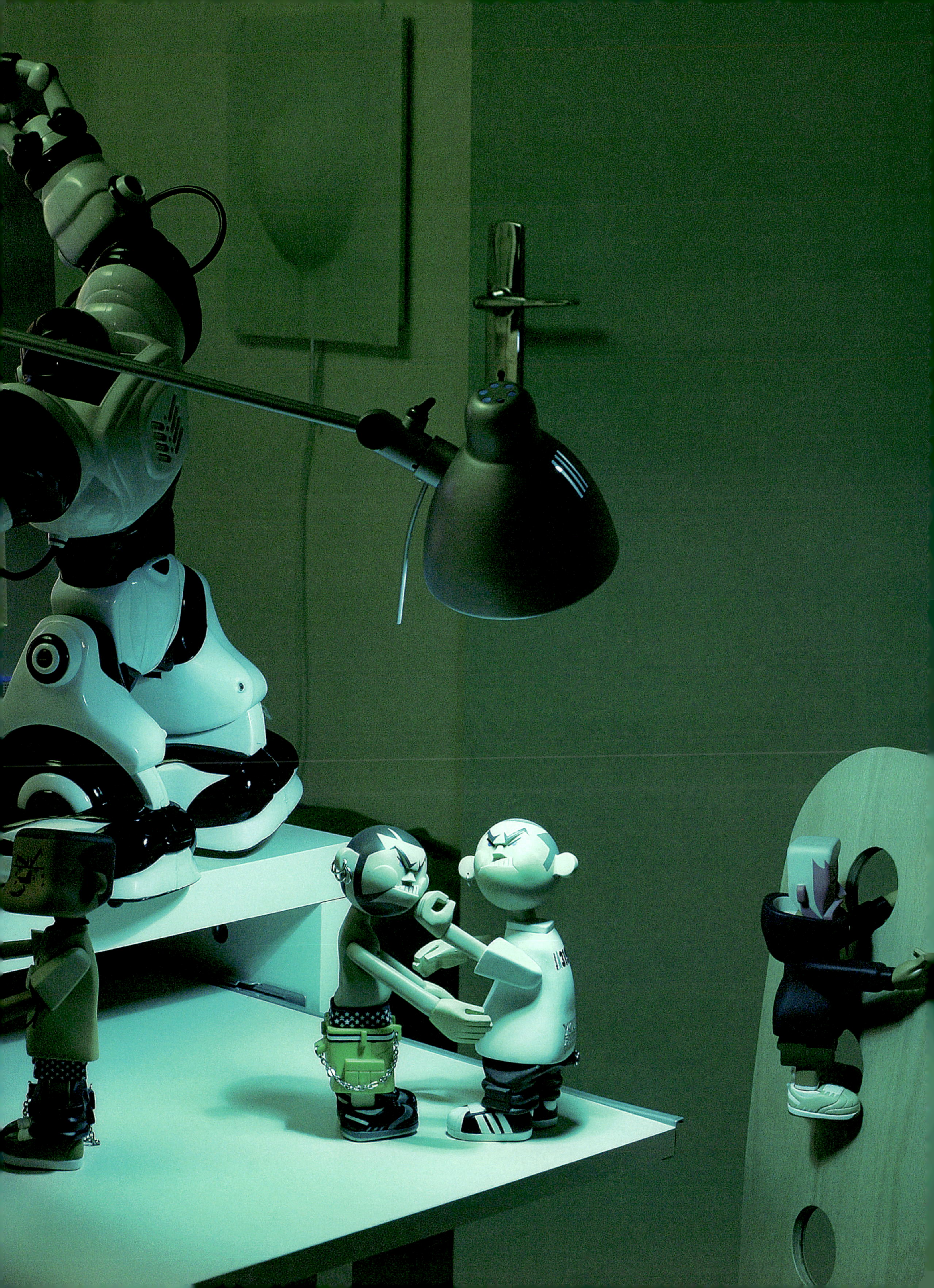

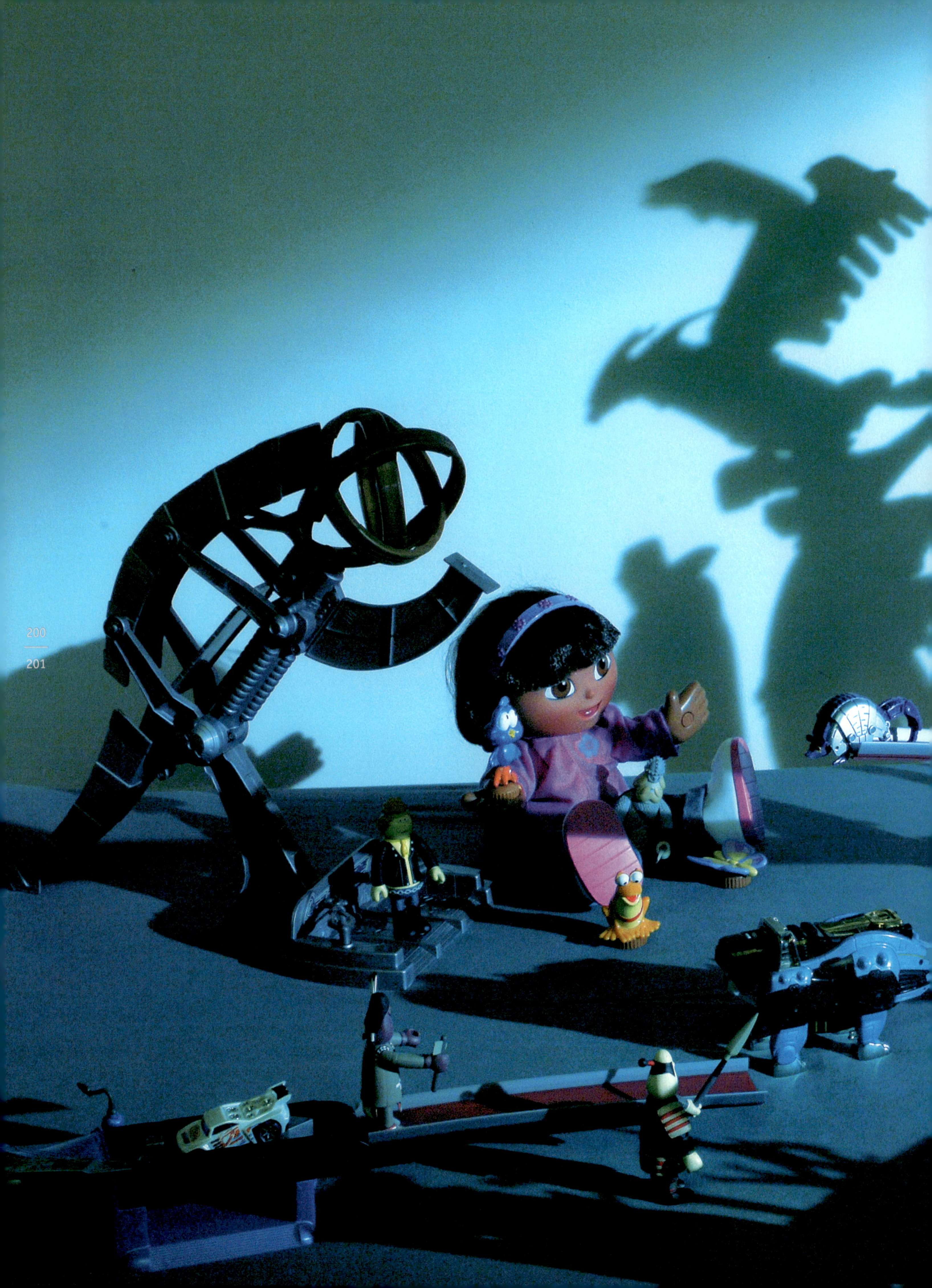

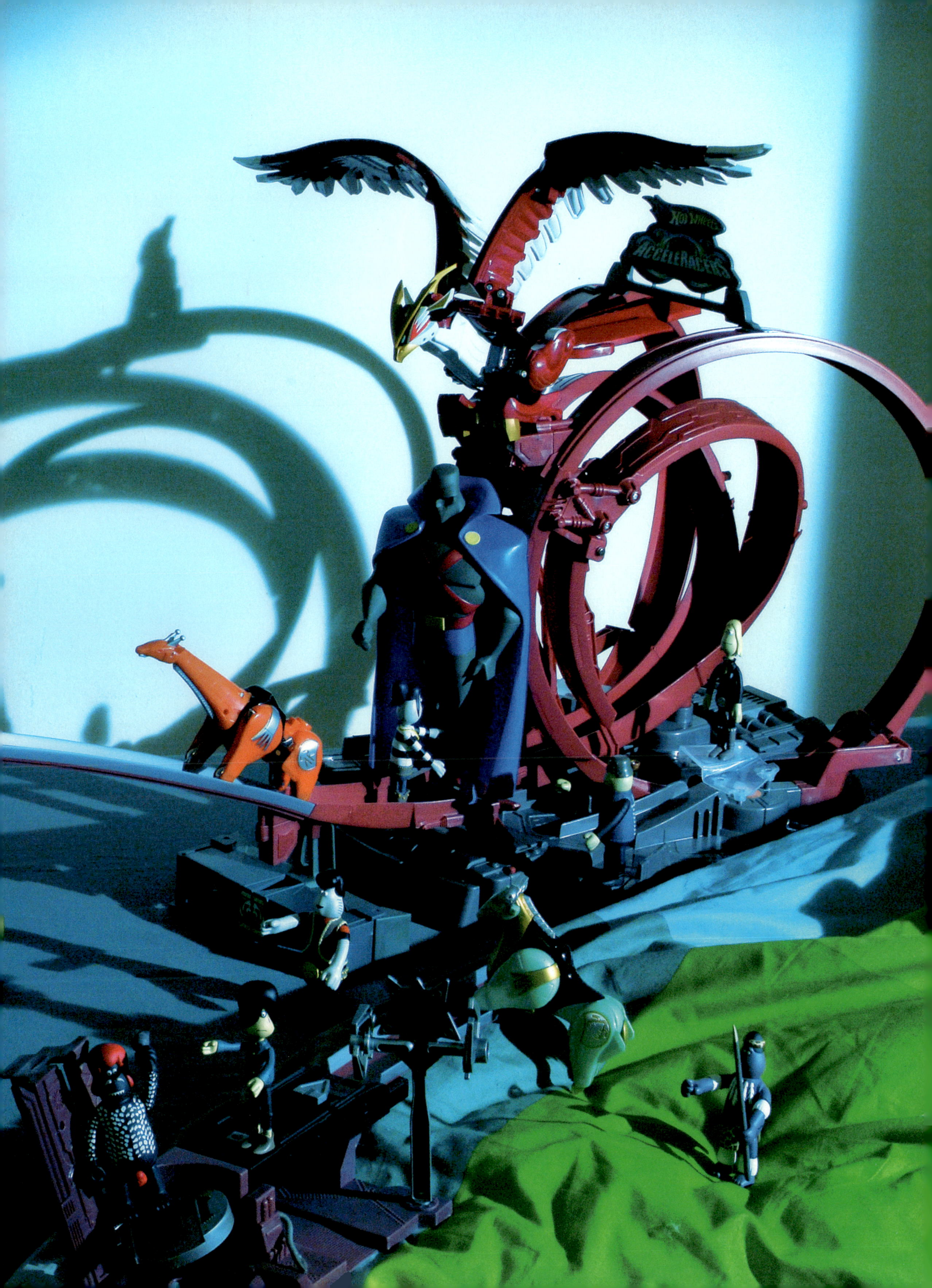
HOT WHEELS
ACCELERACERS

re masks toys? We know that they allow us to be what we are not, or what we are in secret, in the dark. We know that they make us larger or more savage, give us permission to be mad, transform us into something else, something we recognize only in our dreams. Masks make us doubles, grant us a parallel life, superimpose a identity on the one we show to the world.

But are they toys?

In ancient Greece, masks not only represented a god or a person: they *were* that god or that person's incarnation, and were treated as such by the actors. After a performance, the mask was ceremonially dedicated to the god it was supposed to symbolize and left in the theatre. The god's 'otherness' was not supposed to be carried into the outside world, where it might wreak havoc.

Masks continue to be faces even when no one is wearing them. They grin or grimace, show us their teeth or boast of a big red nose, try to frighten or amuse us as they hang on their hooks, waiting for a person of flesh and blood to put them on. Whoever wears a mask feels that he is not truly responsible for his actions; that even though the hands that pull it over the face and the eyes that peer through the slits are his own, the performance is someone else's; that he is not the master of the game. If masks are toys, they are toys that cannot be owned.

Masks toy with us.

he heroes of literature lack toys. Their childhood is told with no reference to a ball, a stuffed animal, a tin car. The young Charles Bovary spends his days reading history notebooks and the *Anacharsis*; the young Marcel Proust enjoys stories and the pictures of his magic lantern; Oliver Twist and David Copperfield have no playthings to speak of, and neither do Tom Sawyer and Huckleberry Finn; the boy Genji is taught manners but not games; Kim plays with other children but not with toys; Poil de Carotte's companions are chickens and dogs; Alice's is a kitten; Cosette is not allowed to play at all. Evelyn Waugh's Sebastian in *Brideshead Revisited* famously carries with him his childhood teddy and Mrs Ramsay's little boy finds consolation in 'a pocket knife with six blades' for not going to the lighthouse, but by and large, the holdings of the literary nursery are very thin. And yet they must have had some kind of secret familiar, some charm or trinket to ward off the miseries and fears of childhood. Where are Julien Sorel's wooden sword, Nana's dolls made by Mademoiselle Remanjou, Tom Jones's hobby-horse?

The nineteenth-century poet Coventry Patmore likened the consolation his son found in his toys, after being punished, to what he himself hoped for in his last hour, and listed the objects the sleeping boy had laid out by his bedside:

A box of counters and a red-veined stone,
A piece of glass abraded by the beach
And six or seven shells,
A bottle with bluebells
And two French copper coins, ranged there with careful art,
To comfort his sad heart.

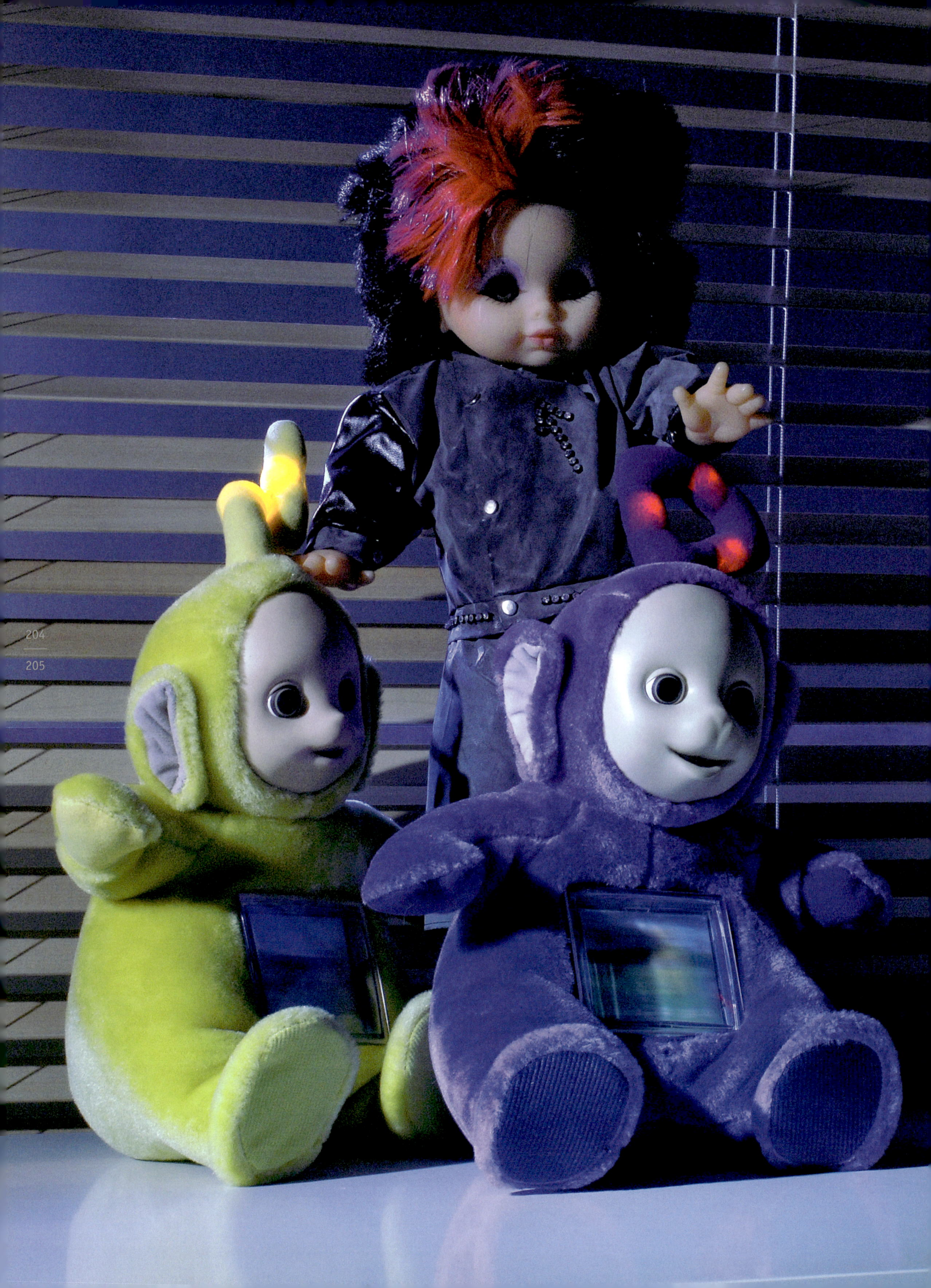

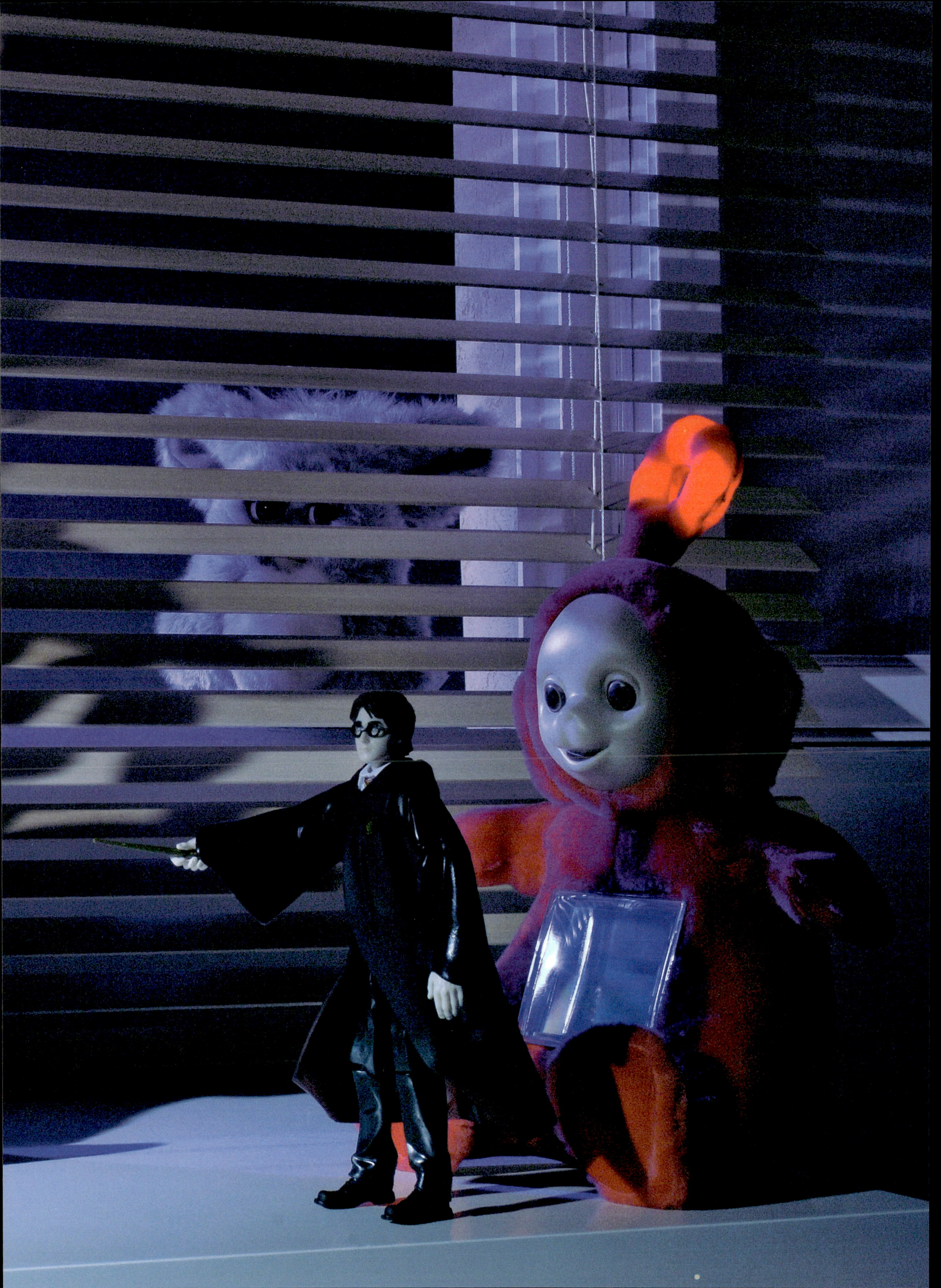

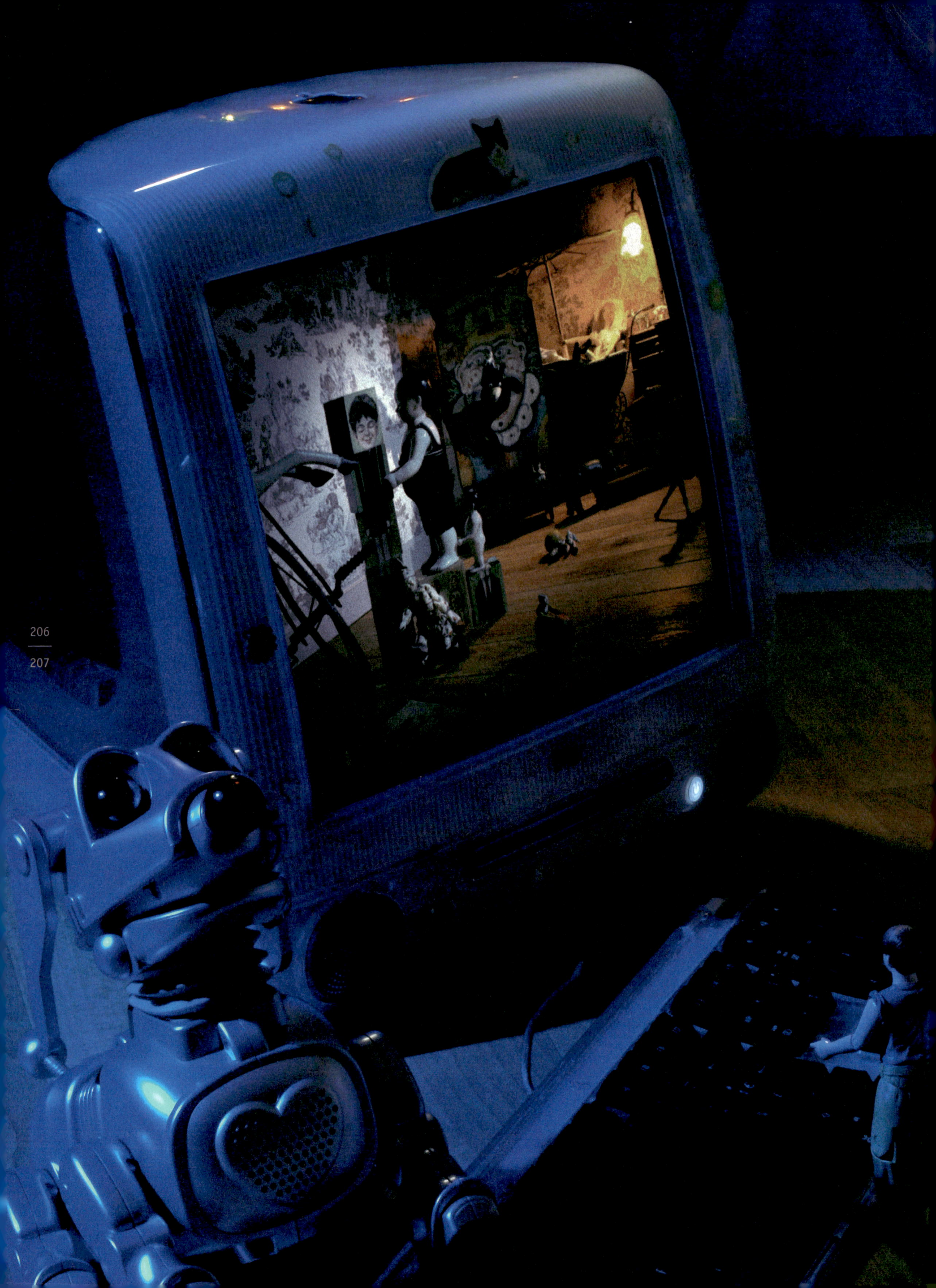

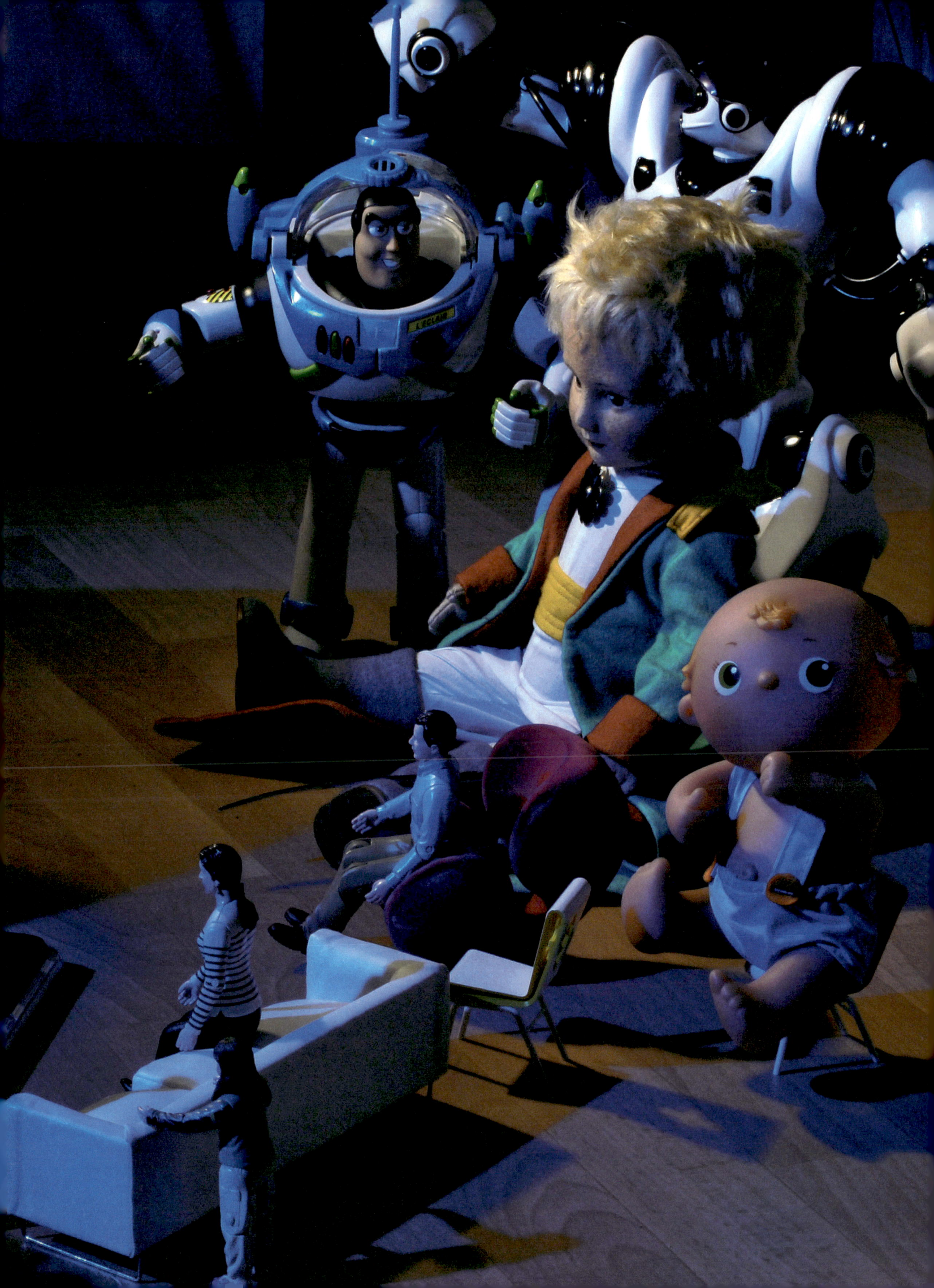

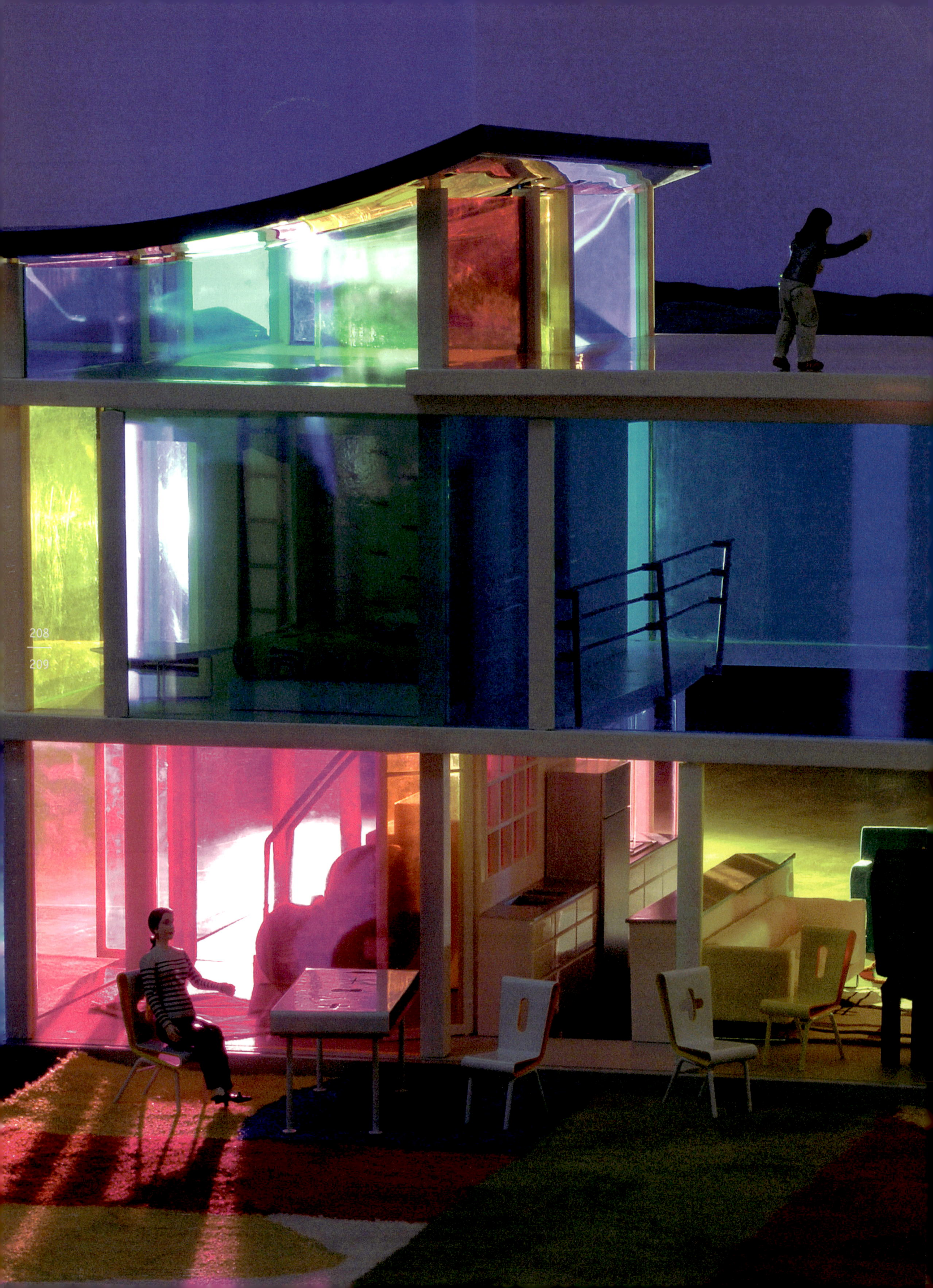

208
209

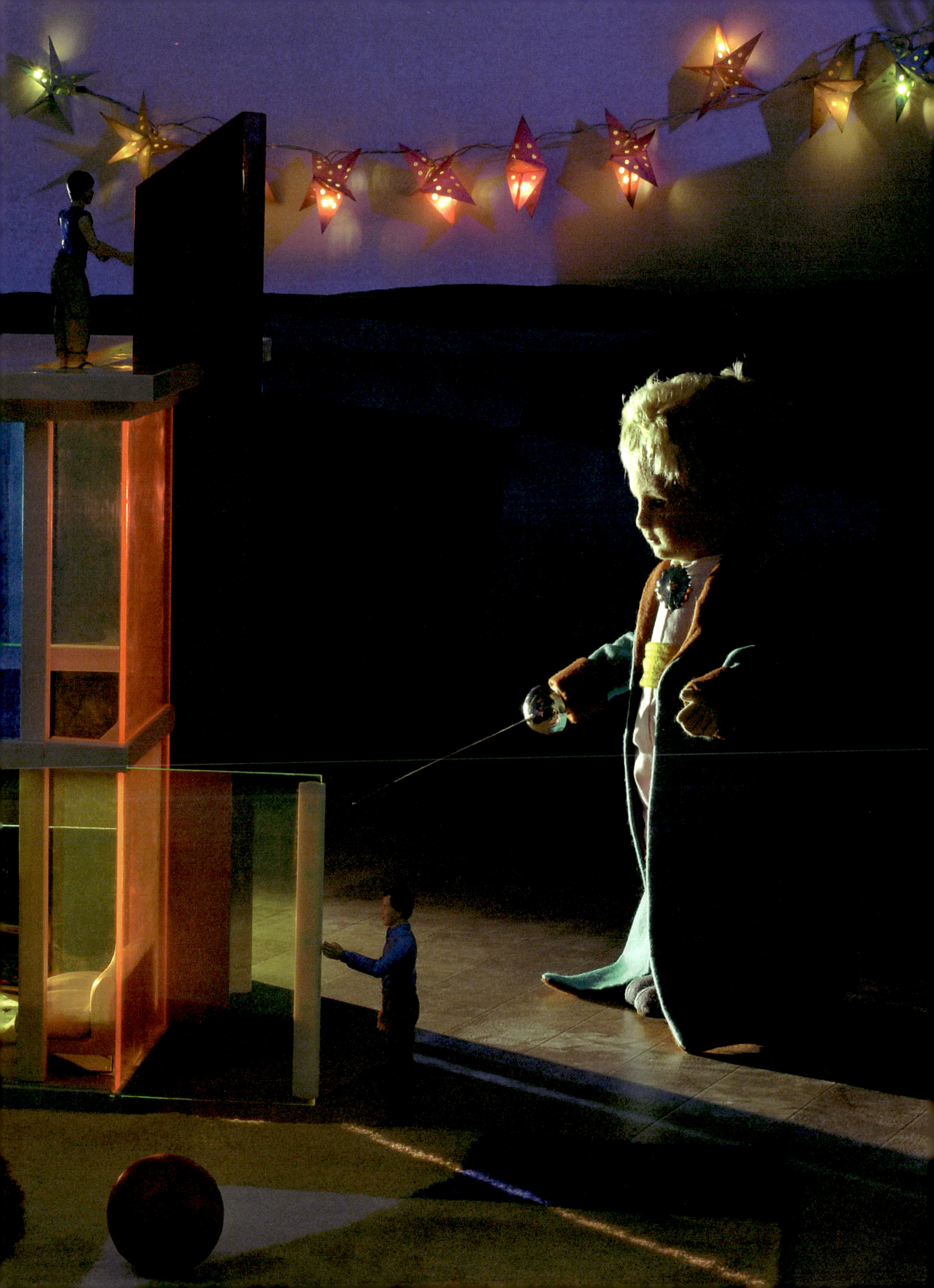

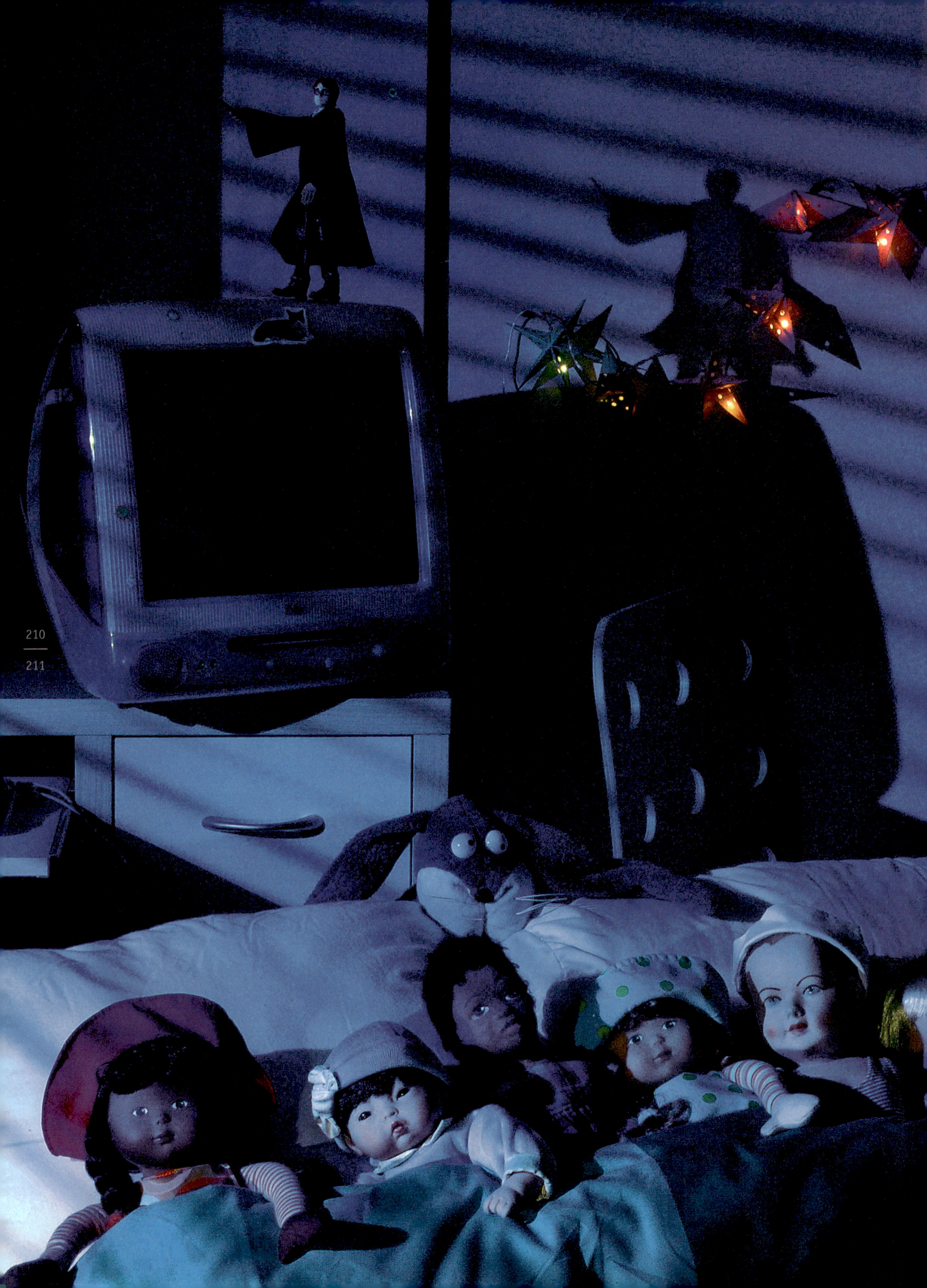

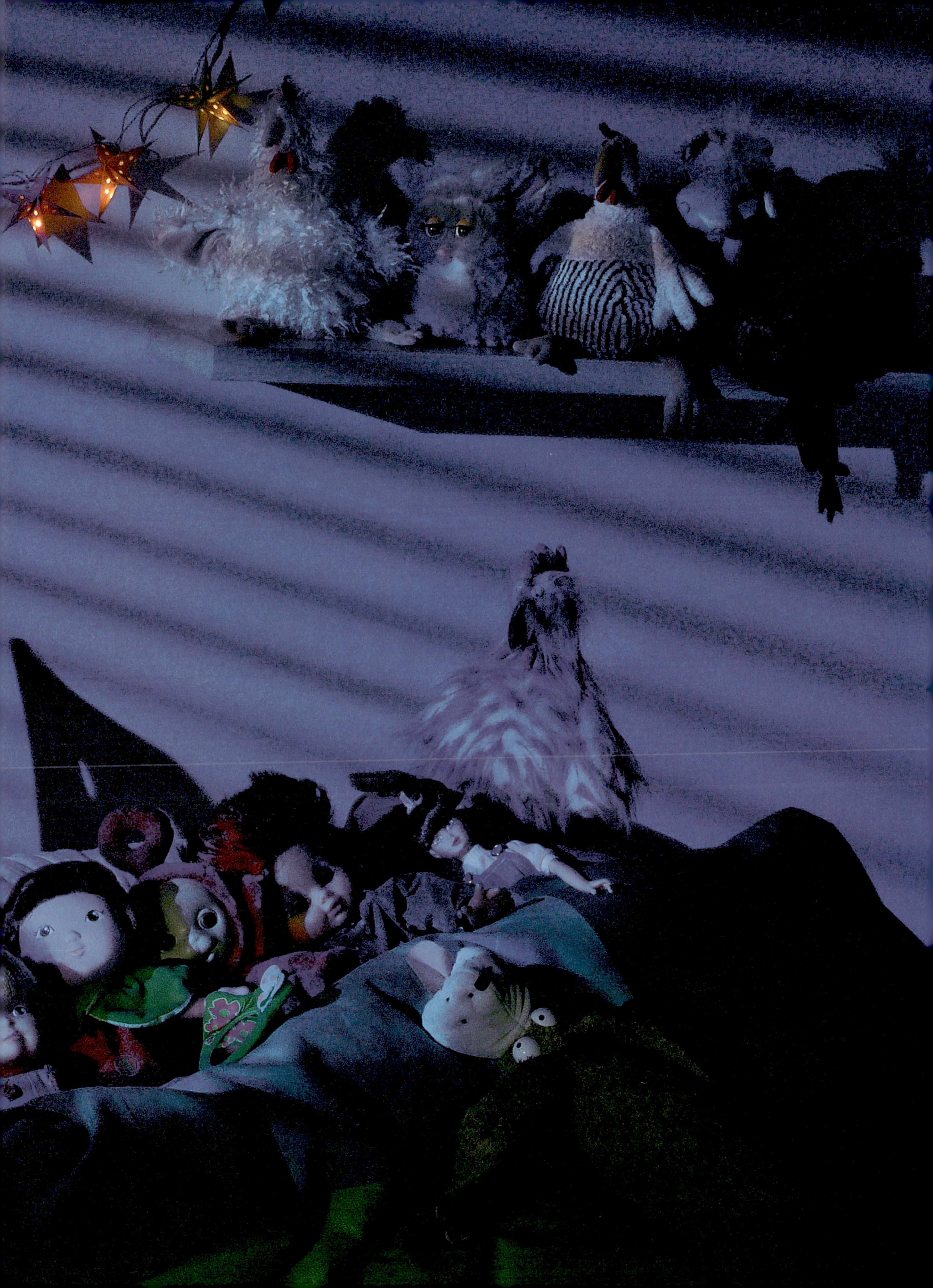

The toy collection of the
Musée des Arts Décoratifs, Paris

1,274 dolls, 275 doll's accessories, 44 doll's houses and kitchens, 458 pieces of furniture, 180 tea sets, 1,474 wooden or stuffed animals, 1,879 early-learning games and toys, 144 circuses and clowns, 27 Noah's Arks, 229 soldiers and tanks, 1,205 figurines, 571 cars, 167 racing cars and tracks, 131 planes and helicopters, 529 trucks and tractors, 189 train sets and stations, 121 boats and submarines, 22 garages, 185 robots, flying saucers and rockets, 123 characters from children's books, films and TV series, 176 construction sets, 984 board games, 458 educational toys, 80 video game consoles: that makes a total of almost 12,000 toys that make up the collection of the Musée des Arts Décoratifs.

Although some pieces pre-date the French Revolution (chess pieces and gambling games), the majority of the collection is made up of acquisitions from the mid-19th century to the present day. The oldest toys are mostly of French and German origin (Germany was the leading producer before the First World War). After the Second World War, the market was open to imports from the US and Japan, while nowadays the leading toy manufacturers are in China, which is responsible for 90 per cent of world production.

The first toy acquired by the museum is a set of furniture from the 19th century. As such, it matched the museum's other collections, whose objective was to trace the history of domestic life from the Middle Ages to the present. But very soon the collection surpassed the remit of representing French domestic taste. A reflection of daily life in miniature form, toys are testimony to social changes. They echo the discoveries of science and the great moments of history. More than simply an illustration of play practices in one time period, toys are images of the world. By bringing together a collection of toys that tell the tale of more than a century of human history, the Musée des Arts Décoratifs offers a unique look at our changing society.

The opening of the Musée des Arts Décoratifs in the Palais du Louvre (1905) coincided with the heyday of industry. The great technological innovations that were on show at the Paris World Fairs of 1889 and 1900 were part of this emergence. The Eiffel Tower, with its 300 metres of steel, was an industrial marvel that became the symbol of the French capital: like the famous Big Wheel from the 1900 fair, it appeared on jigsaws and building blocks that were sold in the store Au Paradis du Jouets (Toy Paradise) before turning up several years later in the museum collection.

The new manufacturing capabilities of the early 20th century, together with growing public demand, encouraged industrial entrepreneurs to expand their businesses. Mass production and mechanization of toy-making allowed the use of new materials (tinplate, metal, celluloid) and innovative techniques (moulding, combustion engines, steam, electricity, clockwork, rack and pinion). After 1900, the industrial landscape of French toy-making changed and small craft houses began to grow. One example was Roullet-Decamps, specialists in clockwork toys and automata, who in 1909 began to produce Christmas window displays for Le Bon Marché department store.

The year 1905 saw the founding of the Société des Amateurs de Jouets et Jeux Anciens (the Society for Lovers of Antique Games and Toys),[1] as well as the Chambre Syndicale des Industriels du Jouet (the Employers' Federation of Industrial Toymakers).[2] Both of these organizations gave French manufacturers a chance to affirm themselves in the face of their German competitors. The quality-control triangle that symbolized any item 'made in France' began to be applied to toys. The merging of organizations such as Le Jouet de Paris[3] and the Société Française de Fabrication de Bébés et Jouets[4] also strengthened the national market.

It was following the wide-ranging education laws passed by Jules Ferry in 1884 that play was first recognized as a method of learning. Building blocks and construction sets began to appear in schools. Toys were democratized and were sold in Paris department stores. Gift catalogues published by Galeries Lafayette, Le Printemps, Le Bon Marché and Le Louvre were illustrated by famous artists who were also toy designers (Benjamin Rabier, André Hellé, Caran d'Ache). These catalogues advertised novelties and exclusive lines for each holiday season.

The creation of parks and gardens aimed at children, which began in the second half of the 19th century, began to intensify. The Jardin d'Acclimation, opened in 1854, the temporary Zoological Garden for the 1931 Colonial Exhibition, and Vincennes Zoo, created in 1934, invited children to discover the lives of plants and animals, and miniature zoo animals began to turn up in children's bedrooms.

In the *Revue des Arts Décoratifs* in 1901, recalling the exhibition 'L'Enfance' (Childhood) held at the Petit Palais in May of the same year, the journalist Léo Claretie wrote: 'The toy industry certainly rises above decorative art, because its caprices and imagination bring together the most precious secrets of all the crafts together.'

He ends the article by saying that if ever an institution
was necessary, it is surely a toy museum.

In 1975, the Department of Toys at the Musée des Arts
Décoratifs was founded by François Mathey,[5] then head
curator of the Union Centrale des Arts Décoratifs (UCAD).
In this way, he gave a privileged place to the world of childhood,
two years after the exhibition of the prestigious toy collection
of the Sonneberg Museum, Germany. The UCAD Department
of Toys built its reputation through some twenty themed and
historical exhibitions:

• 'Le cirque et le jouet' celebrated the world of
  performance through clowns and performing animal toys.

• 'Personnages et héros' opened the permanent rooms
  of the Toy Gallery in 1985 and presented toys based on
  literature, comic books, animated films and TV shows.

• 'Le jouet de bois' traced the universal nature of wood,
  which is used to make toys all over the world.

• 'Du soldat au robot transformable' looked at the
  representation of war through lead soldiers, G.I. Joe,
  Action Man and robots.

• 'Poupées d'hier, créations d'aujourd'hui' used the
  evolution of fashion and technology to tell the story
  of the oldest of toys, the doll.

• 'Histoires d'ours' examined the beloved teddy bear,
  first created in 1905.

• 'La ville en jouets' looked at city life seen through toys.

Supported by the generosity of patrons, collectors, toy-lovers
and toy-makers, these twenty exhibitions have led to many
donations and bequests which have allowed the department to
enlarge its collection. It was also thanks to them that the Centre
for Toy Documentation was founded in 1986: documents, books,
exhibition catalogues, store catalogues, magazines on the world
of toys and games allow the public to consult an archive of
invaluable information.

A century after the opening of the Musée des Arts Décoratifs, the
Toy Gallery reopens to the public in September 2006 and plans
two exhibitions every year.[6] Every project is a chance to look at
this collection with a contemporary eye and build on this
exceptional resource.

The inaugural exhibition celebrates more than a century of toy
history. It has provided the chance to publish this book and also
to make a film about clockwork toys,[7] to start a project on the
history of video games[8] and to team up with a Franco-Swiss toy
manufacturer to create the robot I-Noo. This interactive toy is
designed and produced by Ouaps, and for the Toy Gallery, it has
been given a new look by French designer Matali Crasset. It has
therefore become part of the purest decorative arts tradition as
well as being an ambitious innovation in contemporary toy design.

DOROTHÉE CHARLES
Curator, Department of Toys

Notes
1 The Société des Amateurs de Jouets et Jeux Anciens was founded in 1905 by journalist
Léo Clarentie and historian Henry-René D'Allemagne with the aim of preserving the heritage
of childhood, studying toys and stimulating new research among toy manufacturers.

2 The Chambre Syndicale des Industriels du Jouet was founded following the Lépine
Awards in 1901 and supported industrial toymakers.

3 The company Le Jouet de Paris (1902–68) merged with the Société Industrielle de
Ferblanterie (The Industrial Society of Tinsmiths) in 1910. Its initial became J. de P.
and later JEP.

4 The Société Française de Fabrication de Bébés et Jouets (SFBJ), founded in 1899, brought
together the most prestigious French dollmakers, including Jumeau, Pintel and Bru.

5 François Mathey was head curator of the Union Centrale des Arts Décoratifs from 1965–85.
In 1975, he named Monica Burckhardt as curator of the Department of Toys, who worked on
the collection until 1998. Barbara Spadaccini replaced her until 2004.

6 In 1999, Bernard Desmoulins was named the winner of the competition for the
redesign of the Study Gallery, the Toy Gallery and the Jean Dubuffet Gallery at the
Musée des Arts Décoratifs.

7 The film *Les Rêves de Toto et Tata* was directed by Constance Guisset and Benjamin
Graindorge. It brings together some fifty clockwork toys from the 1880s to the 1950s,
by manufacturers from France (Victor Bonnet, F.V.-D.S., Gégé, Jouets Création, Joustra,
Fernand Martin, Mahé et Gutton, Petitcollin, Roullet-Descamps, VéBé), Germany (Bing,
Blomer & Schüler, Max Carl, Günthermann, Köhler, Ernst Paul Lehmann, Schuco),
Britain (Li-Lo) and Japan (Alps).

8 This project was conceived by Philippe Dubois, president of the association Mo5,
and Jean-Baptiste Clais, curator in this field. It retraces the history of the most significant
video games for consoles and PCs since the creation of *Pong* in 1972.

Toys in order of appearance

Pages 8–9

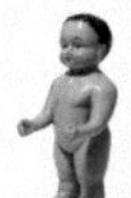

Frozen Charlotte
c. 1870. Germany. Painted porcelain.
H. 17 cm. Inv. 53096

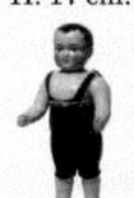

Frozen Charlie
c. 1880. Germany. Painted porcelain
and knit. H. 42 cm. Inv. 988.1111

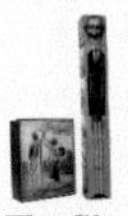

The Giants
c. 1890. A. Sala (1845–1896),
manufacturer, Germany. Set of building
blocks. Printed paper, cardboard and
wood. Max. h. 67 cm. Inv. 58274

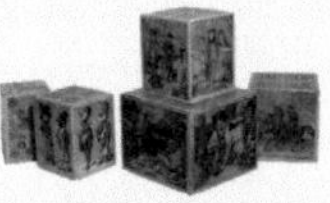

Set of building blocks
1890. France. Printed and varnished
paper and wood. Max. h. 110 cm.
Inv. Fnac 2039.77

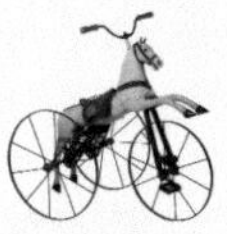

Horse tricycle
c. 1900. France. Wood, iron and leather.
H. 80 cm; L. 86 cm; W. 49 cm. Inv. 54206

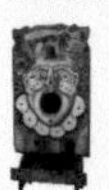

'Gugus and his Donkey' game
c. 1900. France. Game of skill. Painted
wood. H. 80 cm. Inv. 55663

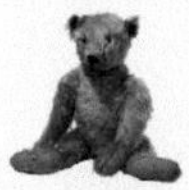

Teddy bear
c. 1905. Steiff (1880), manufacturer,
Germany. Mohair. H. 54 cm. Inv. 999.91.1

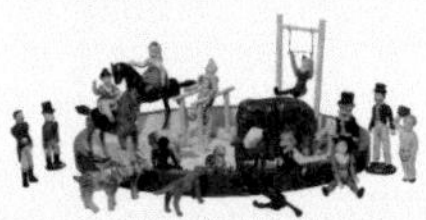

Barnum Circus
c. 1900. France. Painted plaster, fabric
and wood. Max. h. 13 cm. Inv. Fnac 2039.1

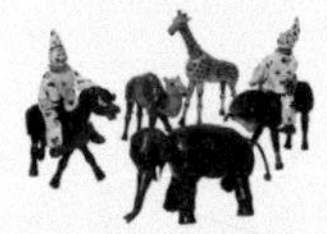

Humpty-Dumpty Circus
c. 1910. Schoenhut (1872), manufacturer,
USA. Painted wood, printed fabric and
string. Max. h. 27 cm. Inv. 990.50.1–7

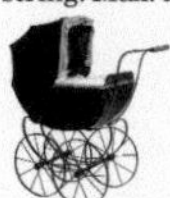

Doll's pram
c. 1910. France. Wood, imitation leather,
metal and fabric. H. 48 cm; L. 64 cm;
W. 24 cm. Inv. 57816

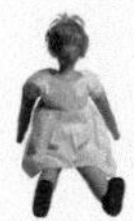

Doll
1916. Georges Lepape (1887–1971),
designer, France. Painted and varnished
wood, fabric, mohair, cotton wool and
imitation leather. H. 51 cm. Inv. 993.114

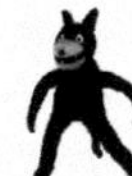

Felix the Cat
c. 1925. From the cartoon *Felix the Cat*
(1919) by Otto Messmer and Pat Sullivan.
Steiff (1880), manufacturer, Germany or
Dean's Rag Book Co., manufacturer, UK.
Fabric and glass. H. 30 cm. Inv. 995.74.1

Pages 10–11

**Frozen Charlie, Felix the Cat,
The Giants, Gugus and his donkey,
Barnum Circus** (see pp. 8–9)

Pages 14–15

Barnum Circus (see pp. 8–9)

Pages 16–17

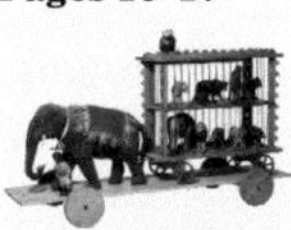

Elephant pulling a menagerie
c. 1910. France. Wood, metal, painted
plaster, papier mâché, velvet and fabric.
H. 35 cm; L. 65 cm; W. 18 cm. Inv. 54043

Humpty-Dumpty Circus, doll's pram
(see pp. 8–9)

Pages 20–21

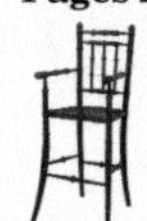

High chair
c. 1885. France. Varnished bamboo
and cane. H. 51 cm. Inv. 56671

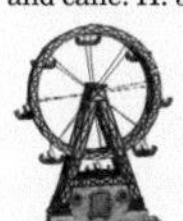

Paris 1900 Big Wheel
c. 1900. Based on the Big Wheel from
the 1900 World Fair, Paris. Au Paradis
des Enfants (c. 1863–1928), store, France.
Wood, painted cardboard and metal.
H. 46 cm; L. 32 cm; W. 10 cm.
Inv. 995.161.1

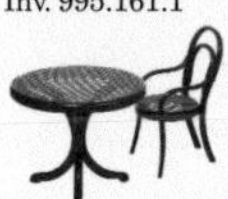

Table and chair
c. 1900. Thonet Frères (1853),
manufacturer, France. Varnished stained
oak and cane. Chair: H. 24 cm. Table:
H. 20 cm; Diam. 23 cm. Inv. 52874.A
and B

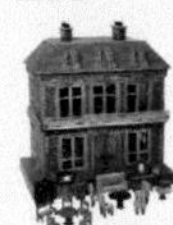

Collapsible doll's house
1904. France. Wood, paper, glass and
metal. H. 63 cm; L. 60 cm; W. 38 cm.
Inv. 994.56

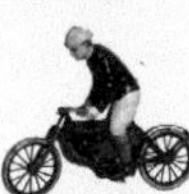

Halloh motorcycle no. 683
c. 1912. Ernst Paul Lehmann (1881),
manufacturer, Germany. Wind-up toy.
Lithographed metal. H. 16 cm; L. 22 cm;
W. 4.5 cm. Inv. 998.136.3

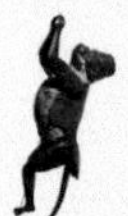

Climbing acrobat monkey
c. 1920. Ernst Paul Lehmann (1881),
manufacturer, Germany. Wind-up toy.
Painted metal and string. H. 21 cm.
Inv. 54218

**Teddy bear, tricycle horse, Barnum
Circus, Felix the Cat, Humpty-
Dumpty circus, doll's pram, doll**
(see pp. 8–9); **elephant pulling a
menagerie** (see pp. 16–17)

Pages 22–23

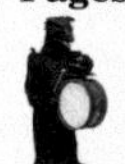

Drumming bear
c. 1885. Jean Roullet (1866–1989),
manufacturer, France. Wind-up toy. Fur,
glass, wood, metal and paper. H. 34 cm.
Inv. 988.1201

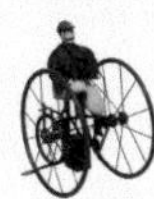

Man on a tricycle
c. 1890. France. Wind-up toy. Painted
bamboo and wood, metal, paper, fabric.
H. 34 cm; L. 35 cm; W. 21 cm. Inv. 993.53

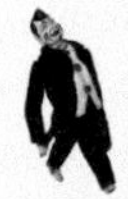

**Guguss the clown, articulated
tumbling toy**
c. 1908. Ets Migault (1878–c. 1930),
manufacturer, France. Wind-up toy.
Painted and moulded plaster and felt.
H. 26 cm. Inv. 54661

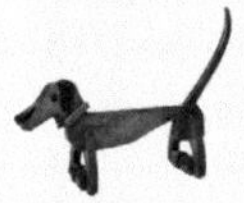

Basset hound
c. 1910. Emmanuel Poiré, known as
Caran d'Ache (1859–1909), designer,
France. Drag-along toy. Painted and
varnished wood. H. 45 cm; L. 62 cm;
W. 18 cm. Inv. 23531.A

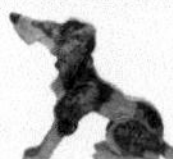

Fox terrier
c. 1900. Emmanuel Poiré, known as
Caran d'Ache (1859–1909), designer,
France. Painted wood. H. 19 cm;
L. 21 cm; W. 5 cm. Inv. 57123

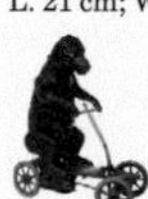

Bear on wheeled trolley
c. 1915. Bing (c. 1880–c. 1934),
manufacturer, Germany. Wind-up toy.
Painted metal. H. 17 cm; L. 15 cm;
W. 6.5 cm. Inv. 994.48

Felix the Cat (see pp. 8–9); **elephant
pulling a menagerie** (see pp.16–17)

Pages 24–25

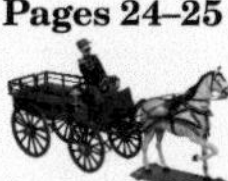

Carriage with soldier
c. 1870. Anonymous prisoner of war,
designer and manufacturer, Germany.
Painted card and wood, metal, leather and
horsehair. H. 42 cm; L. 77 cm; W. 21 cm.
Inv. 2005.2.1.1–2

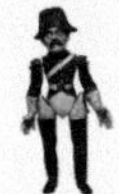

Soldier puppet
c. 1900. France. Painted wood and metal.
H. 35 cm. Inv. 55381

High chair (see pp. 20–21)

Pages 26–27

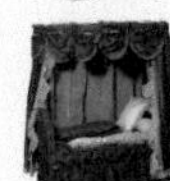

**Four-poster bed and upholstered
chair**
c. 1890. France. Painted wood, cotton,
lace and silk. H. 23 cm; L. 32 cm; W. 7 cm
(bed); H. 26 cm; L. 14 cm; W. 12 cm
(chair). Inv. 35341.A and B

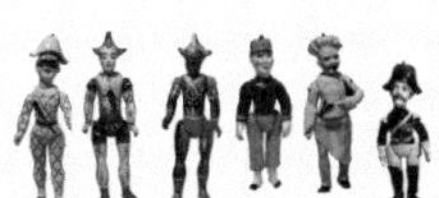

**Marionettes: Harlequin, Geronimo
Medrano Boum-Boum, Raphaël
Padilla a.k.a. Chocolat, soldiers,
cooks and policeman**
c. 1900. France. Painted wood and fabric.
Max. h. 34 cm; Inv. 992.164.1 to 9

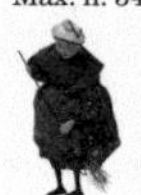

Housekeeper
c. 1912. Fernand Martin (1849–1919),
manufacturer, France. Wind-up toy.
Painted metal, fabric and straw.
H. 18.5 cm. Inv. 993.58

Felix the Cat (see pp. 8–9); **Thonet
chair, high chair** (see pp. 20–21);
soldier puppet, carriage with soldier
(see pp. 24–25)

Pages 28–29

Carriage with soldier (see pp. 24–25);
**clown marionettes: Medrano Boum
Boum and Padilla a.k.a. Chocolat,
four-poster bed and upholstered
chair** (see pp. 26–27)

Pages 32–33

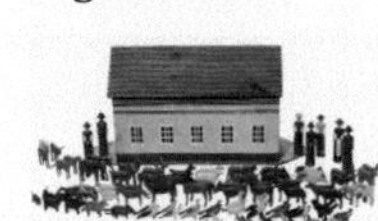

Noah's Ark
c. 1880. Erzgebirge region, Germany.
Carved and painted wood. H. 29 cm;
L. 63 cm; W. 18.5 cm (ark); H. 11 cm
(figure). Inv. 995.66.2.1–126

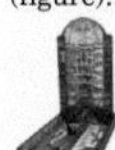

'Ascending the Dome' game
c. 1900. Le Printemps (1865), store and
manufacturer, France. Printed card,
plaster, wood and metal. Max. h. 58 cm.
Inv. 2005.3.1.1–12

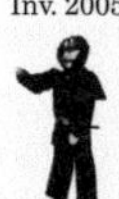

Policeman
1901. Fernand Martin (1849–1919),
designer and manufacturer (1880–1912),
France. Wind-up toy. Painted metal, fabric
and felt. H. 20 cm. Inv. 998.276.1

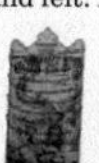

'Toboggan Parisien' game
1903. France. Painted wood, printed
paper and metal. H. 50 cm; W. 20 cm;
Depth 2 cm. Inv. 55822

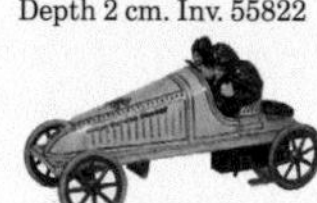

Gordon Bennett Cup racing car
c. 1908. Gunthermann (c. 1877–1965),
manufacturer, Germany. Wind-up toy.
Painted metal and rubber. H. 11 cm;
L. 21 cm; W. 9.5 cm. Inv. 57886

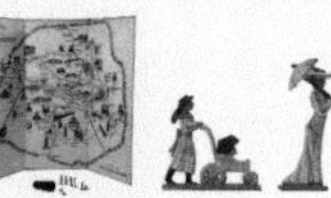

**'Jeu du Métropolitain':
Paris Metro game**
c. 1909. Les Grands Magasins du Louvre
(1855–1974), manufacturer, France.
Printed card and painted lead. L. 91 cm
(board); H. 4 cm (figures). Inv. 995.64.1

Felix the Cat (see pp. 8–9);
housekeeper (see pp. 26–27)

Pages 34–35

Noah's Ark (see pp. 32–33)

Pages 36–37

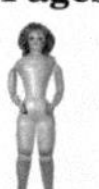

Doll
c. 1870. France. Leather, glass and
porcelain. H. 38 cm. Inv. 35336.C

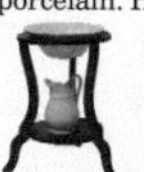

Washstand
c. 1890. France. Wood and porcelain.
H. 16 cm. Inv. 50848

Perfume shop
c. 1890. France. Painted wood, printed
paper, glass and card. H. 44 cm; L. 46 cm;
W. 20 cm. Inv. 38179

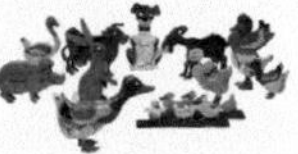

Farm animals
c. 1910. Benjamin Rabier (1864–1939),
illustrator and designer; Le Jouet en Bois
Passerat et Radiguet (1872–c. 1900),
manufacturer, France. Cut and painted
wood. Max. h. 24 cm. Inv. 995.155.1–12

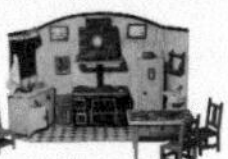

**Kitchen with furniture and
accessories**
c. 1914. France. Painted wood and
metal. H. 35.5 cm; L. 59 cm; W. 24 cm.
Inv. 988.631

Felix the Cat (see pp. 8–9); **table and
chair** (see pp. 20–21), **upholstered
chair** (see pp. 26–27)

Pages 38–39

Doll (see pp. 36–37)

Pages 42–45

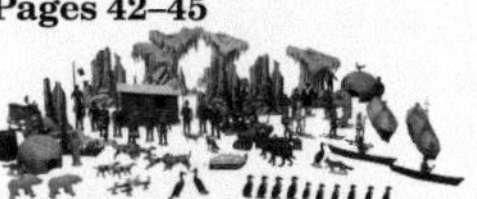

Expedition to the North Pole
c. 1912. C.B.G. Mignot (Cuperly-Blondel-
Gerbeau, 1785), manufacturer, France.
Painted lead and paper. Max. h. 10 cm.
Inv. 993.177.1

Pages 46–47

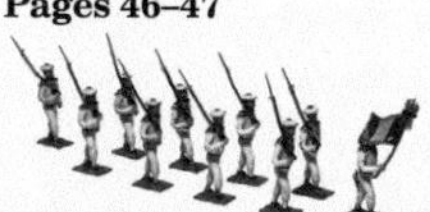

Sailors
c. 1900. C.B.G. Mignot (Cuperly-Blondel-
Gerbeau, 1785), manufacturer, France.
Painted lead. H. 8 cm. Inv. 990.80.1–10

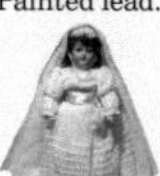

Doll in communion dress
1907. Simon & Halbig (1869–1930),
manufacturer, Germany. Plaster,
biscuit porcelain and fabric. H. 33 cm.
Inv. 998.146.3

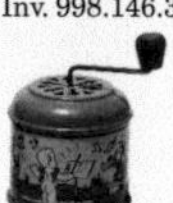

Musical box
1910 to 1960. Camelin (1909–62),
manufacturer, France. Lithographed
metal, lead and nylon thread. H. 9 cm.
Inv. 49696

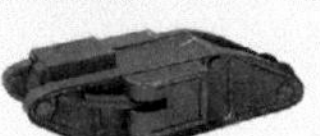

Tank
1916. France. Painted card. H. 8 cm;
L. 26 cm; W. 10 cm. Inv. 55681.2

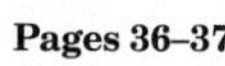

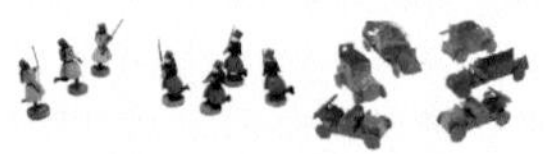

Military figures and vehicles
1916–17. André Hellé (1870–1945) and Charles-Émile Carlègle (1877–1940), illustrators and designers; Le Printemps (1865), store and manufacturer, France. Painted wood. Max. h. 5 cm. Inv. 55676.1, 4, 5, 8, 9, 11, 12, 13, 15, 16, 55676.7, 55676.13, 55676.15 and 55681.1

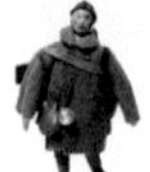

Doll in military dress
c. 1917. Berthe Noufflard (1886–1971), designer, France. Plaster, wood and felt. H. 19 cm. Inv. 55837.1

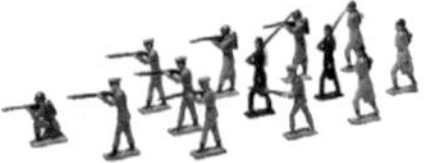

Soldiers
c. 1918. C.B.G. Mignot (Cuperly-Blondel-Gerbeau, 1785), manufacturer, France. Lead. H. 5 cm. Inv. 990.233

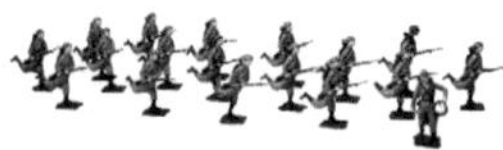

Infantry soldiers
c. 1920. X. R. (1914?–1925?), manufacturer, France. Lead. H. 7 cm; L. 6 cm. Inv. 990.69

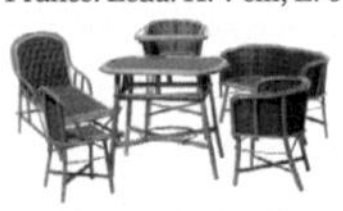

Sitting room furniture: sofa, chair, chaise longue, armchair, high chair and table
c. 1920. France. Wood and wicker. Max. h. 31 cm. Inv. Fnac 2039.16

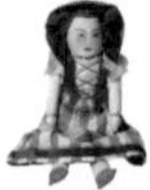

Doll from the Alsace region
c. 1920. France. Fabric, wool, velvet, cotton and silk. H. 37 cm. Inv. 990.490

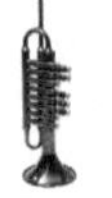

Trumpet
1918–55. Delinot (1868–*c.* 1960), manufacturer, France. Brass. H. 34 cm. Inv. 46890

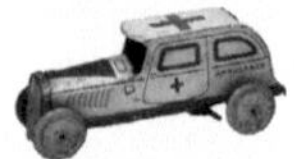

Citroën ambulance
c. 1920. C.R. (Société Rossignol et Roitelet, *c.* 1875–1962), manufacturer, France. Painted metal. H. 6 cm; L. 15 cm; W. 6 cm. Inv. 996.145.8.1

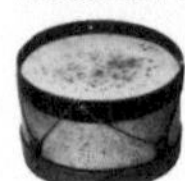

Drum
c. 1920. Ets L. Roulleau, manufacturer, France. Painted wood, metal, cord and leather. H. 14 cm. Inv. Fnac 2039.55.2

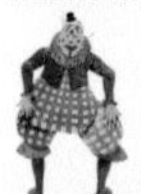

Puppet clown
1920. France. Painted wood and string. H. 36 cm; L. 16 cm. Inv. 54047

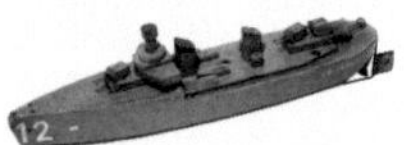

***Le Terrible 12* warship**
c. 1925. France. Painted wood. H. 12 cm; L. 41 cm; W. 8 cm. Inv. 996.121.2

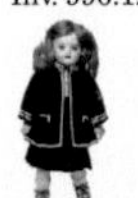

Bleuette doll
1934. S.F.B.J. (Société Française de Fabrication de Bébés et Jouets, 1899–1957), manufacturer, France.

Wood, painted plaster, fabric and biscuit porcelain. H. 28 cm. Inv. 992.163

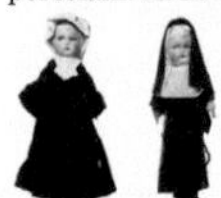

Sisters of Charity of the Order of St Vincent de Paul
c. 1935. France. Moulded and painted board, cotton and fabric. Inv. 988.514.2 to 4

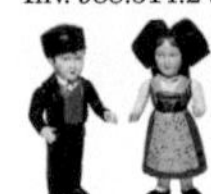

Boy and girl dolls from Alsace
1937. Petitcollin (1860), manufacturer, France. Painted celluloid. H. 17 cm. Inv. 992.674.1 and 2

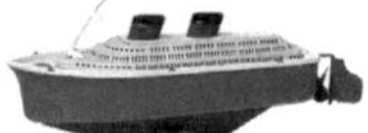

Ocean liner
1937. VéBé (1937–65), manufacturer, France. Wind-up toy. Painted metal. H. 9 cm; L. 22 cm; W. 7 cm. Inv. Fnac 2039.139

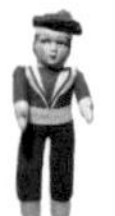

Sailor doll
c. 1940. France. Fabric and cardboard. H. 36 cm. Inv. Fnac 2039.144.4

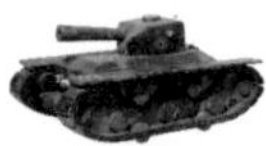

Tank
c. 1940. France. Painted wood. H. 18 cm; L. 36 cm; W. 21 cm. Inv. 54444

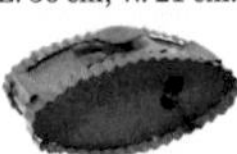

Tank
c. 1940. France. Wind-up toy. Painted metal. H. 9 cm; L. 17 cm; W. 7 cm. Inv. 990.248.1

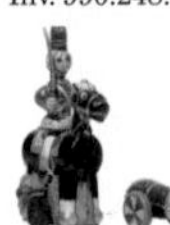

Soldier on horseback and cannon
c. 1960. T.P.S. (Toplay Ltd, 1956), manufacturer, Japan. Wind-up toy. Printed metal. H. 4 cm; L. 7 cm; W. 4.5 cm. Inv. 54638.2

Pages 48–49

Military figures and vehicles
(see pp. 46–47)

Pages 50–51

Military figures and vehicles, Sisters of Charity of the Order of St Vincent de Paul, doll in communion dress
(see pp. 46–47)

Pages 52–53

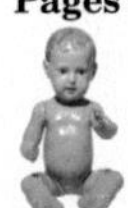

Baby doll
c. 1925. S.I.C. (Société Industrielle de Celluloïd, 1906–27), manufacturer, France or Reich Goldmann & Co (1890–?), manufacturer, Germany. Celluloid and glass. H. 36 cm. Inv. 988.1105.1

Infantry soldiers (see pp. 46–47)

Pages 54–55

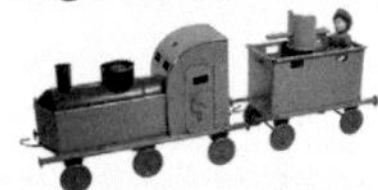

Armoured train with soldier doll
1915. France. Painted metal, plaster and felt. H. 20.5 cm; L. 60 cm; W. 12 cm. Inv. 2000.59.1

Infantry soldiers (see pp. 46–47)

Pages 56–57

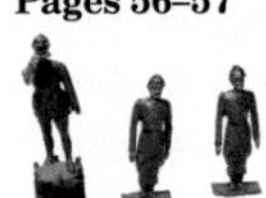

Soldiers
c. 1918. C.B.G. Mignot (Cuperly-Blondel-Gerbeau, 1785), manufacturer, France. Painted lead. Max. h. 7 cm. Inv. 992.423.(1–4)

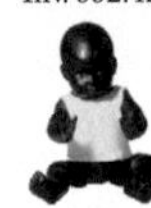

'Negri' baby doll
c. 1930. Petitcollin (1860), manufacturer, France. Painted celluloid and cotton. H. 29 cm. Inv. 46791

Furniture (see pp. 46–47)

Pages 58–59

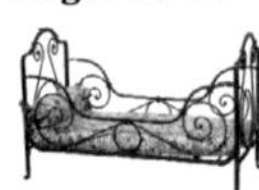

Doll's bed
c. 1900. Painted iron and fabric. H. 31 cm; L. 47 cm; W. 22 cm. Inv. 51345

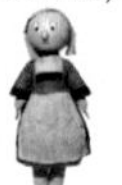

Bécassine doll
c. 1925. From the comic-strip character by J. P. Pinchon (1871–1953), created in 1905 for *La Semaine de Suzette*. France. Painted card, fabric and felt. H. 38 cm. Inv. 46794

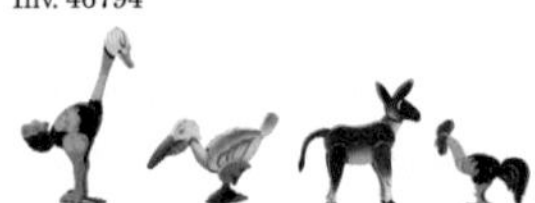

Ostrich, pelican, donkey, rooster and giraffe
1928. Marius Rossillon, a.k.a. O'Galop (1867–1946), designer; Ets Migault (1878–*c.* 1930), manufacturer, France. Painted wood. Max. h. 36 cm. Inv. 987.881.1 to 5

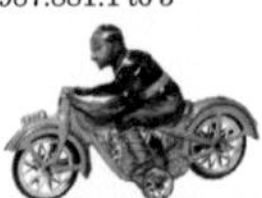

T922 motorcycle
1930. Payá (1905), manufacturer, Spain. Wind-up toy. Stamped and lithographed sheet metal. H. 11 cm; L. 17 cm; W. 4 cm. Inv. 54636.1

Pages 60–61

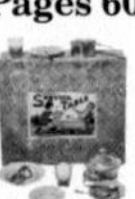

Dinner set
c. 1920. Desrues et Guilleminot (1864–?), manufacturer, France. Aluminium, porcelain and plastic. H. 10 cm; L. 35 cm; W. 25 cm (set). Inv. 49974

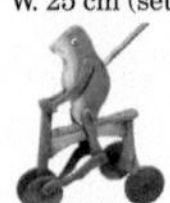

Frog on a tricycle.
c. 1930. France. Painted and unpainted wood. H. 30 cm; L. 23 cm; W. 12 cm. Inv. 57121

Ostrich, pelican, donkey, rooster and giraffe (see pp. 58–59)

Pages 62–63

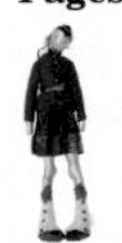

Scottish doll
c. 1925. Paul Poiret (1879–1944), Les Ateliers Martine (1926–29), designers and manufacturers, France. Cloth, silk, wool and leather. H. 54 cm. Inv. 2005.42.1

Infantry soldiers (see pp. 46–47)

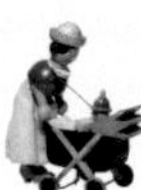

'Ma Nounou' nanny doll
1926. Garcin-Jo, illustrator, designer and manufacturer, France. Wind-up toy. Painted and varnished wood, iron and fabric. H. 27 cm; L. 21 cm; W. 7.5 cm. Inv. 992.376

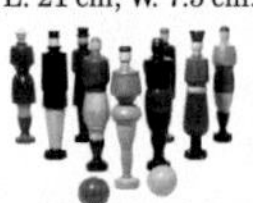

Anthropomorphic skittles
c. 1927. France. Turned and painted wood. H. 25 cm. Inv. 58292

Pages 66–67

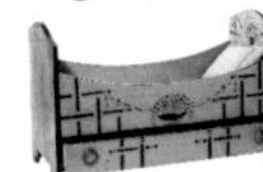

Doll's bed
1923. Workshop of war-wounded soldiers (*c.* 1915–18), designer and manufacturer, France. Painted wood and fabric. H. 36 cm; L. 55 cm; Depth 26.5 cm. Inv. 48411

Pages 66–67

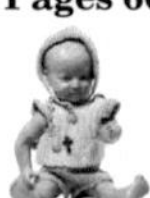

Baby doll
Series IX, *c.* 1924. Petitcollin (1860), manufacturer, France. Painted celluloid, wool and metal. H. 19 cm. Inv. 48421

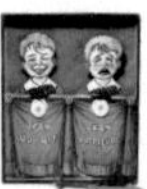

'Laughing John, Crying John' shooting gallery
c. 1920. E.R., manufacturer, France. Painted wood and metal. H. 6 cm; L. 35 cm; W. 29 cm. Inv. 989.193

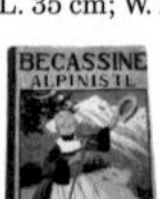

***Bécassine alpiniste* (Bécassine the Mountain-Climber), book**
1923. From the magazine *La Semaine de Suzette*, M.-L. Caumery (1867–1941), text by J. P. Pinchon (1871–1953), illustrations; Gautier et Languereau (1917), publishers, Paris. 64 pp. Inv. DJ 882

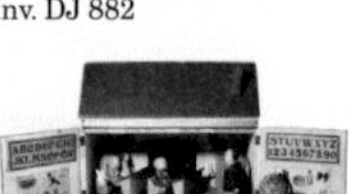

Schoolhouse
c. 1925. France. Painted plaster and wood. H. 27 cm; L. 32 cm; W. 15 cm. Inv. 48416

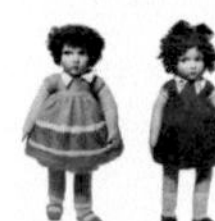

Dolls
c. 1927. Raynal (1922–*c.* 1980), manufacturer, France. Painted fabric, felt and cotton. Max. h. 55 cm. Inv. 53940.1 and 2

Bécassine doll (see pp. 58–59)

Pages 68–69

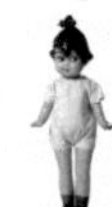

Nella doll
1925. Italy. Painted plaster and fabric. H. 47 cm. Inv. 993.70.1

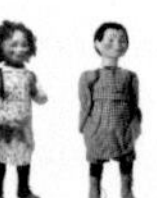

Tata the schoolgirl and Toto the schoolboy
c. 1925. Gaston Decamps (1882–1972), designer; Roullet-Decamps (1889–1995), manufacturer, France. Wind-up toy. Plaster, cardboard, horsehair, cotton, leather and celluloid. H. 35 cm and 36 cm. Inv. 990.1118 and 996.24.2

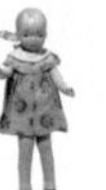

Doll
c. 1925. S.I.C. (Société Industrielle de Celluloïd, 1902–27), manufacturer, France. Painted celluloid and fabric. H. 24 cm. Inv. 48418.A

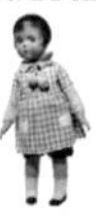

Dominique doll
1927. S.I.C. (Société Industrielle de Celluloïd, 1902–27), manufacturer, France. Painted celluloid, wool and fabric. H. 40 cm. Inv. 987.250

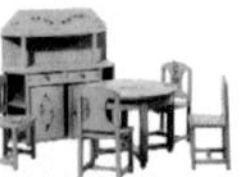

Kitchen furniture: chairs, table and dresser
c. 1930. France. Painted wood. Max. h. 42 cm. Inv. 55884 (1–6)

Bécassine doll (see pp. 58–59); **schoolhouse** (see pp. 66–67)

Pages 70–71

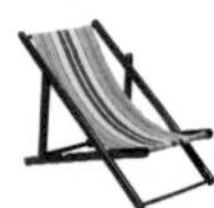

Deckchair
c. 1920. France. Varnished wood and canvas. H. 27 cm. Inv. 995.51.3

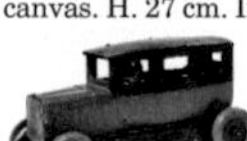

Limousine
c. 1920. C.R. (Société Rossignol et Roitelet, *c.* 1875–1962), manufacturer, France. Wind-up toy. Painted metal. H. 8 cm; L. 17cm; W. 6.5 cm. Inv. 996.123.5

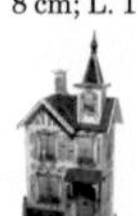

Doll's house
c. 1920. Gottschalk (*c.* 1865–*c.* 1930), manufacturer, Germany. Wood and lithographed paper. H. 60 cm; L. 25 cm; W. 25 cm. Inv. 999.45.3

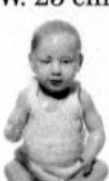

Baby doll
c. 1920. S.I.C. (Société Industrielle de Celluloïd, 1902–27), manufacturer, France. Painted celluloid and fabric. H. 36 cm. Inv. 48419

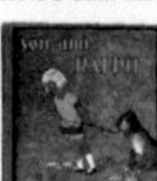

***Son ami Ralph* (Her Friend Ralph), book**
1923. Text by Jean Bonnerot, drawings by Armand Rapeno; published by H. Laurens, Paris. 82 pp. Inv. DJ 883

Sitting-room furniture (see pp. 46–47); **Bécassine doll** (see pp. 58–59); **baby doll, dolls** (see pp. 66–67)

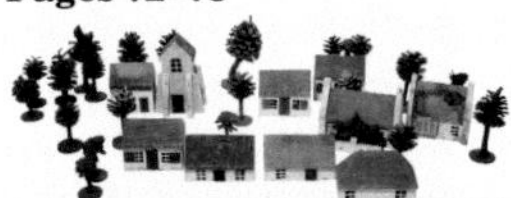

Pages 72–73

Model village and figures
1916–17. André Hellé (1870–1945) and
Charles-Émile Carlègle (1877–1940),
designers; Le Printemps (1865), store
and manufacturer, France. Painted wood.
Max. h. 12.5 cm. Inv. 55676.2 and 3

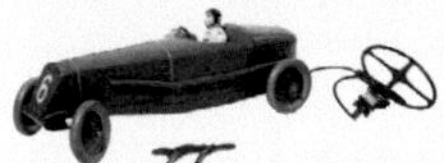

Grand Prix Delage racing car
1928. JEP (Jouet de Paris, 1902–68),
manufacturer, France. Wind-up toy.
Painted metal and rubber. H. 15.5 cm;
L. 43 cm; W. 18 cm. Scale 1:10. Inv. 55997

Pages 74–75

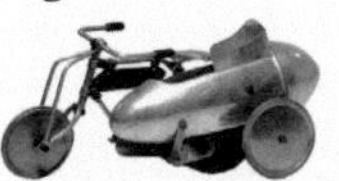

**Tricycle, bicycle, bike with
sidecar and scooter**
c. 1920. Fontaine et Rigot Cie, Jouets
Auto-Cycle (1920?–1938?), manufacturer,
France. Aluminium, rubber and wicker.
Max. h. 21 cm. Inv. 57859.1–4

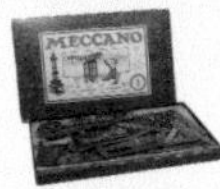

Meccano set
c. 1925. Meccano (1901), manufacturer,
France. Enamelled metal. H. 2.5 cm;
L. 41 cm; W. 25.5 cm (box). Inv. 995.150.4

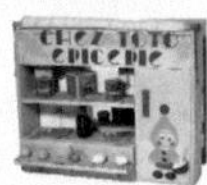

'Chez Toto' grocer's shop
c. 1927. France. Painted wood, cardboard
and fabric. H. 26 cm; L. 64 cm; W. 32 cm.
Inv. 48422

Pages 78–79

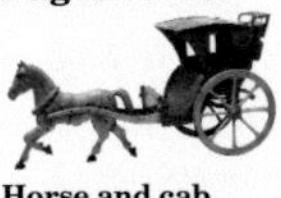

Horse and cab
c. 1920. C. R. (Société Rossignol et
Roitelet, c. 1875–1962), manufacturer,
France. Painted metal. H. 13 cm;
L. 26 cm; W. 9 cm. Inv. 996.124.2

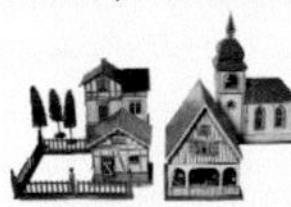

Village
c. 1920. France. Lithographed paper
and wood. Max. h. 41 cm. Inv. 48440

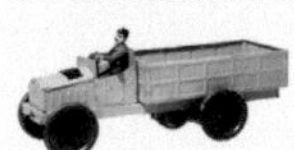

Farm truck
1928. Victor Bonnet et Cie (1920–65),
manufacturer, France. Wind-up toy.
Painted metal. H. 12 cm; L. 25 cm;
W. 9.5 cm. Inv. 56873

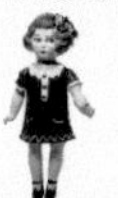

Adette doll
c. 1928. A.D.T (Société Nouvelle
des Établissements, 1893–c. 1960?),
manufacturer, France. Moulded and
painted papier mâché. H. 44 cm.
Inv. 54262

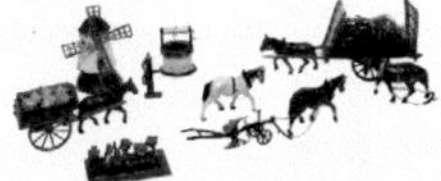

Farm
c. 1930. B.F. (Bourreaux Frères,
c. 1899–?); L.R. (Louis Roussy, 1925–61),
manufacturers, France. Painted lead.
Max. h. 22 cm. Inv. Fnac 2039.106

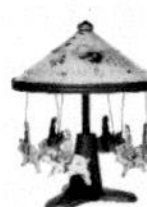

Carousel with pigs
c. 1930. C.I.J. (Compagnie Industrielle du
Jouet, c. 1930–69), manufacturer, France.
Painted metal and wood. H. 32 cm; Diam.
26 cm. Inv. 995.76.2

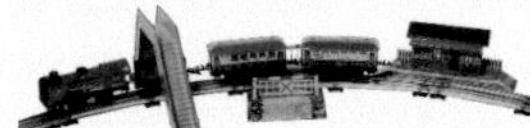

Electric train
1940. Hornby France (c. 1922–73),
manufacturer, France. Painted and
lithographed stamped sheet metal.
Max. h. 15.5 cm. Inv. Fnac 2039.53

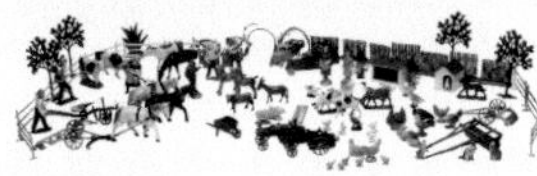

Farm
c. 1945. France. Painted plaster and lead.
Max. h. 12 cm. Inv. 998.145.1 to 89

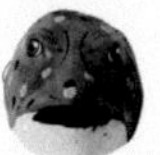

Frog mask
1945. France. Painted moulded
cardboard. L. 19 cm; W. 16 cm;
Depth 10.5 cm. Inv. 55829.13

Pages 80–81

Electric train, farm (see pp. 78–79)

Pages 82–83

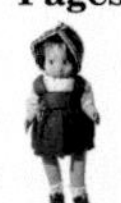

Venus doll
c. 1930. Adrien Carvaillo (1923–39),
manufacturer, France. Fabric, silk and
felt. H. 50 cm. Inv. Fnac 2039.24

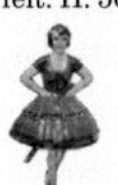

Spanish dancer spinning top
c. 1930. Technofix (1922–78),
manufacturer, Germany. Wind-up toy.
Painted metal. H. 16 cm. Inv. 989.849

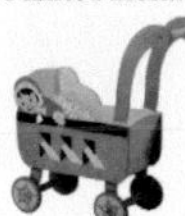

Doll's pram
c. 1930. France. Painted wood and fabric.
H. 50 cm; L. 39 cm; W. 19 cm. Inv. 56876

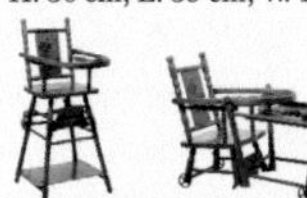

Adjustable high chair
c. 1932. France. Wood and metal.
Max. h. 65 cm. Inv. 992.620

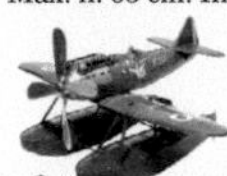

F260 seaplane
1934. JEP (Jouet de Paris, 1902–68),
manufacturer, France. Wind-up toy.
Lithographed metal. H. 16 cm; L. 49 cm;
Wingspan 35 cm. Inv. 997.138

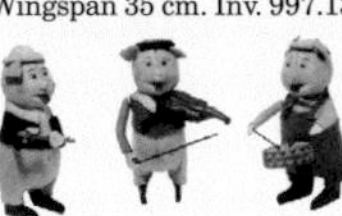

The Three Little Pigs
1934. From the animated film (1933)
directed by Burt Gillett and produced
by Walt Disney. Schuco (1912–78),
manufacturer, Germany. Wind-up toy.
Metal and felt. H. 10 cm. Inv. 56368

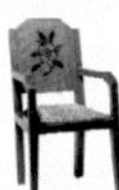

Chair
c. 1935. France. Wood and cotton.
H. 40 cm; L. 20 cm; W. 21 cm.
Inv. 46804

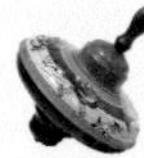

Musical top
c. 1940. Ets Haricot (1922–c. 1960),
manufacturer, France. Painted metal
and wood. H. 17 cm; Diam. 15 cm.
Inv. 46894.A

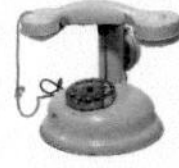

Telephone
1940. JEP (Jouet de Paris, 1902–68),
manufacturer, France. Painted metal.
H. 16 cm. Inv. 50891.A

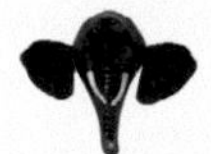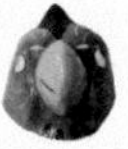

Elephant and parrot masks
1945. France. Painted and moulded
cardboard. L. 39.5 cm; W. 18.5 cm;
Depth 12.5 cm (elephant). L. 20 cm;
W. 16.5 cm; Depth 15.5 cm (parrot).
Inv. 55829.3 and 14

Adette doll, frog mask (see pp. 78–79).

Pages 86–87

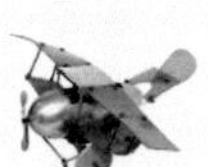

Propeller plane
c. 1925. Fontaine et Rigot Cie, Jouets
Auto-Cycle (1920?–1938?), manufacturer,
France. Metal and plastic. Wingspan
37 cm. Inv. 51306.A

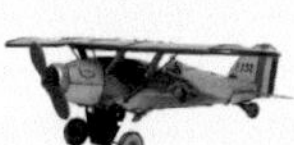

F252 Morane-Saulnier plane
1933. JEP (Jouet de Paris, 1902–68),
manufacturer, France. Wind-up toy.
Painted metal. Wingspan 40 cm.
Inv. 988.1121

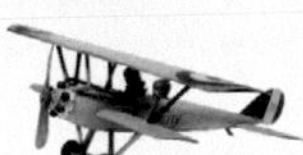

'The Fly' plane
c. 1938. France. Painted wood. Wingspan
39 cm. Inv. 996.121.1

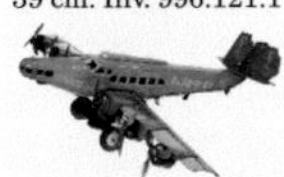

Paris–New York Transatlantic plane
1938. Joustra (1934), manufacturer,
France. Wind-up toy. Lithographed metal.
Wingspan 60 cm. Inv. 994.58.2

F260 seaplane, chair, Venus doll
(see pp. 82–83)

Pages 88–89

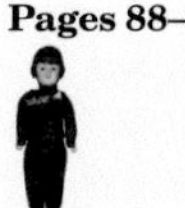

Doll in aviator costume
1928. Homage to Charles Lindbergh
(1902–74). France. Cardboard, glass,
fabric and mica. H. 47 cm. Inv. 58282

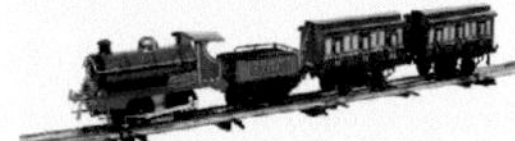

**Train with engine, tender and
two carriages**
1930. Hornby France (c. 1922–73),
manufacturer, France. Painted metal.
L. 17.5 cm (engine). Inv. 988.907

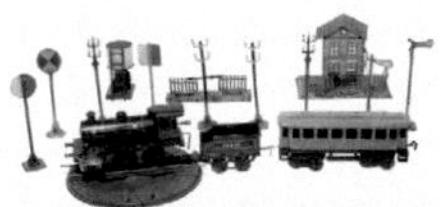

Station, train and signals
c. 1938. JEP (Jouets de Paris, 1902–68),
manufacturer, France. Painted metal.
H. 14 cm (station). Inv. 992.34

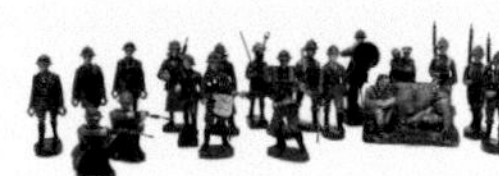

German soldiers
c. 1935. Elastolin (1912–83),
manufacturer, Germany. Painted
aluminium. Max. h. 8 cm. Inv. 54737

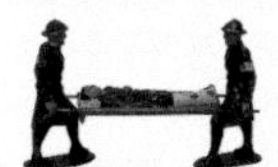

**Stretcher-bearers with
wounded soldier**
c. 1945. France. Painted lead. H. 7 cm.
Inv. 992.408.1

Pages 90–91

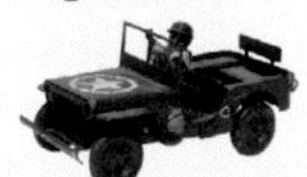

Liberation jeep with soldier
1945. J.R.D. (1935–63), manufacturer,
France. Painted metal and fabric. H. 9 cm;
L. 17.5 cm; W. 8 cm. Inv. Fnac 2039.188

**Station and train, doll in aviator
costume, German soldiers, stretcher-
bearers with wounded soldier**
(see pp. 88–89)

Pages 92–93

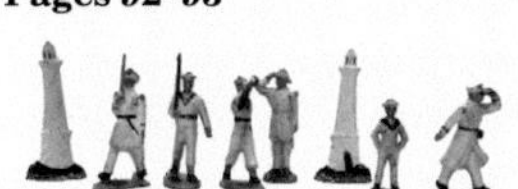

Sailors
c. 1938. Aludo (1937–60), manufacturer,
France. Painted aluminium. Max. h. 8 cm.
Inv. 989.851

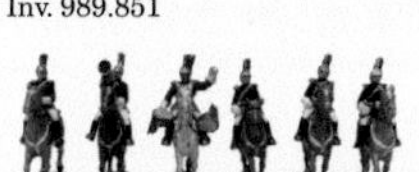

**Cavalry of the Garde Républicaine
and Saint-Cyriens**
1950–60 and 1939–40. Quiralu (1933–61),
France. Painted aluminium. Max. h.
10 cm. Inv. 990.76

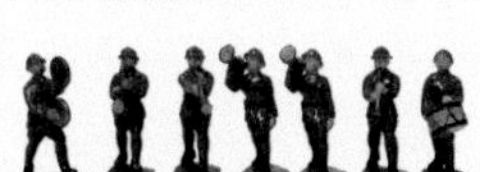

Military band
1933–40. Quiralu (1933–61),
manufacturer, France. Painted
aluminium. Max. h. 6 cm.
Inv. 999.98.40.1–11

Belgian soldiers
c. 1935. Lineol (1906–c. 1969),
manufacturer, Germany. Painted plaster.
Max. h. 13 cm. Inv. 54734.1–28

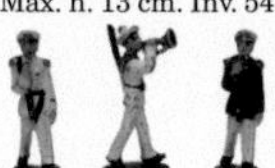

Sailors
1939–45. Quiralu (1933–61),
manufacturer, France. Painted
aluminium. H. 6.5 cm. Inv. 992.406.1–3

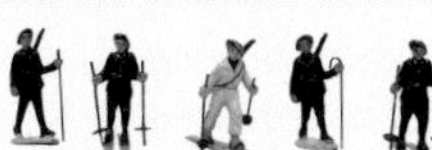

Soldiers with skis
1939. Quiralu (1933–61), manufacturer,
France. Painted aluminium. H. 6.5 cm.
Inv. 53143.A

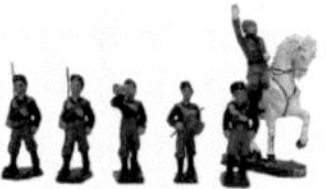

Italian soldiers
c. 1939. Fontanini (1908–45),
manufacturer, Italy. Painted plaster.
Max. h. 12 cm. Inv. 54738.1–6

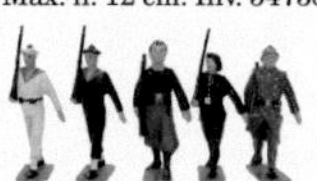

Soldiers, sailors and Zouave soldier
c. 1940. Mignalu (1936–55),
manufacturer, France. Painted
aluminium. H. 14 cm. Inv. 55376

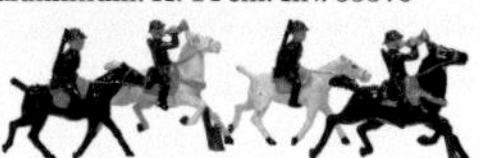

Mounted soldiers
1945. Aludo (1937–60), D.C. (Domage
et Cie, 1920–c. 1965), manufacturers,
France. Painted hollow lead. H. 8 cm.
Inv. 54995.5–8

Venus doll (see pp. 82–83); **doll in
aviator costume** (see pp. 88–89)

Pages 94–95

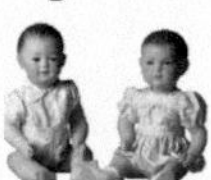

François and Jacky baby dolls
c. 1936. S.N.F. (Société Nobel Française,
c. 1928–63), manufacturer, France.
Painted celluloid and silk. H. 45 cm.
Inv. Fnac 2039.20.A and B

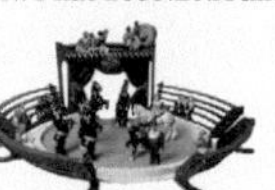

Circus
c. 1948. Jouet Philippe/Les Fonderies de
Suresnes (c. 1950–?), manufacturer,
France. Lead, painted aluminium, cork,
wood and paper. Max. h. 21 cm. Inv. 57829

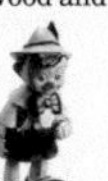

Pinocchio
1949. From the film *Pinocchio* (1940) by
Walt Disney, adapted from the book *The
Adventures of Pinocchio* by Carlo Collodi
(1826–90). Les Jouets Création,
manufacturer, France. Wind-up toy.
Painted wood and metal. H. 19 cm.
Inv. 992.694

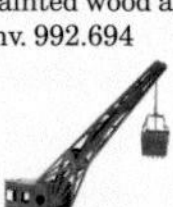

Crane
1958. Ets Rollet (1926), manufacturer,
France. Painted metal. H. 47 cm;
W. 23 cm; Arm 54 cm. Inv. 51077

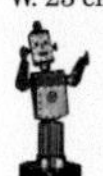

Wakouwa robot
c. 1965. Hong Kong. Plastic. H. 12.5 cm.
Inv. 55989.2

Pages 96–97

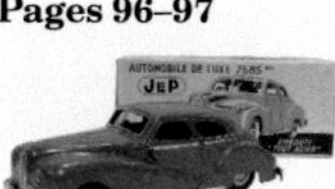

Delahaye luxury car
c. 1950. JEP (Jouet de Paris, 1902–68),
manufacturer, France. Wind-up toy.
Painted and stamped steel. H. 11 cm;
L. 33 cm; W. 15 cm. Inv. Fnac 2039.134

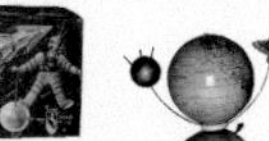

Revolving globe
c. 1950. MS, Germany. Battery operated.
Painted metal. Diam. 8 cm. Inv. 991.441

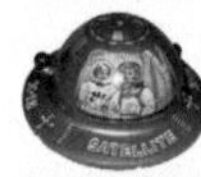

Space Surveyor X-12
1960. T.M. (Masudaya, 1924),
manufacturer, Japan. Battery operated.
Painted metal and plastic. Diam. 22 cm.
Inv. 991.425

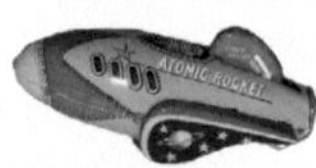

Atomic Rocket
c. 1960. T.M. (Masudaya, 1924),
manufacturer, Japan. Wind-up toy.
Painted metal and plastic. H. 9 cm;
L. 18 cm; W. 7 cm. Inv. 55986.1

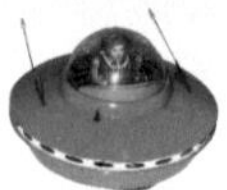

Flying saucer
c. 1960. Japan. Wind-up toy. Plastic.
Diam. 24 cm. Inv. 991.424

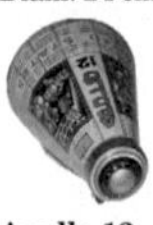

Apollo 12
c. 1960. T.T., manufacturer, Japan. Painted
metal and plastic. L. 10 cm. Inv. 991.438

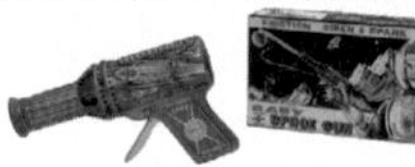

Baby space gun
c. 1960. Daiya (c. 1955–c. 1975),
manufacturer, Japan. Wind-up toy.
Painted metal. L. 15 cm. Inv. 991.446

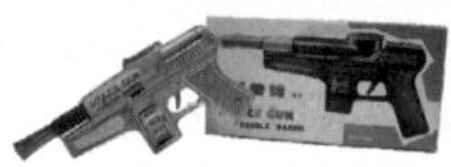

Space gun
c. 1960. Made in China. Wind-up toy.
Painted metal. L. 31 cm. Inv. 991.447

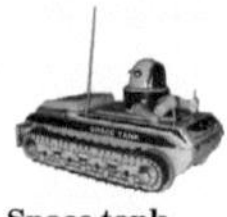

Space tank
c. 1960. Made in China. Battery operated.
Painted metal. L. 25 cm. Inv. 991.435

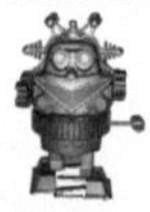

Robot
1965. Yoneya (1950), manufacturer,
Japan. Wind-up toy. Printed metal and
plastic. H. 12.5 cm; W. 7 cm; Depth 6 cm.
Inv. Fnac 2039.143

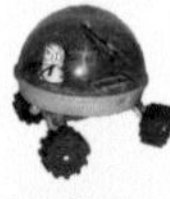

Strolling Space Station
c. 1965. Yoneya (1950), Japan. Plastic.
Diam. 9 cm. Inv. 991.439

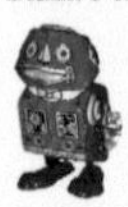

Hopping Robot
c. 1965. Yoneya (1950), manufacturer,
Japan. Wind-up toy. Printed metal and
plastic. H. 9 cm; W. 5 cm; Depth 6 cm.
Inv. 55988

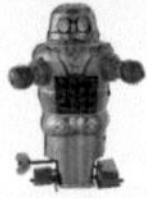

Robot W
c. 1965. Noguchi (c. 1960), manufacturer,
Japan. Wind-up toy. Printed metal and
plastic. H. 16.5 cm; L. 12 cm; W. 7 cm.
Inv. 55987

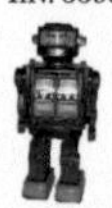

Super Astronaut
c. 1965. S.H. (Horikawa, 1959),
manufacturer, Japan. Battery operated.
Plastic and metal. H. 28 cm; L. 14 cm;
W. 10 cm. Inv. 55980

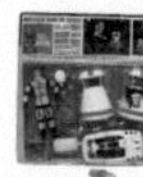

Major Mason with Moon Suit
1966. Mattel (1945), manufacturer, USA.
Plastic. H. 16 cm. Inv. 991.487

Wakouwa Robot (see pp. 94–95)

Pages 98–99

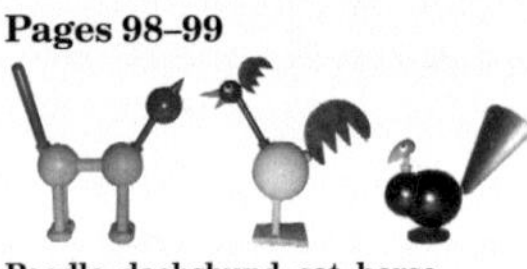

**Poodle, dachshund, cat, horse,
cockerel, turkey, elephant,
llama, rabbit**
1946. Georges Martin (1906–52), designer
and manufacturer, France. Painted
and lacquered wood. Max. h. 22 cm.
Inv. 988.1210

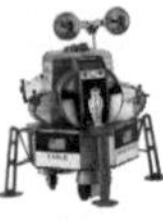

**Apollo 12, American Eagle
Lunar Module**
c. 1969. DSK (Daishin Kogyo),
manufacturer, Japan. Battery operated.
Printed metal and plastic. H. 26 cm;
L. 24 cm; base 18 cm. Inv. 55979

Pinocchio, Wakouwa Robot (see
pp. 94–95); **Space Surveyor X-12,
flying saucer, Atomic Rocket, Super
Astronaut, Robot W, Hopping Robot,
robot** (see pp. 96–97)

Pages 102–103

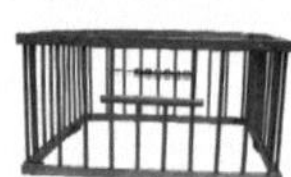

Playpen
c. 1932. France. Painted and varnished
wood. H. 26 cm; L. 50 cm; W. 50 cm.
Inv. 992.619

Wakouwa Robot (see pp. 94–95); **Space
Surveyor X-12, Apollo 12, Strolling
Space Station, space tank, Robot W,
Hopping Robot, robot, Major Mason
with Moon Suit** (see pp. 96–97)

Pages 104–105

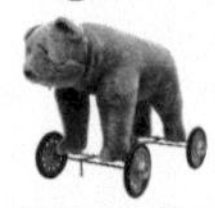

Bear on wheels
c. 1937. Pintel (1887–1973),
manufacturer, France. Mohair fur fabric,
metal and rubber. H. 45 cm; L. 69 cm;
W. 37 cm. Inv. 988.1163

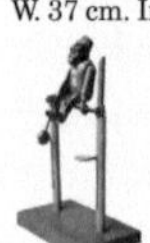

Acrobat monkey on bar
c. 1949. Germany. Wind-up toy. Painted
wood and metal. H. 18.5 cm; L. 12 cm;
W. 7.5 cm. Inv. 54291

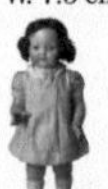

Noëlle walking doll
1949. Petitcollin (1860), manufacturer,
France. Battery operated. Celluloid, glass
and fabric. H. 40 cm. Inv. 49681

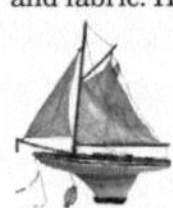

Sailing boat
1950. Borda (1936), manufacturer,
France. Painted wood and cotton.
H. 62 cm; L. 50 cm; W. 14 cm. Inv. 58266.2

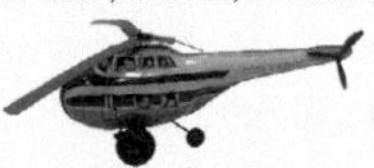

Côte d'Azur helicopter
1950. Joustra (1934), manufacturer,
France. Wind-up toy. Painted metal.

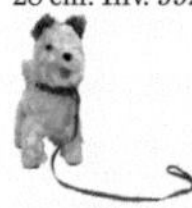

H. 23 cm; L. 34 cm; Rotor span
28 cm. Inv. 992.217

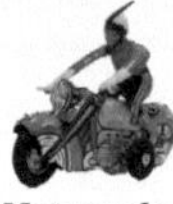

Toutoutrotte walking dog
c. 1950. Pintel (1887–1973),
manufacturer, France. Battery operated.
Fur fabric, glass and plastic. H. 22 cm;
L. 21 cm; W. 10 cm. Inv. 55408

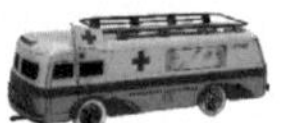

Motorcycle
c. 1950. S.F.A. (Société de Fabrication et
d'Assemblage, 1935–60), manufacturer,
France. Wind-up toy. Lithographed metal
and rubber. H. 14 cm. Inv. Fnac 2039.6

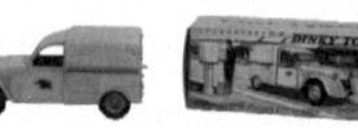

Ambulance
c. 1950. C.R. (Société Rossignol et
Roitelet, c. 1875–1962), manufacturer,
France. Wind-up toy. Painted metal. H.
8 cm; L. 25 cm; W. 5.5 cm. Inv. 996.126.1

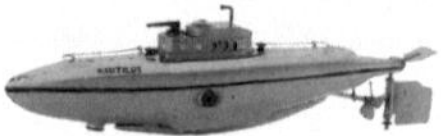

Citroën 2CV post-office van
1951. Dinky Toys France (1934–71),
manufacturer, France. Painted metal.
L. 8 cm. Scale 1:43. Inv. 44545

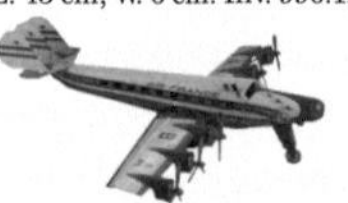

Nautilus 919 submarine
c. 1960. JEP (Jouet de Paris, 1902–68),
manufacturer, France. Wind-up toy.
Enamelled and painted metal. H. 12 cm;
L. 43 cm; W. 6 cm. Inv. 996.123.3

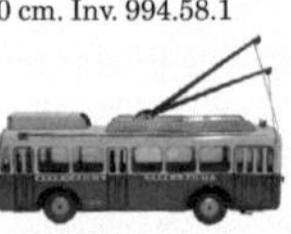

Air France 541 Croix du Sud plane
1954. Joustra (1934), manufacturer,
France. Wind-up toy. Lithographed metal.
H. 13 cm; L. 53 cm; Wingspan
60 cm. Inv. 994.58.1

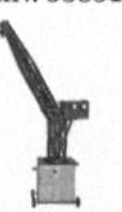

Trolley bus
1954. Joustra (1934), manufacturer,
France. Wind-up toy. Painted metal
and plastic. H. 26 cm; L. 37 cm; W. 12 cm.
Inv. 55851.1

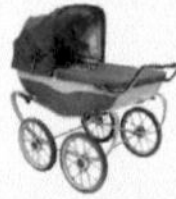

Goliath 434 crane
c. 1955. Joustra (1934), manufacturer,
France. Wind-up toy. Painted metal.
H. 62 cm; W. 16 cm; Arm 26 cm.
Inv. Fnac 2039.109

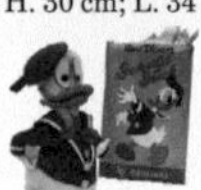

Doll's pram
c. 1955. Edmond Doucet, manufacturer,
France. Metal, plastic, rubber and fabric.
H. 30 cm; L. 34 cm; W. 14 cm. Inv. 992.190

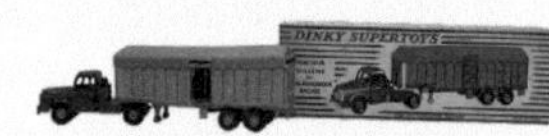

Donald Duck
c. 1957. From the cartoon character
(1934), created by Dick Lundy. Max Carl
(1924–92), manufacturer, Germany.
Wind-up toy. Cardboard, fur fabric,
felt and rubber. H. 21 cm. Inv. 56319

Articulated truck with trailer
Dinky Supertoys series, 1963. Dinky Toys
France (1934–71), manufacturer, France.

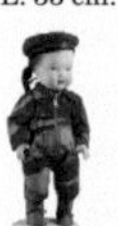

Painted metal and plastic. Scale 1:43.
L. 33 cm. Inv. 41321

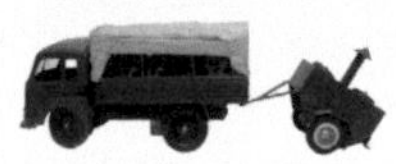

Army truck
1955. C.I.J. (Compagnie Industrielle
du Jouet, c. 1930–69), manufacturer,
France. Painted metal, rubber, plastic
and canvas. H. 16 cm; L. 32 cm; W. 13 cm.
Inv. Fnac 2039.43

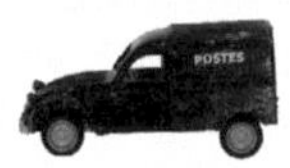

Citroën 2CV post-office van
1955. Norev (1946), manufacturer,
France. Painted metal. L. 8 cm.
Scale 1:43. Inv. 996.138.2

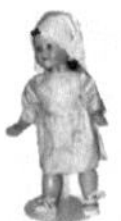

Nurse doll
c. 1955. Vénus (1923), manufacturer,
France. Rhodoid, fabric, ribbon and
plastic. H. 34 cm. Inv. 990.450

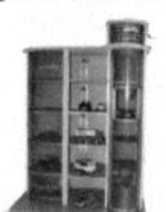

Citroën garage
1955. C.I.J. (Compagnie Industrielle du
Jouet, c. 1930–69), manufacturer, France.
Wind-up toy. Painted wood and plastic.
H. 49 cm; L. 36 cm; W. 36 cm. Inv. Fnac
2039.171

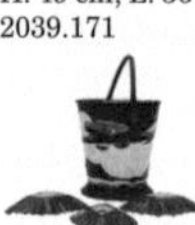

Beach bucket with sandcastle moulds
1955. France. Painted metal.
Diam. 15 cm. Inv. 51286

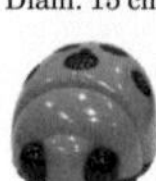

**'Le Cyberson', ladybird toy that
responds to whistles**
1957. Hachette (1876), manufacturer,
France. Battery operated. Plastic and
metal. H. 15 cm; L. 28 cm; W. 18 cm.
Inv. 995.145.1

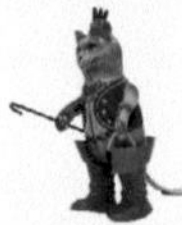

Puss in Boots
c. 1958. From the fairytale *Puss in Boots*
by Charles Perrault (1628–1703), first
published in 1697. Joustra (1934),
manufacturer, France. Wind-up toy.
Enamelled and stamped sheet metal, plastic
and rubber. H. 13 cm. Inv. Fnac 2039.85.1

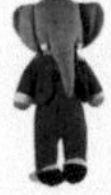

Babar the Elephant
c. 1965. From the character *Babar* (1931),
created by Jean de Brunhoff (1899–1937).
Clodrey (1952–82), manufacturer, France.
Fabric and felt. H. 45 cm. Inv. 990.408

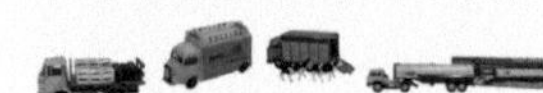

**Renault glass truck, 1963; Citroën
Philips van, 1964; Willème cab with
platform trailer; Berliet breakdown
truck; Berliet brewery truck; Richier
steamroller; Berliet cattle truck;
Berliet dumper truck; Boilot cab and
car-carrier trailer; Willème cab with
container trailer; Peugeot J7 fire
engine, 1965**

Dinky Toys France (1937–71),
manufacturer, France. Painted metal,
plastic, rubber and wood. Max. l. 33 cm.
Scale 1:43. Inv. 41305 to 41310, 41313,
41314, 41322 and 44557

**Circus, François and Jacky baby
dolls, crane, Pinocchio** (see pp. 94–95);
Delahaye luxury car (see pp. 96–97)

Pages 106–107

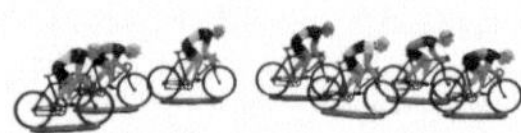

Cyclists
c. 1945. Roger, manufacturer, France.
Moulded aluminium and painted lead.
H. 5.5 cm. Inv. 989.482.1–3

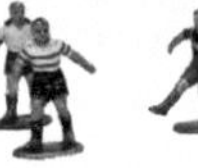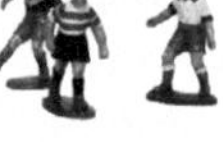

Football players
1950. Quiralu (1933–61), manufacturer,
France. Painted aluminium. H. 5 cm.
Inv. 53143.D

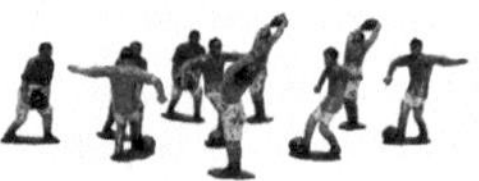

Football players
c. 1950. Aludo (1937–60), manufacturer,
France. Painted metal. Max. h. 8 cm.
Inv. 988.998

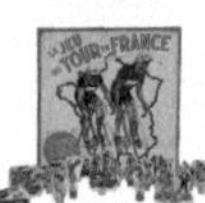

Tour de France game
c. 1948. OGEP, manufacturer, France.
Printed cardboard and wood. H. 36 cm;
L. 36 cm; W. 3 cm (box). Inv. 998.273.2

**Ambulance, nurse doll, Côte d'Azur
helicopter** (see pp. 104–105)

Pages 108–109

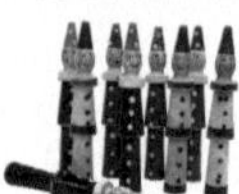

Clown skittles
c. 1950. France. Turned and painted
wood. H. 25 cm. Inv. 988.1109.2

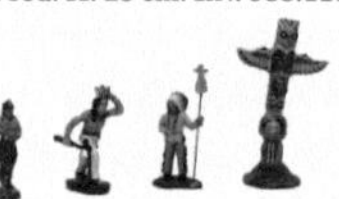

Indians and totem poles
c. 1950. Solido (1932), manufacturer,
France. Painted plaster. Max. h. 14 cm.
Inv. 990.71 and 990.71.1

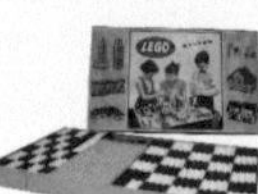

Lego System box set
1958. Lego System and Billund (1948),
manufacturer, Denmark. Plastic. H. 3 cm;
L. 33 cm; W. 20 cm (box). Inv. 997.114.1

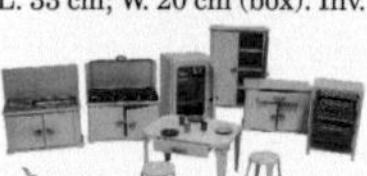

**Kitchen furniture: cupboards, sink
unit, vegetable rack, cooker, table,
stool, fridge and crockery**
1960. C.R. (Société Rossignol et Roitelet,
c. 1875–1962), manufacturer, France.
Lacquered metal. Max. h. 13 cm.
Inv. 995.72.1.1 and 1.2, 995.72.2.1 and
2.2, 995.72.3.1, 3.2, 3.3, 3.5 and 3.8,
995.72.4.1 and 995.72.5

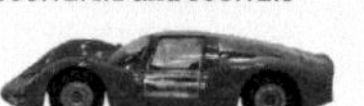

Porsche Carrera 6
1966. Solido (1932), manufacturer,
France. Painted metal. L. 9.5 cm; W. 5 cm.
Inv. 47890.H

Pinocchio (see pp. 94–95); **Citroën
garage, Air France 541 Croix du Sud
plane, collection of Dinky Toys**
(see pp. 104–105)

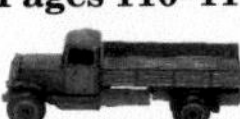

Pages 110–111

Citroën 25 truck
1939. Dinky Toys France (1934–71), manufacturer, France. Painted metal and rubber. H. 3 cm; L. 10.5 cm; W. 3.5 cm. Scale 1:43. Inv. 55900.1

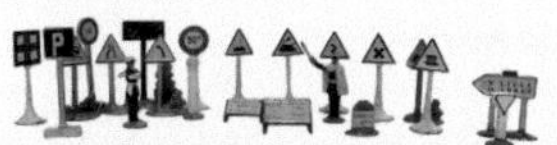

Policemen and road signs
c. 1953. Quiralu (1933–61), manufacturer, France. Painted aluminium. Max. h. 9 cm. Inv. 995.70.1

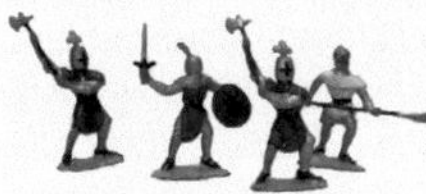

Crusader knights in chain mail
1955. Inco et Guibert, manufacturers, France. Plastic. H. 7 cm. Inv. 55438.1

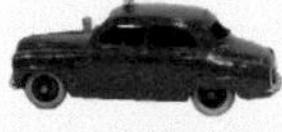

Simca 9 Aronde taxi, c. 1950; **Chrysler New Yorker; Citroën 11 BL**, 1955. Dinky Toys France (1934–71), manufacturer, France. Painted metal and rubber. Max. l. 10 cm; Max. w. 4 cm. Scale 1:43. Inv. 992.157.1, 2 and 4

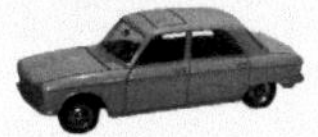

Peugeot 204
1965. Dinky Toys France (1934–71), manufacturer, France. Painted metal and rubber. H. 2.5 cm; L. 9 cm; W. 3.5 cm. Scale 1:43. Inv. 44543

Collection of Dinky Toys (see pp. 105–106); **Indians and totem poles** (see pp. 108–109)

Pages 114–115

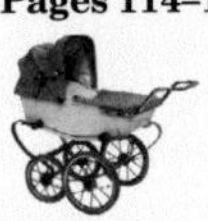

Pram
c. 1937. Au Nain Bleu (1836), store and manufacturer, France. Metal, plastic, rubber and imitation leather. H. 28 cm; L. 19 cm; W. 14 cm. Inv. 48420

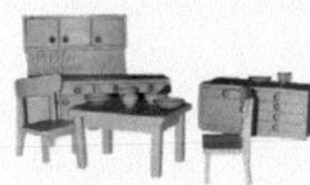

Kitchen furniture: cupboard, chairs, table, dresser and crockery
1948. J.F.J. (Jeux et Jouets Français, 1904–30), manufacturer, France. Painted and lacquered wood. Inv. 46807

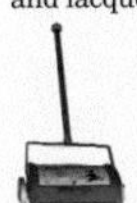

Musical sweeper
1950. Fisher-Price (1931), manufacturer, USA. Painted metal. H. 58 cm. Inv. 997.99.1

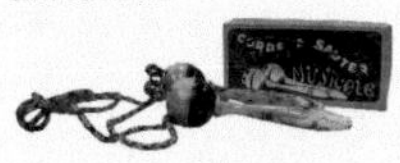

Musical skipping rope
1950. Camelin (1909–62), manufacturer, France. Metal, wood and rope. L. 80 cm. Inv. 46895

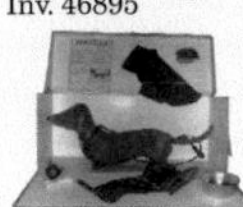

Dachshund
c. 1950. Gaston Decamps (1882–1972), designer and manufacturer, France. Battery operated. Cotton, metal and plastic. H. 17 cm; L. 40 cm; W. 10 cm. Inv. 998.94.14

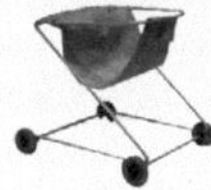

Baby walker
c. 1950. France. Metal, rubber and canvas. H. 14 cm; L. 17 cm; W. 14 cm. Inv. 46812

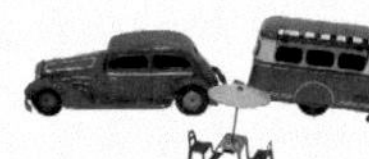

Weekend car with caravan, no. 400/602
1952. Joustra (1934), manufacturer, France. Wind-up toy. Stamped and painted metal. L. 51 cm. Inv. Fnac 2039.90

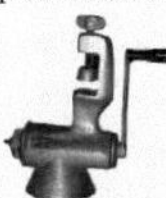

Mincing machine
c. 1955. France. Painted metal. H. 17 cm; L. 14 cm; W. 7 cm. Inv. 988.29

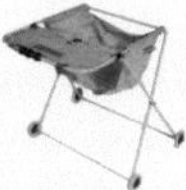

Baby walker
1956. Bébé Confort (1875), manufacturer, France. Metal and fabric. H. 25 cm; L. 29 cm; W. 26 cm. Inv. 41152

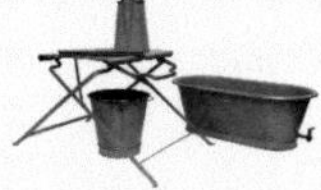

Washstand and accessories
1957. JEP (Jouet de Paris, 1902–68), manufacturer, France. Painted metal. Max. h. 24 cm. Inv. 988.522

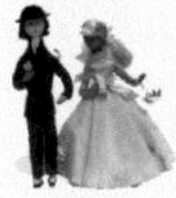

'Les Amoureux de Peynet' boy and girl dolls
1957. Raymond Peynet (1908–99), designer; Technigom (c. 1950–70), manufacturer, France. Winner of Toy Oscar 1957, in Girl's Toys category. Technigom rubber, metal, fabric and felt. H. 21 cm. Inv. 990.411.1

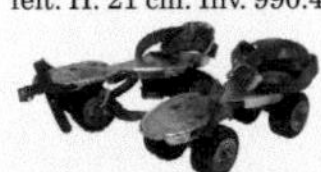

Vitesse roller skates
1955. Ets Rollet (1926), manufacturer, France. Metal and leather. H. 8 cm; L. 22 cm; W. 8 cm. Inv. 49031

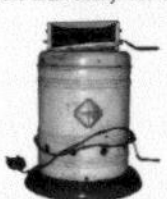

Washing machine
c. 1955. Jouets Charlys-Ets Badet (1903–c. 1960), manufacturer, France. Electric toy. Enamelled metal and rubber. H. 23 cm. Inv. Fnac 2039.29

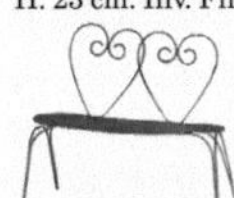

Bench
c. 1956. Raymond Peynet (1908–99), designer and manufacturer, France. Painted metal. H. 12 cm; L. 15 cm; W. 5 cm. Inv. 54657.3

Pinocchio (see pp. 94–95); **Babar, doll's pram, Noëlle doll** (see pp. 104–105); **policemen and road signs** (see pp. 110–111)

Pages 116–117

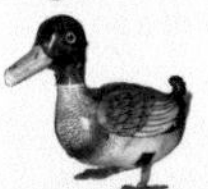

Mallard duck
c. 1947. Germany. Wind-up toy. Painted and printed metal and plastic. H. 7 cm; L. 9 cm; W. 4 cm. Inv. 54627.3

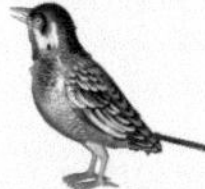

Chaffinch
c. 1950. Köhler (1873), manufacturer, Germany. Wind-up toy. Painted and printed metal and plastic. H. 13 cm; L. 19 cm; W. 6 cm. Inv. 54629.1

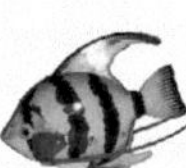

Angel fish
c. 1950. China. Wind-up toy. Printed metal and plastic. H. 13 cm; L. 18 cm; W. 5 cm. Inv. 54633.1

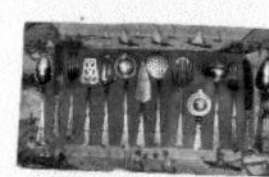

Place settings
1950. France. Metal. Max. l. 10.5 cm; W. 7 cm. Inv. 988.633

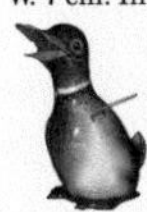

Mallard duck
c. 1955. Joustra (1934), manufacturer, France. Wind-up toy. Lithographed painted metal. H. 15 cm. Inv. 988.1164.1

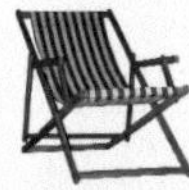

Deckchair
1955. France. Wood and fabric. H. 41 cm; L. 23 cm; W. 39 cm. Inv. 990.444.1

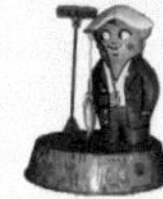

Martin the Fisherman
c. 1955. Joustra (1934), manufacturer, France. Wind-up toy. Stamped, enamelled and painted metal. H. 15 cm; L. 12 cm. Inv. 50870

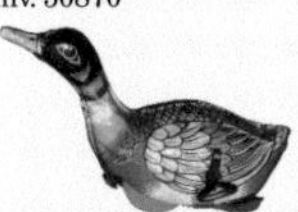

Duck
c. 1955. Alps (1948), manufacturer, Japan. Wind-up toy. Stamped and painted metal and plastic. H. 6 cm; L. 10 cm; W. 5 cm. Inv. 54627.2

Donald Duck (see pp. 104–105)

Pages 118–119

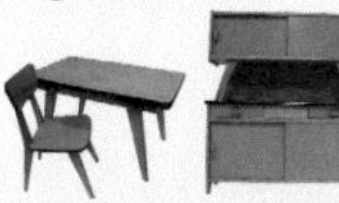

Kitchen furniture: chairs, table and dresser
c. 1950. France. Laminated wood. Max. h. 59 cm. Inv. 46575

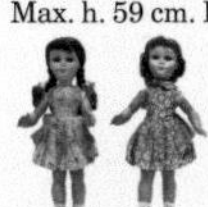

Dolls
1955–60. Bella (1946–84), manufacturer, France. Plastic, fabric and synthetic fibres. Max. h. 41 cm. Inv. Fnac 2039.212.38, 39 and 42

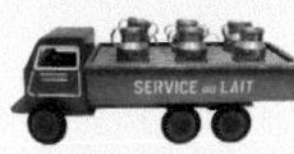

Milk wagon
c. 1959. Joujoulac (1954–69), manufacturer, France. Painted and varnished wood and aluminium. H. 21 cm; L. 55 cm; W. 21 cm. Inv. 988.142

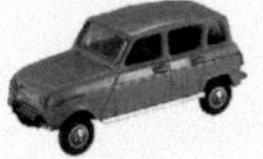

Renault 4L
1962. Joustra (1934), manufacturer, France. Wind-up toy. Plastic, rubber and painted metal. H. 6 cm; L. 19 cm; W. 8.5 cm. Scale 1:43. Inv. 55852

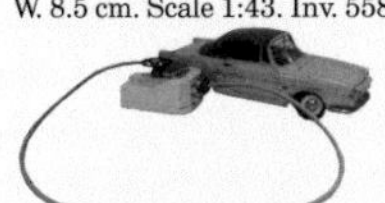

Remote control car
c. 1965. C.I.J. (Compagnie Industrielle du Jouet, c. 1930–69), manufacturer, France. Painted metal and plastic. H. 7.5 cm; L. 29 cm; W. 9.5 cm. Inv. 539744

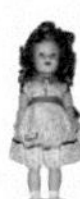

Doll
c. 1965. Raynal (1922–c. 1980), manufacturer, France. Plastic and nylon. H. 46 cm. Inv. Fnac 2039.212.48

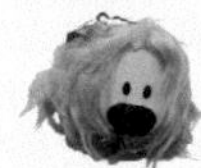

Dougal
1965. From the TV series *The Magic Roundabout* (1964), created by Serge Danot (1931–90); Clodrey (1952–82), manufacturer, France. Synthetic materials and plastic. H. 12 cm; L. 34 cm; W. 18 cm. Inv. 47855

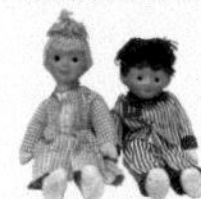

Nicolas and Pimprenelle
1966. From the TV series *Nounours, bonne nuit les petits* (1962), created by Claude Laydu. Clodrey (1952–82), manufacturer, France. Stuffed fabric and plastic. H. 50 cm. Inv. 41137.1 and 2

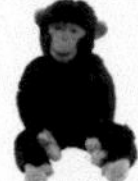

Chimpanzee
c. 1970. Anima (1947), manufacturer, France. Kapok. H. 55 cm. Inv. 43354

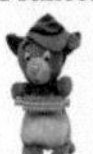

Italian Cat
1970. From the animated film *The Aristocats* (1970) directed by Wolfgang Reitherman and produced by Walt Disney. Pintel (1887–1973), manufacturer, France. Fur fabric and felt. H. 38 cm. Inv. 55382.1

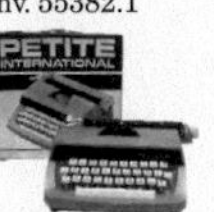

Petite International deluxe typewriter
1970. Mettoy Playcraft (1934–84), manufacturer, Great Britain. Plastic. H. 12 cm; L. 25 cm; W. 24 cm. Inv. 43369

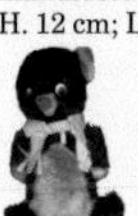

Cuddly bear
1973. Pintel (1887–1973), manufacturer, France. Fur fabric, plastic, jersey and felt. H. 32 cm. Inv. 55407

Pages 120–121

Milk wagon, Nicolas and Pimprenelle, Petite International deluxe typewriter, Dougal, Italian Cat, kitchen furniture (see pp. 118–119)

Pages 122–123

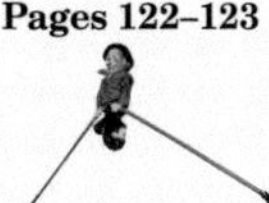

Balancing clown
1960. Fewo (Fenh-Wolf & Co, c. 1950), manufacturer, Germany. Wind-up toy. Painted metal, fabric and plastic. H. 20 cm. Inv. 53870

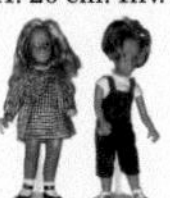

Sasha dolls
1965. Sasha Morgenthaler (1893–1975), designer and manufacturer, Switzerland. Plastic and fabric. H. 43 cm. Inv. 40145.1 and 2

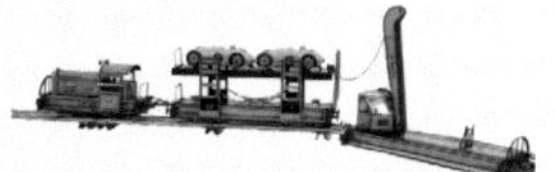

Pages 126–127

Train
1950. Saint-Nicolas, manufacturer, France. Wind-up toy. Painted metal. Max. h. 20 cm. Inv. Fnac 2039.209

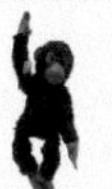

Congo monkey
c. 1960. Hermann Teddy Original (1907), manufacturer, Germany. Mohair, felt and glass. H. 34 cm. Inv. 998.255.1.5

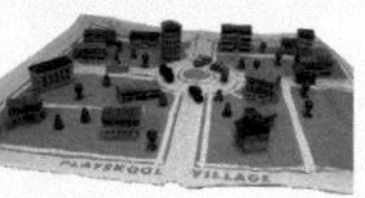

Village
1961. Playskool (1928), manufacturer, USA. Painted wood and fabric. Max. h. 9 cm; L. 79 cm (ground cloth). Inv. 41147

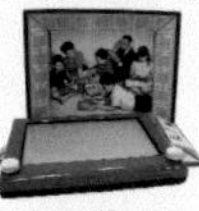

Etch-a-Sketch
c. 1965. Jouets Rationnels (c. 1950–60), manufacturer, France. Winner of Toy Oscar 1966. Plastic. H. 4 cm; L. 24 cm; W. 20 cm. Inv. 40434

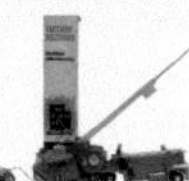

Fire engine
c. 1965. Ets Rollet (1926), manufacturer, France. Battery operated. Plastic. H. 42 cm. Inv. 51085

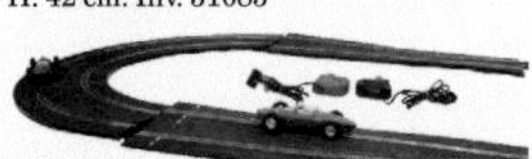

Grand Prix racing track with Matra F1 and Porsche 917 racing cars, accessories and figures
1966. Scalextric (1952), France. Metal and plastic. Max. l. 2.29 m; Min. l. 12 cm (track). L. 14 cm; W. 6 cm (cars). H. 6 cm (figures). Inv. 41301.A–B, 41302, 41272.A–B, 41273, 41282, 41298, 44458 and 44549

Remote control car, Renault 4L, chimpanzee (see pp. 118–119)

Pages 128–129

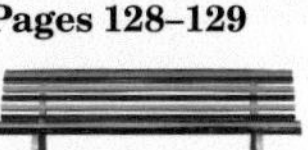

Bench
1960. France. Painted wood. H. 16 cm; L. 40 cm; W. 16 cm. Inv. 990.443.1

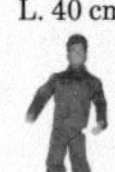

G.I. Joe
1964. Hasbro (1923), manufacturer, USA. Vinyl, plastic and rubber. H. 29 cm. Inv. 41110.A

Girl doll (see pp. 118–119)

Pages 130–131

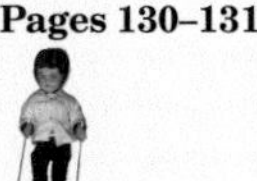

Ketty doll
1960. Jouets Mont Blanc (1947–c. 1980), manufacturer, France. Battery operated. Polyethylene, plastic, wood and fabric. H. 30 cm; L. 31 cm; W. 7.5 cm. Inv. 988.783

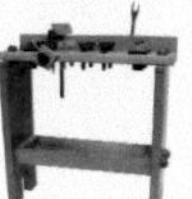

Workbench with tools
1960. Léon Giraud-Sauveur et Fils (1914), manufacturer, France. Painted wood and metal. H. 50 cm; L. 43 cm; W. 17 cm. Inv. 41077

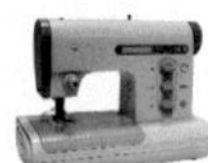

Gabriela sewing machine
c. 1960. France. Plastic. H. 19 cm;
L. 25 cm; W. 15 cm. Inv. 995.140.1

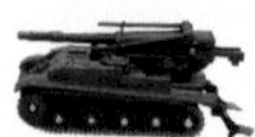

**AMX bridge-layer tank and 155-mm
automatic cannon**
c. 1964 and 1972. Dinky Toys France
(1934–71), manufacturer. Zamac
(zinc/lead alloy) and plastic. H. 7 cm;
L. 34 cm; W. 6.5 cm (tank); H. 5 cm;
L. 9 cm; W. 5 cm (cannon). Scale 1:50.
Inv. 44537 and 44529

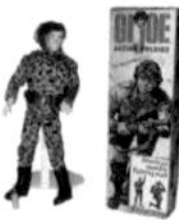

**G.I. Joe Combat Marine, G.I. Joe
Frogman, G.I. Joe Radio Operator,
Combat Fatigues Set**
1964. Hasbro (1923), manufacturer,
USA. Vinyl, plastic and rubber. H. 29 cm.
Inv. 41110.B, C, E and G

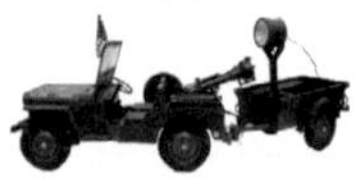

G.I. Joe Official Jeep Combat Set
c. 1965. Hasbro (1923), manufacturer,
USA. Vinyl, plastic and rubber. H. 30 cm;
L. 80 cm. Inv. 41111

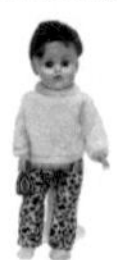

Doll
1965. Palitoy (1909–84), manufacturer,
Great Britain. Vinyl, plastic and fabric.
H. 44 cm. Inv. Fnac 2039.212.61

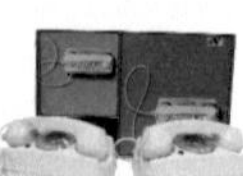

Toy telephones
1969. Vullierme (1946–*c.* 1989),
manufacturer, France. Battery operated.
Plastic. H. 12 cm; L. 20 cm. Inv. 43255

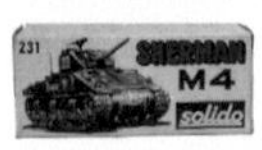

Tanks: Afrika-Korps Tiger, 1969;
AMX-13 Bitube, 1970; **Jagdpanther**,
1971; **Sherman M4; Destroyer M10**,
1972
Solido (1932), manufacturer, France.
Zamac and plastic. Max. h. 6 cm;
Max. l. 19 cm; Max. w. 8 cm. Scale 1:50.
Inv. 44492 to 44497

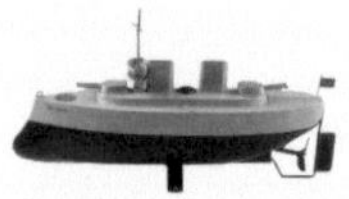

Battleship
c. 1978. Sutcliffe (1920–83),
manufacturer, Great Britain. Wind-up
toy. Painted steel. H. 13 cm; L. 32 cm;
W. 8 cm. Inv. 993.13.13

**Kitchen furniture, chimpanzee,
doll** (see pp. 118–119); **Grand Prix
racetrack, Congo monkey** (see
pp. 126–127); **bench** (see pp. 128–129);
G.I. Joe set (see pp. 130–131)

Pages 132–133

Kitchen furniture (see pp. 118–119);
Congo monkey (see pp. 126–127);
**G.I. Joe set, workbench with tools,
tanks** (see pp. 130–131)

Pages 134–135

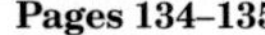
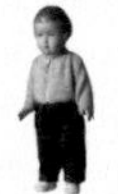

Françoise doll
1951. S.N.F. (Société Nobel Française,
c. 1928–63), manufacturer, France.
With the collaboration of the magazine
Modes & Travaux. Celluloid and fabric.
H. 39 cm. Inv. 56904

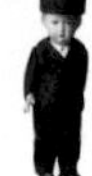

Josette doll in postman's costume
1952. S.N.F. (Société Nobel Française,
c. 1928–63), manufacturer, France.
Celluloid and fabric. H. 39 cm. Inv. 49051

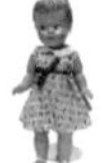

Doll
c. 1955. Clodrey (1952–82), manufacturer,
France. Polyflex, fabric and plastic.
H. 25 cm. Inv. 991.10

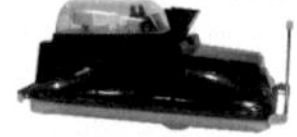

Cybercar
1957. Hachette (1876), manufacturer,
France. Winner of Toy Oscar 1957, in
Boy's Toys category. Battery operated.
Plastic. H. 13 cm; L. 22 cm; W. 17 cm.
Inv. 996.43.1

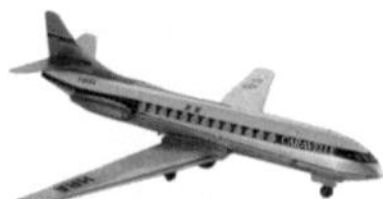

Caravelle plane
c. 1960. Joustra (1934), manufacturer,
France. Wind-up toy. Metal and plastic.
H. 7 cm; L. 43 cm; Wingspan 47 cm.
Scale 1:76. Inv. 996.123.15

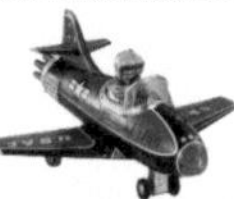

Mystery Action Plane
c. 1960. T.N. (Nomura Toy Industrial Co.
Ltd, 1940), manufacturer, Japan. Winner
of Toy Oscar 1960. Battery operated.
Painted metal. H. 13 cm; L. 30 cm;
Wingspan 27 cm. Inv. 53153

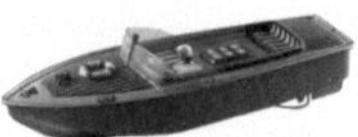

Chris-Craft motorboat
c. 1960. Arnold (1906), manufacturer,
Germany. Electronic toy. Plastic.
L. 30 cm. Inv. Fnac 2039.137

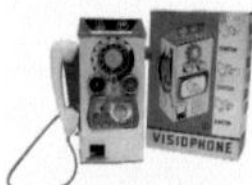

Tintin Visiophone
1960. Ets Rollet (1926), manufacturer,
France. Winner of Toy Oscar 1960.
Plastic and metal. H. 32 cm. Inv. 54996

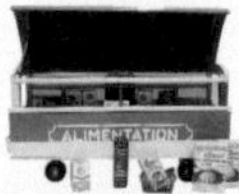

Mobile store
c. 1962. Ets Monart-Joujoulac (1954–69),
manufacturer, France. Painted wood.
H. 25 cm; L. 50 cm; W. 18 cm. Inv. 54447

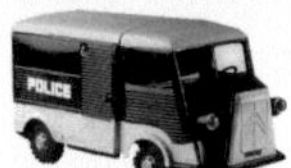

Citroën police van
1963. J.R.D. (1935–63), manufacturer,
France. Painted metal. H. 17 cm;
L. 34 cm; W. 17 cm. Inv. 51078

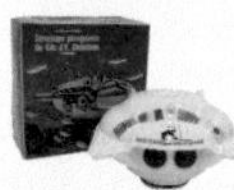

Cousteau submarine
1964. Ets Rollet (1926), manufacturer,
France. Battery operated. Plastic. L. 28 cm;
W. 28 cm; Diam. 28 cm. Inv. 51082

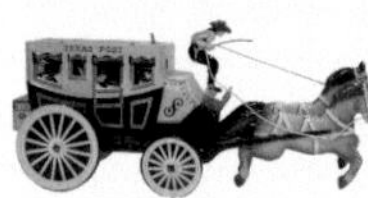

Texas Post stagecoach
1965. Joustra (1934), manufacturer, France.
Wind-up toy. Lithographed metal. H. 14.5
cm; L. 23 cm; W. 11 cm. Inv. Fnac 2039.36

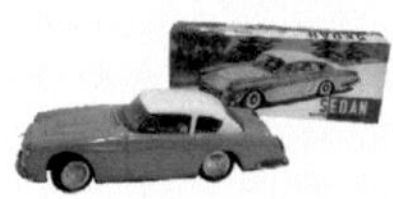

Ferrari sedan
c. 1965. Made in China. Painted metal.
H. 8 cm; L. 25 cm; W. 10 cm (box).
Inv. 41121

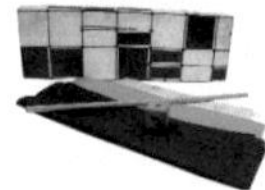

Baubau wooden building set no. 1
1965. Gert Müller (b. 1931), Kurt Naëf
(b. 1926), designers and manufacturers,
Switzerland. Beechwood and canvas.
L. 64 cm (pole); L. 5 cm (cube). Inv. 40137

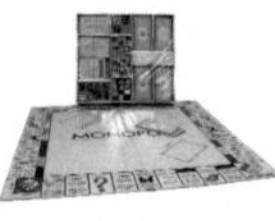

Monopoly deluxe set no. 5
1965. Game created in 1933 by Charles
Darrow (1889–1967). Miro Company
(1936–80), manufacturer, France.
Cardboard and plastic. L. 50.5 cm;
W. 27 cm; Depth 5.5 cm (box). Inv. 40167

**Grand Prix racetrack, Congo
monkey** (see pp. 126–127)

Pages 138–139

Congo monkey (see pp. 126–127);
**Baubau building set, Monopoly set,
Citroën police van, mobile store,
Françoise doll, Josette doll in
postman's costume, Ferrari sedan**
(see pp. 134–135)

Pages 140–141

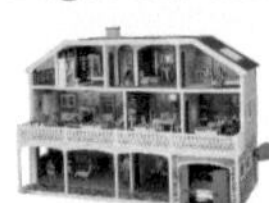

Doll's house, figures and accessories
1980. Lundby (1945), manufacturer,
Sweden. Electronic toy. Plastic, cardboard
and wood. H. 57 cm; L. 87 cm; W. 40 cm.
Inv. 49987

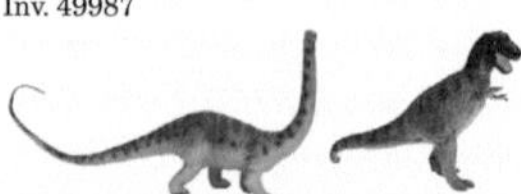

**Dinosaurs: Brachiosaurus,
Apatosaurus, Diplodocus,
Tyrannosaurus, Allosaurus,
Spinosaurus, Triceratops,
Pteranodon, Elasmosaurus**
1988–92. Replicas of models from the
Carnegie Museum collection, Pittsburgh,
USA. Safari Ltd (1980), manufacturer,
USA. Plastic. Max. h. 39 cm. Scale 1:15
and 1:40. Inv. 992.466.1 to 7, 14, 19 and 20

Pages 142–143

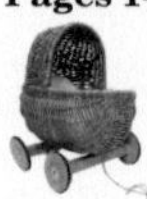

Doll's crib
1974. Catherine Refabert (b. 1938),
designer; Clodrey (1952–82), manufacturer,
France. Wicker, wood and cotton. H. 39 cm;
L. 32 cm; W. 25 cm. Inv. 44723

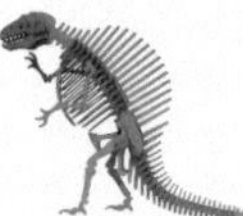

Spinosaurus
1980. Tatsuya Egawa (b. 1961) and
Kazuma Kodaka (b. 1969), designers;
Tatsuya Original, manufacturer, Japan.
Wood. H. 52 cm; L. 75 cm. Inv. 49472

Dinosaurs (see pp. 140–141)

Pages 144–145

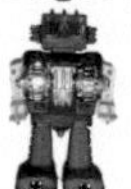

Robot
c. 1975. Made in Japan. Battery operated.
Plastic. H. 22 cm; L. 14 cm; W. 7 cm.
Inv. 54622

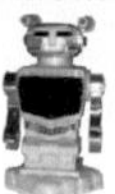

Robot
1975. Soma, manufacturer, Hong Kong.
Battery operated. Plastic. H. 26 cm.
Inv. 55981

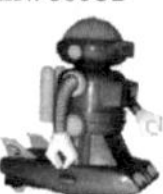

Robot
1975. Solpa (Solakidi brothers, 1946–85),
manufacturer, Greece. Battery operated.
Plastic. H. 25 cm. Inv. 55982

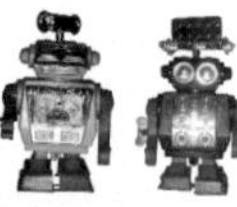

Robots
1975. Japan and Hong Kong. Wind-up toy.
Plastic. Max. h. 18 cm. Inv. 55983.1 to 3

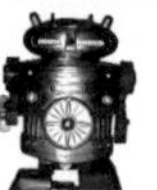

Robot
1975. Toy Hero, manufacturer,
Japan. Wind-up toy. Plastic. H. 10 cm.
Inv. 55984.1

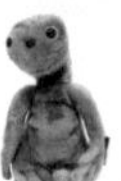

E. T.
1982. From the film *E.T.* (1982), directed
by Steven Spielberg. USA. Synthetic fur
and plastic. H. 34 cm. Inv. 54376.1–2

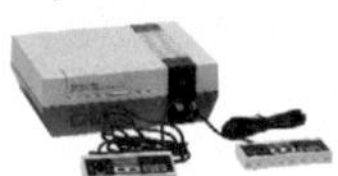

NES games console (released in
Japan as Famicom, 1983) with the game
Gremlins 2, 1990. Nintendo (1889),
manufacturer, Japan. 8-bit console.
H. 9 cm; L. 26 cm; L. 20 cm. Inv. in
progress

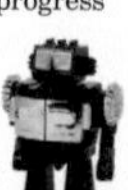

Blackfighter Robot
1983. S.H. (Horikawa, 1959),
manufacturer, Japan. Battery operated.
Plastic and metal. H. 23 cm; L. 12.5 cm;
W. 10 cm. Inv. 54592.1–2

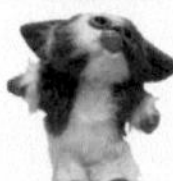

Gizmo
1984. From the film *Gremlins* (1984),
directed by Joe Dante. USA. Made in
Malaysia. Fur fabric and plastic. H. 26 cm.
Inv. 55966

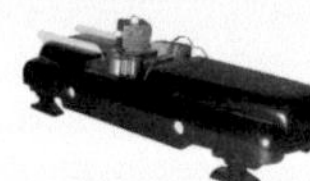

**Robots, rocket on wheels and
space vehicles**
1986–87. Christian Poumeyrol (b. 1947),
designer, France. Plastic and wood
with metallic varnish. Max. h. 30 cm.
Inv. 988.87 and 990.360 to 362

Pages 146–147

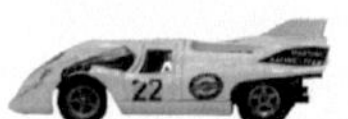

Porsche 917 K Le Mans 1972
1972. Solido (1932), manufacturer,
France. Painted metal. H. 2.5 cm;
L. 10 cm; W. 4.5 cm. Scale 1:43. Inv. 44470

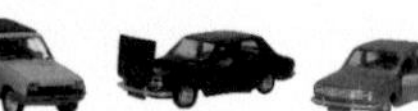

Renault 5 TL and two Renault R12s
1972. Norev (1946), manufacturer,
France. Metal and plastic. Max. h. 3 cm.
Scale 1:43. Inv. 44556.A and 44559.A–B

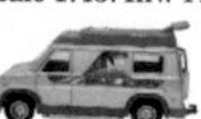

**4x4 Blazer, 4x4 Toyota, Kerian-Nice,
4x4 Blazer, Holiday Van, 4x4 Blazer,
Toyota Raid, Air France bus and
Holiday Van**
1981–82. Majorette (1966), manufacturer,
France. Painted metal and plastic.
Max. h. 7 cm. Scale 1:43. Inv. 51136.A–B,
51137.A–B, 51139.A–C, 51144.A and
53971.2

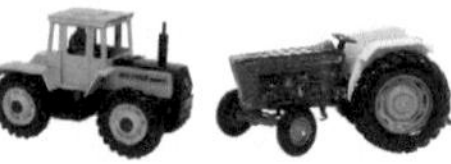

Tractors
1982. Britains (1893–*c.* 1990),
manufacturer, Great Britain. Painted
metal, rubber and plastic. Max. h. 10 cm.
Inv. 989.121.2 and 54361.B

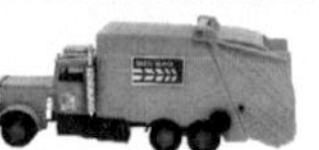

Dust cart
1984. Matchbox (1953), manufacturer,
Great Britain. Made in Macao. Painted
metal and plastic. Scale 1:43. Inv. 55908

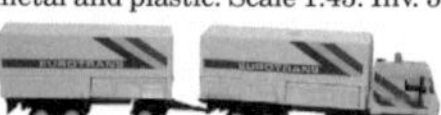

Tanker, 1983; **Ferrari racing car
transporter truck**, 1984; **Tanker**, 1986
Superkings series. Matchbox (1953),
manufacturer, Great Britain. Made in
Macao. Painted metal and plastic. Max. h.
8 cm. Inv. 56184.2; 56936.2; 56937.2

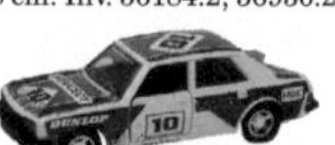

Peugeot 305, 1981; **Mercedes
Benz yacht transporter truck**,
1985; **Mercedes Benz refrigerated
truck**, 1988
Superkings series. Matchbox (1953),
manufacturer, Great Britain. Painted
metal and plastic. Max. h. 10 cm.
Inv. 56933.1, 56936.1, 56938.3

**Robots, Blackfighter Robot, E.T.,
NES with the game *Double Dragon*,**
1988 (see pp. 144–145)

Pages 148–149

Darth Vader
1978. From the film *Star Wars* (1977),
directed by George Lucas. Kenner
Products (1947–95), manufacturer, USA.
Made in Hong Kong. Plastic. H. 38 cm.
Inv. 991.505

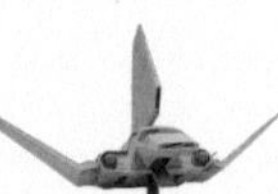

Imperial Shuttle
1984. From the film *Return of the Jedi*
(1983) by George Lucas. Kenner Products
(1947–95), manufacturer, USA. Plastic.
Max. h. 57 cm; L. 51 cm; Wingspan 90 cm.
Inv. in progress

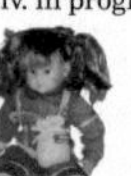

'Copine Aérobic' doll
1984. Corolle (1979), manufacturer,
France. Stuffed and printed fabric and
vinyl. H. 54 cm. Inv. 54952.3

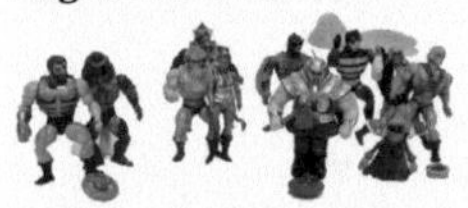

Pages 174–175

Masters of the Universe Heroes:
Man-At-Arms, Orko, Ram Man,
Prince Adam, Man-E-Faces, Stratos,
Teela, Mekaneck, Fisto, Buzz-Off
1983. Mattel (1945), manufacturer, USA.
Made in Hong Kong. Plastic. Max. h.
14 cm. Inv. 56309.1 to 11

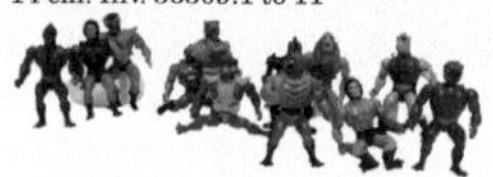

Masters of the Universe Villains:
Jitsu, Kobra Khan, Clawful, Beast
Man, Webstor, Mer-Man, Zodac, Trap
Jaw, Whiplash, Tri-Klops, Skeletor
1983. Mattel (1945), manufacturer, USA.
Made in Hong Kong. Plastic. Max. h.
14 cm. Inv. 56310.1 to 11

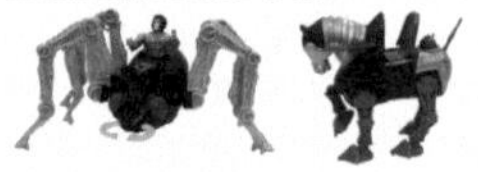

Masters of the Universe:
Spydor and Stridor
1983–84. Mattel (1945), manufacturer,
USA. Made in Mexico. Battery operated.
Plastic. Max. h. 21 cm. Inv. 991.510,
991.514

Pitou the dog (see pp. 172–173)

Pages 176–177

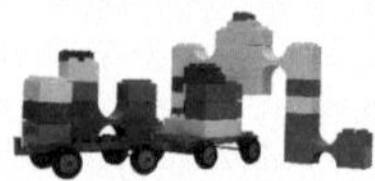

Duplo basic set
c. 1970. Lego/Duplo (1948),
manufacturers, Denmark. Plastic.
H. 7 cm; L. 42 cm; W. 24 cm. Inv. 46620

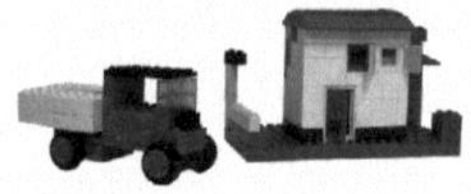

Lego house, 1970–80;
Lego basic set, c. 1972
Lego (1948), manufacturer, Denmark.
Plastic. Max. h. 12 cm. Inv. 46454
and 46615

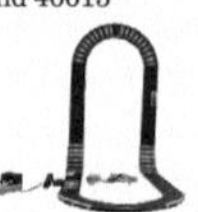

Turbo Team vertical racing set
c. 1980. Tyco (1926–98), manufacturer,
USA. Made in Hong Kong. Electronic toy.
Plastic and paper stickers. Total l. 3.80 m;
Max. h. 75 cm. Inv. 54398

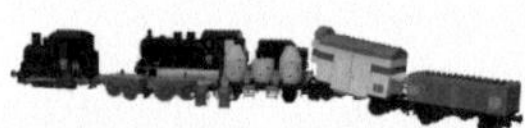

Lego train
1982. Lego (1948), manufacturer,
Denmark. Electronic toy. Plastic.
L. 80 cm. Inv. 51619

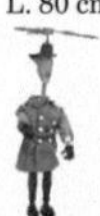

Inspector Gadget
1983. From the cartoon *Inspector Gadget*
(1983), created by Bruno Bianchi, Andy
Heyward and Jean Chalopin. Bandai
(1950), manufacturer, Japan. Made in
Macao. Wind-up toy. Plastic. Max. h.
55 cm. Inv. 54388

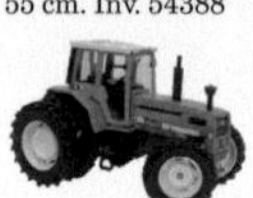

Tractor
1983. R.O.S., manufacturer, Italy. Metal
and plastic. H. 11 cm; L. 17 cm; W. 13 cm.
Inv. 990.84

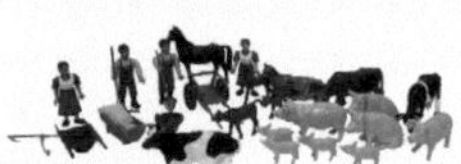

Farm playset
1988. Schleich (1935), manufacturer,
Germany. Plastic. Max. h. 10.5 cm.
Inv. 989.110.1–6

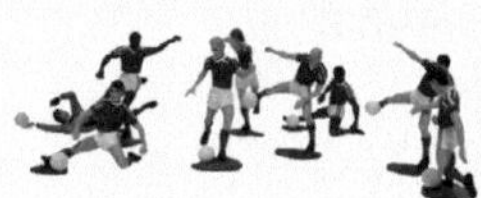

Sportstars footballers: players from
the French national team, Paris
Saint Germain, Olympique de
Marseille and Bordeaux
1989. Tonka Corporation (1946–91),
manufacturer, USA. Made in China.
Painted plastic. H. 10 cm; L. 11 cm.
Inv. 991.294.1 to 3 and 991.260

Pages 180–181

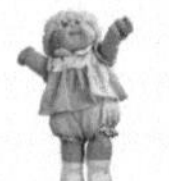

Cabbage Patch Kids
1982. Xavier Roberts (b. 1955), designer;
Ideal (1979–1990?), manufacturer, USA.
Plastic and fabric. H. 42 cm. Inv. 54412

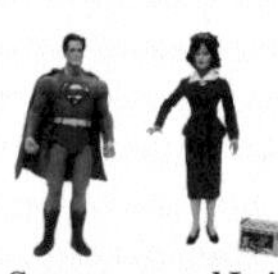

Superman and Lois Lane
1997. From the comic-book characters
(1938) created by Jerry Siegel and
Joe Shuster. Robert Tonner, designer;
Robert Tonner Doll Company (1991),
manufacturer, USA. Porcelain, wool,
fabric and paper. Max. h. 51 cm.
Inv. 999.92. 1 and 2

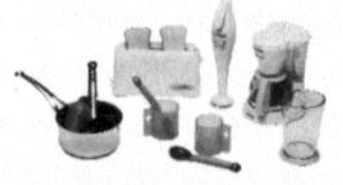

Deluxe kitchen set
2003. Smoby (1978), France. Plastic.
Max. h. 19 cm. Inv. 2006.15.13.1 12

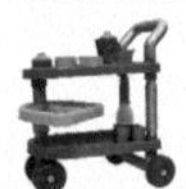 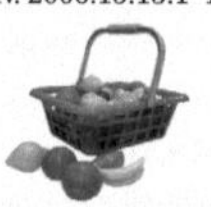

Cool Cook, 2004; **basket of fruit and
vegetables**, 2005
Écoiffier, manufacturer, France. Plastic.
Max. h. 45 cm. Inv. 2006.15.2.1–32 and
2006.15.16.1–21

Pages 182–183

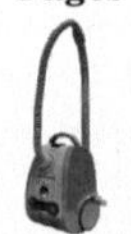

Neo Mini Rowenta vacuum cleaner
2003. Smoby (1978), manufacturer,
France. Made in China. Battery operated.
Plastic and polystyrene beads. H. 61 cm.
Inv. 2006.15.17.1–6

**Pokemon Advanced: Pikachu,
Treecko, Taillow, Wurmple,
Wailmer, Duskull, Mudkip,
Corphish, Wynaut, Latias,
Zigzagoon, Groudon, Poochyena,
Seedot, Azurill and Whismur**
2004. From the video game *Pokemon*
(1996), created by Satochi Tajiri.
Bandai (1950), manufacturer, Japan.
Made in China. Plastic. Max. h. 5 cm.
Inv. 2006.13.14 to 18

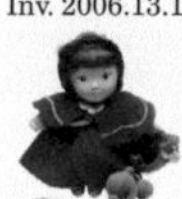

'Coquelicot la Coquette' doll
Pomponnette series, 2004. Sophie
Piégelin, designer; Ouaps (2002),
manufacturer, France. Made in China.
Plastic, polyester, fabric. H. 34 cm.
Inv. 2006.17.5

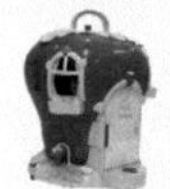 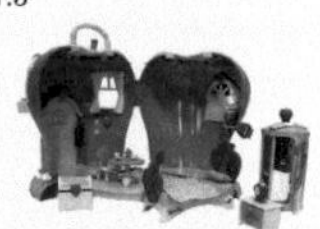

**Strawberry Shortcake Strawberry-
Scented Home**
2005. Bandai (1950), manufacturer,
Japan. Made in China. Battery operated.
Plastic and fabric with artificial scent.
Max. h. 29 cm. Inv. 2006.13.4.1–18

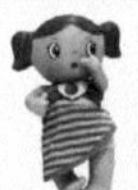

Beedibies girl doll
2005. Corolle (1979), manufacturer,
France. Plastic and fabric. H. 22 cm.
Inv. 2006.16.11

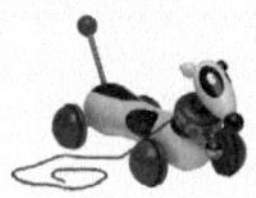

Toby the dog
2006 (1st ed. 1996). Vilac (1911),
manufacturer, France. Drag-along toy.
Painted and lacquered wood, metal and
string. H. 11 cm; L. 35 cm; W. 12 cm.
Inv. in progress

Superman and Lois Lane
(see pp. 180–181)

Pages 184–185

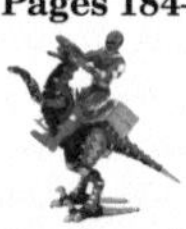

Dino Thunder Red Raptor Rider
2003. From the TV series *Power
Rangers* (1993). Bandai (1950),
manufacturer, Japan. Made in China.
Plastic. H. 17 cm. Inv. 2006.13.11.1–4

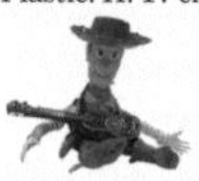

Strummin Singin' Woody
2003. From the animated film *Toy Story*
(1995), directed by John Lasseter. Hasbro
(1923), manufacturer, USA. Battery
operated. Plastic and fabric. Max. h.
35 cm. Inv. 2006.15.8

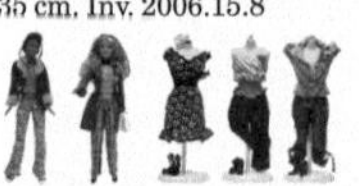

Kayla and Barbie, 2004; **Fashion
Fever outfits**, 2002
Mattel (1945), manufacturer, France.
Plastic and fabric. Max. h. 30 cm.
Inv. 2006.16.3, 4 and 2006.16.5 to 7

Pages 188–189

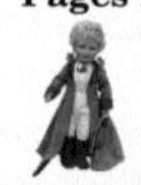

The Little Prince
c. 1983. From the book *The Little Prince*
(1943) by Antoine de Saint-Éxupéry
(1900–44). John Wright, designer; John
Wright Dolls (1976), manufacturer, USA.
Felt. H. 46 cm. Inv. 992.468.1

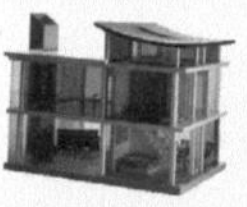 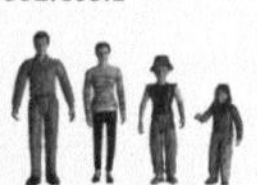

**The Kaleidoscope House: doll's
house and Blue-Green family**
2001. Laurie Simmons (b. 1949), Peter
Wheelwright (b. 1949), designers. Bozart:
Toys by Artists (1996), manufacturer.
Made in China. Plastic. H. 61 cm;
L. 80 cm; Depth 56 cm (house);
Max. h. 15 cm (figures). Scale 1:12.
Inv. 2004.45.1.1–12 and 2004.176.2.1–4

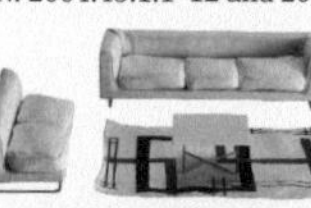

**The Kaleidoscope House:
Sofas, table and rug**
2001. Jasper Morrison (b. 1959),
designer. Bozart: Toys by Artists (1996),
manufacturer. Made in China. Wood,
aluminium, fabric and plastic. Max. h.
6.5 cm; L. 22 cm; W. 25 cm. Scale 1:12.
Inv. 2004.176.1.1–4

**The Kaleidoscope House:
Sofa, armchair, table and rug**
2001. Ron Arad (b. 1951), Karim Rashid
(b. 1960), designers. Bozart: Toys by
Artists (1996), manufacturer. Made in
China. Metal, velvet, plexiglas and cotton.
Max. h. 10.5 cm; Max. w. 18.1 cm; Max.

depth 12 cm. Scale 1:12. Inv. 2004.45.2.1
to 4

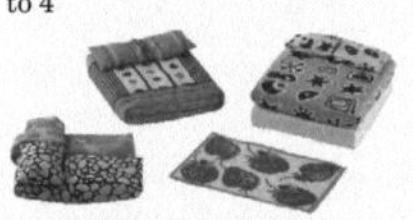

**The Kaleidoscope House:
Bedroom furniture**
2001. Laurie Simmons (b. 1949), Peter
Wheelwright (b. 1949), designers. Bozart:
Toys by Artists (1996), manufacturer.
Made in China. Wood and cotton. Max.
h. 4 cm; Max. l. 14 cm; Max. w. 15.5 cm.
Scale 1:12. Inv. 2004.45.3.1 to 4

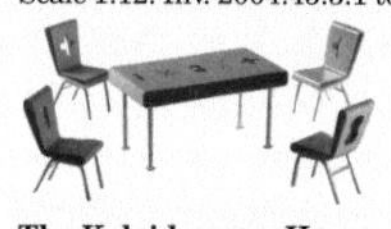

**The Kaleidoscope House:
Dining room furniture**
2001. Karim Rashid (b. 1960), designer.
Bozart: Toys by Artists (1996),
manufacturer. Made in China. Tinted
plastic. Max. h. 8 cm; Max. l. 14 cm; Max.
w. 7.2 cm. Scale 1:12. Inv. 2004.45.4.1 to 5

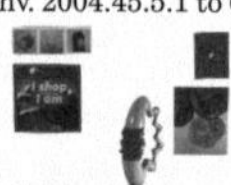

**The Kaleidoscope House:
Art Collection no. 1**
2001. Mel Bochner (b. 1940), Carroll
Dunham (b. 1949), Peter Halley (b. 1953),
Mel Kendrick (b. 1949), Cindy Sherman
(b. 1954), Laurie Simmons (b. 1949),
artists. Bozart: Toys by Artists (1996),
manufacturer. Made in China. Plastic,
wood and digital print on cardboard. Max.
h. 16.1 cm; Max. w. 11.4 cm. Scale 1:12.
Inv. 2004.45.5.1 to 6

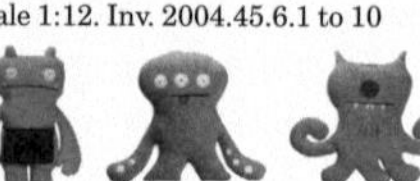

**The Kaleidoscope House:
Art Collection no. 2**
2001. Sarah Charlesworth (b. 1947),
Barbara Kruger (b. 1945), Allan
McCollum (b. 1944), John Newman
(b. 1952), Alexander Ross (b. 1960), Lisa
Yuskavage (b. 1962), artists. Bozart: Toys
by Artists (1996), manufacturer. Made in
China. Plastic, wood and digital print on
cardboard. Max. h. 20 cm; Max. w. 15 cm.
Scale 1:12. Inv. 2004.45.6.1 to 10

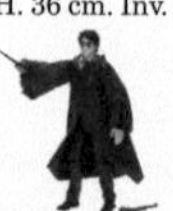

**Uglydolls: Wage, Cinko, Target,
Ice-Bat and Wedgehead**
2003. David Horvath (b. 1971) and Sun-
Min Kim (b. 1976), designers; Prettyugly
LLC (2003), manufacturer, USA. Made
in China. Polyester fibre and fabric.
H. 36 cm. Inv. 2004.181.1, 3, 4, 7 and 8

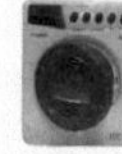

Harry Potter
2003. From the *Harry Potter* film series
(started 2001), adapted from the books by
J.K. Rowling. Mattel (1945), manufacturer,
USA. Made in China. Wind-up toy. Plastic.
H. 22 cm. Inv. 2006.15.19.1–3

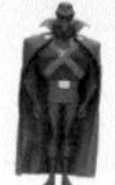

Mini Calor washing machine
2003. Smoby (1978), manufacturer,
France. Made in China. Battery operated.
Plastic. H. 24 cm; L. 19 cm; W. 15 cm.
Inv. 2006.15.12

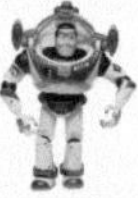

J'onn J'onzz, the Martian Manhunter
2003. From the DC Comics superhero
(1955), created by Joseph Samachson and
Joe Certa. Mattel (1945), manufacturer,
USA. Made in China. Plastic. H. 27 cm.
Inv. 2006.15.18

Buzz Lightyear
2003. From the animated film *Toy Story*
(1995), directed by John Lasseter. Hasbro

(1923), manufacturer, USA. Battery
operated. Plastic and fabric. Max. h.
35 cm. Inv. 2006.15.9.1-4

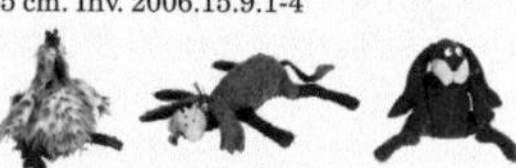

**Felinda Feile the cat; Chicky,
Chucky and Chacky the birds;
Karriere Sau the pig; Börsten Tief
the rabbit; Many Money the dog;
Pirate Punky the cow**
2004. Sigikid (1968), manufacturer,
Germany. Fabric and yarn. Max. h. 53 cm.
Inv. 2006.14.2 to 7, 2006.14.10 and 12

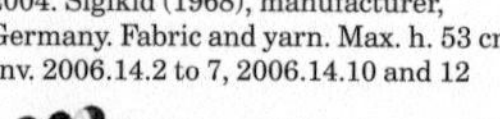

Robosapiens
2004. Wow Wee Ltd (1988), manufacturer,
Hong Kong. Battery operated with remote
control. Plastic. H. 16 cm; L. 18 cm;
W. 9 cm. Inv. 2006.15.21.1–2

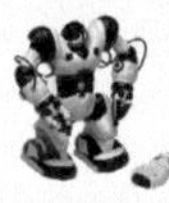

Beedibies boy doll
2005. Corolle (1979), manufacturer,
France. Plastic and fabric. H. 22 cm.
Inv. PR 2006.16.10

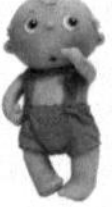

Babal
2005. Alex Hochstrasser (b. 1973),
designer; Active People (1984),
manufacturer, Switzerland. Made in
China. Educational toy. Polyurethane.
Max. diam. 17 cm. Inv. 2005.175.1 to 3

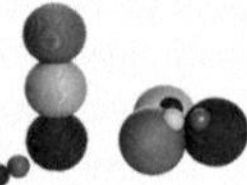

ZGMX-X10A Freedom Gundam
2005. From the cartoon series *Gundam*
(1979), created by Yoshiyuki Tomino
and Hajime Yadate. Bandai (1950),
manufacturer, Japan. Plastic. H. 26 cm.
Inv. 2006.13.22.1–170

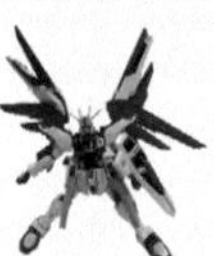

Cacao and Cannelle dolls
Doucette series, 2005. Corolle (1979),
manufacturer, France. Made in China.
Fabric and plastic. H. 39 cm.
Inv. 2006.15.10 and 11

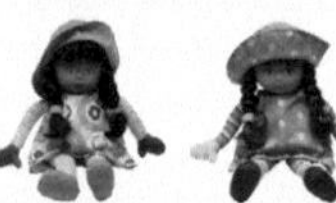

Laa-Laa, Po, Tinkywinky and Dipsy
2005. From the TV series *Teletubbies*
(1997), created by Anne Wood and
Andrew Davenport. Tomy (1924),
manufacturer, Japan. Made in China.
Battery operated. Plastic and polyester.
H. 37 cm. Inv. 2006.15.4–7

**Superman and Lois Lane, Cool Cook
and basket of fruit and vegetables**
(see pp. 180–181); **Pokemon Advanced,
Toby, Beedibies girl doll, Coquelicot
doll** (see pp. 182–183); **Strummin
Singin' Woody** (see pp. 184–185)

Pages 190–191

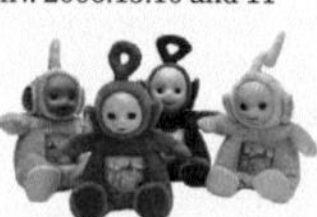

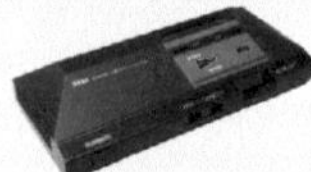

**Sega Master System with *The Ninja*
game cartridge**
1986. Sega (1954), manufacturer, Japan.
8-bit game console. H. 7 cm; L. 37 cm;
W. 17 cm. Inv. in progress

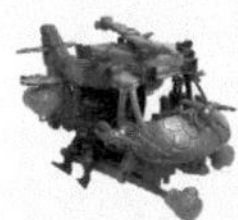

Turtlecopter
1988. From the cartoon *Teenage Mutant Ninja Turtles* (1987), adapted from the comic-book by Kevin Eastman and Peter Laird. Bandai (1950), manufacturer, Japan. Plastic. H. 19 cm; L. 37 cm; W. 16 cm. Inv. 991.1031.B

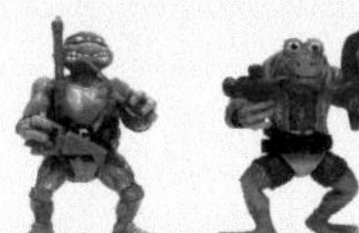

Michaelangelo, Raphael, Leonardo, Splinter, Genghis Frog, Usagi Yojimbo, Mike the Sewer Surfer, Leo the Sewer Samurai, Don the Undercover Turtle, Shredder, Leatherhead
1988, 1990 and 1991. From the cartoon *Teenage Mutant Ninja Turtles* (1987), adapted from the comic-book by Kevin Eastman and Peter Laird. Bandai (1950), manufacturer, Japan. Plastic. Max. h. 12 cm. Inv. 991.1027.B, C, E, F, H, L, M, N, 991.1028.C and H

Pages 192–193

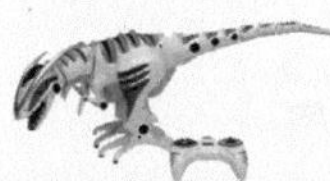

Roboraptor
2005. Wow Wee Ltd (1988), manufacturer, China. Battery operated with remote control. Plastic. H. 25 cm; L. 77 cm; W. 23 cm. Inv. 2006.15.20.1–2

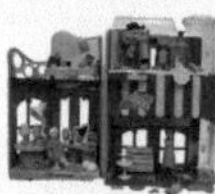 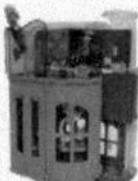

Polly Pocket Quik-Clik House of Style
2005. Mattel (1945), manufacturer, France. Plastic and magnets. H. 32 cm; L. 40 cm; W. 12 cm. Inv. 2006.16.9.1–45

Teenage Mutant Ninja Turtles
(see pp. 190–191)

Pages 194–195

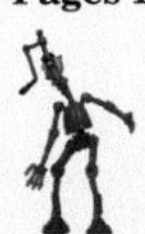

Fender
2004. From the animated film *Robots* (2004), directed by Chris Wedge. Mattel (1945), manufacturer, USA. Made in China. Plastic. H. 19 cm. Inv. 2006.15.15

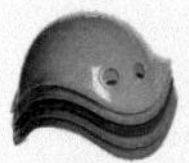 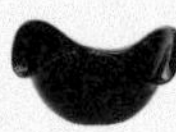

Bilibo
2001. Alex Hochstrasser (b. 1973), designer; Active People (1984), manufacturer, Switzerland. Made in China. Educational toy. Polyethylene. H. 40 cm; L. 37 cm; W. 40 cm. Inv. 2005.175.4 to 6, 8 and 9

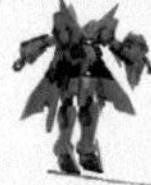

GAT-X303 Aegis Gundam
2005. From the cartoon series *Gundam* (1979), created by Yoshiyuki Tomino and Hajime Yadate. Bandai (1950), manufacturer, Japan. Plastic. H. 21 cm. Inv. 2006.13.23.1–170

Strummin Singin' Woody (see pp. 184–185); **Babal, ZGMX-X10A Freedom Gundam, Cacao and Cannelle** (see pp. 188–189)

Pages 196–197

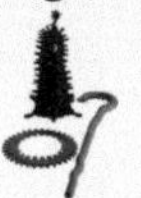

Tactoo-loo, Skinsitive Ghost Robot
2003. Rémi Leclerc (b. 1965), designer,

Hong Kong; Creata International Ltd (1982–2003), manufacturer, Hong Kong. Battery operated. Plastic and semi-transparent rubber. H. 34.5 cm. Inv. 2004.178.1

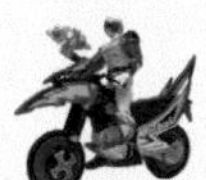

Tsunami Cycle
2003. From the TV series *Power Rangers* (1993). Bandai (1950), manufacturer, Japan. Made in China. Plastic. Max. h. 14 cm. Inv. 2006.13.10.1–3

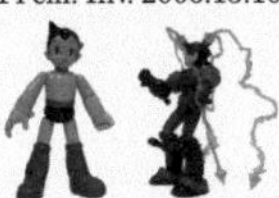

Astro Boy and Astro Boy Atlas
2004. From the cartoon *Astro Boy* (Japan, 1963), adapted from the manga comic by Osamu Tezuka. Bandai (1950), manufacturer, Japan. Battery operated interactive toy. Plastic. Max. h. 28 cm. Inv. 2006.13.24 and 2006.13.20

Pages 198–199

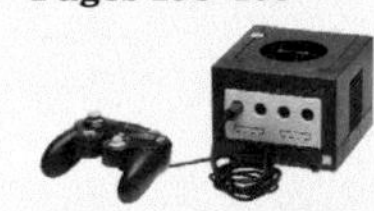

GameCube, 2001 with the platform game *Mario Party 4*, 2002
Nintendo (1889), manufacturer, Japan. H. 11.5 cm; L. 15 cm; W. 14 cm. Inv. in progress

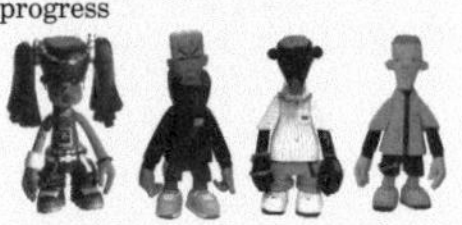

Miss Gardener 002, Square Gardener 007, Young BB Gardener 039, Young Square Gardener 043, Lazy XXX Gardener 067, Fatwest Gardener 010 and Young Fatwest Gardener 046
2003. Michael Lau (b. 1970), designer; Crazysmiles (2000), manufacturer, Hong Kong. Painted vinyl and plastic. Max. h. 18 cm. Inv. 2004.183.1, 3, 7, 8, 10, 2005.18.1 and 4

Robosapiens (see pp. 188–189)

Pages 200–201

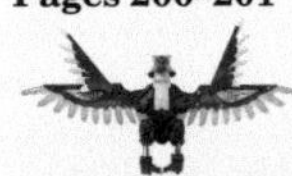

Jumbo Isis Megazord
Wild Force series, 2002. From the TV series *Power Rangers* (1993). Bandai (1950), manufacturer, Japan. Made in China. Battery operated. Plastic. Max. h. 33 cm. Inv. 2005.19.1.1–10

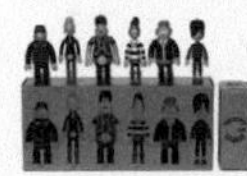 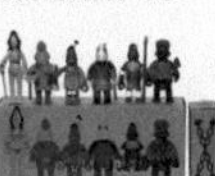

Forever Sensible Motorcycle Club and The Old Guard figures
In-Crowd series, 2004. James Jarvis (b. 1970), designer; Amos (2002), manufacturer, Great Britain. Made in China. Painted vinyl. Max. h. 12.5 cm. Inv. 2005.43.1 and 2005.43.2

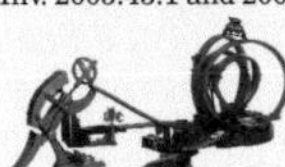

AcceleDrome racing track
2005. Hot Wheels (1968), manufacturer, USA. Made in China. Battery operated. Plastic and metal. H. 80 cm; L. 1 m (track); L. 8 cm (cars). Inv. 2006.15.1

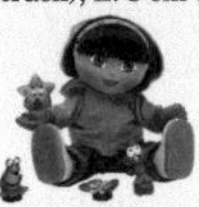

Dora the Explorer
2005. From the cartoon series *Dora the Explorer* (2000), created by Valerie Walsh, Eric Weiner and Chris Gifford. Fisher-Price (1931), manufacturer, USA. Made in China. Battery operated interactive toy. Plastic and fabric. Max. h. 31 cm. Inv. 2006.16.8.1–5

Pages 204–205

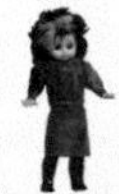

Funky doll
1983. Clodrey-Ajena (1982), manufacturer, France. Plastic and fabric. H. 52 cm. Inv. 54947

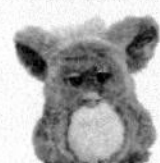

Furby
2005 (1st ed. 1998). Dave Hampton, designer. Tiger Electronica (1998) and Hasbro (1923), manufacturers, USA. Battery operated. Plastic and fur fabric. H. 22 cm. Inv. 2006.15.3.1–2

Teletubbies, Harry Potter
(see pp. 188–189)

Pages 206–207

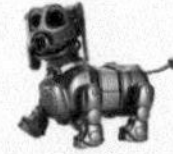

Dog.com, talking interactive dog
2001. Tomy (1924), manufacturer, Japan. Electronic toy. Metal and plastic. H. 22 cm; L. 33 cm; L. 14 cm. Inv. 2002.72.1

The Kaleidoscope House: Blue-Green family and Jasper Morrison furniture, the Little Prince, Robosapiens, Buzz Lightyear, Beedibies boy doll (see pp. 188–189)

Pages 208–209

The Kaleidoscope House set, the Little Prince (see pp. 188–189)

Pages 210–211

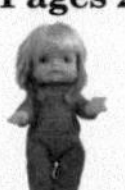

'First Tears' doll
1989. Bandai (1950), manufacturer, Japan. Made in Great Britain. Plastic and fabric. H. 28 cm. Inv. 990.1102

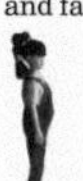

'Mama Surprise' doll
1990. Migliorati, manufacturer, Italy. Made in China. Plastic and fabric. H. 40 cm. Inv. 991.9

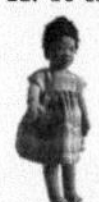

Doll
1990. Helen MacLeod, designer, Great Britain. Stuffed fabric, mohair and jersey. H. 40 cm. Inv. 991.105

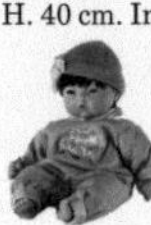

'Grocalin Ciel' baby doll
1995. Corolle (1979), manufacturer, France. Vinyl and fabric. H. 30 cm. Inv. 996.155.2

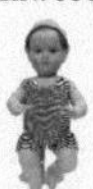

Boy doll
1997. Petitcollin (1860), manufacturer, France. Plastic and cotton. H. 38 cm. Inv. 997.111.4

Coquelicot doll (see pp. 182–183); **Cacao and Cannelle, Teletubbies, Harry Potter, Sigikid soft toys** (see pp. 188–189); **Funky doll, Furby** (see pp. 204–205)

Toy Exhibitions at the Musée des Arts Décoratifs

Jouets artistiques et modernes
(15 May–18 June 1916)

Jouets et ses images artistiques
(21 November 1916–21 January 1917)

*Jeux et jouets** (9 December 1965–31 January 1966)

Jouets, une sélection du musée de Sonneberg and *L'enfant et les images, sélection internationale de livres illustrés* at the Galeries du CCI, Centre de Création Industrielle (23 October 1973–15 January 1974)

*Jouets américains de la petite enfance, 1925–1975** (16 November 1977–16 January 1978)

*Grande exposition des jouets français 1880–1980** and *La crèche de Roland Roure* (24 November 1982–14 February 1983)

Jouets traditionnels du Japon (28 October 1981–3 March 1982)

*Le cirque et le jouet** (18 October 1984–14 January 1985)

*Jouets: Paris 1900** at the town halls of the 10th (October–December 1984) and 13th *arrondissements* (March–April 1985) of Paris, in collaboration with the Musée des Arts Décoratifs

Personnages et héros (22 February–19 October 1986)

L'arche de Noé (25 October 1986–8 February 1987)

*Le jouet de bois de tous les pays, de tous les temps** (12 November 1987–14 February 1988)

Jeux d'esprit, jeux d'adresse (25 October 1989–25 March 1990)

Snoopy fête ses 40 ans (24 January–22 April 1990)

Du soldat de bois au robot transformable (10 May–4 November 1990)

Les sports et les loisirs illustrés par le jouet (28 November 1991–4 October 1992)

Poupées d'hier, créations d'aujourd'hui (11 April–3 November 1991)

*Animaux de tout poil** (21 October 1992–7 November 1993)

*Histoires d'ours** (9 February–26 June 1994)

La ville en jouets (23 October 1996–23 February 1997)

* Exhibition accompanied by a catalogue

Picture credits

Pages 8 to 211
© Les Arts décoratifs / Michel Pintado

Pages 215 to 223
© Les Arts décoratifs/ Laurent-Sully Jaulmes, Jean Tholance

Pages 8–9, 20–21, 36–37 and 46–47
© 2006 ADAGP, Paris: Georges Lepape, Berthe Noufflard, Benjamin Rabier

Page 66–67
© Hachette Livre / Gautier-Languereau

Pages 94–95, 98–99, 104–105, 108–109, 114–115 and 118 to 121
© Disney

Pages 104–105 and 114–115
™ and © Nelvana. All Rights Reserved

Page 104–105 and 134–135
© Hachette Livre

Pages 148 to 151 and 156 to 159
Star Wars: Episode IV – A New Hope © 1977 and 1997 Lucasfilm Ltd & ™. All Rights Reserved. Used under authorization. Unauthorized duplication is a violation of applicable law. COURTESY OF LUCASFILM LTD.

Pages 184–185, 188–189, 194–195 and 206–207
© Disney / Pixar

Pages 134–135, 150–151 and 156–157
© Hergé/Moulinsart 2006

Pages 144–145
© SunSoft

Pages 144–145, 146–147 and 198–199
© Nintendo. All Rights Reserved

Pages 144–145 and 172–173
™ & © Warner Bros. Entertainment Inc. 2006

Pages 146–147
© Tradewest

Pages 188–189 and 206 to 209
With kind permission of the Estate of Antoine de Saint-Exupéry

Pages 188–189, 204–205 and 210–211
™ & © Warner Bros. Entertainment Inc. Harry Potter Publishing Rights © J.K. Rowling 2006

Pages 190–191
© SEGA

Pages 190–191
© Atari

Pages 22–23, 46–47, 48–49, 50–51, 62–63, 72–73, 94–95, 98–99, 104–105, 114–115, 118–119, 126–127, 130–131, 134–135, 144–145, 146–147, 150–151, 156–157, 176–177, 210–211
© All Rights Reserved

Acknowledgments

This book was published on the occasion of the
reopening of the Musée des Arts Décoratifs, Paris.

It was created with the partnership of La Grande Récré
and the enthusiasm that Franck Mathais, director of communications,
has brought to the Toy Gallery.

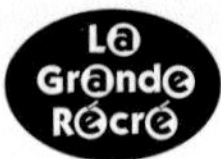

This book brings together more than 700 games and toys, most of which entered the collection
of the Musée des Arts Décoratifs through the painstaking work of Monica Burckhardt, curator
of the Department of Toys from 1975 to 1997.

Our warmest thanks to the patrons who have generously contributed to the building of the collection:

Robert Alazet, Camille Alsac, Jean and Gisèle Alsac, Madame Louis Amic,
Michel Aroutcheff, M. Badin, Mme Beche, Cosette Bellancourt, Joëlle Berthaut,
Maurice Bisson, Robert Bordaz, Colette Boulard, Mme Boyer, M. Braquenié,
Maurice Brunhammer, Mathilde Bulteau, Jean-Louis and Monica Burckhardt,
Claude Chapelon, Guillaume de Chazournes, Marie-Ange and Brigitte Delamarche,
Mme Deledalle, Raoul Esquene, Guy de Faramoud, Sylvie de Fayet, Mme Ferré,
Odile Jacquot, Anatole Jakowsky, Germaine Joly, Anne de Labriffe, Mme Latil,
Michael Lau, Simone Laurenceau-Serrière, Baudoin Lebon, N. Lhortolary, Bernard Macaire,
Adrien Maeght, Mme Milhomme, Colette Mouzon, Henriette and Geneviève Noufflard,
M. Parguez, M.A.C. Person-Zia, Christian Poumeyrol, Catherine Refabert, M. Rein,
Michèle Rosier, M. Sarda Annie Scheppers, Robert Tcherkhoff, Anna Ternot,
Michel and Hélène David-Weill, Guy and R. de Wouters, Elizabeth de Wouters

Association Naja, Centre de Création Industrielle,
Chambre Syndicale des Industries du Jouet

Active People, Ajena, Anima, Anselme, Arbois, L'Association, Bandai, Bébé Confort, Bella,
Berchet, Le Bon Marché Rive Gauche, CEJI, Clodrey, Coqueval, Corolle, Dagobert, Fisher-Price,
General Mills, Hefa Société, Interjouet, Ideal Loisirs, Isotra, John Wright Dolls, Jouets Rationnels,
Joustra, Lego System, Maison Rollet, Majorette, Matchbox, Mattel and Mattel France, Meccano,
Miro Company, Moquin et Breuil, Norev, Obertal, Orli-Jouet, Ouaps, Playmobil, Prettyugly LLC,
Rainbow Promotion, Rehbock, Robert Tonner Doll Company, Sigikid, Smoby, Solijouets,
Tonka Société, Vilac, Vulli, Vullierme

and to the Fonds National d'Art Contemporain
for the many donations of toys.

Thanks also to:

All the manufacturers and copyright-holders who kindly gave us
permission to reproduce this collection of toys

The association Mo5.com and Karine Mestrejean from Laboîte Com Concept for the loan of the game
consoles; Philippe Hourdé for the loan of the *Star Wars* posters; Maider Mainingue and Charlyse Lenoir
from IKEA for the loan of the furniture for the 21st-century bedroom; Chancelia Debraux from the
store Les Temps Modernes in Paris for the loan of the 1950s furniture

Thierry Haag, director of the Musée du Jouet in Moirans-en-Montagne; Carola Jiulleig, Deutsches
Historisches Museum, Berlin; Josep Maria Joan Rosa, director of the Museo del Joguet de Catalunya,
Figueres; Friederike Lindner, Deutsches Spielzeugmuseum; Bartomeu Mari and Tatiana Verbi for
their valuable assistance

Tamara Charles, Guillaume Dejardin, Pauline Duclos,
Marie Fialon, Maïra Gabriel Anhorn, Antoine Haas,
Noémi Joly, Camille Lansival, Émilia Philippot, Jules Saulnier,
Thomas Valette and the collection management team at the Musée
des Arts Décoratifs for all their help